# PHOTOSHOP CS5

## for Windows and Macintosh
## Visual QuickStart Guide

Elaine Weinmann
Peter Lourekas

 Peachpit Press

# For Alicia

Visual QuickStart Guide
**Photoshop CS5 for Windows and Macintosh**
Elaine Weinmann and Peter Lourekas

**Peachpit Press**
1249 Eighth Street
Berkeley, CA 94710

510/524-2178
510/524-2221 (fax)

Find us on the Web at: www.peachpit.com
To report errors, please send a note to errata@peachpit.com
Peachpit Press is a division of Pearson Education

Copyright © 2010 by Elaine Weinmann and Peter Lourekas

Cover Design: RHDG/Riezebos Holzbaur, Peachpit Press
Logo Design: MINE™ www.minesf.com
Interior Design: Elaine Weinmann
Production: Elaine Weinmann and Peter Lourekas
Illustrations: Elaine Weinmann and Peter Lourekas, except as noted

ISBN-13: 978-0-321-70153-4

ISBN-10:    0-321-70153-4

9 8 7 6 5 4 3 2 1

Printed and bound in the United States of America

# Acknowledgments

Nancy Aldrich-Ruenzel, publisher at Peachpit Press, has been able to adapt the company's products not only to perpetually changing subject matter, but also to a complex and rapidly changing delivery system.

Victor Gavenda, choir master and longtime editor at Peachpit Press, tech edited this book in Windows with sharp eyes, keen intelligence, and wit.

Susan Rimerman, editor at Peachpit, was responsive to our every question and request.

Production editor Lisa Brazieal did an expert job of spearheading the prepress production before sending the files off to Courier Printing.

Nancy Davis, editor-in-chief; Gary-Paul Prince, promotions manager; Keasley Jones, associate publisher; and many other terrific, hard-working people at Peachpit contributed their respective talents.

Elaine Soares, photo research manager, and Lee Scher, photo research coordinator, of the Image Resource Center at Pearson Education (the parent company of Peachpit Press) quickly procured the stock photos from Shutterstock.com that we requested.

Rebecca Pepper did a thorough, thoughtful, and meticulous job of copy editing.

Steve Rath produced a comprehensive index.

Scout Festa did the final round of proofreading, just when our eyes were too strained to focus on another comma or period.

Adobe Systems, Inc., produces creative software tools that are a pleasure to use and write about. For allowing us to beta test Photoshop CS5 while it was in development, and for helping us untangle its mysteries by way of the online forum, we thank John Nack, principal product manager for Adobe Photoshop; Vishal Khandpur, project manager – prerelease; Bryan O'Neil Hughes and Zorana Gee, Photoshop product managers; and the many other members of the Adobe Photoshop CS5 beta team.

Most important, to Alicia and Simona, our pride and joy, who teach us as much as we teach them.

—Elaine Weinmann and Peter Lourekas

★ New or improved Photoshop features are identified by red stars in this table of contents and throughout this book.

# Contents

## 6: Panels

## 7: Pixel Basics

## 8: Layer Basics

## 9: Selections & Masks

## 10: History

## 11: Colors & Blending Modes

## 12: Adjustment Layer Basics

## 13: Adjustments in Depth

## 14: Combining Images

## 15: Brushes

## 16: Retouching

## 17: Refocusing

## 18: More Layers

## 19: Filters

## 20: Type

## REGISTER THIS BOOK!

Purchasing this book entitles you to more than just a couple of pounds of paper. If you register the book with Peachpit Press, you're also entitled to download copies of most of the images used throughout the book, which you can use to practice with as you follow the step-by-step tutorials. To get started, follow this link: www.peachpit.com/photoshopcs5vqs. This takes you to the book's page at the Peachpit Press website. Once there, click Register your book to log in to your account at peachpit.com. If you don't already have an account, it takes just a few seconds to create one, and it's free.

After logging in, you'll need to enter the book's ISBN code, which you'll find on the back cover, and answer a security question. Click Submit, and you're in! You'll be taken to a list of your registered books. Find Photoshop CS5 Visual QuickStart Guide on the list, and click Access to protected content to get to the download page.

Note: These images are low-resolution (not suitable for printing), and they are copyrighted by their owners, who have watermarked them to discourage unauthorized reproduction. They are for your personal use only, not for distribution. You're not limited to using them in the order shown, and of course you're welcome to use your own photos instead.

## Downloadable images

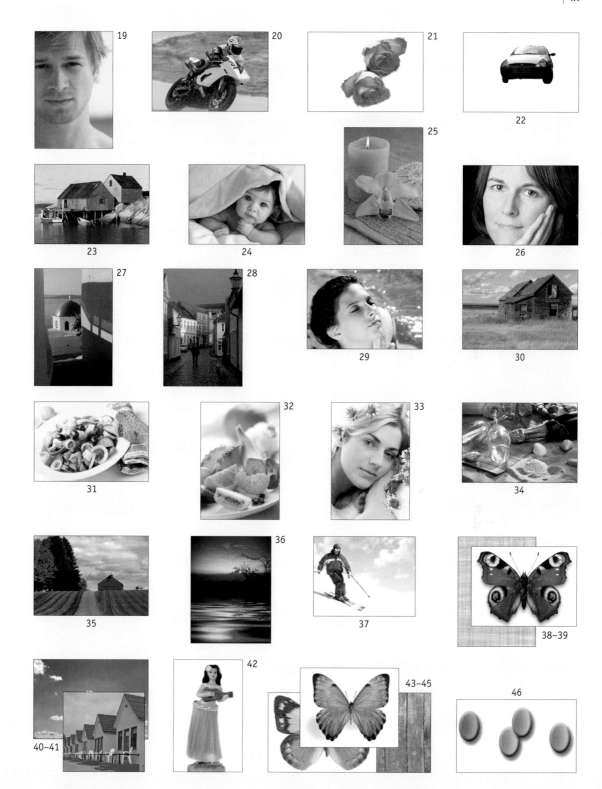

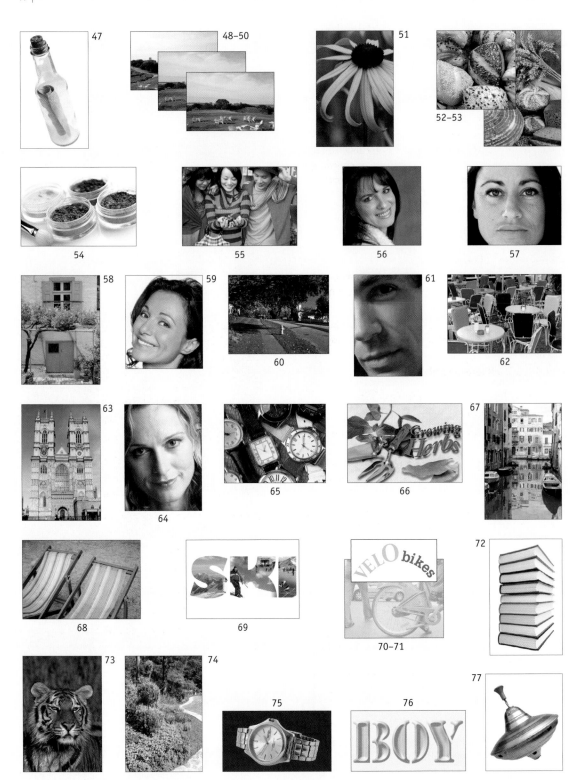

Welcome to Photoshop! In this chapter, you'll launch the application and familiarize yourself with Photoshop color basics, such as displays, document color modes, and channels. Most important, before you start editing images — and also before outputting any files — you need to incorporate color management into your workflow. You'll accomplish this by calibrating your display, choosing color settings, and downloading the necessary printer profiles.

## Launching Photoshop

### To launch Photoshop in Windows:

Do one of the following:

In a 32-bit version of Windows, click the Start button on the taskbar, choose All Programs, then click Adobe Photoshop CS5.

In a 64-bit version of Windows, click the Start button, choose All Programs, then click Adobe Photoshop CS5 (64-bit).

Double-click a Photoshop file icon.

### To launch Photoshop in the Mac OS:

Do one of the following:

Click the Photoshop icon  in the Dock. (If you haven't created the icon yet, open the Adobe Photoshop CS5 folder in the Applications folder, then drag the Adobe Photoshop CS5 application icon into the Dock.)

Open the Adobe Photoshop CS5 folder in the Applications folder, then double-click the Adobe Photoshop CS5 application icon.

Double-click any Photoshop file icon.

---

**WANT TO SEE MORE ONSCREEN?**

If you want to open a file quickly to make the screen more "live" as you read through this chapter, navigate to the Samples folder inside the Photoshop application folder, then double-click a .psd image file, such as "Fish.psd." (Don't worry...you'll soon learn how to open photos and create documents.)

**FINDING THE NEW STUFF**

This symbol ★ identifies Photoshop features that are new or improved.

---

## COLOR MANAGEMENT

1

### IN THIS CHAPTER

## Displays, modes, and channels

Onscreen, your Photoshop image is a bitmap — a geometric arrangement, or mapping, of dots on a rectangular grid. Each dot, or pixel, represents a different color or shade. If you drag with a painting tool, such as the Brush, across an area of a layer, pixels below your pointer are recolored. With a high zoom level chosen for your document, you can see (and edit) individual pixels. **A** Bitmap programs like Photoshop are best suited for editing and producing photographic, painterly, or photorealistic images that contain subtle gradations of color, which are called "continuous tones." The images you edit in Photoshop can originate from a digital camera, from a photo print that you have scanned, from a file saved in another application, or from scratch using program features, such as painting and cloning tools.

To enable color images to be viewed onscreen, your display projects red, green, and blue (RGB) light. Combined in their purest form, these additive primaries produce white light. If you were to send your Photoshop file to a commercial print shop for four-color process printing, it would be rendered with cyan (C), magenta (M), yellow (Y), and black (K) inks. Because computer displays use the RGB model, they can only simulate the CMYK inks that are used in commercial printing.

The successful translation of a digital image to a printed one isn't as simple as you might think. To begin with, the same document may look surprisingly different on different displays due to such variables as the temperature of the display, the lighting in the room, and even the colors on your wall. Moreover, many colors that you see in the natural world or that can be displayed onscreen can't be printed (have no ink equivalents), and conversely, some printable colors can't be displayed onscreen. The color management techniques that we outline in this chapter will help smooth out the kinks in the color workflow from digital input to display onscreen, then finally to print.

➤ In Photoshop, you can choose colors using the Grayscale, RGB (red-green-blue), HSB (hue-saturation-brightness), CMYK (cyan-magenta-yellow-black), or Lab (lightness, a-component, and b-component) color model, and you can choose colors from a color matching system, such as PANTONE.

### Photoshop channels

All Photoshop images are composed of one, three, or four channels (see the sidebar below). In an RGB image, for example, the three channels store the intensity of red, green, or blue at each pixel as a level of gray. Most likely you will work with images that store 256 levels of gray for each channel. Because the 256 gray levels are represented by 8 bits (short for "binary digits") of computer data, the bit depth of such an image is said to be 8 bits per channel. Files that have a higher bit depth of 16 or 32 bits per channel contain more color information (see page 19).

➤ Open an RGB Color image and display the Channels panel. Click Red, Green, or Blue on the panel to display only that channel, then click the topmost channel name on the panel to restore the composite display. Although you

**A** *In this extreme close-up of a photo in Photoshop, you can see the individual pixels that the image is made of.*

| DEFAULT NUMBER OF CHANNELS FOR EACH IMAGE MODE | | |
|---|---|---|
| One | Three | Four |
| Bitmap | RGB | CMYK |
| Grayscale | Lab | |
| Duotone | Multichannel | Multichannel |
| Indexed Color | | |

can make adjustments to individual channels, normally you will edit all the channels at once while viewing the composite image.

In addition to the core channels we just discussed, you can add two other types of channels. You can save a selection as a mask in a grayscale (alpha) channel, or add channels for individual spot colors.**A**

The more channels a document contains, the larger its file storage size is. A document in RGB Color mode, which contains three channels (Red, Green, and Blue), will be three times larger than it would be if converted to Grayscale, a single-channel mode. If you were to convert it to CMYK Color mode, the file would contain four channels (Cyan, Magenta, Yellow, and Black) and would be larger still.

## Photoshop document color modes

A document can be converted to, displayed in, and edited in any of these color modes: Bitmap, Grayscale, Duotone, Indexed Color, RGB Color, CMYK Color, Lab Color, or Multichannel. The ones you will work in the most are RGB Color and CMYK Color. To convert a document to a different mode, use the Image > Mode submenu.**B** If a mode is dimmed on the menu, it means you must convert

the file to a different mode first in order to make it available. For example, a file must be in Grayscale mode to be converted to Duotone mode. The availability of some Photoshop commands and options will vary depending on the color mode of your document.

Some mode conversions can cause noticeable color shifts. For example, if you convert a file from RGB Color mode to CMYK Color mode, printable colors will be substituted for RGB colors. The fewer times you convert a file, the better, as its color data is altered with each conversion change. Some conversions flatten layers, such as a conversion to Indexed Color, Multichannel, or Bitmap mode. Other conversions give you the option to preserve layers via a Don't Flatten button in an alert dialog.

Digital cameras and medium- to low-end scanners produce RGB images. For faster editing, and in order to access all the filters in Photoshop, we recommend keeping your files in RGB Color mode. In fact, most desktop color inkjet printers, especially those that use six or more ink colors, can process RGB Color files directly from Photoshop.

➤ To "soft-proof" your RGB document as a simulation of CMYK Color mode without performing an actual mode change, see pages 404–405.

*Continued on the following page*

*Main image channels*

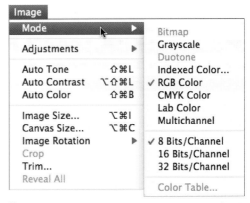

**A** *An alpha channel*  A spot color channel

**B** *Use the Mode submenu to change the color mode of your document.*

The following is a brief summary of the color modes that a document can be converted to in Photoshop:

In **Bitmap** mode, pixels are either 100% black or 100% white, and no layers, filters, or adjustment commands are available. (To convert a file to this mode, you must convert it to Grayscale mode first.)

In **Grayscale** mode, pixels are black, white, or up to 254 shades of gray (a total of 256). If you convert a file from a color mode to Grayscale mode and then save and close it, its luminosity (light and dark) values will be preserved, but its color information will be deleted permanently. In Chapter 13, we'll show you how to convert a layer to grayscale without changing the document color mode.

To produce a **duotone**, two or more extra plates are added to a grayscale image to enhance its richness and tonal depth. This requires special preparatory steps in Photoshop and expertise on the part of your commercial printer.

Files in **Indexed Color** mode contain a single channel, as well as an 8-bit color table (which contains a maximum number of 256 colors or shades). When you optimize a file in the GIF format via the Save for Web & Devices dialog, the file is converted to this color mode automatically (see pages 423–424).

**RGB Color** 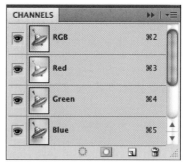 A is the most versatile mode of all and the one you'll use most often. It's the mode in which digital cameras save your photos, the only mode in which all the Photoshop tool options and filters are accessible, the mode of choice for online output, and the mode of choice for export to video and multimedia programs.

In Photoshop, although you can display and edit your files in **CMYK Color** mode, B we recommend editing them in RGB Color mode, then converting a copy of them to CMYK Color mode only when required for commercial printing or for export to a page layout application. Exceptions to this rule are images that are saved by high-end scanners in CMYK Color mode; keep them as CMYK to preserve their original color data.

**Lab Color** is a three-channel mode that was developed for the purpose of achieving consistency among various devices, such as printers and displays. Lab Color files are device-independent, meaning their color definitions stay the same regardless of how each output device defines color. The channels represent lightness (the image details), the colors green to red, and the colors blue to yellow. The lightness and color values can be edited independently of one another. Although Photoshop uses Lab Color to produce conversions between RGB and CMYK color modes internally, there's rarely a need for Photoshop users like us to convert our files to Lab Color mode.

**Multichannel** images contain multiple 256-level grayscale channels. If you convert an image from RGB Color to Multichannel mode, its Red, Green, and Blue channels are converted to Cyan, Magenta, and Yellow. As a result, the image may become lighter and the contrast may be reduced. Some Photoshop pros assemble individual channels from several images into a single composite image by using this mode, but this takes expertise.

With this foundation in color basics, you're ready to take the plunge into color management.

A *Because the mode of this document is RGB Color, it contains three channels.*

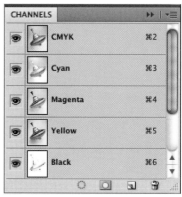

B *We converted the document to CMYK Color mode; now it contains four channels.*

# Introduction to color management

Problems with color inconsistency can arise due to the fact that hardware devices and software packages read or output color differently. If you were to compare how an image looks in an assortment of imaging programs and Web browsers, the colors might look completely different in each case, and worse still, may not match the picture you originally shot with your digital camera. Print the image, and you'll probably find the results are different yet again. In some cases, these differences might be slight and unobjectionable, but in other cases such color shifts can wreak havoc with your design or turn a project into a disaster!

A color management system can prevent most color discrepancies by acting as a color interpreter. It knows how each particular device and program interprets color, and adjusts those colors when necessary. The result is that the colors in your files will display and output more consistently as the files are shuttled among various programs and devices. Applications in Adobe Creative Suite 5 use standardized ICC (International Color Consortium) profiles, which tell your color management system how each specific device defines color.

Each particular device ca n capture and reproduce only a limited range (gamut) of colors, which in the jargon of color management is known as the **color space**. The mathematical description of the color space of each device, in turn, is called its **color profile**. Furthermore, each input device, such as a camera, attaches its own profile to the files it produces. Photoshop will use that profile in order to display and edit the colors in your document; or if the document doesn't contain a profile, Photoshop will use the current **working space** (a color space you choose for Photoshop) instead.

Color management is especially important when the same image is used for multiple purposes, such as for online output and print output. Note: For print output, be sure to consult with your prepress service provider or commercial printer (if you're using one) about color management to ensure that your color management setup works smoothly with theirs.

The "meat" of this chapter consists of instructions for choosing color management options, which we strongly recommend you follow before editing your images in Photoshop. Our instructions are centered on using Adobe RGB as the color space for your image-editing work to create color consistency throughout your workflow. We'll show you how to set the color space of your digital camera to Adobe RGB, calibrate your display, specify Adobe RGB as the color space for Photoshop, acquire the proper profiles for your inkjet printer and paper type, and assign Adobe RGB as the profile of choice for files that don't use that color space.

You'll need to focus on color management again when you prepare your file for printing. In Chapter 25 (Print), you will create a soft-proof setting for your particular inkjet printer and paper using the acquired profiles, and then use it to view a soft proof of your document onscreen. The profile will also be used for outputting files to a color inkjet printer, a device that expects files to be in RGB color. Finally, we'll show you how to use the appropriate profiles when outputting either to the Web or to a commercial press.

The first step in color management is to establish Adobe RGB as the color space for your camera.

## Setting a camera's color space to Adobe RGB

Most high-end, advanced amateur digital cameras and digital SLR cameras have an onscreen menu, which you can use to customize how the camera processes digital images. Although we'll use a Nikon D700 as our representative model for setting a camera to the Adobe RGB color space, you can follow a similar procedure to set the color space for your camera.

Note: If you shoot photos in the JPEG format, you should choose Adobe RGB as the color space for your camera, regardless of which model it is. If you shoot raw files, these steps are optional, as you will have the opportunity to assign the Adobe RGB color space when you convert your photos via the Camera Raw plug-in (see page 66).

*Continued on the following page*

## To set a camera's color space to Adobe RGB:

1. On the back of your Nikon camera, press the Menu button to access the menu on the LCD screen, and then, if necessary, press the up or down arrow on the multi selector to select the **Shooting Menu** tab.

2. On the Shooting Menu, press the down arrow on the multi selector to select the **Color Space** category **A** (Canon EOS Rebel cameras label this category as Parameters). Press the right arrow on the multi selector to move to the submenu.

3. Press the down arrow to select **Adobe RGB**.**B**

4. Press the OK button to set your choice,**C–D** then press the Menu button to exit the Menu screen.

**NIKON D700**

A *On the Nikon Shooting Menu, we selected the Color Space category.*

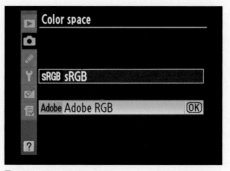

B *We pressed the right arrow, then chose Adobe RGB from the Color Space submenu.*

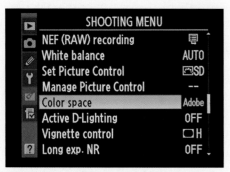

C *After pressing OK, the Color Space for our camera is now Adobe RGB.*

**CANON EOS REBEL**

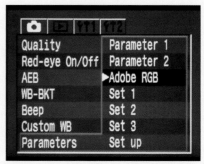

D *On a Canon EOS Rebel, we selected the Parameters category, pressed Set to get to the submenu, then chose Adobe RGB from the submenu.*

# Calibrating your display

## Display types

There are two main types of computer displays: a CRT (cathode ray tube, as in a traditional TV set) and the more common LCD (liquid crystal display, or flat panel display). The display performance of a CRT fluctuates due to its analog technology and the fact that its display phosphors (which produce the glowing dots that you see onscreen) fade over time. A CRT display can be calibrated reliably for only around three years.

LCD displays use a grid of fixed-sized liquid crystals that filter color coming from a back light source. Although you can adjust only the brightness on an LCD (not the contrast), the LCD digital technology offers more reliable color consistency than a CRT, without the characteristic flickering of a CRT. The newest LCD models provide good viewing angles, display accurate color, use the desired daylight temperature of 6500K for the white point (see below), and are produced under tighter manufacturing standards than CRTs. Moreover, the color profile that's provided with an LCD display (and that is installed in your system automatically) usually describes the display characteristics accurately.

➤ Both types of displays lose calibration gradually, and you may not notice the change until the colors are way off. To maintain the color consistency of your display, stick to a regular monthly calibration schedule. Thankfully, our calibration software reminds us to recalibrate our display via a monthly onscreen alert.

## Understanding the calibration settings

Three basic characteristics are adjusted when a display is calibrated: The brightness (white level) is set to a consistent working standard; the contrast (dark level) is set to the maximum value; and a neutral gray (gray level) is established using equal values of R, G, and B. To adjust these characteristics, calibration devices evaluate the white point, black point, and gamma in the display.

➤ The **white point** data enables the display to project a pure white, which matches an industry-standard color temperature. Photographers favor using D65/6500K as the temperature setting for the white point.

➤ The **black point** is the darkest black a display can project. All other dark shades are lighter than this darkest black, which ensures that shadow details display properly.

➤ The **gamma** defines how midtones are displayed onscreen. A gamma setting of 1.0 reproduces the linear brightness scale that is found in nature. Human vision, however, responds to brightness in a nonlinear fashion, so this setting makes the screen look washed out. A higher gamma setting redistributes more of the midtones into the dark range, which our eyes are more sensitive to, and produces a more natural-looking image. Photography experts recommend using a gamma setting of 2.2 for both Windows and Macintosh displays.

## Buying a calibration device

The only way to calibrate a display properly is by using a hardware calibration device, which produces a profile containing the proper white point, black point, and gamma settings for your display. The Adobe color management system, in turn, will use that profile to display colors in your Photoshop document more accurately.

If you're shopping for a calibration device, you'll notice a wide range in cost, from a $100 to $300 colorimeter to a much more costly, but more precise, high-end professional gadget, such as a spectrophotometer. A colorimeter and its step-by-step wizard tutorial will enable you to calibrate your display more precisely than you could by using subjective "eyeball" judgments.

Among moderately priced calibrators, our informal reading of hardware reviews and other industry publications has yielded the following as some of the current favorites: Spyder3Pro and Spyder3Elite by Datacolor; i1 Display 2 and i1 Display LT by X-Rite; and hueyPro, which was developed jointly by PANTONE and X-Rite.

Note: If, after calibrating your display, you intentionally or unintentionally adjust the display's brightness and contrast settings or change the room lighting (or repaint your walls!), remember to recalibrate it!

For Mac OS users who don't have a calibration device, your system supplies a display calibration utility; look for it in System Preferences > Displays > Color. Click Calibrate and follow the instructions that appear onscreen.

The steps outlined here apply loosely to the three hardware display calibrators that are mentioned on the preceding page. We happen to use Spyder3Pro.

## To calibrate your display using a hardware device:

1. Set the room lighting to the level that you normally use for work. If you have a CRT, let it warm up for 30 minutes for the display to stabilize.

2. Increase the brightness of your display to its highest level. In the Mac OS, if you have an Apple display, choose System Preferences > Displays and drag the Brightness slider to the far right. For a third-party display or any Windows display, use either a mechanical button on the display or a menu command in the OnScreen Display (OSD).

3. Launch the calibration application that you've installed, then follow the straightforward instructions on the step-by-step wizard screens. **A–B** You will need to tell the application the following important information: your display type (CRT or LCD), the white point to be used (choose D65/6500K), and the desired gamma value (choose 2.2 for both Windows and Macintosh).

For a CRT display, you may see a few more instructional screens requesting further display setting choices.

4. After entering your display information (**A**, next page), you'll be prompted to drape the colorimeter (hardware calibration sensor) over the monitor (**B**, next page). For an LCD, if a baffle is included with the calibration device, clip it on to prevent the suction cups from touching and potentially damaging the screen. Follow the instructions to align the sensor with the image onscreen. Click OK or Continue to initiate the series of calibration tests, which will take from 5 to 8 minutes.

5. After removing the calibration sensor, you'll be prompted to name your new display profile (**C**, next page). Include the date in the profile name, for your own reference. The application will place the new profile in the correct location for your Windows or Macintosh operating system. The wizard will step you through one or two more screens, and then you're done. When launched, Photoshop will automatically be aware of the new display profile.

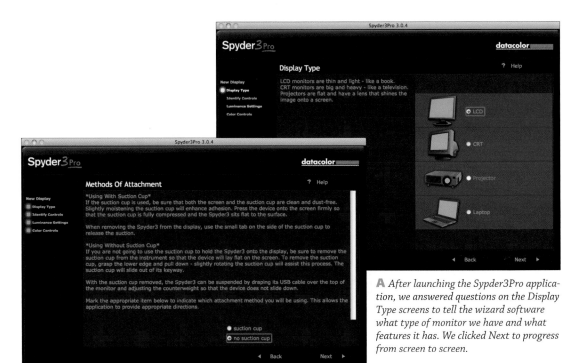

**A** *After launching the Sypder3Pro application, we answered questions on the Display Type screens to tell the wizard software what type of monitor we have and what features it has. We clicked Next to progress from screen to screen.*

**B** *On this Methods of Attachment screen, we clicked No Suction Cup.*

**A** *The resulting settings appeared on this Current Settings screen. Click Continue with These Settings.*

*Note: If you have already used the device to calibrate your monitor, a screen entitled CheckCAL will appear instead of this one. Click CheckCAL – Check Current Calibration.*

**B** *When this Measuring Display screen appeared, we draped the colorimeter over the monitor and aligned it with the onscreen image, then clicked Continue to initiate the actual calibration process.*

**C** *When the calibration was finished, we clicked Next, and this Specify Profile Name screen appeared. In our profile name, we included the monitor name and the current date.*

*After we clicked Next again, the SpyderProof screen appeared. We clicked Switch to compare the pre- and postcalibration results. Finally, we clicked Next, chose Quit, then clicked Next one last time to exit the software.*

# Choosing a color space for Photoshop

Continuing with our recommended steps for color management, you'll use the Color Settings dialog to set the color space for Photoshop. If you want to get up and running quickly by establishing Adobe RGB as the color space without wading through all the options in the Color Settings dialog, you can make one simple preset choice by following the first set of instructions below — that is, if you use the program primarily to produce images for print output on a commercial or color inkjet printer and you've followed our instructions for color management thus far.

## To choose a color settings preset:

1. Choose Edit > **Color Settings** (Ctrl-Shift-K/ Cmd-Shift-K). The Color Settings dialog opens (**A**, next page).

2. Choose **Settings**: **North America Prepress 2** (readers residing outside North America, choose an equivalent for your output device and geographic location). This preset changes the RGB working space to Adobe RGB (1998), and sets all the color management policies to the safe choice of Preserve Embedded Profiles so each file you open in Photoshop will keep its own profile.

3. Click OK.

If you want to explore the Color Settings dialog in more depth, follow these instructions instead. Pick and choose among the options, depending on your output requirements.

## To choose color settings options:

1. Choose Edit > **Color Settings** (Ctrl-Shift-K/ Cmd-Shift-K). The Color Settings dialog opens (**A**, next page).

2. From the **Settings** menu, choose one of these presets, depending on your output needs:

   **Monitor Color** sets the RGB working space to your display profile. This is a good choice for video output, but not for print output.

   **North America General Purpose 2** meets the requirements for screen and print output in North America. All profile warnings are off.

   **North America Newspaper** manages color for output on newsprint paper stock.

   **North America Prepress 2** manages color to conform with common press conditions in

North America. The default RGB color space that is assigned to this setting is Adobe RGB. When CMYK documents are opened, their values are preserved.

**North America Web/Internet** is designed for online output. All RGB images are converted to the sRGB color space.

3. The **Working Spaces** settings control how RGB and CMYK colors are treated in a document that lacks an embedded profile. You can either leave these settings as they are or choose other options (the RGB options are discussed below). For the **CMYK** setting, ask your output service provider which working space to choose.

   We recommend choosing one of these **RGB** color spaces, depending on your output needs:

   **Monitor RGB** [current display profile] sets the RGB working space to your display profile, and is useful if you know that other applications you'll be using for your project don't support color management. Keep in mind, however, that if you share files that use your monitor profile (as the color space) with another user, their monitor profile will be substituted for the RGB working space, and this may undermine the color consistency that you're aiming for.

   **ColorSync RGB** (Mac OS only) matches the Photoshop RGB space to the space that's specified in the Apple ColorSync Utility. If you share this configuration with another user, it will use the ColorSync space that's specified in their system.

   **Adobe RGB (1998)** contains a wide range of colors and is useful when converting RGB images to CMYK. You may have gotten our drift by now that this option is recommended for print output but not for online output.

   **ProPhoto RGB** contains a very wide range of colors and is useful for output to high-end inkjet and dye sublimation printers.

   **sRGB IEC61966-2.1** is a good choice for Web output, as it reflects the settings on the average computer display. Many hardware and software manufacturers use this as the default space for scanners, low-end printers, and software.

4. Click OK.

➤ The Adobe RGB (1998) color space, which is recommended for print output, includes more colors in the printable CMYK gamut than the sRGB IEC61966-2.1 color space, which is designed for online output. Although sRGB IEC61966-2.1 is the default listing on the Working Spaces: RGB menu in the Color Settings dialog, it can spell disaster for print output.

**DOCUMENT-SPECIFIC COLOR**

Photoshop supports document-specific color, meaning that each document keeps its own color profile. The profile controls how colors in the file are previewed onscreen, edited, and converted on output. For documents that lack an embedded profile, Photoshop generates a preview using the current working space.

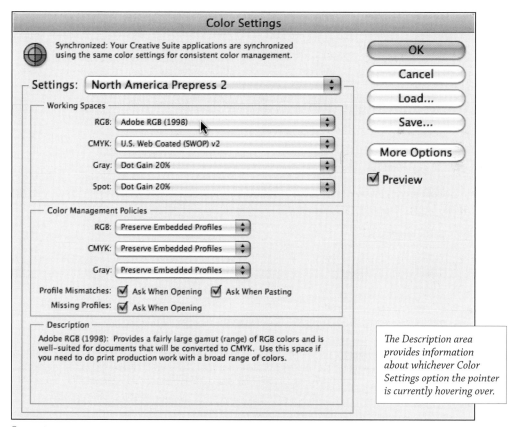

The Description area provides information about whichever Color Settings option the pointer is currently hovering over.

**A** *We chose North America Prepress 2 from the Settings menu in the Color Settings dialog.*

# Synchronizing color settings

If the color settings in another Adobe Creative Suite program that you have installed on your system (such as Illustrator or InDesign) don't match the settings in Photoshop, an alert will display at the top of the Color Settings dialog (as in **A**, next page). If you haven't installed one of the full Adobe Creative Suites, you'll have to start up the errant application and fix its color settings by hand. If you do have a suite installed, you can use the Suite Color Settings dialog in Bridge to synchronize the color settings for all of the color-managed Adobe programs on your system.

Before synchronizing the color settings via Bridge, make sure you've chosen the proper settings in Photoshop (see the preceding two pages).

### To synchronize the color settings among Creative Suite applications using Bridge:

1. On the Application bar in Photoshop, click the **Launch Bridge** button. Br

2. In Bridge, choose Edit > **Creative Suite Color Settings** (Ctrl-Shift-K/Cmd-Shift-K). The Suite Color Settings dialog opens.**A**

3. Click the same settings preset you chose in the Color Settings dialog in Photoshop, then click **Apply**. Bridge will change (synchronize) the color settings of the other Adobe Creative Suite applications to conform to the selected preset.

---

**MATCHING THE SETTINGS**

The presets in the Suite Color Settings dialog are the same as on the Settings menu in the Color Settings dialog (see page 10). Keep Show Expanded List of Color Settings Files unchecked to display just the five basic presets.

---

**A** *Use the Suite Color Settings dialog to synchronize the color settings of all the applications in the Adobe Creative Suite that you have installed on your system.*

## Customizing your color policies

The current color management policies govern whether Photoshop honors or overrides a document's settings if the color profile in the file, when opened or imported, doesn't conform to the current color settings in Photoshop. If you chose the North America Prepress 2 setting in the Color Settings dialog (page 10), the Ask When Opening policy (the safest option, in our opinion) is already chosen for you, and you can skip these instructions.

### To customize the color management policies for Photoshop:

1. Choose Edit > **Color Settings** (Ctrl-Shift-K/ Cmd-Shift-K). The Color Settings dialog opens. **A**

2. From the **Color Management Policies** menus, choose an option for files that are to be opened or imported into Photoshop:

   **Off** to prevent Photoshop from color-managing the files.

   **Preserve Embedded Profiles** if you expect to work with both color-managed and non-color-managed documents, and you want each file to keep its own profile.

**Convert to Working RGB** or **Convert to Working CMYK** to have all documents that you open or import into Photoshop adopt the program's current color working space. This is usually the best choice for Web output.

3. Do any of the following optional steps:

   For **Profile Mismatches**, if you check **Ask When Opening**, Photoshop will display an alert if the color profile in a file you're opening doesn't match the current working space. Via the alert, you will be able to override the current color management policy for each file.

   Check **Ask When Pasting** to have Photoshop display an alert if it encounters a color profile mismatch when you paste or drag and drop color imagery into a document. The alert lets you override your color management policy when pasting.

   For files with **Missing Profiles**, check **Ask When Opening** to have Photoshop display an alert offering an option to assign a profile.

4. Click OK.

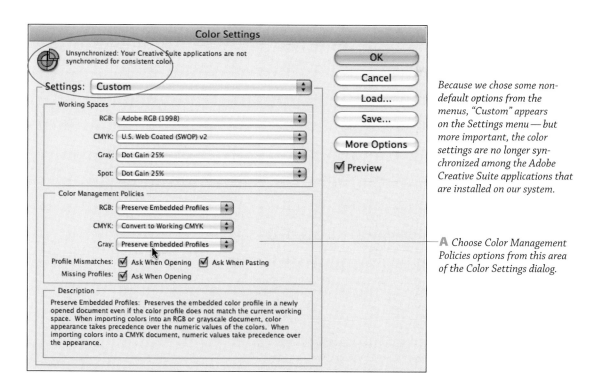

*Because we chose some non-default options from the menus, "Custom" appears on the Settings menu — but more important, the color settings are no longer synchronized among the Adobe Creative Suite applications that are installed on our system.*

**A** *Choose Color Management Policies options from this area of the Color Settings dialog.*

# Saving custom color settings

For desktop color printing, we recommended choosing North America Prepress 2 as the color setting for Photoshop (see page 10). For commercial printing, let the pros supply the proper color settings: Ask your print shop to send you a .csf file with all the correct Working Spaces and Color Management Policies settings for their particular press. Then all you'll need to do is install that custom color settings file in the proper location by following the instructions below and, when needed, choose it from the Settings menu in the Color Settings dialog.

## To save custom color settings as defaults for the Creative Suite:

1. In Windows, put the file in Program Files\
   Common Files\Adobe\Color\Settings.

   In the Mac OS, put the file in Users/[user name]/Library/Application Support/Adobe/Color/Settings.

2. To access the newly saved settings file, open the Color Settings dialog, then choose the name of the .csf file from the Settings menu.

If your print shop gives you a list of recommended settings for the Color Settings dialog — but not an actual .csf file — you can choose and then save that collection of settings as a .csf file by following these instructions.

## To save custom color settings:

1. Choose Edit > **Color Settings** (Ctrl-Shift-K/Cmd-Shift-K). The Color Settings dialog opens.

2. Enter the required settings by choosing and checking the appropriate options.

3. Click Save and enter a file name (we recommend including the printer type in the name), keep the .csf extension and the default location, then click Save.

4. Click OK to exit the Color Settings dialog.

# Acquiring printer profiles

Thus far, we've shown you how to set your camera to the Adobe RGB color space, calibrate your display, and specify Adobe RGB as the color space for Photoshop. Next you'll learn how to acquire the proper printer profile(s) so you can incorporate color management into your specific printing scenario.

## To download the printer profile for an inkjet printer:

Most printer manufacturers have a website from which you can download either an ICC profile for a specific printer/paper combination or a printer driver that contains a collection of specific ICC printer/paper profiles. Be sure to choose a profile that conforms to the particular printer/paper combination you will be using.

1. On the following page, we step you through a few pages on the websites for two manufacturers of widely used printers: Epson, focusing on the Stylus Photo R series (Epson.com) (**A–C**, next page) and Canon (Canon.com) (**D–F**, next page).

   Another option is to also download an ICC profile for a specific printer/paper combo from the website for a paper manufacturer, such as ilford.com or crane.com/museo.

   Note: The profiles for the newest printer models may not be available yet on these sites. Check back periodically.

2. After visiting the website, install the profile you downloaded by following the instructions that accompany it.

   On pages 404–405, we'll show you how to use the profile to soft-proof a document onscreen.

## FINDING A PROFILE FOR AN EPSON STYLUS PRINTER, PHOTO R SERIES

**A** *On the Epson.com home page for your region, choose Drivers & Support > Printers.*

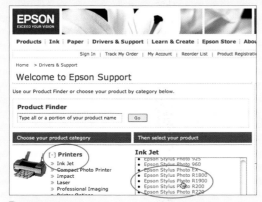

**B** *Click Ink Jet under Printers, then click your printer model on the list of printers.*

**C** *On the page for the printer model, below Drivers & Downloads, click the link for your operating system. On the Drivers & Downloads page (shown above), click the link for Premium ICC Profiles for [printer name].*

*On the Premium ICC Printer Profiles page (not shown), click the profile for your chosen paper type.*

## FINDING A PROFILE FOR A CANON INKJET PRINTER

**D** *On the Canon.com home page for your region, choose Downloads > Consumer.*

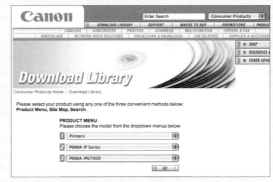

**E** *From the menus, choose the Printers category, product type (printer series), and printer model, then click Go.*

**F** *On the Drivers & Downloads page, select your operating system, then click the correct printer driver. The driver will install the profiles automatically.*

# Changing color profiles

When a file's profile doesn't conform to the current working space (Adobe RGB, in our case) or the color profile is missing altogether, you can use the Assign Profile command to assign the correct one. You may notice visible color shifts if the color data of the file is reinterpreted to conform to the new profile, but rest assured, the color data in the actual image is preserved. Do keep Preview checked, though, so you can see what you're getting into.

## To change or remove a file's color profile:

1. With a file open in Photoshop, choose Edit > **Assign Profile**. If the file contains layers, an alert may appear, warning you that the appearance of the layers may change; click OK. The Assign Profile dialog opens.**A**

2. Check Preview, then click one of the following:

   To remove the color profile, click **Don't Color Manage This Document**.

   To assign your current working space to the file, click **Working** [document color mode and the name of your chosen working space]. If you followed our instructions for color management, you've already specified Adobe RGB as the Working RGB space, but you can click this option for any photo that wasn't shot or scanned using that color space.

   To assign a different profile, click **Profile**, then choose a profile that differs from your current working space.

3. Click OK.

The Convert to Profile command lets you preview the conversion of a document to an assortment of output profiles and intents, and then converts the color data to the chosen profile. Note: This command performs a mode conversion and changes the actual color data in your file!

## To convert a file's color profile:

1. Choose Edit > **Convert to Profile**. In the Convert to Profile dialog,**B** check Preview.

2. Under Destination Space, from the **Profile** menu, choose the profile you want to convert the file to (it doesn't necessarily have to be the current working space).

3. Under Conversion Options, choose an **Intent** (for the intents, see the sidebar on page 405).

4. Leave the default Engine as **Adobe (ACE)** and keep **Use Black Point Compensation** and **Use Dither** checked.

5. *Optional:* Check Flatten Image to Preserve Appearance to merge all layers and adjustment layers in the document.

6. Click OK.

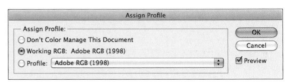

**A** *Use the Assign Profile dialog to either remove a color profile or assign a different one.*

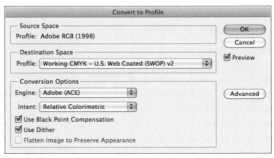

**B** *Use the Convert to Profile dialog to convert your document to a different color profile. Here, we're switching from the Adobe RGB profile to our working CMYK profile for a standard web press that uses coated paper.*

---

**WHERE A DOCUMENT'S PROFILE IS LISTED**

➤ If Document Profile is chosen from the Status bar menu at the bottom of the application frame, the current profile will be listed on the bar.

➤ In the File > Save As dialog, if you save a file in a format that supports embedded profiles, such as Photoshop (PSD) or Photoshop PDF, you can check ICC Profile... (Windows)/Embed Color Profile... (Mac OS) to embed the profile with the file — if one has been assigned.

➤ In the File > Print dialog, the profile name appears in the upper right, under "Document."

We start this chapter with a few basic pointers for buying a digital camera and shooting digital photos. Following that, you'll learn how to calculate the correct resolution for a file, create a new blank document, create document presets, save and copy your files, use the Status bar, and close up shop. In the next chapter, you will learn how to download photos from your camera and how to use Bridge to open and manage files. In Chapter 4, you will learn how to open and correct your photos using the Camera Raw plug-in before opening them into Photoshop.

Although Photoshop lets you create, open, edit, and save files in over a dozen different formats,**A–B** on a frequent basis, you'll probably encounter or use only a handful of those formats, namely Photoshop (PSD, the native Photoshop file format), Photoshop EPS, Photoshop PDF, JPEG, and TIFF. The Large Document format, or PSB (nicknamed "Photoshop Big"), is used only for huge files; see the sidebar on page 22.

Because Photoshop reads so many different file formats, you can use the program to open images from many sources, such as digital cameras, scanners, drawing applications, and video captures. You can edit a single image, create a montage of imagery from multiple files, or create images entirely within Photoshop by using brushes, filters, and other commands.

*Continued on the following page*

# CREATING FILES

2

```
Photoshop (*.PSD;*.PDD)
BMP (*.BMP;*.RLE;*.DIB)
CompuServe GIF (*.GIF)
Dicom (*.DCM;*.DC3;*.DIC)
Photoshop EPS (*.EPS)
Photoshop DCS 1.0 (*.EPS)
Photoshop DCS 2.0 (*.EPS)
FXG (*.FXG)
IFF Format (*.IFF;*.TDI)
JPEG (*.JPG;*.JPEG;*.JPE)
JPEG 2000 (*.JPF;*.JPX;*.JP2;*.J2C;*.J2K;*.JPC)
Large Document Format (*.PSB)
PCX (*.PCX)
Photoshop PDF (*.PDF;*.PDP)
Photoshop Raw (*.RAW)
Pixar (*.PXR)
PNG (*.PNG)
Portable Bit Map (*.PBM;*.PGM;*.PPM;*.PNM;*.PFM;*.F
Scitex CT (*.SCT)
Targa (*.TGA;*.VDA;*.ICB;*.VST)
TIFF (*.TIF;*.TIFF)
```

```
✓ Photoshop
  Large Document Format
  BMP
  CompuServe GIF
  Dicom
  Photoshop EPS
  IFF Format
  JPEG
  JPEG 2000
  PCX
  Photoshop PDF
  Photoshop 2.0
  Photoshop Raw
  Pixar
  PNG
  Portable Bit Map
  Scitex CT
  Targa
  TIFF
  Photoshop DCS 1.0
  Photoshop DCS 2.0
```

**A** *Files can be saved in these formats in Windows.*

**B** *Files can be saved in these formats in the Mac OS.*

# Buying, and choosing settings for, a digital camera

## Buying a digital camera

If you're shopping for a digital camera, the first step is to figure out which model suits your output requirements and, of course, your budget. Two factors to consider in this regard are a camera's megapixel value and the size of its digital light sensor.

Camera manufacturers usually list the resolution of a model as width and height dimensions in pixels (such as 3000 pixels x 2000 pixels). Multiply the two values, and you'll arrive at a number in the millions, which is the number of pixels the camera captures in each shot. This is known as the camera's megapixel value. If your camera captures a sufficient number of pixels, you'll be able to print high-quality closeups and enlargements of your photos.

Compact, inexpensive "point-and-shoot" cameras offer few or no manual controls and have a resolution of 6 to 10 megapixels. They capture enough detail to produce decent-quality 5" x 7" prints but not larger, and acceptable Web output.

Advanced amateur camera models have a resolution of 8 to 12 megapixels. You can get high-quality 8" x 10" prints from these cameras, and they offer more manual controls.

Professional camera models (such as digital SLRs) have a resolution of 12 megapixels or higher and can produce high-quality 11" x 14" prints or larger — but they're costly. More importantly, the digital light sensors in such cameras are larger and more sensitive than those in lesser cameras. They record more precise detail and produce a higher-quality image, with less visual noise. High-megapixel cameras with large sensors aren't for everyone — and not just because of their price tag. Images with a high megapixel count have larger file sizes, take longer to upload from the camera to the computer, and require a larger hard drive for storage. (See our comparison of megapixels and print size on page 22.) Unless you tend to crop your photos or output large prints, an 8- to 10-megapixel camera will be better suited to your needs.

Aside from the megapixel count and the size of the sensor, make sure the camera you buy can accommodate a wide assortment of lenses.

For more advice about buying a camera, you can visit the website for *PC Magazine* (pcmag.com) or *Macworld* (macworld.com). Photography magazine websites are also good sources of information.

## Choosing settings in your digital camera

You've acquired a camera (congratulations!) — now you may want some pointers on how to use it. To get good-quality photographs, in addition to establishing the right lighting conditions, composing the shot artistically, etc., you need to choose your camera settings wisely. Here are some basic guidelines:

➤ Medium- and high-end digital cameras let you choose an **ISO** setting, which controls the sensitivity of the camera's digital sensor to light (and is comparable to film speed in film photography). High ISO settings tend to produce digital noise in low-light areas, so it's best to choose the lowest ISO setting that still enables you to get the desired exposure.

➤ Decide whether to have your camera capture the photos in the **JPEG** format (see pages 425–426), or even better, as unprocessed **raw** files.*

➤ Choose a **color space** for your camera: sRGB for onscreen or Web output, or Adobe RGB for print output.

➤ For JPEG photos, choose a **white balance** setting that's appropriate for the lighting conditions in which the photos will be shot; the camera will process the image data based on this setting. For raw files, you can ignore the white balance setting, as the images won't be processed inside the camera.

➤ If your camera has a histogram display, use it to verify that your shot was taken with the correct **exposure** settings (aperture and shutter speed). In an overexposed image, insufficient details are captured in the highlight areas; in an underexposed image, insufficient details are captured in the shadow areas. Photoshop can process and adjust only the details that your camera captures. (For a discussion of histograms, see pages 203–204.)

Regardless of whether you shoot JPEG or raw photos, most exposure deficiencies, color casts, and other imaging problems can be corrected via the Camera Raw dialog (see Chapter 4) and then the photo can be further corrected via an assortment of adjustment commands in Photoshop.

*Each camera model produces its own variation of a raw file. In this book, we refer to such files collectively as "raw files."*

# Working with 16 bits per channel

To get good-quality output from Photoshop, a wide range of tonal values must be captured at the outset. The wider the dynamic range of your chosen input device, the finer the subtleties of color and shade it can capture. Most advanced amateur and professional digital SLR cameras capture at least 12 bits of accurate data per channel. Like cameras, scanners range widely in quality: Consumer-level scanners capture around 10 bits of accurate data per channel, whereas the high-end professional ones capture up to 16 bits of accurate data per channel.

Shadow areas in particular are notoriously difficult to capture well. But if your camera can capture 12 to 16 bits per channel (or you work with high-resolution scans), you will have a head start, because your files will contain an abundance of pixels in all levels of the tonal spectrum.

Photoshop can process files that are in 8, 16, or 32 Bits/Channel mode. All Photoshop commands are available for 8-bit files. Most Photoshop commands are available for 16-bit files (e.g., on the Filter menu, the Liquify and Lens Correction filters are available, as are some or all of the filters on the Blur, Noise, Render, Sharpen, Stylize, and Other submenus, whereas filters on the other submenus are not). Too few Photoshop commands are available for 32 Bits/Channel files to make such files a practical choice.

Although you can lower the bit depth of your files via the Image > Mode submenu, it's better to keep them in 16 Bits/Channel mode. The editing and resampling commands in Photoshop can degrade the image quality, but the extra pixels in 16-bit images make this less of a problem. 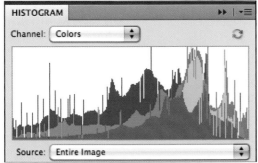–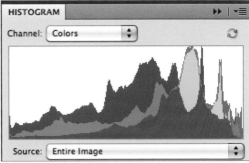 The tonal adjustment commands in particular, such as Levels and Curves, remove pixel data and alter the distribution of pixels across the tonal spectrum. Signs of pixel loss from destructive edits will be more visible in a high-end print of an 8-bit image than in a 16-bit image. Because 16-bit images contain an ample number of pixels in all parts of the tonal spectrum at the outset, more tonal values are preserved, and the resulting output is higher quality.

To summarize, these are some basic facts about 16-bit files to consider:

➤ Photoshop can open 16-bit files in CMYK or RGB mode.

➤ 16-bit files can be saved in many formats, such as Photoshop (.psd), Large Document (.psb), Photoshop PDF (.pdf), PNG (.png), TIFF (.tif), and JPEG 2000 (.jpf).

➤ From the Mac OS, you can print 16-bit files, provided your printer supports 16-bit printing.

➤ For commercial print output, your output service provider may request 8-bit files, in which case you will need to convert them after image-editing.

Note: If system or storage limitations prevent you from working with 16-bit images, consider following this two-stage approach: Perform the initial tonal corrections (such as Levels and Curves adjustments) on the 16-bits-per-channel image, then convert it to 8 bits per channel for further editing.

**A** *As a result of a Levels command adjustment to this 8-bit image, some image data was discarded, as shown by the spikes and gaps in the histogram.*

**B** *Here, the same Levels adjustment was made to a 16-bit version of the same image. Because of the higher bit depth, the smooth tonal transitions were preserved.*

# Calculating the correct file resolution

## Resolution for print

If you shoot digital photos, your camera will preserve either all the pixels that are captured as raw files or a portion of the pixels that are captured as small, medium, or large JPEG files. If you use a scanner to acquire images, you can control the number of pixels the device captures by setting the input resolution in the scanner software.

High-resolution photos contain more pixels, and therefore finer details, than low-resolution photos, but they also have larger file sizes, take longer to render onscreen, require more processing time to edit, and are slower to print. Low-resolution images, however, look coarse and jagged and lack detail when printed. Your files should have the minimum resolution to obtain the desired output quality from your intended output device at the desired output size — but not much higher. There are three ways to set the resolution value for your digital files.

➤ If you open raw digital or JPEG photos into the Camera Raw dialog, which we highly recommend, you can specify an image resolution there. See page 66.

➤ After opening your files into Photoshop, you can change the image resolution in the Image Size dialog (see pages 122–124).

➤ When scanning photos, you'll set the image resolution using the scanning software for that device.

The print resolution for digitized images (from a camera or scanner) is calculated in pixels per inch (ppi). **A–C** For output to an inkjet (desktop) printer, the file resolution should be between 240 and 300 ppi.

Commercial print shops have specific requirements for their particular output devices, so it's important to ask them what resolution and halftone screen frequency settings they're going to use before choosing a resolution for your files. For a grayscale image, the proper resolution will usually be around one-and-a-half times the halftone screen frequency (lines per inch) setting of the output device, or 200 ppi; for a color image, the resolution will be around twice the halftone screen frequency, or 250–350 ppi.

**A** *72 ppi*

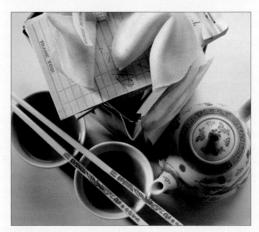

**B** *150 ppi*

**C** *300 ppi*

## Resolution and dimensions for the Web

Choosing the correct file resolution for Web output is a no-brainer: It's always 72 ppi.

Choosing the correct dimensions for Web output requires a little more forethought, because it depends on how your Photoshop images are ultimately going to be used in the Web page layout. To quickly create a document with the proper dimensions and resolution for Web output, choose a preset in step 3 at right. To determine a maximum custom size for a Photoshop image to be displayed on a Web page, first estimate how large your user's browser window is likely to be, then calculate how much of that window the image is going to fill. Currently, the most common monitor size is 1024 pixels wide by 768 pixels high. Most viewers have their browser window open to a width of approximately 1000 pixels. If you subtract the space occupied by the menu bar, scroll bars, and other controls in the browser interface, you're left with an area of up to 800 x 600 pixels; you can use those dimensions as a guideline. If your Photoshop file is going to be used as a small element in a Web page layout, you can choose smaller dimensions.

# Creating a new, blank document

In these instructions, you will create a new, blank document. You can drag and drop or copy and paste imagery into this document from other files, or draw or paint imagery by hand using brushes. The images can then be edited with Photoshop commands, such as effects and filters.

### To create a new, blank document:

1. Choose File > **New** (Ctrl-N/Cmd-N). The New dialog opens.**A**

2. Type a name in the **Name** field.

3. Do either of the following:

   Choose a preset size option from one of the three categories on the **Preset** menu: the Default Photoshop Size; a paper size for commercial and desktop printers; or a screen size for Web, mobile, film, and video output. Next, choose a specific size for that preset from the **Size** menu.

   Choose a unit of measure from the menu next to the Width field; the same unit will be chosen automatically for the Height (or to change the unit for one dimension only, hold down Shift while choosing it). Next, enter custom **Width** and **Height** values (or use the scrubby sliders).

*Continued on the following page*

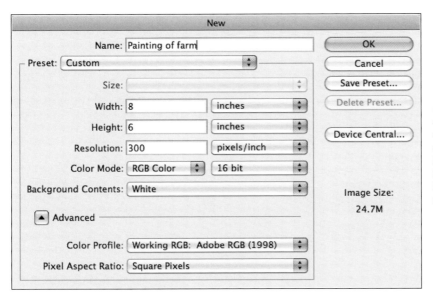

**A** *In the New dialog, enter a file Name; either choose a Preset size or enter custom Width, Height, and Resolution values; choose RGB Color Mode and a Background Contents option; and choose a Color Profile.*

**4.** Enter the **Resolution** required for your target output device — be it an imagesetter or the Web. For the Web, enter 72; for print output, see our discussion of resolution on page 20. You can use the scrubby slider here, too.

**5.** Choose a document **Color Mode** (RGB Color is recommended), then from the adjacent menu, choose **8 bit** or **16 bit** as the color depth (see page 19). You can convert the image to a different color mode later, if needed (see "Photoshop document color modes" on pages 3–4).

**6.** Note the **Image Size**, which is listed on the right side of the dialog. If you need to reduce that size, you can choose smaller dimensions, a lower resolution, or a lower bit depth.

**7.** For the Background of the image, choose **Background Contents**: **White** or **Background Color**; or choose **Transparent** if you want the bottommost tier of the document to be a layer. (To choose a Background color, see Chapter 11. To learn about layers, see Chapter 8.)

**8.** Click the Advanced arrowhead, if necessary, to display additional options, then choose a **Color Profile**. This list of profiles will vary depending on the document Color Mode. (Note: you can also assign or change the profile later in the Edit > Assign Profile dialog. To learn more about color profiles, see pages 10–11 and 16.)

For Web or print output, leave the Pixel Aspect Ratio on the default setting of Square Pixels. For video output, choose an applicable option (see Photoshop Help).

**9.** Click OK. A new, blank document window appears onscreen. To save it, see page 24.

➤ To force the New dialog settings to match those of an existing open document, open the New dialog, then from the bottom of the Preset menu, choose the name of the document that has the desired dimensions.

➤ If the Clipboard contains graphic data (say, that you copied from Adobe Photoshop or Illustrator), the New dialog will automatically display the dimensions of that content. Choosing Clipboard from the Preset menu in the New dialog accomplishes the same thing. If you want to prevent the Clipboard dimensions from displaying, and display the last-used file dimensions instead, hold down Alt/Option as you choose File > New.

---

### MEGAPIXELS, RESOLUTION, AND PRINT SIZES

| Image Resolution | Megapixels in Inches (rounded off)* | | | |
|---|---|---|---|---|
| | 6 | 8 | 10 | 12 |
| 150 ppi | 13 x 20 | 16 x 22 | 17 x 24 | 18 x 28 |
| 300 ppi | 7 x 10 | 8 x 11 | 8 x 13 | 9 x 14 |

*These print sizes are approximate. For a more exact listing, search the Web for "megapixels to print size chart."*

### PHOTOSHOP BIG

In Photoshop, you can create and save files as large as 300,000 x 300,000 pixels — or over 2 gigabytes (GB) — and they can contain up to 56 user-created channels. The Large Document (.psb) format is designed specifically for saving these gonzo files, but they can be opened and edited only in Photoshop (versions CS through CS5).

What can you do with PSB files? If you have the disk space to store and work with them and have access to a wide-format printer that can output super-large images (up to 32,000 x 32,000 pixels), great. In order to output a PSB file on an ordinary printer, though, you would have to lower its resolution drastically (remember to duplicate the file first).

# Creating document presets

If you tend to use the same document size, color mode, or other settings repeatedly in the New dialog, take the time to create a document preset for those settings. Thereafter, you'll be able to access your settings via the Preset menu, which will save you startup time as you create new files.

## To create a document preset:

1. Choose File > **New** or press Ctrl-N/Cmd-N. The New dialog opens.

2. Choose settings, such as the width, height, resolution, color mode, bit depth, background contents, color profile, and pixel aspect ratio. Ignore any setting that you don't want to include in the preset; you'll exclude it from the preset in step 5.

3. Click **Save Preset**. The New Document Preset dialog opens. **A**

4. Enter a **Preset Name**.

5. Under **Include in Saved Settings**, uncheck any New dialog settings that you don't want included in the preset.

6. Click OK. Your new preset will appear on the Preset menu in the New dialog.

➤ To delete a user-created preset, choose it from the Preset menu, click Delete Preset, then click Yes (this can't be undone).

**CHOOSE YOUR DEFAULTS**

In Edit/Photoshop > Preferences > Units & Rulers, under New Document Presets Resolutions, you can enter Print Resolution and Screen Resolution values. Thereafter, one of those values will appear in the Resolution field in the File > New dialog when you choose a preset from the Preset menu. The Print Resolution value is used for the Paper and Photo presets (the default value is 300 ppi); the Screen Resolution value is used for the Web, Mobile & Devices, and Film & Video presets (the default value is 72 ppi).

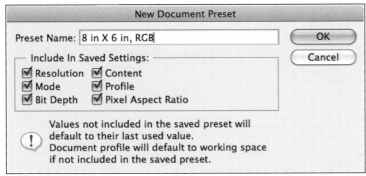

**A** *Use the New Document Preset dialog to control which of the current settings in the New dialog will be saved in your new document preset.*

# Saving your file

If you're not sure which format to use when saving a file for the first time, you can safely go with the native Photoshop format, PSD. One good reason to do so is that PSD files are more compact than TIFF files (see also the sidebar on the following page).

## To save an unsaved document:

1. If the document window contains any imagery, you can choose File > **Save** (Ctrl-S/Cmd-S); if it's completely blank, choose File > **Save As** (Ctrl-Shift-S/Cmd-Shift-S). The Save As dialog opens.

2. Type a name in the **File Name** field A/**Save As** field (A, next page).

3. Choose a location for the file.

   In Windows, if you need to navigate to a different folder or drive, use the Save In menu at the top of the dialog.

   In the Mac OS, click a drive or folder in the Sidebar panel on the left side of the window. To locate a recently used folder, use the menu below the Save As field.

4. Choose a file format from the **Format** menu. Only the native Photoshop (PSD), Large

Document Format (PSB), TIFF, and Photoshop PDF formats support layers (see the information about flattening layers on pages 134 and 146).

5. If you're not yet familiar with the features listed in the **Save** area, leave the settings as is. The As a Copy option is discussed on page 26.

6. If the file contains an embedded color profile and the format you're saving to supports such profiles, in the **Color** area, you can check **ICC Profile/Embed Color Profile**: [profile name] to save the profile with the file. (To learn about embedded profiles, see pages 10, 13, and 16.)

7. Click Save.

➤ In the Mac OS, to have Photoshop append a three-character extension (e.g., .tif, .psd) to the file name automatically when a file is saved for the first time, in Edit/Photoshop > Preferences > File Handling, choose Append File Extension: Always. Extensions are required when exporting Macintosh files to the Windows platform and when posting files to a Web server.

➤ To learn about the Maximize PSD and PSB File Compatibility option in the File Handling panel of the Preferences dialog, see page 390.

**A** *This is the Save As dialog in Windows.*

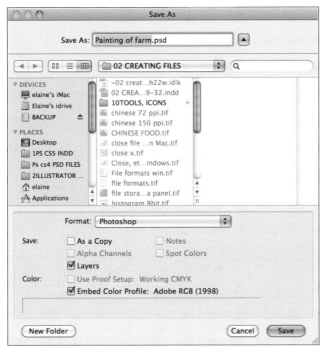

**A** *This is the Save As dialog in the Mac OS.*

---

### CHOOSING THE CORRECT FORMAT

Photoshop (PSD), Large Document (PSB), TIFF, and Photoshop PDF are the only formats that preserve the following Photoshop features:

► Multiple layers and layer transparency

► Shape layers

► Smart Objects

► Adjustment layers

► Editable type layers

► Layer effects

► Alpha channels

► Grids and guides

ICC color management profiles are preserved by the above-mentioned formats (and also by the JPEG and Photoshop EPS formats).

To prepare your document for printing from another application or to export it to an application that doesn't read Photoshop layers, read about the TIFF, EPS, and PDF formats on pages 417–420. Or for Web output, read about the GIF and JPEG formats on pages 421–426.

---

Once a file has been saved for the first time, each subsequent use of the Save command overwrites (saves over) the last version.

### To save a previously saved file:

Choose File > **Save** (Ctrl-S/Cmd-S).

The simple Revert command restores your document to the last-saved version.

Note: We know you can't learn everything at once, but keep in mind for the future that the History panel, which Chapter 10 is devoted exclusively to, serves as a full-service multiple undo feature. Also, a use of the Revert command shows up as a state on the History panel, so you can undo a revert by clicking an earlier history state.

### To revert to the last saved version of a file:

Choose File > **Revert**.

► To undo the most recent modification, choose Edit > Undo (Ctrl-Z/Cmd-Z). Not all edits can be undone by this command. For the other undo and redo commands, see page 113.

The Save As command lets you save a copy of your file under a new name (say, to create a design, document color mode, or adjustment variation) or with different options. Another important use of this command is to save a flattened copy of a file in a different format, for export to another application. This is necessary because most non-Adobe applications can't import Photoshop PSD files or read Photoshop layers.

### To save a new version of a file:

1. Choose File > **Save As** (Ctrl-Shift-S/Cmd-Shift-S). The Save As dialog opens.

2. Change the name in the **File Name/Save As** field. This is important!

3. Choose a location for the new version from the Save In menu in Windows or by using the Sidebar panel and columns in the Mac OS. (Read about the new Save As to Original Folder preference on page 390. ★)

4. *Optional:* From the Format menu, choose a different file format. Only formats that are available for the file's current color mode and bit depth are listed. Note: If you try to save a 16-bit file in the JPEG (.jpg) format, Photoshop will produce a flattened, 8-bit copy of the file automatically. ★

   *Beware!* If the format you've chosen doesn't support layers, the Layers option becomes dimmed, a yellow alert icon displays, and layers in the new version are flattened.

5. Check any available options in the **Save** area, as desired. For example, you could check **As a Copy** to have the copy of the file remain closed and the original file stay open onscreen, or uncheck this option to have the original file close and the copy stay open.

   Depending on the current File Saving settings in Edit/Photoshop > Preferences > File Handling (and depending on whether you're working on a Windows or Mac OS machine), some preview and extension options may be available in the Save As dialog. See pages 389–390.

6. In the **Color** area, check ICC **Profile/Embed Color Profile**: [profile name], if available (see pages 10, 13, and 16), to include the profile, for color management.

7. Click Save. Depending on the chosen file format, another dialog may appear. For the TIFF format, see page 417; for EPS, see pages 418–419; or for PDF, see page 420. For other formats, see Photoshop Help.

➤ If you don't change the file name or format in the Save As dialog but do click Save, an alert will appear. Click Yes/Replace to replace the original file, or click No/Cancel to return to the Save As dialog.

➤ To optimize a file in the GIF or JPEG format for Web output, see pages 423–426.

---

**A DESIGNER'S BEST FRIEND**

To create document variations within the same file, explore the Layer Comps panel; see pages 382–384.

## Using the Status bar

Using the Status bar and menu at the bottom of the document window, you can read data about the current file or find out how Photoshop is currently using memory.

### To use the Status bar:

From the menu next to the Status bar at the bottom of a floating or tabbed document window, choose the type of data you want displayed on the bar:

**Document Sizes** to list the approximate file storage size of a flattened version of the file if it were saved in the PSD format (the value on the left) and the storage size of the current file including layers (the value on the right).

**Document Profile** to list the embedded color profile (the words "Untagged [RGB or CMYK]" appear if a profile hasn't been assigned).**A**

**Document Dimensions** to list the image dimensions (its width, height, and resolution).

**Scratch Sizes** to list the amount of RAM Photoshop is using to process all currently open files (the value on the left) and the amount of RAM that is currently available to Photoshop (the value on the right). If the first value is greater than the second, it means Photoshop is currently utilizing virtual memory on the scratch disk.

**Efficiency** to list the percentage of program operations that are currently being done in RAM as opposed to the scratch disk (see page 391). When this value is below 100, it means the scratch disk is being used.

**Current Tool** to list the name of the current tool.

To view detailed data about a particular file, use the Metadata panel in Bridge.

### To find out the storage size (and other data) of a file:

1. On the Application bar in Photoshop, click the Bridge button.![Br] In Bridge, click an image thumbnail (see page 36).

2. In the Metadata panel on the right, under File Properties, note the **File Size** value.**B**

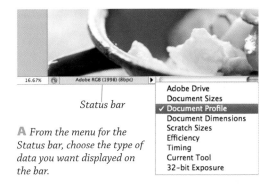

**A** *From the menu for the Status bar, choose the type of data you want displayed on the bar.*

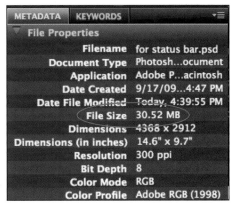

**B** *To learn the storage size of a file, click its thumbnail in Bridge, then in the File Properties category of the Metadata panel, note the File Size listing.*

---

**GETTING DOCUMENT INFO FAST**

Regardless of which info category is chosen on the Status bar menu, you can always click and hold on the Status bar to display the following data about the current image: its dimensions, number of channels, color mode, bit depth, and resolution.

# Ending a work session

## To close a document:

1. Do one of the following:

   Click the ⊗ on a document tab. A

   Choose File > **Close** (Ctrl-W/Cmd-W).

   Click the Close button in the upper right corner of a floating document window in Windows, **B** or the upper left corner of a floating document window in the Mac OS. **C**

2. If you try to close a file that was modified since it was last saved, an alert dialog will appear. **D** Click No (N)/Don't Save (D) to close the file without saving it, or click Yes (Y)/Save (S) to save the file before closing it (or click Cancel to cancel the close command).

➤ An asterisk on a document title bar or tab indicates that the document contains unsaved changes.

➤ To quickly close multiple open documents, press Ctrl-Alt-W/Cmd-Option-W. In the alert dialog that appears, you can check Apply to All, ★ if desired, to have your response apply to all the open documents, then click Don't Save or Save.

➤ In Photoshop, to close a file and launch or go to Bridge, choose File > Close and Go To Bridge (Ctrl-Shift-W/Cmd-Shift-W).

## To exit/quit Photoshop:

1. In Windows, choose File > **Exit** (Ctrl-Q) or click the Close button for the application frame.

   In the Mac OS, choose Photoshop > **Quit Photoshop** (Cmd-Q).

2. All open Photoshop files will close. If any changes were made to any open file since it was last saved, an alert dialog will appear. Click No (N)/Don't Save (D) to close the file without saving it, or click Yes (Y)/Save (S) to save it before exiting/quitting Photoshop (or click Cancel to cancel the exit/quit command).

**A** *In Windows and the Mac OS, you can close a tabbed document by clicking the X on the tab.*

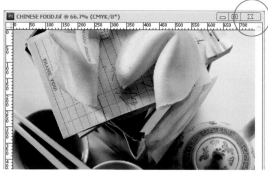

**B** *In Windows, click the Close (X) button on a floating document window.*

**C** *In the Mac OS, click the Close (red) button on a floating document window.*

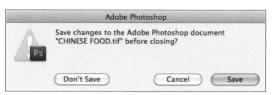

**D** *If you try to close a file that contains unsaved changes, this alert prompt will appear. A similar prompt will appear if you exit/quit Photoshop and any open files contain unsaved changes.*

The Bridge application ships with Photoshop and is aptly named because it serves as a bridge to programs in the Adobe Creative Suite. In Chapter 1, you learned how to use Bridge to synchronize the color settings for your Creative Suite programs. With its large thumbnail previews of files from Adobe Creative Suite applications, Bridge is the best vehicle for opening files, and it offers a host of other useful features.

This chapter begins with instructions for downloading photos from a digital camera. Following that, you will use Bridge to preview, examine, label, rate, sort, and filter your file thumbnails; customize the Bridge workspace; organize thumbnails into collections and collapsible stacks; search for, move, copy, and assign keywords to files; and open files into Photoshop. You will also use Mini Bridge, a panel that lets you access the Bridge features in Photoshop. There's a lot to learn in this comprehensive chapter — progress through it at your own pace.

## Launching Adobe Bridge

### To launch Adobe Bridge:

To open the Adobe Bridge window, do one of the following:

In Windows or in the Mac OS, on the Application bar in Photoshop, click the **Launch Bridge** button [Br] (Ctrl-Alt-O/Cmd-Option-O).

In Windows, click the Start button, choose All Programs, then click **Adobe Bridge CS5**.

In the Mac OS, double-click the **Adobe Bridge CS5** application icon [Br] or click the **Bridge** icon [Br] on the Dock.

➤ There is a Bridge feature that lets it launch automatically at startup and stay in the background in stealth mode. We suggest that beginning users turn this feature off by going to the Edit/Adobe Bridge CS5 > Preferences dialog for Bridge (Ctrl-K/Cmd-K), Advanced panel, and unchecking Start Bridge at Login.

**A** *On the Application bar in Photoshop, click the Launch Bridge button to launch Bridge (or to switch to Bridge if it's already running).*

**BRIDGE 3**

# Downloading photos from a camera

When you use a digital camera, your photos are stored on a removable memory card — most likely a CompactFlash (CF) or Secure Digital (SD) card. Rather than having to tether your camera directly to a computer, you can remove the memory card and insert it into a card reader device, then download your photos from the card reader to your computer via a USB cable or Firewire cable, depending on which connection your camera supports (Firewire is the faster of the two).

When you start downloading images from a camera, your system's default application or dialog for acquiring images may launch automatically. Instead of using the system dialog, we recommend using the Photo Downloader application that is included with Bridge. Instructions are provided here.

## To download photos via a card reader and Photo Downloader:

1. Take the card out of your camera and insert it into the appropriate slot in the card reader.

2. Plug the card reader into your computer. If the default system application for acquiring photos launches, exit/quit it.

3. Launch **Bridge**, then click the **Get Photos from Camera** button at the top of the Bridge window. The Photo Downloader dialog opens. **A** If an alert dialog appears and you want to make Photo Downloader the default capture application, click Yes (as we do); if not, click No.

4. From the **Get Photos From** menu in the Source area, select your card reader.

5. In the **Import Settings** area, do the following:

   To change the save location, click **Browse/Choose**, then navigate to the desired folder. Click OK/Choose again to assign that folder and return to the Photo Downloader dialog.

   To create a new subfolder within the folder you just selected, choose a naming convention from the **Create Subfolder(s)** menu, or choose Custom Name and enter a folder name (or choose None for no new subfolder).

   *Optional:* To assign your digital images recognizable names and shorter sequential numbers in lieu of the long default number, choose a Custom Name option from the Rename Files menu, then enter a name and a starting number. A sample of your entries displays in the Example field.

Check **Open Adobe Bridge** to have the photos display in Bridge when the download is completed.

Keep the Preserve Current Filename in XMP, Convert to DNG, and Delete Original Files options unchecked.

We recommend that you check **Save Copies To** then click **Browse/Choose** to send copies of your photos to a designated folder on an external hard drive, as a backup.

**A** *This is the Standard dialog of the Photo Downloader.*

**6.** If you want to download select photos (instead of the whole batch) from your memory card, click **Advanced Dialog** to display the larger Advanced dialog. 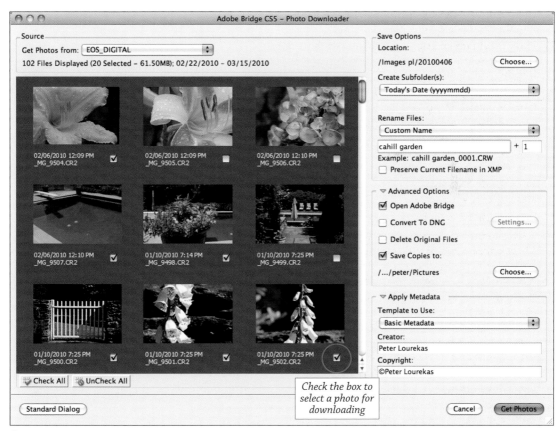A Below the thumbnail window, click **UnCheck All**, then check the box below each photo to be downloaded. Or click, then Shift-click a sequence of photos, then check the box for one of them; a check mark will appear below each selected photo.

*Optional:* In the Apply Metadata area, enter Creator and Copyright info to be added to the metadata of all downloaded photos. This data will display in Bridge.

➤ To switch back to the smaller Standard dialog at any time, click Standard Dialog.

**7.** Click Get Photos to start the downloading process. When the downloading is finished, the Photo Downloader dialog is dismissed automatically. If you checked the Open Adobe Bridge option, your photos will display in a new window in Bridge. Don't worry about previewing or opening them just yet. We'll step you through that process later.

**8.** Now that you're done using the Photo Downloader, you should insert a blank DVD and burn the copies of your photo files to the DVD as a permanent backup copy. In the Mac OS, you can do this via drag-and-drop in the Finder. If you need to learn how to copy files to a DVD, consult the Help files for your operating system.

**A** *This Advanced dialog of the Photo Downloader contains the same options as the Standard dialog, plus metadata features and an area for checking which photos are to be downloaded.*

# Features of the Bridge window

First, we'll identify the main sections of the Bridge window, starting from the top (**A**, next page). The two rows of buttons and menus running across the top of the window are jointly referred to as the toolbar. The second row of the toolbar is also called the Path bar.

In the Essentials workspace, the main window is divided into three panes: a large pane in the center and a vertical pane on either side. Each pane contains one or more panels, which are accessed via tabs: Favorites, Folders, Filter, Collections, Export, Content, Preview, Metadata, and Keywords. Panels in the side panes let you manage files, filter the display of thumbnails, and display file data; the large central panel displays file thumbnails. At the bottom of the Bridge window are controls for changing the thumbnail size and format. (To customize the Bridge workspace, see pages 34–35 and 41–43.)

We'll explore the toolbar features and most of the panels in depth in this chapter, but for the moment, here is a brief description of the panels:

The **Favorites** panel displays a list of folders that you've designated as favorites, for quick access. See page 36.

The **Folders** panel contains a scrolling window with a hierarchical listing of all the top-level and nested folders on your hard drive. See page 36.

The **Filter** panel lists data specific to files in the current folder, such as their label, star rating, file type, date created, and date modified. By clicking various listings in the **Filter** panel on or off, you can quickly control which files from the current folder display in the Content panel. To expand or collapse a category, click the arrowhead. See page 45.

The **Collections** panel displays the names (and folder icons) of collections, which are user-created groups of image thumbnails. Using the collection features, you can organize and access your file thumbnails without relocating the actual files. See pages 52–53.

The **Content** panel displays image thumbnails (and optional thumbnails for nested folders) within the currently selected folder. In the lower right corner of the Bridge window, you can click a View Content button to control whether, and in what format, metadata pertaining to the current files displays in the Content panel (see page 42). For any view type, you can change the thumbnail size via the Thumbnails slider. The Content panel is used and illustrated throughout this chapter.

The **Preview** panel displays a large preview of the image (or folder) thumbnail that you have selected in the Content panel. If the thumbnail for a video or PDF file is selected, a controller for playing the video or for viewing the pages displays in this panel. Two or more selected image thumbnails can be previewed in this panel, for quick comparison, and it has a loupe mechanism that you can use to magnify the details of the previewed image. See pages 36–38.

Detailed information about the currently selected file displays in two locations in the **Metadata** panel: a quick summary in the placard at the top (see the sidebar on page 36) and detailed listings within the categories below. The File Properties category, for example, lists the file name, format, date created, date modified, etc. To expand or collapse a category, click the arrowhead. You can use the IPTC Core category in the Metadata panel to attach creator, description, copyright, and other information to the currently selected file (see the sidebar on page 54). When the thumbnail for a digital photo is selected, the Camera Data (EXIF) category displays the camera settings that were used to capture the photo. If the photo was edited in Camera Raw, the panel will have a Camera Raw category in which those settings will be listed.

Use the **Keywords** panel to assign one or more descriptive subkeywords to your images, such as an event, name, or location, so they can be located more quickly (see page 55). You can run a search to find image thumbnails based on keyword criteria, or display images by checking keywords in the Filter panel (see page 45).

Note: The Export and Inspector panels aren't covered in this book.

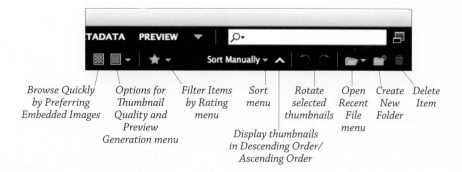

Browse Quickly by Preferring Embedded Images

Options for Thumbnail Quality and Preview Generation menu

Filter Items by Rating menu

Sort menu

Rotate selected thumbnails

Display thumbnails in Descending Order/ Ascending Order

Open Recent File menu

Create New Folder

Delete Item

Get Photos from Camera

Return to last Adobe Creative Suite application ★

Refine menu (Review Mode, Batch Rename, File Info)

Open in Camera Raw

Output menu (Web or PDF)

Name of currently displayed folder

Workspace switcher

Workspace menu

For navigation controls on the toolbar, see page 36.

Path bar

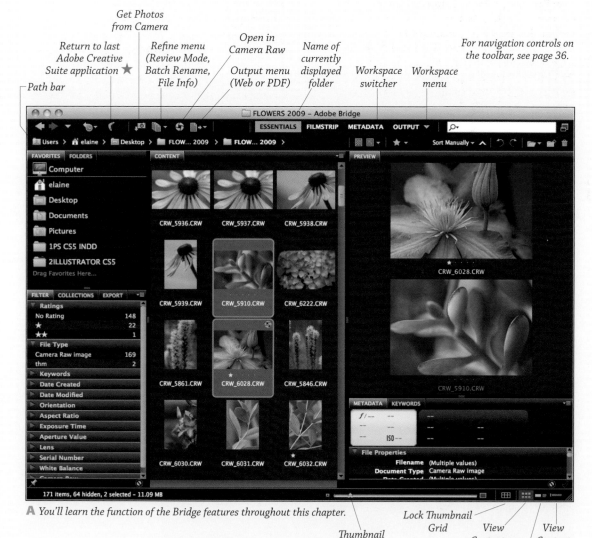

**A** You'll learn the function of the Bridge features throughout this chapter.

Thumbnail Size slider

Lock Thumbnail Grid

View Content as Thumbnails

View Content as List

View Content as Details

# Choosing a workspace for Bridge

To reconfigure the Bridge window quickly, choose one of the predefined workspaces. (To create and save custom workspaces, see pages 41–43.)

## To choose a workspace for Bridge:

Do one of the following:

On the upper toolbar, click **Essentials**, **Filmstrip**, **Metadata** (List View for the thumbnails), **Output**, **Keywords**, **Preview**, **Light Table**, **Folders**, or a custom workspace.**A** (To display more workspace names, pull the gripper bar to the left.)

From the **Workspace** menu on the workspace switcher, choose a workspace **B–C** (and **A–C**, next page).

Press the shortcut for one of the first six workspaces on the switcher (as listed on the Workspace menu): Ctrl-F1/Cmd-F1 through Ctrl-F6/Cmd-F6. The shortcuts are assigned automatically to the first six workspaces on the switcher, according to their current order from left to right.

➤ To change the order of workspaces on the switcher, drag any name to the left or right.

➤ To learn how to resize the thumbnails in the Content panel, see page 41.

*To reveal more workspace names, drag the gripper bar to the left.*

**A** *Click a workspace name on the workspace switcher...*

**B** *...or choose a workspace name from the Workspace menu*

**C** *The Filmstrip workspace features a large preview of the currently selected thumbnail(s).*

**A** *In the Essentials workspace, all the panels are showing.*

**B** *In the Preview workspace, the Metadata and Keywords panels are hidden to make room for a larger preview, and the thumbnails display in a vertical format (the opposite arrangement from the Filmstrip workspace).*

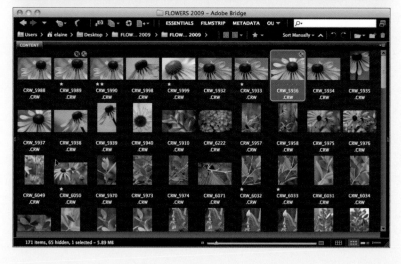

**C** *In the Light Table workspace, the Content panel occupies the entire Bridge window. Use this workspace when you need to view a large number of thumbnails.*

# Previewing images in Bridge

## To add a folder to the Favorites panel:

Do either of the following:

Drag a folder icon from the Content panel or the Explorer/Finder into the Favorites panel (the pointer will be a plus sign).

Right-click a folder in the Folders or Content panel and choose **Add to Favorites**.

➤ Via check boxes in the Favorite Items area of Edit/Adobe Bridge CS5 > Preferences > General, you can control which system folders appear in the Favorites panel.

➤ To remove a folder from the Favorites list, right-click it and choose Remove from Favorites.

## To display and select images in Bridge:

1. Do any of the following:

In the **Folders** panel, navigate to a folder. You can use the scroll arrows, and you can expand or collapse any folder by clicking its arrowhead.

Display the contents of a folder by clicking its icon in the **Folders** panel or by double-clicking its thumbnail in the **Content** panel. Note: For folder icons thumbnails to display in the Content panel, View > Show Folders must be checked.

Click the **Go Back** button ◀ on the toolbar **A** to step back through the last folders viewed, or the **Go Forward** button ▶ to reverse those steps.

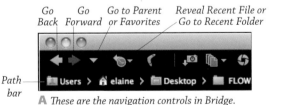

Go Back  Go Forward  Go to Parent or Favorites  Reveal Recent File or Go to Recent Folder

Path bar

**A** *These are the navigation controls in Bridge.*

Click a folder name in the **Favorites** panel.

From the **Go to Parent or Favorites** menu ⬛ on the toolbar, choose a parent or favorites folder.

Click a folder name on the **Path** bar (Window > Path Bar).

From one of the menus ▶ on the Path bar, choose a folder. If another submenu displays, click yet another folder; repeat until you reach the desired folder.

➤ To display thumbnails for images in all the nested subfolders inside the current folder, choose Show Items from Subfolders from its menu. ▶ To restore the normal view, click the Cancel button ⬛ on the Path bar.

2. In the **Content** panel, click an image thumbnail. A colored border appears around it, and data about the file is listed in the Metadata panel. An enlarged preview of the image also displays in the **Preview** panel, if that panel is showing. Or to select multiple images, Ctrl-click/Cmd-click nonconsecutive thumbnails (**A**, next page); or click the first thumbnail in a series of consecutive thumbnails, then Shift-click the last one you want to select.

➤ A number in the upper left corner of an image thumbnail indicates that it's in a group, called a stack. To display all the image thumbnails in a stack, click the number. To collapse the stack, click the number again (see page 48).

➤ When an image thumbnail is selected, you can cycle through other thumbnails in the current folder by pressing an arrow key. To quickly locate and select a particular thumbnail, start typing the file name.

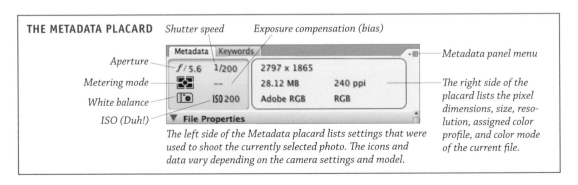

**THE METADATA PLACARD**    *Shutter speed*    *Exposure compensation (bias)*

*Aperture*

*Metering mode*

*White balance*

*ISO (Duh!)*

*Metadata panel menu*

*The right side of the placard lists the pixel dimensions, size, resolution, assigned color profile, and color mode of the current file.*

*The left side of the Metadata placard lists settings that were used to shoot the currently selected photo. The icons and data vary depending on the camera settings and model.*

**A** *Ctrl-click/Cmd-click to select multiple consecutive or nonconsecutive image thumbnails.*

You can control whether thumbnails and the preview render quickly but at low resolution, or slower and color-managed at high resolution.

## To choose quality options for the thumbnails and previews:

From the **Options for Thumbnail Quality and Preview Generation** menu ▓ on the Bridge toolbar, choose a preference for the thumbnail quality:

**Prefer Embedded (Faster)** displays low-resolution thumbnails and is useful when you need to display many images quickly.

**High Quality on Demand** displays high-resolution, color-managed thumbnails and previews for selected thumbnails (generated from the source files) and low-resolution previews for unselected ones. This is a good compromise between the two other options.

**Always High Quality,** the default setting, displays high-resolution thumbnails and previews, whether the thumbnails are selected or not. Rendering is the slowest with this option.

➤ For lower quality but faster previewing, click the Browse Quickly by Preferring Embedded Images button ▓ on the Bridge Path bar; this enables the Prefer Embedded (Faster) option. Click the button again to return to the current setting on the Options for Thumbnail Quality and Preview Generation menu.

➤ The Generate 100% Previews option saves actual-size JPEG versions of thumbnails to disk so Bridge can generate higher-quality previews when the loupe is used or when images are displayed at 100% view in the Full Screen Preview or in Slideshow mode. Since this option uses a lot of disk space, we recommend keeping it unchecked.

## To compare two or more image previews:

1. In Bridge, click or choose the Filmstrip or Preview workspace.

2. In the Content panel, Ctrl-click/Cmd-click up to nine thumbnails. **A** Large versions of those thumbnails will display in the Preview panel.

3. *Optional:* Ctrl-click/Cmd-click an unselected thumbnail in the Content panel to add it to the Preview panel, or do the same for a selected thumbnail to remove it from the Preview panel.

## To display a full-screen image preview:

1. Press the Spacebar to display a full-screen preview of the currently selected thumbnail and hide the Bridge window temporarily.

2. To zoom in or out, press + or – or use the scroll wheel on your mouse (you can drag the magnified preview). If desired, press the right arrow key to cycle through other thumbnails in the same folder.

3. To redisplay the Bridge window, press the Spacebar or Esc.

## To inspect image details with an onscreen loupe:

1. To make the loupe appear, click an image in the Preview panel or click the frontmost image in Review mode (see the next page). **B**

   Note: If the loupe doesn't appear, it's because the Ctrl-Click/Cmd-Click Opens the Loupe When Previewing or Reviewing option is checked in Edit/Adobe Bridge CS5 > Preferences > General (for Bridge). If this is the case, Ctrl-click/Cmd-click the image to make the loupe appear.

2. Click the area to be examined. By default, pixels display in the loupe at 100% view (the zoom level is listed below the preview). Press + to zoom in on the loupe display (up to 800%) or press – to zoom out, or use the scroll wheel on your mouse. To examine a different area, click that area or drag the loupe to it.

3. *Optional:* If you're previewing two images using two loupes, you can Ctrl-drag/Cmd-drag either loupe to move them simultaneously.

4. Click the loupe to remove it.

**A** *We Ctrl/Cmd clicked two image thumbnails to display them in the Preview panel, then clicked a preview to display the loupe.*

When selected thumbnails are put into Review mode, the Bridge window is hidden to make room for a very large preview on a black background, and you can cycle through the images as if they're on a carousel.

### To preview images in Review mode:

1. Do one of the following:

   Open a folder of images.

   Alt-click/Option-click a thumbnail stack.

   Select five or more image thumbnails (Ctrl/Cmd or Shift-click them).

2. Press Ctrl-B/Cmd-B (or from the Refine menu 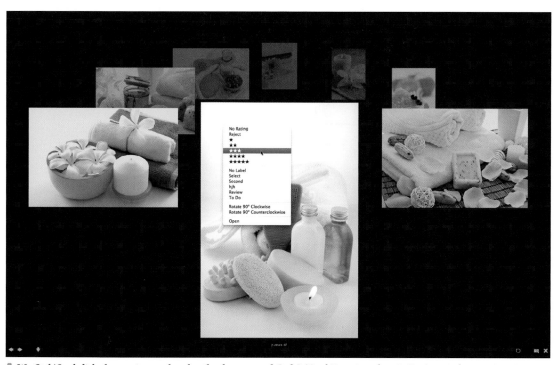 at the top of the Bridge window, choose Review Mode). The Bridge window is hidden temporarily, and the images display on a black background.**A**

3. To rotate the carousel, do any of the following:

   Drag any image preview to the left or right.

   Click one of the smaller previews to bring it to the forefront.

Click (and keep clicking) the Go Forward ▶ or Go Backward ◀ button in the lower left corner, or press the left or right arrow key.

4. To examine the frontmost (enlarged) image with a loupe, click it. Drag the loupe to move it. Click the loupe again to remove it.

5. To rate the frontmost thumbnail, right-click it and choose a star rating or a label from the context menu. To view a list of keyboard shortcuts onscreen, press H.

6. To take the frontmost image out of the carousel, click the down-pointing arrow ⬇ in the lower left corner, or drag the image to the bottom of your screen. This won't delete the actual file.

   ➤ You can pare down a selection of images this way before grouping them as a stack (see pages 48–49) or as a collection (see pages 52–53).

7. To exit Review mode, press Esc or click the ✖ in the lower right corner.

8. Click any image thumbnail to deselect the rest.

**A** *We Ctrl/Cmd clicked seven image thumbnails, then pressed Ctrl-B/Cmd-B to view them in Review mode.*

# Opening files from Bridge

You can open as many files into Photoshop as the currently available RAM and scratch disk space on your computer allow.

Note: To open a raw, JPEG, or TIFF digital photo into Camera Raw (to apply corrections before opening the files into Photoshop), see pages 62–63.

## To open files from Bridge into Photoshop:

1. In the Content panel, display the thumbnail for the image(s) to be opened.

2. Do either of the following:

   Double-click an image thumbnail.

   Click an image thumbnail or select multiple thumbnails, then double-click one of them or press Ctrl-O/Cmd-O.

   Photoshop will launch, if it isn't already running, and the image(s) will appear onscreen.

   If any alert dialogs appear, see page 58.

➤ If a photo has been opened in Camera Raw and settings were applied to it in that dialog, the ☻ icon displays in the top right corner of its thumbnail. If you're confident about the photo's current Camera Raw settings and are ready to open it into Photoshop, Shift-double-click it.

➤ To locate a file in Explorer/Finder, right-click its thumbnail in Bridge and choose Reveal in Explorer/Reveal in Finder from the context menu. The folder that the file resides in will open in a window in Explorer/Finder and the file icon will be selected.

➤ By default, the Bridge window stays open after you use it to open a file. To minimize/close the Bridge window as you open a file, hold down Alt/Option while double-clicking the file thumbnail.

➤ To open an image into Photoshop from Review mode, right-click it and choose Open from the context menu.

## To reopen a recently opened file:

To reopen a file that was recently opened and then closed, choose the file name in one of these locations:

In Bridge, choose from the **Open Recent File** menu 🖼 on the right side of the Path bar.

In Bridge or Photoshop, choose from the File > **Open Recent** submenu.

In Bridge, from the **Reveal Recent File or Go to Recent Folder** menu, 🖼 choose **Adobe Photoshop > Recent Adobe Photoshop Files**, then click the thumbnail for a file to open it. To redisplay an "actual" folder when you return to Bridge, click the Go Back arrow 🔙 or a Favorites folder.

In Photoshop, on the toolbar of the Mini Bridge panel, from the **Go to Parent, Recent Items, or Favorites** menu, 🔍 choose **Recent Folders > Recent Adobe Photoshop Files**, then click the thumbnail for a file to open it. To redisplay an "actual" folder in Mini Bridge, click the Go Back arrow. 🔙 ★

---

**GETTING TO PHOTOSHOP QUICKLY**

If Photoshop was the last Creative Suite application open, you can go to it quickly from Bridge by clicking the Return to Adobe Photoshop button 🔲 on the toolbar. ★ Photoshop will launch, if it isn't already running.

**ALAS, THE POOR OPEN COMMAND**

➤ With Bridge now the best vehicle for opening files, the Open command is relegated to this sidebar. To use the Open command in Photoshop, choose File > Open (Ctrl-O/Cmd-O). In Windows, choose Files of Type: All Formats; in the Mac OS, choose Enable: All Readable Documents. Locate and click the desired file name, then click Open.

➤ Another way to open a file is by double-clicking its file icon in Explorer/Finder. Photoshop will also be launched, if it's not already running.

# Customizing the Bridge window

## To display or hide the panels:

On the **Window** menu, check which panels you want to show or hide.

➤ To quickly hide (and then show) the side panes, press Tab or double-click the dark vertical bar between the side and middle panes.

➤ To display just the Content panel in a compact window, click the Switch to Compact Mode button in the upper right corner of the Bridge window. Click it again to restore the full window.

## To configure the Bridge panes and panels manually:

Do any of the following:

To make a panel or panel group taller or shorter, drag its horizontal gripper bar upward or downward. **A**

To make a whole pane wider or narrower, drag its vertical gripper bar horizontally; **B** the adjacent pane will resize accordingly.

To minimize a panel to just a tab (or to restore its former size), double-click its tab. (This doesn't work for all panels.)

To move a panel into a different group, drag the panel tab, and release the mouse when the blue drop zone border appears around the desired group.

To display a panel as a separate group, drag its tab between two panels, and release the mouse when the horizontal blue drop zone line appears.

## To resize the image thumbnails:

At the bottom of the Bridge window, drag the **Thumbnail Size** slider **C** or click the **Smaller Thumbnail Size** button or **Larger Thumbnail Size** button.

➤ To display only full thumbnails, with grid lines between them, click the Lock Thumbnail Grid button at the bottom of the Bridge window. With this option on, no shuffling of thumbnails will occur if you resize the Content panel.

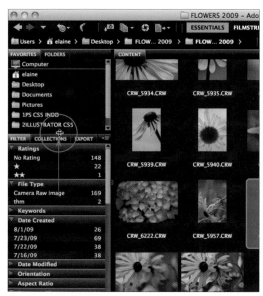

**A** *Moving the horizontal bar upward shortens the Favorites and Folder panels and lengthens the Filter, Collections, and Export panel group.*

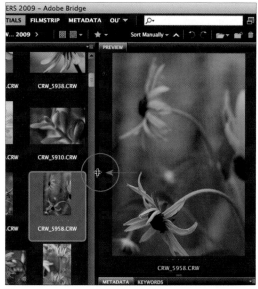

**B** *Moving the vertical bar for the right pane to the left widens the Preview, Metadata, and Keywords panels.*

**C** *Use the Thumbnail Size slider at the bottom of the Bridge window to resize your image thumbnails.*

## To control how metadata is displayed in the Content panel:

1. In the lower right corner of the Bridge window, click a View Content button: **A** **View Content as Thumbnails** (minimal file data), **View Content as Details** (more file data),**B** or **View Content as List** (small icons with columns of data).

    ➤ With View Content as List chosen, you can change the column order by dragging any column header to the left or right.

2. To control which categories of metadata display below or next to the image thumbnails when the View Content as Thumbnails option is chosen, go to Edit/Adobe Bridge CS5 > Preferences > Thumbnails, then select from any or all of the **Details**: **Show** menus. For example, to display exposure settings, you would choose Exposure.

    ➤ When the View Content as Thumbnails option is chosen, you can toggle the display of data on and off by pressing Ctrl-T/Cmd-T.

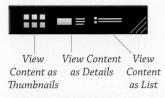

*View Content as Thumbnails*    *View Content as Details*    *View Content as List*

**A** *The View Content buttons control the display of metadata in the Content panel.*

### METADATA IN THE TOOL TIPS

If Show Tooltips is checked in Edit/Adobe Bridge CS5 Preferences > Thumbnails and you rest the pointer on an image thumbnail, the tool tip will list the metadata for that image. You can turn this feature off if it becomes annoying.

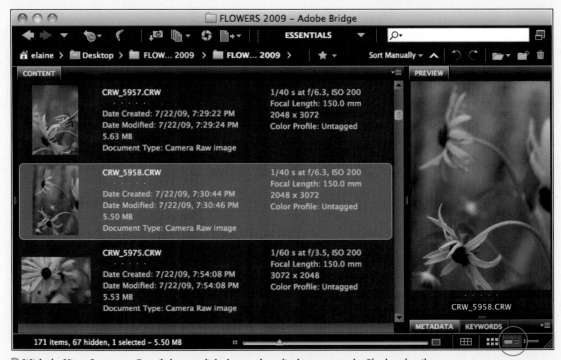

**B** *With the View Content as Details button clicked, metadata displays next to the file thumbnails.*

## Saving custom workspaces

If you save your customized workspaces, you'll be able to access them again quickly at any time and will avoid having to set up your workspace each time you launch Bridge.

### To save a custom workspace for Bridge:

1. Do all of the following:

   Choose a size and location for the overall Bridge window.

   Arrange the panel sizes and groups as desired.

   Choose a thumbnail size for the Content panel.

   Choose a sorting order from the Sort menu at the top of the Bridge window (see page 45).

   Click a View Content button.

2. From the **Workspace** menu on the workspace switcher, choose **New Workspace**.

3. In the New Workspace dialog, **A** enter a Name for the workspace, check Save Window Location as Part of Workspace and/or Save Sort Order as Part of Workspace (both are optional), then click Save.

   Note: Your new workspace will be listed first on the workspace switcher, and will be assigned the first shortcut (Ctrl-F1/Cmd-F1). To change the order of workspaces on the bar, drag any workspace name horizontally to a different slot. When you do this, the shortcuts will be reassigned based on the new order.

➤ To delete a user-saved workspace, from the Workspace menu, choose Delete Workspace. From the menu in the dialog, choose the workspace to be deleted, then click Delete.

## Resetting the Bridge workspaces

When you make a manual change to a saved workspace, the change sticks with the workspace even when you switch to a different one. As an example, if you were to change the thumbnail size for the Filmstrip workspace, click the Essentials workspace, then click back on the Filmstrip workspace, the new thumbnail size would still display. Via the commands for resetting workspaces, you can restore the default settings to any individual predefined (standard Adobe) or user-saved workspace or to all the predefined workspaces.

### To reset the Bridge workspace:

Do either of the following:

To restore the default settings to one workspace, right-click the workspace name and choose **Reset**.

To restore the default settings to all the Adobe predefined workspaces, choose **Reset Standard Workspaces** from the Workspace menu.

**A** Use the New Workspace dialog to name your workspace and choose options for it.

---

**CHOOSING COLORS FOR THE BRIDGE INTERFACE**

In Edit/Adobe Bridge CS5 > Preferences > General (Ctrl-K/Cmd-K), under Appearance, you can choose a User Interface Brightness (gray) value for the side panes; a different Image Backdrop value for the Content and Preview panels and for the background behind images when displayed in Full Preview View, Slideshow, or Review Mode; and an Accent Color for the border around selected folders, thumbnails, and stacks.

# Rating and labeling thumbnails

If you assign star ratings and/or color labels to your thumbnails, you'll be able to control which ones display based on their ranking, and locate them easily via the Filter panel or the Find command. In addition, you can apply a Reject rating to any image thumbnails that you want to hide from the Content panel but aren't ready to delete from your hard drive.

## To rate and label thumbnails:

1. Select one or more image thumbnails in the Content panel.

2. Do any of the following:

   From the Label menu, choose a **Rating** (to assign a star ranking) and/or a **Label** (to add a color-coded strip below the thumbnail).

   Click a thumbnail, then click any one of the five dots below it; stars will appear. To remove one star, click the star to its left. To remove all the stars from a thumbnail, click to the left of the first one. (If you don't see the dots or stars, enlarge the thumbnails via the Thumbnail Size slider.)

   Press one of the keyboard shortcuts that are listed on the Label menu.

   Right-click a thumbnail in the Content panel, then choose a category from the **Label** submenu on the context menu.

   Right-click in the Preview panel and choose a star rating and/or label for that image.

   To label the losers with a red "Reject" label,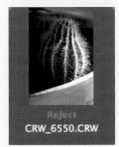 choose Label > **Reject** or press Alt-Del/Option-Delete. Note: If Show Reject Files is unchecked on the View menu, all rejected thumbnails will be hidden.

➤ If tool tips get in the way of your adding or removing stars, go to Edit/Adobe Bridge CS5 > Preferences > Thumbnails and uncheck Show Tooltips.

➤ You can assign custom names to the label categories in Edit/Adobe Bridge CS5 > Preferences > Labels.

## To remove ratings or labels from thumbnails:

1. Select one or more image thumbnails.

2. From the Label menu, choose **No Rating** or press Ctrl-0/Cmd-0 (zero), and/or choose **No Label**.

**A** *This thumbnail has an Approved (green) rating.*

**B** *We clicked the third dot on this thumbnail to give it a 3-star rating...*

**C** *...but then we changed our minds, so we clicked to the left of the stars to remove them.*

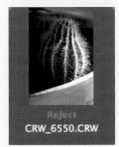

**D** *This poor fellow has a Reject rating.*

---

**RATING THUMBNAILS IN REVIEW MODE**

To rate or label images in Review mode, right-click the large, frontmost image and choose from the context menu.

## Choosing a sorting order

The order in which thumbnails display in the Content panel is determined by the criterion checked on the Sort menu. This order applies to all folders and thumbnails in Bridge, not just to the currently selected one. By applying ratings and/or labels, choosing a sorting order, and checking categories in the Filter panel (see below), you'll be able to locate the files you need more quickly and efficiently. Note that the sorting order also affects the batch and auto-mate commands in Bridge, because they process files based on the current sequence of thumbnails.

### To choose a sorting order for thumbnails:

From the **Sort** menu on the Path bar, choose a sorting order (such as By Date Created). **A** All thumbnails (except those in stacks) will be rearranged in the Content panel. To restore the last manual sort (by dragging), choose Manually.

➤ To reverse the current order, click the Ascending Order ▲ or Descending Order ▼ arrowhead.

## Filtering the display of thumbnails

The Filter panel lists data specific to files in the current folder, such as their label, star rating, date created, or keywords. When you check specific criteria in the panel, only thumbnails meeting those criteria display in the Content panel; thumbnails in stacks are ignored.

### To filter the display of thumbnails:

Do either of the following:

On the **Filter Items by Rating** menu on the Bridge toolbar, **B** check the desired criteria.

On the **Filter** panel, click the arrowhead to expand any category, such as Labels or Ratings, then check a criterion. **C** To require additional criteria to be met, check more listings, either in the same category or in other categories. For example, to display only files that have a 3-star rating, check the 3-star listing under Ratings. (To remove a criterion, click the listing again.)

➤ To prevent the current filters (check marks) from clearing when you display other folders, click the Keep Filter When Browsing 📌 button on the panel; the button will display a highlight color.

➤ To remove all check marks from the Filter panel, click the Clear Filter 🚫 button at the bottom of the panel or press Ctrl-Alt-A/Cmd-Option-A.

**A** *From the Sort menu on the Path bar, choose a sorting order for your selected thumbnails.*

**B** *Control which thumbnails display via the Filter Items by Rating menu.*

**C** *Because we checked the three-star ranking in the Filter panel (under the Ratings category), only thumbnails matching that criterion (that have three stars) will display in the Content panel.*

---

### THE FILTER PANEL IS DYNAMIC

The categories that are listed on the Filter panel (e.g., Ratings, Keywords, Exposure Time) change dynamically depending on what data is available for files in the currently selected folder and what categories are checked on the Filter panel menu. For instance, if you haven't applied ratings to any files in the current folder, you won't see a Ratings category; should you apply a rating to one of the thumbnails, the Ratings category will appear.

# Using Mini Bridge ★

A wonderful new feature of Photoshop CS5 is Mini Bridge, a miniature version of "big" Bridge in a panel format. Love it. What are known as panels in Bridge are called pods in Mini Bridge.

### To preview files in Mini Bridge:

1. In Photoshop, click the **Mini Bridge** button ▣ on the Application bar or choose File > **Browse in Mini Bridge**. The resizable Mini Bridge panel opens (**A**, next page).

2. Click the **Browse Files** button ▣ on the Home Page (if you don't see this button, click the **Home Page** button ⌂ at the top of the panel).

3. On the **Panel View** menu,▣ make sure **Path Bar**, **Navigation Pod**, and **Preview Pod** are checked.

4. To navigate to a folder, do one of the following:

   Click a folder on the Path bar.

   In the **Navigation** pod, click Favorites or Recent Folders, then click a folder, or click Recent Files, or the folder for a collection (see pages 52–53).

   Make a choice from the **Go to Parent**, **Recent Items**, or **Favorites** menu ▣ on the Toolbar.

   Click the **Search** button ▣ on the Toolbar, enter a file name, then click Search.

5. Use controls at the bottom of the panel to customize the display of file thumbnails:

   Adjust the thumbnail size via the **Thumbnail Size** slider (we keep our thumbnails small).

   From the **View** menu,▣ choose to view content **As Thumbnails** (file names below the thumbnails), **As Filmstrip** (thumbnails in one row), **As Details** (large thumbnails and more data), or **As List** (tiny thumbnails and columns of data).

6. At the top of the **Content** pod, you have access to the following menus for sorting and filtering thumbnails:

   The **Select** menu ▣ gives you access to the Refresh command (see the tip at right); the Show Reject Files, Show Hidden Files, and Show Folders commands; and the Select All, Deselect All, and Invert Selection commands.

   The **Filter Items by Rating** menu ▣ offers even more options than the one in Bridge, such as Keep Filter When Browsing and Show 1 or More Stars.

   The **Sort** menu ▣ lets you sort thumbnails, such as by Filename, Type, or Date Created.

7. To preview a thumbnail, select it, then do any of the following (only one file previews at a time):

   View the thumbnail in the **Preview** pod.

   To view the image as a large preview in the Content pod, press **Shift-Spacebar**. To enlarge the preview, click it; you can drag the image in the preview. To exit the preview, click Close (or in the Mac OS, you can also press Esc).

   For a full-screen preview, press the **Spacebar**. To go back to Mini Bridge, press the Spacebar again or Esc.

   To preview multiple thumbnails as a slideshow or in Review mode, Ctrl-click/Cmd-click to select them, then choose Slideshow or Review Mode from the **Preview** menu ▣ ▾ at the bottom of the panel or from the context menu.

➤ To close a pod, click its Close button.▣

➤ The Mini Bridge panel can be docked to the bottom of the document window (drag the top bar until you see a blue drop zone line).

➤ To add a folder to the Favorites area, right-click it in the Content pod and choose Add to Favorites.

### To open files from Mini Bridge into Photoshop:

1. Select the thumbnails for the file(s) to be opened.

2. Do either of the following:

   Double-click one of the selected thumbnails.

   Right-click a thumbnail and choose **Open** or **Open Image**.

➤ If a file is in a format that can be opened into Camera Raw, you can right-click its thumbnail and choose Open in Camera Raw. See page 63.

➤ The Tools menu ▣ in Mini Bridge provides access to some useful Photoshop commands, such as Place > In Photoshop (see page 309), Photoshop > Load Files into Photoshop Layers (see page 241), and Photoshop > Photomerge (see pages 250–251).

➤ After you change a thumbnail in some way in Bridge (say you rename, duplicate, or move it), if the Content pod doesn't update automatically, choose Refresh from the Select menu.▣

➤ To view a selected image thumbnail in Bridge, click the Go to Adobe Bridge button ▣ at the top of the panel, or right-click the thumbnail and choose Reveal in Bridge.

Via settings, you can control when Bridge is launched, a requirement for running Mini Bridge, and also change the colors for the Mini Bridge interface.

## To choose settings for Mini Bridge:

1. Click the **Home Page** button 🏠 at the top of the panel, then click the **Settings** button.

2. Do either or both of the following:

   Click **Bridge Launching**, then choose the desired settings.**B**

   To change the colors for the Mini Bridge panel, click **Appearance**, then adjust the User Interface Brightness and/or Image Backdrop sliders. Also check Color Manage Panel to have Photoshop color-manage the thumbnails and preview based on the color profile that is currently assigned to your primary display.

3. Do either of the following:

   To choose the other settings category, click **Settings**.

   To go back to the main Mini Bridge pods, click the **Browse Files** button. 🖼

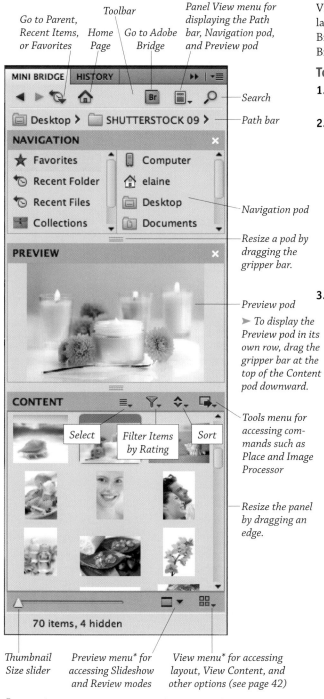

*Go to Parent, Recent Items, or Favorites* — *Toolbar* — *Home Page* — *Go to Adobe Bridge* — *Panel View menu for displaying the Path bar, Navigation pod, and Preview pod*

*Search*

*Path bar*

*Navigation pod*

*Resize a pod by dragging the gripper bar.*

*Preview pod*
▶ *To display the Preview pod in its own row, drag the gripper bar at the top of the Content pod downward.*

*Select* — *Filter Items by Rating* — *Sort*

*Tools menu for accessing commands such as Place and Image Processor*

*Resize the panel by dragging an edge.*

*Thumbnail Size slider* — *Preview menu\* for accessing Slideshow and Review modes* — *View menu\* for accessing layout, View Content, and other options (see page 42)*

**A** *Here the Navigation, Preview, and Content pods are showing.*

*\*This icon changes depending on what option is currently selected on the menu.*

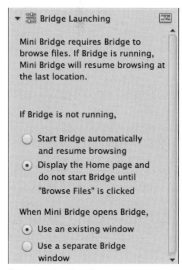

**B** *In Mini Bridge, choose settings to control how Bridge is launched.*

# Using thumbnail stacks

Before learning about stacks, you need to know how to rearrange thumbnails in the Content panel.

### To rearrange thumbnails manually:

Drag any thumbnail (or select, then drag multiple thumbnails) to a new location. Okay, that was a no-brainer. The header on the Sort menu switches to "Sort Manually."

➤ Thumbnails remain where you place them unless you change the sorting order or perform a stacking operation.

Another good way to control how many thumbnails display at a given time is by grouping them in stacks. Think of categories for them, such as landscapes or portraits, shots of the same subject, shots taken with a particular camera setting, etc. This is easy, too.

### To group thumbnails into a stack:

1. Shift-click or Ctrl-click/Cmd-click to select multiple thumbnails.**A** The thumbnail listed first in your selection is going to be the "stack thumbnail" (will display on top of the stack).

2. Press Ctrl-G/Cmd-G or right-click one of the selected thumbnails and choose Stack > **Group as Stack**.**B** A stack looks like a couple of playing cards in a pile, with the stack thumbnail on top. The number in the upper left corner (called the "stack number") tells you how many thumbnails the stack contains.

### To select the thumbnails in a stack:

To select and display all the thumbnails in a stack, click the stack number (click it again to collapse the stack). The stack will remain selected.

To select all the thumbnails in a stack while keeping the stack collapsed, click the stack border (the bottom "card") or Alt-click/Option-click the stack thumbnail (the top image in the stack). Note that although the stack is collapsed, because it is selected, all the thumbnails it contains are displaying in the Preview panel, if that panel is showing.

### To rearrange thumbnails within a stack:

To move a thumbnail to a different position in an expanded stack, click it to deselect the other selected thumbnails, then drag it to a new spot (as shown by the vertical drop zone line).

**A** *We selected the thumbnails to be grouped into a stack,...*

**B** *...then chose the Group as Stack command.*

## To move a whole stack:

1. Collapse the stack, then Alt-click/Option-click the stack thumbnail. The borders of both "cards" in the stack should now be highlighted.

2. Drag the image thumbnail (not the border).

➤ If you drag the top thumbnail of an unselected stack, you'll move just that thumbnail, not the whole stack.

## To add a thumbnail to a stack:

Drag a thumbnail over a stack thumbnail or into an open stack.

## To remove a thumbnail from a stack:

1. Click the stack number to expand the stack.

2. Click a thumbnail to be removed (to deselect the other thumbnails), then drag it out of the stack.

## To ungroup a stack:

1. Click the stack number to expand and select all the thumbnails in the stack.

2. Press Control-Shift-G/Cmd-Shift-G (Stacks > Ungroup from Stack) or right-click the stack and choose Stack > **Ungroup from Stack**. The stack number and border disappear.

# Managing files using Bridge

## To create a new folder:

1. Via the Folders panel or the Path bar, navigate to the folder that you want to add a folder to.

2. Click the **New Folder** button 📁 at the right end of the Bridge toolbar, type a name in the highlighted field below the new folder, then press Enter/Return.

You can move your actual files to a different folder either by dragging their thumbnails or by using a command.

## To move or copy files between folders:
### Method 1 (by dragging)

1. Select one or more thumbnails in the Content panel.

2. In the Folders panel, navigate to (but don't click) the folder or subfolder that you want to move the selected files into.

3. To move the selected files, drag them over the folder name in the Folders panel, or to copy them, hold down Ctrl/Option while dragging.

### Method 2 (via the context menu)

1. Select one or more thumbnails in the Content panel.

2. Right-click one of the selected thumbnails, then from the **Move To** or **Copy To** submenu on the context menu, do either of the following:

   Select a folder name under **Recent Folders** or **Favorites**.

   Select **Choose Folder**. Locate a folder in the Choose a Folder dialog, then click OK/Choose.

## To delete a file or folder:

1. Click an image or folder thumbnail (or Ctrl-click/Cmd-click multiple thumbnails or Shift-click a series of them).

2. Do either of the following:

   Press Ctrl-Backspace/Cmd-Delete, then click OK in the alert dialog.

   Press Del/Delete on your extended keyboard, then click Delete in the alert dialog, if it appears.

➤ Oops! Change your mind? To retrieve a deleted file or folder immediately, choose Edit > Undo. Or to dig it out of the trash, double-click the Recycle Bin/Trash icon for your operating system, then drag the item into the Content panel in Bridge. Phew.

## To rename a file or folder:

1. Click a thumbnail, then click the file or folder name. The name becomes highlighted. **A**

2. Type a new name **B** (for an image file, don't try to delete the extension), then press Enter/Return or click outside the name field.

**A** *To rename a file, click the existing file name…*   **B** *…then type a new name.*

When you download digital photos from your camera to your computer, they keep the sequential numerical labels (e.g., "CRW_0016") that your camera assigned to them. Via the Batch Rename command in Bridge, you can assign more recognizable names to your photos, to make them easier to identify.

### To batch-rename files: ★

1. Display the folder containing the files to be renamed, then select the thumbnails for the files to be renamed.

2. From the **Refine** menu ![icon] at the top of the Bridge toolbar, choose Tools > **Batch Rename** (Ctrl-Shift-R/Cmd-Shift-R). The Batch Rename dialog opens.**A**

3. From the **Preset** menu, choose **Default**.

4. Under **Destination Folder**, click one of the following:

   **Rename in Same Folder** to rename the files and leave them in their current location.

   **Move to Other Folder** to rename the files and move them to a new location.

   **Copy to Other Folder** to leave the original files unchanged but rename the copies and move them to a new location—for a quick way to duplicate your photos. We recommend using

this option, especially if you didn't duplicate your files when you downloaded them.

For the Move or Copy option, click **Browse**, choose or create a new folder location, then click OK/Choose.

5. Under **New Filenames**, specify which data you want included in the names: Text, a good choice (enter text); Date Time (choose options); or Sequence Number to include an incremental number in the names (enter a starting number and choose a digit option).

   To add another row of criteria fields, click the ⊕ button, or to remove a row of fields, click the ⊖ button.

   Click **Preview** to view a listing of the new file names, then click OK.

6. Under **Options**, you can leave Preserve Current Filename in XMP Metadata unchecked, but for **Compatibility**, do check any other operating system that you need your renamed files to be readable in.

7. *Optional:* To save the current New Filenames and Options settings as a preset (to be listed on the Preset menu), click Save, enter a name, then click OK.

8. Click Rename.

**A** *Via the Batch Rename dialog, you can quickly and easily rename a whole folder full of photos.*

# Searching for files

## To find files via Bridge:

1. In Bridge, choose Edit > **Find** (Ctrl-F/Cmd-F). The Find dialog opens. 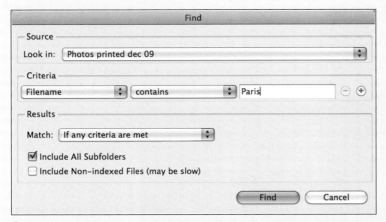A

2. From the **Look In** menu in the Source area, choose the folder to be searched (the current folder is listed by default). To select a folder that's not on the list, choose Look In: Browse, locate the desired folder, then click OK/Choose.

3. From the menus in the **Criteria** area, choose search criteria (e.g., Filename, Date Created, Keywords, Label, Rating, or specific camera settings), choose a parameter from the adjoining menu, and enter data in the field. To add another criterion to the search, click the ⊕ button, or to remove a row of fields, click ⊖.

4. From the **Match** menu, choose "If any criteria are met" to find files based on one or more of the criteria you have specified, or choose "If all criteria are met" to narrow the selection to files that meet all of your criteria.

5. Check **Include All Subfolders** to also search through any of the subfolders that are contained within the folder chosen in step 2.

6. *Optional:* Check Include Non-indexed Files to search through files that Bridge hasn't yet indexed (any folder Bridge has yet to display). This could slow down the search.

7. Click Find. The search results will be placed in a temporary folder called Search Results: [name of source folder] and will display in the Content panel. B The folder will be listed on the Path bar and on the Reveal Recent File or Go to Recent Folder menu 📷▾ on the Bridge toolbar.

8. To create a collection from the search results, see the following page.

➤ To discard the current search results and perform a new search, click New Search, or to cancel the results, click the Cancel button.✕

A *Use the Find dialog to search for and locate files based on various criteria.*

B *After you click Find, the search results display in the Content panel. The parameters used for the search and the name of the folder that was searched are listed as the Find Criteria.*

# Creating and using collections

The collection features in Bridge provide a useful way to catalog and access files without your actually having to relocate them. There are two kinds of collections: a Smart Collection that is created from the results of a Find search, and what we call a "nonsmart" collection which is created by dragging thumbnails manually into a collection icon.

## To create a Smart Collection:

1. Click the tab for the Collections panel. (If it's hidden, choose Window > Collections Panel.)

2. Perform a search via the Edit > Find command (see the preceding page). When the search is completed, click the **Save as Smart Collection** button ▦ at the top of the Content panel. **A**

3. A new Smart Collection icon ▦ appears in the Collections panel. Type a name in the highlighted field, then press Enter/Return. **B**

➤ To add a collection to the Favorites panel, right-click the icon and choose Add to Favorites.

➤ To delete a collection, click it, click the Delete Collection button, ▦ then click Yes in the alert. Not to worry: This won't delete the actual files.

## To display the contents of a collection:

Click its icon ▦ in the Collections panel.

If you edit an existing Smart Collection based on added or new criteria in a new search, the collection contents will update automatically.

## To edit a Smart Collection:

1. In the Collections panel, click the icon for an existing Smart Collection. ▦

2. At the top of the Content panel or in the lower left corner of the Collections panel, click the **Edit Smart Collection** button. ▦ **C**

3. The Edit Smart Collection dialog opens. It looks like the Find dialog, which is shown on the preceding page. To add another criterion, click the next ⊕ button, choose and enter the criterion, and choose "If any criteria are met" from the Match menu. You can also change the source folder and/or change the original criteria.

4. Click Save. The results of the new search will display in the Content panel.

   Note: If you move a thumbnail from a Smart Collection into a folder that wasn't used in the search (or do the same with the actual file), it will be removed from the collection, but not from your hard drive. Don't delete a thumbnail from a Smart Collection unless you want to delete it from your hard drive!

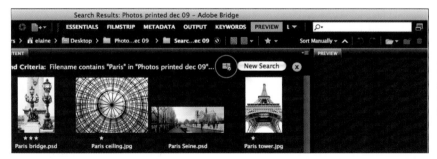

**A** *To create a Smart Collection, click the Save as Smart Collection button in the Content panel.*

**B** *A new Smart Collection appears on the Collections panel. Type a name for it in the field.*

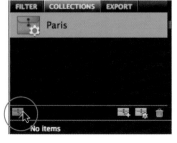

**C** *To edit a Smart Collection, click a Smart Collection icon on the Collections panel, then click the Edit Smart Collection button at the bottom of the panel.*

A collection can also be created without running a search first. We call this a "nonsmart" collection. You can add to a nonsmart collection by dragging thumbnails into it (not so for a Smart Collection).

## To create a nonsmart collection:

1. Do either of the following:

    On the Content panel, select the image thumbnails to be placed into a collection. On the **Collections** panel, click the **New Collection** button, then click Yes in the alert dialog.

    While viewing files in **Review mode** (Ctrl-B/Cmd-B), drag any files you don't want to include in the collection out of the carousel, then click the **New Collection** button.

2. On the panel, rename the collection, A then press Enter/Return. The number of thumbnails in the collection is listed next to the name. ★

A *To create a new collection, click the New Collection button, then type a name for it in the highlighted field.*

## To add thumbnails to a nonsmart collection:

1. Display the Collections panel.

2. Drag one or more thumbnails from the Content panel over a nonsmart collection icon. **B**

➤ You can copy and paste thumbnails from a Smart Collection into a nonsmart one, or from one nonsmart collection into another.

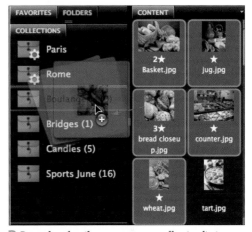

B *Drag thumbnails to a nonsmart collection listing.*

## To remove thumbnails from a nonsmart collection:

1. On the Collections panel, click the icon for a nonsmart collection to display its contents.

2. Select the thumbnails to be removed, then click **Remove From Collection** at the top of the Content panel. **C**

If you rename a file or move it from its original location on disk, Bridge tries to update the link to any nonsmart collections the file is a member of. If Bridge is unsuccessful at this, follow these steps.

C *To take selected thumbnails out of the currently selected collection, click Remove from Collection.*

## To relink a missing file to a nonsmart collection:

1. On the Collections panel, click the collection to which you want to relink a file or files.

2. Next to the Missing File Detected alert at the top of the Content panel, click **Fix**. **D**

3. In the Find Missing Files dialog, click Browse, locate and select the missing file, then click Open. Click OK to exit the dialog.

D *To relink a file that's missing from a collection, click Fix.*

# Exporting the Bridge cache

When the contents of a folder are displayed in the Content panel in Bridge for the first time, the program creates a cache file containing information about those files, such as the data it uses to display ratings, labels, and high-quality thumbnails. Having the cache helps speed up the display of thumbnails when you choose that folder again. If you want this data to be included with files that you copy to a removable disc or to a shared folder on a network, you have to build the cache files and export them to the current folder first.

### To export the Bridge cache to the current folder:

1. Choose Edit/Adobe Bridge CS5 > Preferences > Cache. In the Cache area, check **Automatically Export Cache to Folders When Possible**, then click OK.

2. Display a folder in Bridge.

3. Choose Tools > Cache > **Build and Export Cache**. In the dialog, check **Export Cache to Folders**, keep the Build 100% Previews option off, and click OK.

4. Two hidden cache files will be placed in the current folder, one named .BridgeCache (metadata cache) and the other named .BridgeCacheT (thumbnail cache).

   Now if you use the File > Move To (or Copy To) command in Bridge to move (or copy) selected thumbnails, the folder cache you just created will also move or copy, thanks to the export preference that you checked.

➤ To display the cache file icons in the Content panel, choose View > Show Hidden Files.

Thumbnail cache files sometimes cause display problems. Purging the cache for the current folder may solve the problem, because it prompts Bridge to rebuild the cache.

### To purge the cache files from Bridge:

Do either of the following:

To purge the cache files from the current folder, choose Tools > Cache > **Purge Cache for Folder** "[current folder name]." Two new (hidden) cache files will be generated.

To purge the cache files for multiple selected thumbnails, right-click one of them and choose **Purge Cache for Selection**.

---

**ATTACHING IPTC INFO TO A FILE**

Via the IPTC Core category in the Metadata panel, you can attach creator, description, copyright, and other information to the currently selected file. Click the field next to a listing, enter or modify the file description information, press Tab to progress through other fields and enter data, then click the Apply button ✓ in the lower right corner of the panel. (IPTC is an information standard that is used for describing photos and providing information about them.)

# Assigning keywords to files

Keywords (words that are assigned to files) are used by search utilities to locate files and by file management programs to organize them. In Bridge, you can create parent keyword categories (for events, people, places, themes, etc.), and nested subkeywords within those categories, and then assign them to your files. You can locate files by entering keywords as search criteria in the Find dialog, build a Smart Collection based on a search for keywords, or display files by checking listings below Keywords in the Filter panel.

## To create keywords and subkeywords:

1. Display the Keywords panel. To create a new parent keyword category, click the **New Keyword** button, ⊞ then type a keyword.

2. To create a nested subkeyword, click a parent keyword, click the **New Sub Keyword** button, ⊞ type a word, then press Enter/Return. **A** To add more subkeywords, click the parent keyword first. You can also create nested sub-subkeywords.

➤ You can move (drag) any subkeyword from one parent keyword category into another.

➤ Read about the Keywords Preferences on page 397. For more about keywords, see Adobe Bridge Help.

## To assign keywords to files:

1. Select one or more image thumbnails in the Content panel. If an image has keywords assigned to it already, they will be listed at the top of the Keywords panel; you can assign more.

2. Check the box for one or more subkeywords. **B** (Although you can assign a parent keyword to a file, we can't think of a reason for doing so.) To remove a keyword from a file, uncheck the box.

➤ The keywords that are assigned to the files in the current folder are also listed in the Keywords category in the Filter panel.

➤ To assign keywords via the File Info dialog, select one or more thumbnails, then from the Refine menu 🖿 on the Bridge toolbar, choose File Info (Ctrl-I/Cmd-I). In the Description tab, Keywords field, enter keywords, separated by semicolons or commas. Be on the alert for typing errors!

➤ If you import a file into Bridge that contains keywords that you want to add as permanent subkeywords, right-click each subkeyword under Other Keywords in the Keywords panel and choose Make Persistent from the context menu.

**A** *We created a new parent keyword entitled "Food," kept that category selected, then via the New Sub Keyword button, added subkeywords to it.*

**B** *We clicked an image thumbnail, then assigned subkeywords to it by checking the boxes.*

## USING THE KEYWORDS PANEL

| | |
|---|---|
| Rename a parent keyword or subkeyword | Right-click the word, choose Rename from the context menu, then type a name (this won't alter any already embedded data). |
| Delete a parent keyword or subkeyword | Click the word, then click the Delete Keyword button. 🗑 If that keyword is assigned to any files, it will now be listed in italics. |
| Find a keyword or subkeyword on the list | Type the word in the search field at the bottom of the panel. Choose a search parameter from the menu. 🔍▾ |

# Opening PDF and Illustrator files

When you open PDF or Adobe Illustrator (AI) files into Photoshop, they are rasterized automatically (converted from their native vector format into the Photoshop pixel format). For a PDF, you can either open one or more whole PDF pages or extract raster images from them. Follow these instructions to open a PDF or Adobe Illustrator file from Bridge as a new rasterized document, or follow the instructions on page 309 to place a PDF or Illustrator file as a Smart Object into an existing Photoshop document.

## To open a PDF or Adobe Illustrator file as a new Photoshop document:

1. In Bridge, locate and click the PDF or AI file to be opened. Choose File > Open With > **Adobe Photoshop CS5** or right-click the image thumbnail and choose Open With > Adobe Photoshop CS5 from the context menu. If an alert dialog appears at any time while following these instructions, see page 58.

   ➤ From the Thumbnail Size menu, choose a size for the thumbnail display.

2. The Import PDF dialog opens in Photoshop. Under **Select**, do the following:

   Click **Pages** to view the whole PDF pages **A** or click **Images** to view just the images that are contained in the PDF file. **B** For the latter, click the image (or select multiple images) to be opened, then click OK—you're done.

   If you clicked Pages, follow the remaining steps.

   Note: If the PDF file you're opening contains multiple pages, click the thumbnail for the desired page, or Shift-click or Cmd-click to select multiple pages. Each page you select is going to open as a separate Photoshop file.

3. Under **Page Options**, do the following:

   *Optional:* Type a Name for the new document.

   Choose a **Crop To** option. We keep this on the default setting of Bounding Box to exclude any white areas outside the artwork.

   Check **Anti-aliased** to reduce jaggies and soften the edge transitions.

4. For **Image Size**, do the following:

   For a whole PDF page, you can enter the desired maximum **Width** and **Height** for the Photoshop document(s) or keep the current dimensions. Check **Constrain Proportions** to preserve the

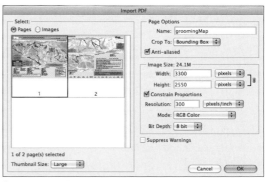

**A** *To open a whole PDF page, in the Import PDF dialog, click Pages, click a page, then choose options for the Photoshop file.*

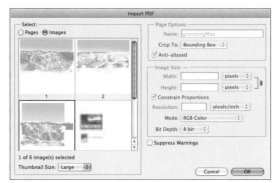

**B** *Or if you prefer to open just one image from a PDF file, click Images, click an image, then click OK.*

### GETTING ILLUSTRATOR FILES INTO PHOTOSHOP

| | |
|---|---|
| Open command (this page) | Opens the file as a new document and converts paths into pixels |
| Place command (see page 309; or for type, see page 340) | Opens the file as a Smart Object layer in an existing Photoshop document |
| Drag a path from an Illustrator document into a Photoshop document (see the last tip on page 309) | Arrives as a new Smart Object layer |
| Copy an object in Illustrator, then Paste it into a Photoshop document (see the next page) | Via the Paste dialog, choose to Paste As a Smart Object, Pixels, Path, or Shape Layer (vectors are preserved, unless you click Pixels) |

aspect ratio of the original PDF, to prevent distortion.

Enter the **Resolution** required for your output device. Entering the correct resolution for the image here, before it's rasterized, will produce a higher-quality image.

From the **Mode** menu, choose a color mode for the document (preferably one that is consistent with the Adobe RGB color space you were directed to establish in Chapter 1). If the file contains an embedded RGB color profile, that profile will be the default listing on the menu and should be kept as your choice. If not, select RGB Color.

Choose a **Bit Depth** of 8 Bit or 16 Bit.

Leave **Suppress Warnings** unchecked to allow an alert to display should a color profile conflict arise.

5. Click OK.

➤ If you try to open an Adobe Illustrator file that wasn't saved with the Create PDF Compatible File option checked, the thumbnail in the Import PDF dialog will display only a text message. Reopen the file in Illustrator, choose File > Save As, rename or replace the file, then click Save. In the Illustrator Options dialog, check Create PDF Compatible File, then click OK. Now you can go ahead and open the file in Photoshop.

➤ To create a solid Background for an imported PDF in Photoshop, create a new layer, fill it with white via Edit > Fill, then choose Layer > New > Background from Layer.

## To paste Adobe Illustrator art into Photoshop:

1. In Illustrator, go to Edit/Illustrator > Preferences > File Handling & Clipboard, check the **Copy As: PDF** and **AICB** options, click **Preserve Appearance and Overprints**, then click OK.

2. Copy an object via Edit > **Copy** (Ctrl-C/Cmd-C).

3. In a Photoshop document, choose Edit > **Paste** (Ctrl-V/Cmd-V). The Paste dialog opens.

4. Click **Paste As: Smart Object** or **Shape Layer** to keep the vector object editable, or click **Pixels** to rasterize it, then click OK.

5. If you clicked Smart Object or Pixels in the dialog, you need to accept the placed object. Click the Commit Transform button ✔ on the Options bar or press Enter/Return. To learn about editing Smart Object layers, see pages 310–311.

---

### BRINGING EPS FILES INTO PHOTOSHOP

You have different options for bringing EPS files into Photoshop than for AI or PDF files:

➤ If you open an EPS file into Photoshop via the File > Open command in Photoshop or via the File > Open With command in Bridge, the Rasterize EPS Format dialog appears. Make Image Size, Resolution, and Mode choices, then click OK.

➤ If you use the File > Place command in Photoshop or the File > Place > In Photoshop command in Bridge, the EPS file will open directly into Photoshop without an import dialog opening. The file will appear in a bounding box at first (to allow for scaling, rotating, and moving), and will become a Smart Object layer when you press Enter/Return.

➤ The Rasterize EPS Format dialog also displays if you use the File > Open as Smart Object command in Photoshop to bring an EPS file into Photoshop. Click OK, and the file will import as a Smart Object layer.

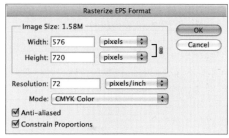

*The Rasterize EPS Format dialog displays when you use the Open or Open as Smart Object command to open an EPS file in Photoshop.*

### CMYK COLORS FROM ILLUSTRATOR

When importing an Illustrator file that contains CMYK colors, in Photoshop, use the File > Place command. It will arrive as a Smart Object (see page 309). This way, the Photoshop file can stay in RGB Color mode but the CMYK colors in the Smart Object will be preserved. For print output, you can convert the whole file to CMYK Color mode.

# Responding to alert dialogs upon opening a file

➤ If you open a file in Photoshop in which a **missing font** is being used (the font isn't available or installed), an alert dialog will appear.**A** ★ If you click OK to open the file, an alert icon will display on the offending layer(s) on the Layers panel.**B** If you try to edit the layer, yet another alert dialog will appear, indicating that font substitution will occur if you click OK.**C** ★ You can either click OK to allow the missing font to be replaced or click Cancel, make the required fonts available, then reopen the document.

➤ If the file's color profile doesn't match the current working space for Photoshop, the Embedded Profile Mismatch alert dialog will appear.**D** Click **Use the Embedded Profile (Instead of the Working Space)** if you must keep the document's current profile, or for better consistency with your color management workflow, we recommend clicking **Convert Document's Colors to the Working Space** to convert the profile to the current working space. Click OK. See also pages 10, 13, and 16.

➤ If the Missing Profile alert dialog appears,**E** click **Assign Working RGB: Adobe RGB (1998)** to assign the profile that you chose as the working space for Photoshop in Chapter 1.

Note: If you're unable to open a file, it may be because the required plug-in module for its format (such as Scitex CT or JPEG 2000) isn't currently installed in the Photoshop Plug-Ins folder. Install the required plug-in, then open the file.

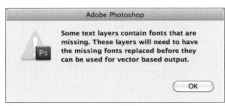

**A** *This alert dialog appears if fonts that are being used in the file you're opening are missing.*

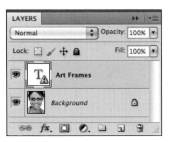

**B** *A missing fonts alert icon displays in the editable type layer thumbnail.*

**C** *This alert dialog appears if you try to edit an editable type layer that's using a missing font.*

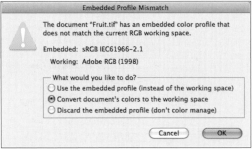

**D** *If this Embedded Profile Mismatch alert dialog appears, indicate whether you want to continue to use the embedded profile or convert the file to the current working space.*

**E** *If this Missing Profile alert dialog appears, click Assign Working RGB: Adobe RGB (1998) to convert the file to the default working space for Photoshop.*

Using the powerful controls in the Adobe Camera Raw plug-in,* you can apply corrections to your photos before opening them into Photoshop. In this chapter, you'll learn how to open digital photos into the Camera Raw dialog (called "Camera Raw," for short), and then use the many tabs in Camera Raw to correct your photos for under- or overexposure, blurriness, color casts, poor contrast, and other defects.

## Why use Camera Raw?

Whereas amateur-level digital cameras store images in the JPEG or TIFF format, advanced amateur and pro models offer the option to save images as raw data files, which has substantial advantages. The camera applies internal processing to photos captured as JPEG or TIFF, such as sharpening, setting the white balance, and making color adjustments. With raw files, you get only the original raw information that the lens captured onto its digital sensor, leaving you with full control over subsequent image processing and correction. Each camera manufacturer creates its own variation of a raw file. (For a further discussion of raw files versus JPEG and TIFF files, see page 61.)

These are some of the advantages to using the Camera Raw plug-in:

➤ Camera Raw processes raw photos from most digital camera models, as well as digital TIFF and JPEG photos.

➤ Camera Raw offers powerful controls for adjusting the exposure, color, tonal range, noise, and other characteristics of your photos, and you can monitor the corrections in a large preview.

➤ For raw files, Camera Raw edits (stored as instructions) are saved in either a separate "sidecar" file or in the Camera Raw database. For TIFF and JPEG files, the instructions are saved in the photo file. When you open a file from Camera Raw into Photoshop, regardless of the format, the instructions are applied to a copy of the file, and the original digital file is preserved.

➤ You can convert your photos to some standard formats (e.g., PSD, JPEG) through Camera Raw, or you can change their format in Photoshop.

Note: Don't confuse the raw files that a camera produces with Photoshop Raw, which is one of the choices on the Format menu in the File > Save and Save As dialogs in Photoshop.

*The Camera Raw plug-in is included with Photoshop.

## 4

### IN THIS CHAPTER

## More reasons to use Camera Raw

In case you're not fully convinced, we'll outline some compelling reasons for using the Camera Raw plug-in instead of opening your digital photos directly into Photoshop. It offers powerful and unique controls that you won't find in Photoshop.

**Raw preview**: The only way to preview a raw photo is through a raw converter, such as Camera Raw. (The image you see on your digital camera's LCD screen is based not on the raw capture, but on the JPEG preview that accompanies the raw capture.)

**Less destructive**: Exposure, white balance, color, and other corrections made in Camera Raw cause less destruction to a photo than adjustment commands in Photoshop. The goal, when applying corrections, is to cause as little destruction as possible while preserving as much original data as possible.

**16 bits per channel**: To preserve the full tonal range of a raw photo, you can use Camera Raw to convert it to a 16-bits-per-channel file. Having more original data at the outset helps offset the data loss from image edits made in Photoshop. The end result is a better-quality photo.

**Tonal redistribution**: A bonus feature of Camera Raw is that it fixes a problem inherent in all digital photos: the fact that the digital sensor in a camera records data in a linear fashion. The sensor captures the existing range of tonal values in a scene as is, without skewing the data. More data is used to capture light values than dark values. **A** The

human eye, however, is more sensitive to lower light levels than to higher light levels. That is, we're more likely to notice when shadows lack detail and less likely to notice extra details in the highlights.

By shifting data into the midtone and shadow ranges, Camera Raw produces a photo that more closely approximates human vision. **B** When a photo contains insufficient data in the shadow range, tonal adjustments made in Photoshop will cause posterization and a noticeable loss of detail. With its extra data in the midtone and shadow ranges, a photo converted by Camera Raw will be better equipped to withstand those Photoshop edits.

**Noise reduction** and **sharpening**: Not to knock Photoshop, but the noise reduction and sharpening features in Camera Raw are easier to use, less destructive, and more effective than similar commands in Photoshop.

**You're halfway there**: You will be able to build on the skills learned in this chapter, because the Camera Raw controls that you'll use to correct the tonal and color balance in your photos are similar to many of the adjustment controls in Photoshop that you will learn about in later chapters (such as Levels, Curves, and Hue/Saturation).

**The skinny**: To correct and enhance digital photos in preparation for further edits in Photoshop, Camera Raw is an ideal launch pad.

---

**CAPTURING TONAL VALUES: A CAMERA VERSUS THE HUMAN EYE**

*50% light value*

*50% light value*

**A** *The digital sensor in a camera captures tonal values in a linear fashion, from light to dark, without altering the incoming data. Note that a light value of 50% is at the midpoint of the tonal range.*

**B** *Camera Raw alters the incoming data, redistributing some tonal values to the shadows and midtones. Note that the 50% light value has been shifted past the midpoint. Now the lower tonal values, in the ranges the human eye is more sensitive to, contain more data.*

## Raw, JPEG, or TIFF?

In addition to raw files, photos that a camera saves in the JPEG or TIFF format can also be opened and edited in Camera Raw. Although more Camera Raw features are available for raw photos than for JPEG and TIFF photos, if your camera doesn't shoot raw photos or you acquire JPEG or TIFF photos from other sources, you can still use most of the Camera Raw features to process them.

Unfortunately, Camera Raw can't correct deficiencies in digital JPEG and TIFF photos as fully as it can in raw photos, for several reasons. First, JPEG and TIFF photos have a bit depth of only 8 bits per channel, unlike raw photos, which have a bit depth of 16 bits per channel. Second, color and tonal processing is applied to JPEGs and TIFFs by the camera ("in camera"). Camera Raw must reinterpret this processed data, with less successful results than when it has access to the raw, unprocessed data. And finally, the editing instructions are saved in the files themselves (processing is applied when the files are opened and saved in Photoshop), not in the sidecar or database file, as is the case with raw files. Nonetheless, you can use the many outstanding correction and adjustment features in Camera Raw to improve your JPEG and TIFF photos.

Note: In this chapter, we focus only on processing raw and JPEG files in Camera Raw—not TIFFs. The JPEG format is mentioned only when a particular feature treats JPEGs differently from the way it treats raw files.

---

### KEEPING CAMERA RAW UP TO DATE

Of the many proprietary raw "formats," some are unique to particular manufacturers (such as Nikon or Canon) and some are unique to particular camera models. To ensure that the latest interpreters for the raw formats that Camera Raw supports are installed in your system, visit www.adobe.com periodically and download any Camera Raw updates that have been posted for your camera.

---

### JPEG...

#### JPEG pluses

➤ JPEG files have smaller storage sizes than raw files, so your digital camera is able to store more of them.

➤ JPEG files have shorter transfer speeds, so they can be captured and stored more quickly by a camera than raw files. For sports, nature, and other quick-motion photography, this faster shot sequencing is a necessity.

➤ Most software programs can read JPEG files.

#### JPEG minuses

➤ The JPEG compression methods destroy some image data and can produce defects, such as artifacts, banding, and a loss of detail.

➤ The pixel data in a JPEG photo is processed by the camera. Although Camera Raw can be used to improve your JPEG photos, it—and you—won't have access to the original pixel data.

### ...COMPARED WITH RAW

#### Raw pluses

➤ The raw compression methods are nondestructive.

➤ The raw formats preserve the original, unprocessed pixel data and full range of tonal levels that were captured by the camera. Because Camera Raw has all the data to work with, the result after adjustments is a higher-quality image.

➤ Because the white point setting isn't applied to raw pixels when a photo is shot (it's merely stored in the metadata of the file), you can adjust this setting in Camera Raw.

➤ Camera Raw does a better job of redistributing tonal values in raw files, so they are better candidates for Photoshop edits.

➤ Raw files can be opened as 16-bits-per-channel files into Photoshop.

#### Raw minuses

➤ Digital cameras create and store raw files more slowly than JPEG files, which is a potential problem for fast-action photographers.

➤ Raw files have larger storage sizes than JPEG files.

#### The bottom line

Despite the advantages of speed and storage size that JPEG has to offer, raw is the clear winner.

# Choosing preferences for opening photos

To standardize your workflow, we recommend setting a preference so your JPEG or TIFF photos will open directly into Camera Raw instead of into Photoshop.

## To set a preference to have your raw photos open directly into Camera Raw:

In Photoshop, go to Edit/Photoshop > Preferences (Ctrl-K/Cmd-K) > File Handling. Check **Prefer Adobe Camera Raw for Supported Raw Files**, then click OK. With this option on, when double-clicked, raw files will open into the Camera Raw dialog (as opposed to other software that converts raw files).

## To set a preference to have your JPEG or TIFF photos open directly into Camera Raw:

In Bridge, choose Edit/Adobe Bridge CS5 > Camera Raw Preferences. At the bottom of the dialog, from the JPEG menu, choose **Automatically Open JPEGs with Settings**, and from the TIFF menu, choose **Automatically Open TIFFs with Settings**.

From now on, when you click a JPEG or TIFF photo thumbnail in Bridge, then click the Open in Camera Raw button 🔄 or press Ctrl-R/Cmd-R, the file will open into Camera Raw.

➤ If you have chosen both Automatically Open options suggested above but for some reason you want to open a JPEG or TIFF photo directly into Photoshop instead of into Camera Raw (and if the file hasn't yet been edited in Camera Raw), click the thumbnail, then press Ctrl-O/Cmd-O.

➤ If the Open in Camera Raw button 🔄 is available when you click a thumbnail, you know that the file can be opened into Camera Raw.

## To choose a host for Camera Raw:

In Bridge, choose Edit/Adobe Bridge CS5 > Preferences (Ctrl-K/Cmd-K), then click General on the left side. Check **Double-Click Edits Camera Raw Settings in Bridge** if you want the Camera Raw dialog to be hosted by Bridge when you double-click the thumbnail in Bridge for a raw photo or a JPEG that was previously edited in Camera Raw. If this preference is unchecked and you double-click a thumbnail for either of those two file types, the file will open into Camera Raw, but hosted by Photoshop.

Note: When Bridge is the host for Camera Raw, the default button for exiting that dialog is labeled Done, whereas when Photoshop is the host for Camera Raw, the default button is Open Image. (If the button is labeled Open Object instead of Open Image, see the first tip on page 86.)

---

**OUR APPROACH**

If you shoot only raw or JPEG photos (as we do) — not TIFF photos — you can follow these two suggestions to have your raw and JPEG photos always open into Camera Raw and your TIFF files always open directly into Photoshop:

➤ In the Edit/Adobe Bridge CS5 > Camera Raw Preferences dialog, under JPEG and TIFF Handling, choose JPEG: Automatically Open JPEGs with Settings and choose TIFF: Disable TIFF Support.

➤ In Edit/Adobe Bridge CS5 > Preferences, check Double-Click Edits Camera Raw Settings in Bridge.

**UPDATING PHOTOS FROM CR 5.X ★**

Using updated profiles, Camera Raw 6.x applies improved processing, such as default sharpening and color calibration. If you want to update a raw photo that was processed by Camera Raw 5, before applying any new adjustments, click the ⚠ icon in the bottom right of the preview window; the Process menu in the Camera Calibration tab 📷 changes to the setting of 2010 (Current). (This Process choice controls which version of the Camera Raw noise reduction, demosaic, sharpening, and postcrop vignette methods are used for rendering and adjusting photos.) Note: If you want to preserve access to the older rendering of the photo, take a snapshot of it before updating it (see page 83).

**WHAT'S THAT WEIRD SYMBOL?**

If a file has been opened and edited previously in Camera Raw, this badge 🔄 appears in the upper right corner of the thumbnail in Bridge, and the current Camera Raw settings are reflected in the appearance of the thumbnail and preview. Also, if the currently selected file has been edited in Camera Raw, a Camera Raw category appears in the Metadata panel.

➤ Each digital camera model attaches a different extension to the names of the raw files it captures, such as .nef for Nikon, .crw or .cr2 for Canon, and .dcr for Kodak.

# Opening photos into Camera Raw

Below is a summary of the steps you will be following in this chapter. Note: If you shoot JPEG photos, start by following the steps in "To set a preference to have your JPEG or TIFF photos open directly..." on the preceding page.

## To open a raw or JPEG digital photo into Camera Raw:

1. Launch Bridge, display the thumbnail for the raw or JPEG photo to be opened, then do either of the following:

   For a raw photo, double-click the thumbnail.

   For a raw or JPEG photo, click the thumbnail, then press Ctrl-R/Cmd-R or click the **Open in Camera Raw** button on the Bridge toolbar.

2. The Camera Raw dialog opens. A An alert symbol may display in the upper right corner of the preview window while the image data is reading in, but will disappear when it's done.

   Information about your photo (taken from the metadata the camera embedded into it) can be found in several locations: the camera model in the title bar at the top of the dialog; the file name below the preview; and the camera settings used to take the photo (aperture, shutter speed, ISO, and focal length) below the histogram.

The image adjustment options are distributed among 10 tabs — Basic, Tone Curve, Detail, HSL/Grayscale, Split Toning, Lens Corrections, Effects, ★ Camera Calibration, Presets, and Snapshots ★ — which you'll use to correct your photo. Many of these tabs are explored in this chapter.

When you're done correcting the photo, you can either click Open Image to open the photo into Photoshop or click Done to close Camera Raw without opening the photo. In either case, the Camera Raw settings stick with the photo but the original data is preserved.

➤ To open a file from Mini Bridge into Camera Raw, right-click the thumbnail and choose Open in Camera Raw. ★

*A The Camera Raw dialog      Toolbox      Camera model      Toggle Full-Screen Mode/previous dialog size (F)*

*Histogram*

*Camera settings*

*Tabs (access to settings)*

*Camera Raw Settings menu*

*Preview*

*Zoom controls      Link to the Workflow Options dialog (see page 66)*

# The Camera Raw tools

In the upper left corner of the dialog,**A** click the **Zoom** tool, then click the image preview to zoom in or Alt-click/Option-click it to zoom out.

Use the **Hand** tool to move a magnified preview image in its window (or hold down the Spacebar for a temporary Hand tool).

For the **White Balance** tool, see the sidebar on page 68.

Choose the **Color Sampler** tool, then click in the image preview to place up to nine samplers. A readout of the RGB components for the pixels below each sampler displays below each tool, and updates as you make color and tonal adjustments. To reposition a sampler, drag it with the Color Sampler tool. To remove all samplers, click Clear Samplers.

For the **Targeted Adjustment** tool, see pages 73 and 74.

For the **Crop** and **Straighten** tools, see the following page.

For the **Spot Removal** tool, see page 82.

The **Red Eye Removal** tool works like the Red Eye tool in Photoshop (for that tool, see page 286).

For the **Adjustment Brush** tool, see pages 79–81.

For the **Graduated Filter** tool, search for "graduated filter tool" in Photoshop Help.

Note: If tool settings are displaying on the right side of the Camera Raw dialog (say you had been using the Adjustment Brush tool) and you want to redisplay the tabs, click one of the first seven tools.

➤ The tools in Camera Raw are "memory-loaded," meaning that you can press a tool shortcut key to select a tool, then press the same key again to reselect the last-used tool.

Other buttons at the top of the dialog:

➤ The Open Preferences Dialog button (or press Ctrl-K/Cmd-K) opens the Camera Raw Preferences dialog.

➤ The Rotate 90° Counterclockwise button and the Rotate 90° Clockwise button rotate the image. The results preview in the dialog.

---

**OTHER WAYS TO ZOOM IN THE PREVIEW**

➤ Press Ctrl–/Cmd–(hyphen) to zoom out or Ctrl-+/ Cmd-+ to zoom in.

➤ Use the Zoom Level menu or zoom buttons (– or +), located below the image preview.

➤ Double-click the Zoom tool to change the zoom level to 100%.

➤ Double-click the Hand tool to fit the image in the preview window.

---

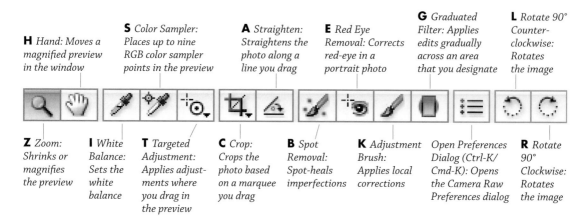

**H** *Hand: Moves a magnified preview in the window*

**S** *Color Sampler: Places up to nine RGB color sampler points in the preview*

**A** *Straighten: Straightens the photo along a line you drag*

**E** *Red Eye Removal: Corrects red-eye in a portrait photo*

**G** *Graduated Filter: Applies edits gradually across an area that you designate*

**L** *Rotate 90° Counter-clockwise: Rotates the image*

**Z** *Zoom: Shrinks or magnifies the preview*

**I** *White Balance: Sets the white balance*

**T** *Targeted Adjustment: Applies adjustments where you drag in the preview*

**C** *Crop: Crops the photo based on a marquee you drag*

**B** *Spot Removal: Spot-heals imperfections*

**K** *Adjustment Brush: Applies local corrections*

*Open Preferences Dialog (Ctrl-K/ Cmd-K): Opens the Camera Raw Preferences dialog*

**R** *Rotate 90° Clockwise: Rotates the image*

**A** *The shortcuts for the Camera Raw tools are listed in boldface above.*

# Cropping and straightening photos

With the Crop tool, you can control which portion of a photo opens in Photoshop. You can readjust the crop marquee at any time, and it will remain available even after you click Save, Done, or Open. All the raw pixels are preserved.

## To crop a photo:

1. Open a photo into Camera Raw (see page 63). Choose the **Crop** tool ⊠ (C).

2. Drag a marquee on the preview image.**A** To move the marquee, drag inside it; to resize it, drag a handle. Only the area within the marquee will import into Photoshop.

3. To preview the crop results, press Enter/Return or click another tool.

You can also straighten a photo before opening it into Photoshop.

## To straighten a crooked photo:

1. Choose the **Straighten** tool ⊿ (A).

2. In the preview, drag along an edge in the photo that you want to align to the horizontal or vertical axis.**B** A crop marquee will display, aligned to the angle you drew.**C** When you open the image into Photoshop, that edge will be aligned with the document window.**D**

➤ To preview the crop results, press Enter/Return or click another tool.

➤ To redisplay a crop (or straighten) marquee after using another tool, choose the Crop (or Straighten) tool again. To remove it, press Esc.

**A** *With the Crop tool, drag a marquee in the preview window.*

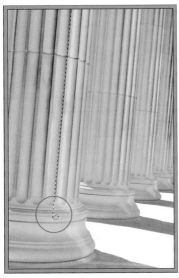

**B** *With the Straighten tool, we are dragging along an edge that we want to align to the vertical or horizontal axis.*

**C** *A marquee displays in Camera Raw.*

**D** *We opened the straightened image into Photoshop.*

# Choosing default workflow settings

Via the Workflow Options dialog, you can change the color space, dimensions, bit depth, and resolution of a photo before opening it into Photoshop —without altering the original digital file. Your choices will become the new default settings.

## To choose default workflow settings:

1. Open a photo into Camera Raw, then at the bottom of the dialog, click the underlined link that lists the color space, bit depth, etc. The **Workflow Options** dialog opens.**A**

2. From the **Space** menu, choose a color profile to be used for converting the raw file to RGB: Adobe RGB (1998), ColorMatch RGB, ProPhoto RGB, or sRGB IEC61966-2.1 (or "sRGB," for short). In Chapter 1, you assigned Adobe RGB as the default color space for color management, so we suggest choosing it here, too.

3. From the **Depth** menu, choose a color depth of 8 Bits/Channel or 16 Bits/Channel (see page 19). If you have a large hard drive and a fast system with a lot of RAM, choose 16 Bits/Channel. With the extra pixels, more of the original tonal levels in your photo will be preserved when it's edited in Photoshop.

4. If you need to resize the image, from the **Size** menu, choose a preset size (in megapixels) that matches the proportions of the raw image. (The default size is the one without a minus sign – or plus sign +.) Resampling will occur if you choose a larger size than the original. Avoid choosing the largest size, to help prevent pixelization. (Experts disagree on whether it's

better to resample an image in Camera Raw or in Photoshop. Until a consensus is reached, you can decide for yourself.) Note: If a crop marquee is present, the Size menu will be labeled Crop Size, and it will list the current crop size.

5. Enter a **Resolution**. This value affects only the print output size. (For instance, a resolution of 240–300 ppi would be appropriate for an image that is 2000 x 3000 pixels or larger, for output to an inkjet printer or a commercial press.)

6. *Optional:* From the Sharpen For menu, choose None, Screen, Glossy Paper, or Matte Paper to apply predefined output sharpening to your photo for the chosen medium. Also choose the desired amount of sharpening from the Amount menu (Standard is usually a good choice).

   Note: The sharpening values that are applied via this dialog aren't listed anywhere. For greater control over capture sharpening, choose None from the Sharpen For menu here and use the sliders in the Detail tab instead (see page 76).

7. Click OK. The new workflow settings will be listed below the preview. They will be applied to the current photo and to photos that you subsequently open into Camera Raw.

➤ To have future photos open from Camera Raw into Photoshop as a Smart Object layer when you click Open Object, check Open in Photoshop as Smart Objects in the Workflow Options dialog (see page 86). Turn this feature on only if it suits your normal workflow.

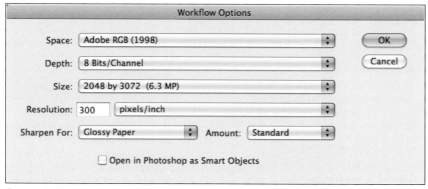

**A** *Use the Workflow Options dialog to choose color space, bit depth, size (dimensions), and resolution settings for the current photo, and to establish the default settings for future photos.*

# Using the Camera Raw tabs

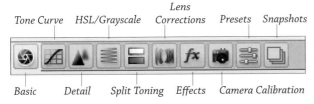

*Tone Curve*  *HSL/Grayscale*  *Lens Corrections*  *Presets*  *Snapshots*

**A** *Click a tab icon to access the specialized options it has to offer.*

*Basic*  *Detail*  *Split Toning*  *Effects*  *Camera Calibration*

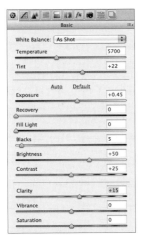 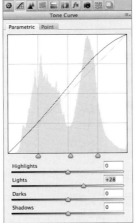  

*Basic tab: Adjust the white balance and exposure (see pages 68–71).*

*Tone Curve tab: Fine-tune the exposure (see pages 72–73).*

*Detail tab: Apply capture sharpening and reduce noise (see pages 76–77).*

*HSL/Grayscale tab: Adjust individual colors (see pages 74–75).*

**B** *In Camera Raw, we perform most of our correction work in the four tabs that are shown above.*

## To restore the default settings to sliders in the Camera Raw tabs:

Double-click a slider to restore the default value to just that slider.

Shift-double-click a slider to restore the **Auto** setting to just that slider.

Click **Default** in the Basic or HSL/Grayscale tab to reset the sliders in just the current tab to their default values (that is, to remove any custom settings).

Choose **Camera Raw Defaults** from the Camera Raw Settings menu ≣◢ to reset all the sliders in all the tabs to the default settings for the camera model that was used to take the photo.

Learn about the Camera Raw Settings menu on the next page.

Hold down Alt/Option and click **Reset** (Cancel becomes Reset) to restore the dialog settings that were in place when the dialog was opened.

---

**TOGGLING THE PREVIEW**

Check Preview (P) at the top of the Camera Raw dialog to preview changes made in all the tabs; or uncheck Preview to view the result of changes made in all the tabs except the current one, so you will be able to evaluate the most recent changes.

When you open a photo into Camera Raw, by default, it's adjusted according to the built-in profile for your camera model. To assign a different collection of settings to your file or to restore the original settings, see the choices listed below.

### To restore settings via the Camera Raw Settings menu:

Choose one of these settings from the Camera Raw Settings menu: 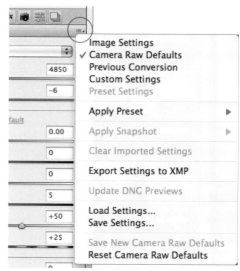 **A**

**Image Settings** to restore the settings that were attached to the file from either the initial photo shoot or a prior Camera Raw session. When you first open a photo, these settings will match the Camera Raw Defaults settings.

**Camera Raw Defaults** to remove any custom settings and reapply the default settings for your camera model, your specific camera, or the ISO setting that was used to take the photo.

**Previous Conversion** to apply the settings from the prior image that was adjusted in Camera Raw.

**Custom Settings** to reapply any custom settings that were chosen since the Camera Raw dialog was opened.

If a user-saved preset is currently applied to the photo, that preset will be listed (see page 83).

**A** *Use the Camera Raw Settings menu to reapply the default settings or the previous settings.*

## Using the Basic tab

When you first open a JPEG photo into Camera Raw, all the sliders in the Basic tab are reset to zero automatically, whereas when you open a raw file into Camera Raw, the sliders are set to the default settings for your camera model. The first step is to use the Basic tab to make any needed corrections to the white balance (see the sidebar at right), exposure, contrast, and saturation. For this first round of adjustments, we recommend using the sliders in the order in which they're listed. The good news is that they cause far less destruction than the adjustment controls in Photoshop do.

As you perform adjustments in the Basic tab, keep your eye on the histogram (in the dialog) so you can monitor how tonal values are being redistributed in the photo.**B** Red, green, and blue pixels are superimposed upon one another at each tonal level in the graph, with shadow pixels on the left and highlight pixels on the right. The white areas indicate where the three colors overlap.

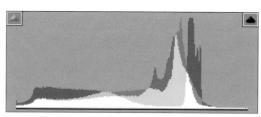

**B** *The Camera Raw histogram charts the number of pixels at each tonal level in your photo.*

---

**WHITE BALANCE, IN PHOTOGRAPHY**

The color temperature of the lighting in which a photo is shot, whether that lighting is natural or artificial, affects the relative amounts of red, green, and blue that a digital camera records. The camera attempts to balance those three colors to produce an accurate white, and then uses the balanced white to make other colors in the photo more accurate. You can refine the white balance of a photo in Camera Raw.

Note: In the Camera Raw dialog, you could adjust the white balance that was produced by your camera with the White Balance tool 🖊 (you click a grayish white area in a photo that contains some detail, to be used by the tool as a sample area). However, deciding which area to click can be tricky, so we recommend using the Temperature and Tint sliders instead, as described on the next page.

## To apply white balance adjustments using the Basic tab:

1. Click the **Basic** tab, ◉ **A–B** and double-click the Hand tool 🖐 to fit the photo in the preview.

2. The white balance (color temperature) should be adjusted first, because this setting affects the overall photo. Do either of the following:

   From the **White Balance** menu, choose a preset that best describes the lighting conditions in which the photo was taken (this is for a raw file only). Choose As Shot at any time to restore the original camera settings.

   To correct the color temperature manually, lower the **Temperature** value to add blue and make the image cooler,**C** or raise it to add yellow and make the image warmer.**D** To fine-tune the temperature correction, move the **Tint** slider slightly to the left to add green or to the right to add magenta. The listing on the White Balance menu will change to Custom.

**B** *When a photo is opened into Camera Raw for the first time, the setting on the White Balance menu in the Basic tab is As Shot.*

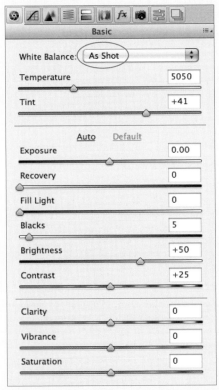

**A** *These are the As Shot settings for the photo shown in* **B***.*

**C** *A lower Temperature value makes the photo cooler. Now there is a noticeable blue cast in the metal and grass.*

**D** *A higher Temperature value makes the photo warmer (note the metal and grass again).*

## To apply tonal adjustments using the Basic tab:

1. When the Camera Raw dialog opens, the tonal sliders in the Basic tab — Exposure, Recovery, Fill Light, Blacks, Brightness, and Contrast — are set to their default values, and the word "Default" is dimmed. For the heck of it, click **Auto** to see which settings Camera Raw deems appropriate for your photo. Next, for better results, click **Default** to restore the default values, and follow the remaining steps.

2. The **histogram** reflects the current Camera Raw settings and redraws as you change them. Study the graph to see if any highlight or shadow pixels are being pushed to the edge (are being clipped). Clipping occurs if the tonal range of a scene is wider than the range the camera can capture. Your goal will be to bring the pixels into the range of your chosen RGB color space, in order to minimize clipping. (In our setup, we have chosen the Adobe RGB color space for our camera; we have also chosen it for Camera Raw via the Workflow Options dialog.)

3. To minimize the clipping of highlight and shadow pixels, do the following:

   In the top left corner of the histogram, click the **Shadow Clipping Warning** button (U) to display a representation of shadow clipping as blue in the preview. In the top right corner, click the **Highlight Clipping Warning** button (O) to display highlight clipping as red **A** (and **A**, next page). Monitor this display of clipping as you apply corrections to your photo.

   To bring out details in the highlights, use the Exposure and Recovery sliders as a duo. For an overexposed photo, move the **Exposure** slider to the left and the **Recovery** slider far to the right until only a trace remains of the red highlight warning color (you can use either the sliders or the scrubby sliders) (**B**, next page).

   To bring out shadow details, use the Blacks and Fill Light sliders as a duo. For an underexposed photo, move the **Fill Light** slider slightly to the right. For a raw photo, also move the **Blacks** slider to the left until only a trace remains of the blue shadow warning color (**C**, next page).

   To minimize clipping another way, Alt-drag/Option-drag the **Exposure** and/or **Recovery** sliders and release the mouse when small

amounts of white (representing all three color channels) display in the black preview. Alt-drag/Option-drag the **Blacks** slider and release the mouse when small amounts of color or black display in the white preview. The color areas represent clipping in those channels.

4. *Optional:* Adjust the Brightness to enhance details in the midtones, and the Contrast to increase or decrease contrast (**D**, next page). Note: For an even better way to adjust the midtones in a photo, see page 72.

Finally, you can use the Clarity slider in the Basic tab to adjust the edge contrast and the Vibrance slider to adjust the color saturation. Note: Although both the Vibrance and Saturation sliders affect color saturation, the latter can cause oversaturation and highlight clipping, whereas the former is much less likely to (move the Saturation slider to the far right, and you'll see what we mean). Even at a moderately high setting, Vibrance doesn't cause oversaturation of skin tones.

## To adjust edge contrast and color saturation using the Basic tab:

1. To add depth by adjusting the edge contrast in the midtones, increase the **Clarity** value, or reduce this value if you want to deliberately soften a photo, such as a portrait or landscape.

2. Adjust the **Vibrance** value to increase or reduce the color saturation (**E**, next page).

3. Turn off the Clipping Warnings by pressing U, then O.

➤ To adjust the saturation of specific colors, see pages 74–75.

*Shadow Clipping Warning button*                    *Highlight Clipping Warning button*

**A** *Activate the Clipping Warning buttons above the histogram (when a warning is on, it has a white border). This is the histogram for the original photo, which is shown in* **A** *on the next page. Most of the pixels are clustered at the left edge of the graph, which indicates that the image is underexposed.*

## CORRECTING AN UNDEREXPOSED PHOTO

**A** *The original photo is underexposed, as you can see by the blue and red clipping warning colors in the preview.*

**B** *We raised the Exposure value in the Basic tab to lighten and recover details in the highlights and midtones.\* We also raised the Recovery value to recover some details in the bright, metallic highlights, but left some clipping because we want some of those highlights to remain pure white, with no details.*

**C** *We used the Fill Light and Blacks sliders to recover details in the shadows (the lower front area of the car and in the grass). The blue and red clipping warning areas have now been minimized.*

**D** *We increased the Brightness value to recover more details in the midtones; we also increased the Contrast value, which had the effect of intensifying the shadows.*

**E** *Finally, we increased the Clarity value to enhance the edge contrast and increased the Vibrance value to boost the color saturation. Now this classic MG really shines!*

*\*The settings on this page were applied to a raw photo. If you downloaded and are working on the JPEG version of this photo, choose a Recovery value of 90, a Fill Light value of 20, a Blacks value of 0, and a Brightness value of +28.*

## Using the Tone Curve tab

After making adjustments in the Basic tab, the next step is to improve the contrast in the photo. Using the Parametric sliders in the Tone Curve tab, you can adjust the highlights, lights, darks, and shadows separately. Although you could also adjust the curve manually (employing the same techniques as for a Curves adjustment layer in Photoshop), if you don't click and drag the curve in just the right way, the image could become posterized. For this reason, we encourage you to use the sliders instead. If you use Adobe Photoshop Lightroom, the Parametric curve and sliders here will look familiar.

### To apply tonal adjustments using the Parametric sliders in the Tone Curve tab:

1. Click the **Tone Curve** tab, then the nested **Parametric** tab. **A–B** Behind the curve you'll see a static display of the current histogram.

2. Increase the **Highlights, Lights** (upper midtones), **Darks** (lower midtones), or **Shadows** value to lighten that tonal range and thereby raise the corresponding portion of the curve above the diagonal line, **C** or reduce the value to darken that tonal range and thereby lower that portion of the curve below the straight diagonal line) (**A–B**, next page). If you need to intensify the contrast, try moving the Highlights and Lights sliders in opposite directions.

3. After adjusting the sliders, you can move the region control (located below the graph) to expand or contract the range of tonal values that each slider adjustment affects. The left region control affects the Shadows slider, the right region control affects the Highlights slider (**C–D**, next page), and the middle region control affects the Lights and Darks sliders. The more a control moves the curve away from the straight diagonal line, the more adjacent tonal ranges are affected; the more a control moves the curve closer to the diagonal line, the fewer adjacent tonal ranges are affected.

➤ Except for the Recovery slider, the sliders in the Basic and Tone Curve tabs shouldn't be pushed to the extreme left or right.

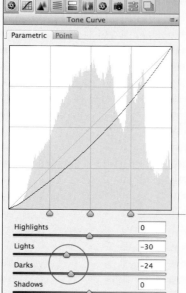

**A** In this photo, the highlights lack detail and the midtones lack contrast.

**B** In the Parametric tab (Tone Curve tab), we reduced the Lights and Darks values, which had the effect of lowering the midsection of the curve.

Region controls

**C** The Lights adjustment darkened the upper midtones, and the Darks adjustment darkened the lower midtones.

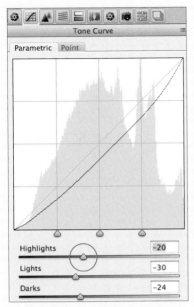

**A** *To darken the highlights, we reduced the Highlights value. This had the effect of lowering the top of the curve.*

**B** *To reduce the highlights, instead of moving a Tone Curve slider, we clicked the Targeted Adjustment tool, ✛ⓞ then dragged downward over a highlight area. This lowered the Highlights value (pushed some highlight areas into the upper midtone range) and recovered details, most noticeably in the clouds. Overall, the image contrast is improved.*

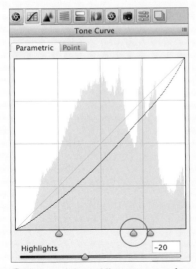

**C** *We moved the middle region control to the right (to 68), which had the effect of lowering the midsection of the curve.*

**D** *The adjustment to the region control expanded the darkening effect of the Lights and Darks sliders, which further darkened both the light and dark tonal ranges. In this final image, the exposure looks just right.*

## Using the HSL/Grayscale tab

In the HSL/Grayscale tab, you can adjust the hue, saturation, or luminance of individual colors. The sliders in this tab are powerful! (They can be used as sliders or scrubby sliders.)

### To adjust individual colors via HSL sliders:

1. Click the **HSL/Grayscale** tab, ▤ and double-click the Hand tool 🖑 to fit the image in the preview.**A**

2. Click the nested **Hue** tab. Move any slider to shift that color toward its adjacent hues, as shown in the bar. For example, you could shift the Greens toward yellow to make a photo warmer, or toward aqua to make it cooler.

3. Click the **Saturation** tab (**A–B**, next page). Move any slider to the left to desaturate a color (make it grayer) or to the right to make it more vivid (more pure). Avoid oversaturation, to keep the photo from looking unnatural and from becoming unprintable.

   ➤ To make a sky look more vivid, increase the saturation of the Blues and Aquas; or to make a sunset warmer, increase the saturation of the Yellows or Greens; or to make the lighting look gray and hazy, lessen the saturation of the Yellows or Greens.

4. Click the **Luminance** tab (**C–D**, next page). Move a slider to the left to make that color darker (by adding black) or to the right to make it lighter (by adding white). Avoid overlightening the colors, to prevent clipping of the highlights.

---

**USING THE TARGETED ADJUSTMENT TOOL**

With the Targeted Adjustment tool ⊕ in Camera Raw, you can apply local adjustments to a photo. After choosing the tool, click a nested HSL tab or click and hold on the tool and choose Hue, Saturation, or Luminance from the menu. Next, drag over a specific color area to apply a correction: Drag upward or to the right to increase the slider values, or downward or to the left to decrease those values. The sliders corresponding to the color under the pointer will shift automatically.

**A** *In the original photo, the sky lacks contrast and the greens and yellows in the field are oversaturated.*

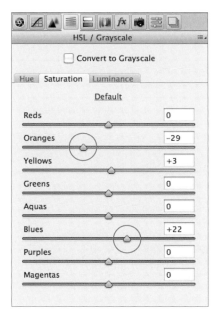

**B** *The Saturation adjustments lessened the intensity of the oranges in the field and added richness to the blues in the sky.*

**A** *In the nested Saturation tab of the HSL/ Grayscale tab, we reduced the saturation of the Oranges and increased the saturation of the Blues.*

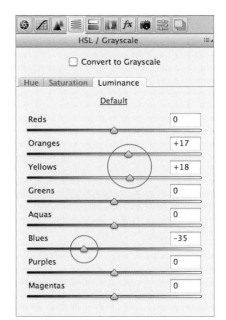

**D** *The Luminance adjustments lightened the colors in the field and darkened the colors in the sky. Overall, the colors in the top part of this photo are now in better balance with those in the lower part.*

➤ *Choose a zoom level of 66% for the Camera Raw preview to see a more accurate rendering of the adjusted pixels.*

**C** *In the nested Luminance tab, we lightened the Oranges and Yellows and darkened the Blues. A negative Blues adjustment can produce an effect similar to a polarizing filter used during a photo shoot.*

# Using the Detail tab

Via sliders in the Detail tab, you can preview and adjust the sharpness of your photo, and also reduce any unwanted color noise. Using these nondestructive sharpening controls is the best way to apply what is called capture, or input, sharpening.

## To sharpen edges using the Detail tab:

1. Click the **Detail** tab ▲ **A** and choose a zoom level of 100% for the preview. Note: If the words "(Preview Only)" display in the Detail tab, click the Open Preferences button ▤ in the toolbox. In the Camera Raw Preferences dialog, choose Apply Sharpening To: All Images, then click OK.

2. In the **Sharpening** area, use the **Amount** slider to adjust the edge definition. For subject matter that needs a lot of sharpening, such as hard objects or architecture, set this slider to 100; if less sharpening is needed, try a value of 50–60.

   ➤ To evaluate sharpening in a grayscale preview, Alt-drag/Option-drag the Amount slider.

3. Alt-drag/Option-drag the **Detail** slider slightly to the right to sharpen edge details and textures, and Alt-drag/Option-drag the **Masking** slider to around 50 to protect low-contrast areas with a black mask and sharpen only high-contrast areas.

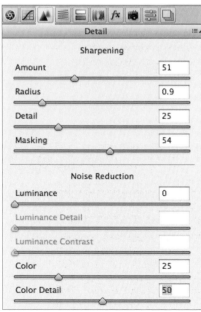

**A** *In the Detail tab, we adjusted the Sharpening sliders.*

All digital cameras produce some luminance (grayscale) noise and color artifacts. Although budget cameras tend to produce the most noise, it can also be produced by a high-end camera if used with a high ISO (light sensitivity) setting to capture a poorly lit scene. Before opening your photo into Photoshop, you should try to remove as much noise from it as possible, as it can become accentuated by image editing. When you follow these instructions, you'll see that shifting one slider value often requires adjusting another.

## To reduce luminance and color noise using the Detail tab: ★

1. With a photo open in Camera Raw (**A**, next page), click the **Detail** tab ▲ and choose a zoom level of 200–300% for the preview.

2. To reduce grayscale noise (graininess), increase the **Luminance** value (**B**, next page). Try a value between 20 and 70.

3. Raising the Luminance value smoothed out the high-contrast edges in the photo. To resharpen those edges, raise the **Luminance Detail** value (**C**, next page). Note that a high Luminance Detail value may reintroduce noise along the edges.

   ➤ With the Hand tool (H), you can move the photo in the preview window, to examine different edges.

4. Raise the **Luminance Contrast** value to restore some edge contrast. The effect of this slider is most noticeable in photos that contain a lot of noise.

5. Defects such as color artifacts and random speckling tend to be most noticeable on solid-color surfaces, particularly those in the shadow areas. To reduce these defects, increase the **Color** value from the default value of 25 to around 40–50, depending on the subject matter of the photo.

6. Raising the Color value may lower the intensity of colors in areas of the photo that were poorly lit. To restore some saturation and intensity to those areas, increase the **Color Detail** value (**D**, next page) from the default value of 50 to around 75, or until the color saturation looks just right. To judge the overall effect of the settings you have chosen in this tab, lower the zoom level.

**A** *This is a close-up of a photo of a shop window (viewed at a zoom level of 300%), with the Noise Reduction: Luminance and Color sliders set to zero (no noise reduction applied). Grayscale noise is evident in the signage, and color artifacts are evident in the poorly lit interior behind the letters.*

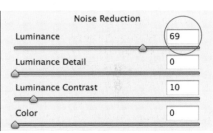

**B** *To remove graininess from the letters, we changed the Luminance value to 69, but this also diminished the edge definition.*

**C** *To resharpen the edges of the letters, we increased the Luminance Detail value to 78.*

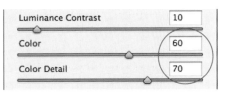

**D** *To remove color artifacts from the dark areas, we increased the Color value to 60. This had the effect of desaturating the colors, though, so to revive the color saturation and intensity, our last adjustment was to increase the Color Detail value to 70. The final image is shown at left.*

## Adding a grain texture

In the world of traditional film stock, the faster the speed, the larger and more apparent the grain. By using the Grain controls in Camera Raw, you can simulate this grainy texture. Pick a photo that won't suffer aesthetically when its details lose definition.

### To add a grain texture to a photo: ★

1. Click the **Effects** tab, *fx* and double-click the Hand tool 🖑 to fit the image in the preview. **A**

2. Under **Grain**, to control the amount of grain applied, choose an **Amount** value of around 50 to make the grain noticeable.

3. To emulate the fine grain of a slow film speed or the coarser grain of fast film speed, do as follows:

   Raise the **Size** value for the size of the grain particles. **B** When this value is greater than 25, a small degree of blurring is also applied, to help blend the grain with the imagery.

   Lower the **Roughness** value below the default value of 50 to produce a more uniform grain; or raise it to produce an uneven, coarse grain. **C** Zoom in to examine the grain, then readjust the Amount value, if needed.

**A** *This photo will be a good candidate for the Grain effect in Camera Raw, because it contains soft, muted colors and the details don't need to stay crisp.*

**B** *The first settings we chose were Grain Amount 50 and Size 80 (the Roughness control was left at the default value of 50). The food textures are starting to blend with the soft background.*

**C** *We changed the Amount to 75, the Size to 60, and the Roughness to 65. The coarser grain (increased Roughness) further unifies the highlights and background with the food textures. Please pass the Parmesan...*

# Using the Adjustment Brush

Unlike settings chosen in the Camera Raw tabs, which apply to the overall photo, the Adjustment Brush lets you apply local adjustments to specific areas. For example, you could adjust the exposure, brightness, or color saturation of a few key details that you want to emphasize in a composition. You draw brush strokes in the preview to define which areas are to be adjusted, then you apply the correction by adjusting the sliders. If most of the sliders for this tool look familiar, it's because they're like the ones in the Basic tab.

## To apply Adjustment Brush edits:

1. After making adjustments in the Basic and Tone Curve tabs,  click the **Adjustment Brush** ✐ (K). The sliders for the tool display. You will paint over specific areas to mask them first, then adjust the sliders for those masked areas.

2. To "zero out" all the sliders except one to make the tool operational, click the + or – button for one of the sliders.

3. Choose a **Feather** value of 60–95 to allow the edits to fade into surrounding areas. Set the **Flow** to 50 (for the smoothness of the stroke), and set the **Density** to 60 (for the level of transparency in the stroke).

4. Check **Show Mask** (Y), adjust the brush size by pressing [ or ], then draw strokes over the areas of the photo that need adjustment. **B** A tint covers the areas that you apply strokes to.

   ➤ The brush size is represented by the solid circle in the pointer, and the feather value is represented by the black-and-white dashed circle.

*Continued on the following page*

**A** *The original photo is lit evenly. We want to apply local exposure edits to lighten and darken some of the areas in the center.*

**B** *On the Adjustment Brush panel, we clicked New, zeroed out the sliders, then applied strokes to mask (mark) the areas to be darkened.*

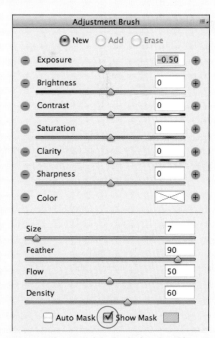

*Because Show Mask is checked, we're able to see where the mask is being brushed on.*

**5.** Uncheck Show Mask, then move the various sliders to apply adjustments to the masked areas.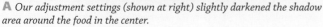

**6.** To apply an adjustment to another area of the photo, click New, then repeat steps 2–5 (**A–B**, next page).

➤ To edit an existing adjustment, click one of the pins that marks the first location you clicked (a black dot appears in the pin), then add to the mask and/or change the slider settings.

➤ To show or hide all the pins, press V or check or uncheck Show Pins.

### To remove Adjustment Brush edits:

**1.** With the Adjustment Brush tool ✐ selected (K), check **Show Mask** (Y) to display the current mask.

**2.** Do either or both of the following:

To remove adjustments locally, click an existing pin, click the **Erase** button, then apply strokes where you want to erase the mask.

To remove an entire pin and its adjustments, click the pin, then press Backspace/Delete.

➤ To remove all Adjustment Brush tool edits and reset the mode to New, click the Clear All button.

**A** *Our adjustment settings (shown at right) slightly darkened the shadow area around the food in the center.*

---

#### USING THE AUTO MASK OPTION WITH THE ADJUSTMENT BRUSH

To mask a specific color area, zoom in on it, check Auto Mask, scale the brush to cover only that area, and start a stroke with the Adjustment Brush over that color. The mask will cover only the areas that match that specific color. We used this method to limit an exposure adjustment to the yellow of the flowers shown at right.

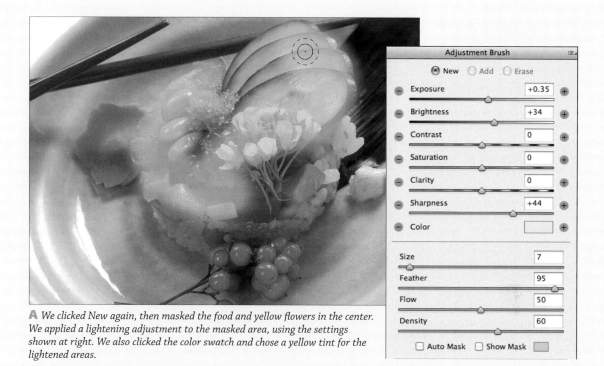

**A** *We clicked New again, then masked the food and yellow flowers in the center. We applied a lightening adjustment to the masked area, using the settings shown at right. We also clicked the color swatch and chose a yellow tint for the lightened areas.*

**B** *We added one last pin, which we used to desaturate the red berries at the bottom of the photo. Because the berries are now subdued, the food and flowers in the center command more attention.*

# Retouching a photo

The Spot Removal tool can be used to remove blemishes or other imperfections, such as spots caused by dust on the camera lens.

## To remove blemishes or spots:

1. Choose the **Spot Removal** tool ✏. (B), and zoom in on the area to be repaired.

2. Position the pointer at the center of the area that needs repair, then drag outward to scale the target circle so it surrounds the blemish **A** (the Radius slider will readjust). When you release the mouse, a green and white source circle appears (which is linked to the red and white target circle), and the area within the target circle is repaired.**B**

3. Drag inside the target or source circle to reposition them, if necessary.**C**

4. From the **Type** menu, choose **Heal** to blend source pixels into the texture and luminosity values of the target pixels or **Clone** to copy the source pixels exactly without healing.

5. *Optional:* Lower the Opacity value to lessen the retouching effect. You can also drag the edge of either circle to resize both of them simultaneously, or add more circle pairs to correct other blemishes. To hide the circles, press V or choose a different tool.

➤ The retouching circles will remain available even after you click Done or Open. To redisplay them, choose the Spot Removal tool. To remove a selected pair, press Backspace/Delete, or to remove all pairs, click Clear All.

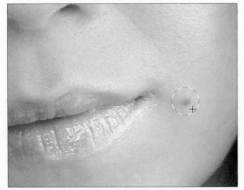

**A** *With the Spot Removal tool, drag a target circle around the blemish to be removed.*

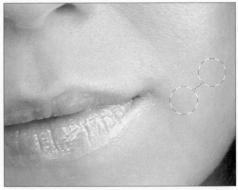

**B** *Camera Raw will display and position a linked source circle in a suitably similar area, and will use pixels from within the source circle to repair the blemish within the target circle.*

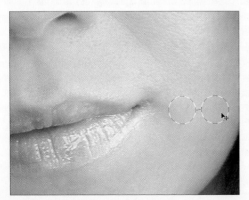

**C** *To control where source pixels are sampled from manually, drag to reposition the source circle. Pixels within the target circle will update instantly.*

# Saving and applying Camera Raw settings

After carefully choosing custom settings for a photo in Camera Raw, you'll be happy to know that you can save those settings as a preset, which you can apply to other photos, such as photos from the same shoot that need the same or similar corrections. You can apply a preset to a single photo via Camera Raw, to multiple photos via Camera Raw (see the next page), or to multiple selected thumbnails in Bridge via the Edit > Develop Settings submenu (see the tip below).

### To save Camera Raw settings as a preset:

1. With your corrected photo open in Camera Raw, choose **Save Settings** from the Settings menu.≡ ◢ The Save Settings dialog opens.**A**

2. Check which categories of settings you want saved in the preset. Or to filter out the number of checked boxes, choose a category (tab name) from the **Subset** menu, then recheck any boxes, if needed.

3. Click Save. A different Save Settings dialog opens (yes, this is confusing). Enter a name (preferably one that describes the function of the preset), keep the .xmp extension and the location as the Settings folder, then click Save.

4. The saved settings preset is now available in the Presets tab ▦ for any photo (see the instructions below).

You can apply a user-defined preset (saved collection of settings) to any photo in Camera Raw.

### To apply a Camera Raw preset:

With a photo that needs correction open in Camera Raw, do either of the following:

Click the **Presets** tab,▦ then click a preset name.

From the **Apply Preset** submenu on the Settings menu, choose a preset.

➤ To apply a Camera Raw preset to one or more selected photos in Bridge, right-click one of the selected thumbnails, then from the Develop Settings menu, choose the desired preset.

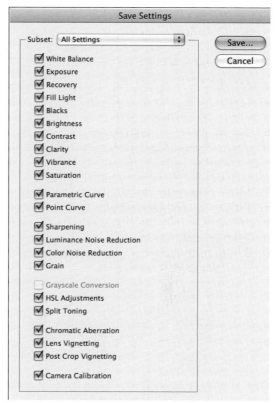

**A** In the Save Settings dialog, specify which of your custom Camera Raw settings are to be saved in a preset.

---

**TAKING SNAPSHOTS OF YOUR EDITS**

If you save an editing stage of your photo (and the current Camera Raw settings) as a snapshot, you will be able to restore the photo to that stage at any time. Snapshots save with the Camera Raw file.

➤ To create a snapshot of the current settings, click the Snapshots tab,▦ then click the New Snapshot button ▣ at the bottom of the tab. In the New Snapshot dialog, enter a name, then click OK. You can continue editing the photo.

➤ To restore the photo to a snapshot version at any time, click a snapshot name in the Snapshots tab. (If you need to restore your last custom settings, choose Custom Settings from the Settings menu.)

# Synchronizing Camera Raw settings

When you open multiple photos into Camera Raw, they are represented by thumbnails in a filmstrip panel on the left side of the dialog. After adjusting one photo or choosing a settings preset, you can click Synchronize to apply those settings to all the open photos. In practice, it's unlikely that every single adjustment that is needed for one photo will work perfectly on all the rest, even if they're from the same shoot. The Synchronize option is useful, however, for applying settings incrementally. For example, you could apply an adjustments preset or some adjustments in the Basic tab to a whole group of photos (perhaps to correct the white balance and exposure), click Synchronize, then select smaller and smaller batches for more targeted adjustments.

### To synchronize the Camera Raw settings of multiple photos:

1. In Bridge, select two or more image thumbnails, preferably for photos that were shot under the same lighting conditions and that require the same type of correction (they should be all raw files or all JPEG files). Double-click one of the selected thumbnails.

2. A filmstrip panel displays on the left side of the Camera Raw dialog.**A** Click one of the thumbnails.

3. Make the necessary adjustments to the selected image, including cropping if all the images are to be cropped in exactly the same way. You could also click a preset in the Presets tab.▦

4. Click **Select All** at the top of the filmstrip panel or Ctrl-click/Cmd-click the thumbnails that you want to apply the corrections to, then click **Synchronize**. The Synchronize dialog opens (it looks like the Save Settings dialog, which is shown on the preceding page).

5. Either manually check the setting(s) to be applied or choose a category from the Synchronize menu (and check any additional boxes).

6. To apply the current settings in the categories you checked to all the selected thumbnails, click OK.

➤ To cycle through the photos in the filmstrip panel, click the left or right arrowhead below the preview (in the lower right). If more than one thumbnail is selected, Camera Raw will cycle through only those photos.

**A** *When you open multiple photos into Camera Raw, the thumbnails for those images display in the filmstrip panel on the left side of the dialog.*

# Converting, opening, and saving Camera Raw files

Still with us? Terrific! Finally, you get to open your Camera Raw file into Photoshop. (After reading this page, also see our instructions for opening a Camera Raw file as a Smart Object layer on the next page.)

## To convert a Camera Raw file and open it into Photoshop (saving its settings):

After correcting an image in Camera Raw, click **Open Image**. The current settings will be saved as instructions for converting the photo without altering the original file. (Or to open multiple images, click Open Images.)

Note: The settings for a raw photo are saved either as part of the internal Camera Raw database in your system or as a hidden sidecar .xmp file, which is placed in the same folder as the raw file. This internal file is different from any user-created settings file that you may have created via the Save Settings command on the Settings menu.

➤ To close the Camera Raw dialog without opening your file, click Done. Your current settings will still be saved as instructions and will be accessible if you reopen the file in Camera Raw.

### WHAT IS DNG?

Photographs capture unrepeatable moments, and archiving them is both a priority and a concern for photographers. Ideally, there would be one standard file format for digital photos that photographers could depend on with confidence, knowing their photos will be stable and accessible for eternity — or at least for many, many years. At the present time, each camera maker uses a unique, proprietary format for creating raw files. Should a manufacturer discontinue its own proprietary format, raw photos from their cameras might be unreadable by Photoshop or other image-editing applications.

Enter DNG (short for Digital Negative), a format developed by Adobe. It preserves all the raw, unprocessed pixel information that the camera records. The coding for the DNG format is nonproprietary (open standard), which means it is available to interested companies. This format may be the long-term solution that photographers will come to rely on — provided it is adopted as the standard by most camera and software manufacturers.

Alternatively, you can open a copy of a Camera Raw file without recording the settings into the metadata of the raw file or into the actual JPEG file.

## To open a copy of a Camera Raw file:

In the Camera Raw dialog, hold down Alt/Option and click **Open Copy** (Open Image becomes Open Copy). The file will be converted using the current settings and will open into Photoshop, but those settings won't be recorded over any existing instructions in the raw or JPEG file.

Using the Save Options dialog, which is accessed via the Save Image button in Camera Raw, you can convert and save a copy of your digital photos in the DNG (Digital Negative), JPEG, TIFF, or Photoshop format. The main reason you're likely to use this dialog is to archive your photos in the DNG format (see the sidebar at left). Camera Raw settings are preserved in DNG files, and are accessible and editable if the files are reopened in Camera Raw.

Note: Camera Raw settings are applied permanently to photos that are converted to the JPEG, TIFF, and PSD formats. JPEG and TIFF files can be reopened in Camera Raw (whereas PSD files cannot), but the settings saved in those files won't display and aren't editable — well, except for JPEG photos that are opened and edited in Camera Raw and then closed by clicking Done; settings for such files will remain available in Camera Raw.

## To save a file as DNG, JPEG, TIFF, or PSD:

1. In the lower left corner of the Camera Raw dialog, click **Save Image**. The Save Options dialog opens.

2. For the Destination, choose **Save in Same Location** or **Save in New Location**. For the latter, choose a location in the Select Destination Folder dialog, then click Select.

3. In the **File Naming** area, enter a file name; also choose a naming or numbering convention from the adjacent menu, if desired.

4. As the **Format**, choose Digital Negative, JPEG, TIFF, or Photoshop, then choose format-related options. For example, if you cropped the photo in Camera Raw, for the Photoshop format, check whether you want to Preserve Cropped Pixels.

5. Click Save.

# Opening and placing photos into Photoshop as Smart Objects

If you open or place a Camera Raw file into Photoshop as a Smart Object, you'll be able to readjust it at any time via Camera Raw. To learn more about Smart Object layers, see pages 308–311.

## To open a Camera Raw file as a Smart Object in Photoshop:

**Method 1 (open as a new document)**

When you're done correcting a photo in Camera Raw, hold down Shift and click **Open Object**. A new document opens in Photoshop, and the photo appears on a Smart Object layer.

➤ If you want Camera Raw to convert and open all files as Smart Objects by default, click the underlined link at the bottom of the dialog, then in the Workflow Options dialog, check Open in Photoshop as Smart Objects. The Open Image button is now labeled Open Object.

**Method 2 (place into an existing document)**

1. Open a Photoshop document.

2. In Bridge, click the thumbnail for a raw or JPEG photo that you have finished editing in Camera Raw. It should have this badge: 🔳.

3. Choose File > Place > **In Photoshop**. The Camera Raw dialog opens.

4. Make any further adjustments to the photo, if desired, then click OK. The image will appear on its own layer in the currently active Photoshop document, within a transform box.**A**

5. Apply any needed scale or shape transformations to the placed image, then to accept it and convert it to a Smart Object layer, press Enter/Return or double-click inside it.**B**

## To edit a Smart Object photo:

1. In Photoshop, double-click a Smart Object layer thumbnail to reopen an embedded copy of the photo into Camera Raw.

2. Make any desired adjustments, then click OK to apply your edits to the Smart Object layer. The original photo won't be affected by your edits.

➤ You can scale a Smart Object layer at any time. Photoshop will use the pixel data from the original file to scale the image, so its quality won't be diminished (that is, provided you don't enlarge it beyond its original size).

**A** *We opened a Photoshop document, then from Bridge, chose File > Place > In Photoshop. When the photo opened in the Camera Raw dialog, we clicked OK; the photo appeared in the Photoshop file. Here, we are Shift-dragging a corner handle of the transform box to scale the placed image. The last step will be to accept it.*

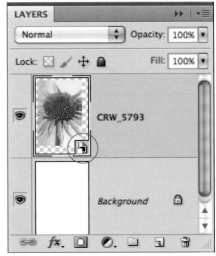

**B** *When we accepted the placed image, the Smart Object icon appeared on the new layer.*

Now that you know how to create and open documents, you're ready to customize your workspace. In this chapter, you'll learn about the main features of the Photoshop interface, such as the Application frame and document tabs. You'll also learn how to change the zoom level and screen mode, rotate the canvas view temporarily, configure the panels, choose a workspace, save custom workspaces, and use the Application and Options bars. In the next chapter, you'll be introduced to the individual panels, including the Tools panel.

## Using the Application frame

Upon launching Photoshop in Windows, you'll see an Application frame* onscreen, which houses the Application bar, Options bar, panels, and your currently open documents. A In the Mac OS (unlike in Windows), the display of the Application frame is optional, but we always keep ours showing and encourage you to do the same.

Although document windows can be left to float freely as in older versions of Photoshop, we recommend docking them as tabs within the Application

*Continued on the following page*

*Application bar*     *Menu bar*     *Options bar*

**A** *This is the onscreen environment for Photoshop in Windows.*

*\*For the sake of simplicity, we will also refer to the Windows application window as the "Application frame."*

frame. When documents are docked as tabs, it's easier to arrange and switch among them, and the Photoshop interface is more streamlined.

In the Mac OS, we also recommend keeping the Application bar, Options bar, and other panels within the Application frame. If your Desktop is anything like ours, it contains a lot of distracting clutter. One of the advantages of using the frame is that it blocks out the Desktop. Secondly, open images are displayed against a light gray background, which provides a neutral backdrop for color work.**A** And thirdly, when Photoshop is in Standard Screen mode, the viewing area for the document resizes dynamically as you hide or show the panels or collapse or expand the panel docks.

## To show (or hide) the Application frame in the Mac OS:

To show the Application frame, check Window > **Application Frame** (to hide it, uncheck the command).

➤ To resize the Application frame, drag one of its edges or corners.

➤ To minimize the Application frame in Windows, click the Minimize button; in the Mac OS, double-click the Application bar.

➤ To learn about the Application and Options bars, see page 100.

*The document tab (or title bar) lists the file name, format, zoom level, current layer, color mode, and bit depth. An asterisk indicates the file contains unsaved changes. To close a document, click the X.*

*Application bar*

*Use the Options bar to choose settings for the current tool.*

*The Standard version of Photoshop has 24 movable panels, which are used for image editing. On most panels, you can enter values or move sliders; a few panels, such as Info and Histogram, serve only to provide information.*

**A** *The Application frame in the Mac OS is shown above.*

# Using tabbed document windows

Whether you're a Windows or Mac OS user (and in the Mac OS, whether the Application frame is showing or not), you can dock multiple open document windows as a series of tabs, and then display any document easily by clicking its tab.

## To dock document windows as tabs into the Application frame:

Do any of the following:

To dock a floating document window manually, drag its title bar to the tab area (just below the Options bar) of the Application frame, and release when the blue drop zone bar appears.**A**

If one or more documents are already docked as tabs and you want to dock all floating document windows into the Application frame, right-click a tab and choose **Consolidate All to Here** from the context menu.**B** Another method is to click the **Consolidate All** icon ◼ on the Arrange Documents menu ◼ (Application bar); the icon is available even when all documents are floating.

To set a preference so that all documents you susequently open are docked as tabs automatically, right-click any panel tab and choose Interface Options, check **Open Documents as Tabs** in the preferences dialog, then click OK.

➤ To cycle among the currently open documents, press Ctrl-Tab/Control-Tab.

➤ To turn a tabbed document window into a floating one, either right-click the tab and choose Move to New Window, or drag the tab downward out of the tab area. To float all currently open document windows, on the Arrange Documents menu ◼ on the Application bar, click Float All in Windows. To dock one floating document window into another, drag its title bar to just below the title bar of the other window. Note: We don't recommend floating document windows when documents are also docked as tabs in the Application frame, because if you were to click in the frame, any floating windows would be obscured behind it.

**A** *To dock one floating document window as a tab manually, drag its title bar to the tab area of the Application frame, and release the mouse when the blue drop zone bar appears.*

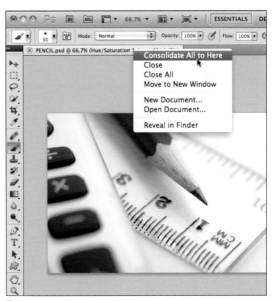

**B** *To dock all floating windows into the Application frame, one method is to right-click a document tab and choose Consolidate All to Here.*

# Arranging document windows

By clicking different icons on the Arrange Documents menu on the Application bar, you can quickly display multiple documents in various tabbed layouts, such as two documents arranged side by side or vertically, or four or six documents in a grid.

## To display multiple tabbed document windows:

On the Application bar, click the **Arrange Documents** menu icon to open the menu, then click one of the available icons (the availability of icons varies depending on how many documents are open).**A**

➤ If any open documents are floating when you click an option on the Arrange Documents menu, they will be docked as tabbed windows automatically.

Just as effortlessly, you can go back to displaying one document at a time.

## To display one tabbed document window:

Do either of the following:

Right-click a tab and choose **Consolidate All to Here** from the context menu.

On the Arrange Documents menu on the Application bar, click the **Consolidate All** (first) icon.

---

**DISPLAYING ONE IMAGE IN TWO WINDOWS**

To open a second window for the same document, choose New Window from the Arrange Documents menu. You could display the document at a different zoom level, turn View > Proof Colors on for one document but not for the other, or choose different Proof Setup menu settings for them.

---

**A** *To arrange these tabbed documents in quadrants, we clicked the 4-Up icon on the Arrange Documents menu.*

# Changing the zoom level

You can display the whole image in the document window or magnify part of it when you need to work on a small detail. The current zoom level percentage is listed in four locations: on the Application bar, on the document title bar or tab, in the lower left corner of the document window, and on the Navigator panel.

Note: For smoother and more continuous zooming, check Animated Zoom in Edit/Photoshop > Preferences > General, and check Enable OpenGL Drawing in Preferences > Performance. The latter preference must also be checked to use the Scrubby Zoom feature, which is discussed below. For the other Zoom preferences, see page 386.

## To change the zoom level using the Zoom tool:

Do any of the following:

Choose the **Zoom** tool, 🔍 then check **Scrubby Zoom** on the Options bar. In the document window, drag immediately to the right to zoom in **A** or to the left to zoom out.* ★

➤ To spring-load the Zoom tool with its current settings, hold down Z.

In the **Zoom Level** field on the Application bar or in the lower left corner of the document window, enter the desired zoom percentage.

Right-click in the document window and choose a zoom option from the context menu.

Click a zoom button on the Options bar: **Actual Pixels** to set the zoom level to 100%; **Fit Screen** to display the entire image at the largest size that can fit in the window; **Fill Screen** to have the image fill the window (only part of the image may be visible); or **Print Size** to display the image at an approximation of its print size.

| SHORTCUTS FOR ZOOMING IN AND OUT | | |
|---|---|---|
| | Windows | Mac OS |
| Zoom in incrementally | Ctrl-+ (plus) | Cmd-+ (plus) |
| Zoom out incrementally | Ctrl-– (minus) | Cmd-– (minus) |
| Zoom in | Ctrl-Spacebar click or drag | Cmd-Spacebar click or drag |
| Zoom out | Alt-Spacebar click or drag | Option-Spacebar click or drag |
| Actual pixels (100% view) | Ctrl-Alt-0 (zero) | Cmd-Option-0 (zero) |
| Fit on Screen | Ctrl-0 (zero) | Cmd-0 (zero) |

*Note: The zoom shortcuts also can be used when some dialogs are open.*

**A** *With the Zoom tool and Scrubby Zoom checked on the Options bar, drag to the right to zoom in (or to the left to zoom out).*

*The Animated Zoom feature kicks in if you don't drag immediately (when scrubby zooming). If you want to prevent this, uncheck the Animated Zoom preference. To change the zoom level without scrubby zooming, click to zoom in or Alt-click/Option-click to zoom out.*

Using the Navigator panel, you can change the zoom level of an image. And when the zoom level is greater than 100%, you can also use the panel to move the image in the document window, to bring an area you want to edit or examine into view.

### To change the zoom level or move the image in the window by using the Navigator panel:

1. Display the Navigator panel. ❋

2. To change the zoom level, do any of the following:

   Ctrl-drag/Cmd-drag across an area of the image thumbnail to marquee it for magnification.

   Type the desired percentage in the zoom field, then press Enter/Return. Or to zoom to a percentage while keeping the field highlighted, press Shift-Enter/Shift-Return.

   Drag the Zoom slider.

   Click the Zoom Out or Zoom In button.

3. If the zoom level is above 100%, you can move the image in the window by dragging the view box on the panel. **A**

Another way to move a magnified image in the document window is by using the Hand tool.

### To move a magnified image in the window with the Hand tool:

Choose the **Hand** tool 🖑 (H) or hold down the Spacebar for a temporary Hand tool, then drag in the document window.

Note: If the document is in a tabbed window in the Application frame and is magnified, you can overscroll it — that is, drag it farther off to the side than you can in a floating window.

➤ You can also move a magnified image in the document window by clicking the up or down scroll arrow in the lower right corner of the document window. Or to move the image more quickly, drag the horizontal or vertical scroll bar.

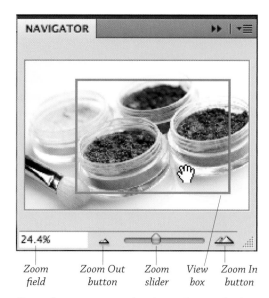

Zoom     Zoom Out     Zoom     View     Zoom In
field        button       slider     box     button

**A** *Use the Navigator panel to change the zoom level of your document and, if the image is magnified, to move it in the window.*

---

**MATCHING THE ZOOM LEVEL OR LOCATION**

If multiple documents are open in Photoshop, from the Arrange Documents menu ▦ on the Application bar, you can choose Match Zoom to match the zoom level of all the windows to that of the currently active image, or Match Location to synchronize the position of all the images in their windows, or Match Zoom and Location to perform both of those functions at once.

**FLICK PANNING**

If the image is magnified and you're working on an OpenGL system, try this: Do a quick little drag in the document, then release; the document will float across the screen. Click once more to stop the motion. For this nifty little feature to work, Enable OpenGL Drawing must be checked in Edit/Photoshop > Preferences > Performance and Enable Flick Panning must be checked in Preferences > General.

When you have multiple documents open (say, in a 2-Up or 3-Up layout), you can save time by scrolling or zooming all of them simultaneously.

### To scroll or zoom in multiple windows:

1. Open two or more documents, then on the Arrange Documents menu,▦ click a 2-Up, 3-Up, 4-Up, 5-Up, or 6-Up icon.

2. Do either of the following:

   To scroll or zoom all the open Photoshop document windows, hold down Shift while using the Hand or Zoom tool.

   Check Scroll All Windows on the Options bar before using the Hand tool, or check Zoom All Windows on the Options bar before using the Zoom tool.

## Rotating the canvas view

OpenGL is a cross-platform API (application programming interface), or language, that was developed by Silicon Graphics for 2D and 3D computer graphics applications. To use the OpenGL features in Photoshop, such as Animated Zoom (see the Note on page 91), Scrubby Zoom, flick panning (see the last tip on the preceding page), or the Rotate View tool (discussed below), your system must contain a video driver or card that provides OpenGL acceleration. To enable OpenGL drawing in Photoshop, go to Edit/Photoshop > Preferences > Performance, then under GPU Settings, check Enable OpenGL Drawing. Relaunch Photoshop.

Unlike the Image > Image Rotation commands, which rotate the image permanently, the Rotate View tool tilts the canvas temporarily so you can draw or paint at a particular angle.

### To rotate the canvas view by using the Rotate View tool:

1. Choose the **Rotate View** tool 🖑 (R), or hold down R to spring-load the tool.

2. Do either of the following:

   Drag in the image.**A**

   On the Options bar, enter a **Rotation Angle** value, use the scrubby slider, or move the dial.

### To reset the canvas to the default angle:

1. Choose the **Rotate View** tool 🖑 (R).

2. Click **Reset View** on the Options bar.

**A** With the Rotate View tool, drag to tilt the canvas area temporarily.

# Changing the screen mode

The three screen modes control which Photoshop interface features are displayed onscreen.

## To change the screen mode:

Press F to cycle through the screen modes, or from the **Screen Mode** menu  on the Application bar,**A** choose one of the following:

**Standard Screen Mode** (the default mode) to display the Application frame (if turned on), document tabs, the Photoshop menu bar, Application bar, Options bar, and panels — with the Desktop visible behind everything.

**Full Screen Mode with Menu Bar** to display the current document on a full-screen gray (default color) background, obscuring the Desktop, with all of the above-mentioned interface features showing.**B**

**Full Screen Mode** to display the current document on a black (default color) background, with the Photoshop interface features and Desktop hidden and the panels visible only upon rollover (see "To make hidden panel docks reappear" on the next page).

➤ When color accuracy is important to us (which, come to think of it, is all the time!), we like to keep the area around the image gray. If you want to change the color of the area around the image for just the current screen mode, right-click that area and choose Gray, Black, or Custom (the last chosen custom color) from the context menu, or choose Select Custom Color and choose a color from the picker. You can also change the color around the image for any or all of the three screen modes via the Preferences dialog; see page 388.

# Choosing a predefined workspace

The quickest way to change your panel setup is by choosing a predefined workspace. They're designed for different kinds of tasks. (To create and save custom workspaces, see pages 98–99.)

## To choose a predefined workspace: ★

On the Application bar in Photoshop, do either of the following:

Click a workspace name, such as **New in CS5**, **Design**, **Photography**, **Essentials**, or **Painting**.**C**

Choose a workspace from the **Workspace** menu on the Application bar.

➤ To display more workspace names on the bar, drag the vertical gripper bar to the left.

**A** *Choose an option from the Screen Mode menu on the Application bar.*

**B** *When performing color correction work, we choose Full Screen Mode with Menu Bar as the screen mode for Photoshop.*

*Drag this bar to the left to reveal more workspace names.*

**C** *To quickly change your panel setup, click a workspace name on the Application bar.*

# Configuring the panels

When you need to fully maximize your screen space, you can hide all the currently open panels and easily make them reappear only when needed.

### To hide (or show) the panels:

Do either of the following:

Press Tab to hide (or show) all currently open panels, including the Tools panel.

Press Shift-Tab to hide (or show) all currently open panels except the Tools panel.

➤ To open a panel individually, choose the panel name from the Window menu.

### To make hidden panel docks reappear:

1. Hide the panels as just described or choose Full Screen Mode from the Screen Mode menu 🔲 on the Application bar.

2. If the document is in Standard Screen mode, let the pointer pause on the dark gray vertical bar at the right edge of the Application frame; or if your document is in either one of the Full Screen modes, let it pause at the edge of your monitor.**A** The panel docks will redisplay temporarily (but freestanding panels will remain hidden).**B** Move the pointer away from the panels, and they'll disappear again.

Note: If this mechanism doesn't appear to be working, right-click any panel tab or icon and choose Auto-Show Hidden Panels from the context menu. That should do the trick.

➤ If you prefer to keep your panels visible onscreen but want to minimize how much space they occupy, shrink them to icons (see the last paragraph on the next page).

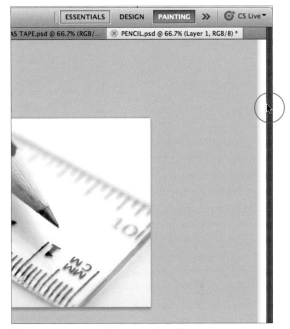

**A** *With the panels hidden, if you let the pointer pause on the dark vertical bar at the right edge of the monitor or Application frame...*

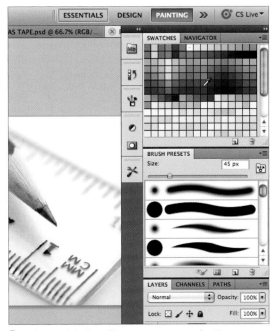

**B** *...the panel docks will reappear temporarily. If you move the pointer away from the panels, they'll disappear again.*

Most of the edits that you will make in Photoshop will require the use of one panel or another. A clever interface makes the panels easy to store, expand, and collapse so they don't intrude on the document space when you're not using them. Note: The individual panels are illustrated in the next chapter.

In the predefined workspaces (which are accessed via the Application bar), the panels are arranged in docks on the right side of your screen — except for the Tools panel, which is on the left side. Each dock can hold one or more panels or panel groups. **A** In this section, we'll show you how to reconfigure them.

### To reconfigure the panel groups and docks:

**Open or close a panel**: Open a panel by choosing its name from the Window menu (a few panels can also be opened or closed via a keyboard shortcut, which is also listed on the menu). The panel will display either in its default group and dock or in its last location. To bring a panel to the front of its group, click its tab (panel name).

**Expand a panel that's collapsed to an icon**: Click the icon or panel name. If Auto-Collapse Iconic Panels is checked in Edit/Photoshop > Preferences > Interface and you open a panel from an icon, it collapses back to the icon when you click elsewhere. With this preference unchecked, the panel stays expanded; to collapse it back to an icon, you must click either the Collapse to Icons button 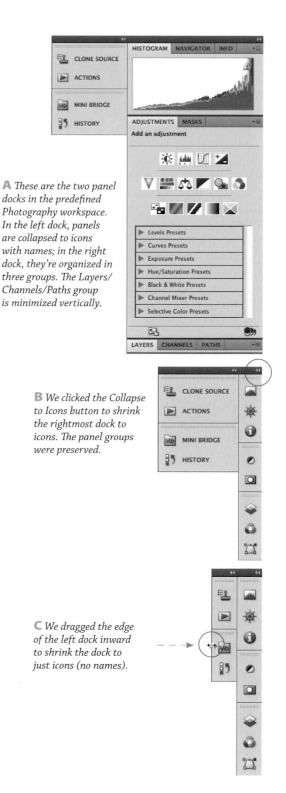 on the panel bar or the panel icon in the dock.

➤ To quickly access the Auto-Collapse Iconic Panels option from a context menu, right-click any panel tab, bar, or icon.

**Maximize or minimize an expanded panel or group vertically** (to toggle the full panel to just a panel tab, or vice versa): Double-click the panel tab or title bar (the gray bar next to the panel tabs).

**Use a panel menu**: Click the icon to access the menu for whichever panel is in front within its group.

**Close a panel or group**: To close a panel, right-click the panel tab and choose Close from the context menu. To close a whole panel group, choose Close Tab Group from the same context menu.

**Collapse a whole dock to either icons or icons with names**: Click the Collapse to Icons button at the top of the dock, or double-click the dark horizontal gray bar. **B** To expand icons to icons with names, or vice versa, drag the vertical edge of the dock horizontally. **C**

**A** *These are the two panel docks in the predefined Photography workspace. In the left dock, panels are collapsed to icons with names; in the right dock, they're organized in three groups. The Layers/Channels/Paths group is minimized vertically.*

**B** *We clicked the Collapse to Icons button to shrink the rightmost dock to icons. The panel groups were preserved.*

**C** *We dragged the edge of the left dock inward to shrink the dock to just icons (no names).*

**Widen or narrow a dock and panels**: Position the pointer over the vertical edge of the dock (↔ cursor), then drag horizontally.

**Lengthen or shorten a panel or group**: Position the pointer over the bottom edge of the panel or group, and when you see this pointer, ↕ drag upward or downward. Panels docked in the same group will resize accordingly. Note that some panels can't be lengthened or shortened.

**Move a panel to a different group**: Drag the panel tab over the title bar of the desired group, and release when the blue drop zone border appears. **A**

**Move a panel to a different slot in the same group**: Drag the panel tab (name) to the left or right.

**Move a panel group upward or downward in a dock**: Drag the title bar, then release it when the horizontal blue drop zone bar is in the desired location. **B**

**Create a new dock**: Drag a panel tab or title bar sideways to the vertical edge of the dock, **C** and release the mouse when the blue vertical drop zone bar appears.

**Reconfigure a dock that's collapsed to icons**: Use methods similar to those for an expanded group. Drag the group "title" bar (the double dotted line) ▦▦▦▦▦ to the edge of a dock to create a new dock; or drag the title bar vertically between groups to restack it (look for a horizontal drop zone line); or drag the title bar into another group to add it to that group (look for a blue drop zone border).

**Make a docked panel or group into a floating one**: Drag the panel tab, icon, or title bar out of the dock. To stack floating panels or groups, drag the top bar of one to the bottom of another.

**Resize a floating panel**: Drag the resize box ▦ (located in the lower right corner) inward or outward, or drag the right edge of the panel horizontally. To resize the Adjustments panel, click the Expanded View button. ⬚ Not all panels are resizable. ➤ To keep a floating panel from docking while it's being moved, hold down Ctrl/Cmd.

**To redock floating panels into the Application frame**: Drag the dark gray bar at the top of the panel group to the right edge of the Application frame, and release the mouse when the pointer is at the edge of the frame and a vertical blue drop zone line appears.

➤ For any tool that uses a brush, you can show the Brush panel by clicking the Toggle Brush Panel button 🖌 on the Options bar or Brush Presets panel. ★ For the Type tool, you can show the Character panel by clicking this button: 🔳.

**A** *A blue drop zone border appears as we drag a panel into a different group.*

**B** *A blue horizontal drop zone bar appears as we move our Channels/Layers panel group upward within the same dock.*

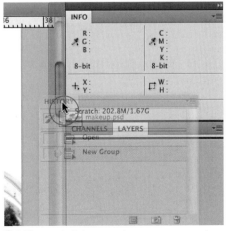

**C** *A blue vertical drop zone bar appears as we drag the History panel out of a dock to create a new dock for it.*

# Saving custom workspaces

Now that you have learned how to customize your working environment in Photoshop, the next step is to save theme-related workspaces for different kinds of tasks. This will shorten your setup time when you begin your work sessions. A In Photoshop CS5, the current panel locations are included automatically when you save a custom workspace. ★ Optionally, the workspace can include custom keyboard shortcuts, as well as menu sets, which control the color label and visibility settings for menu commands.

Your custom workspaces should reflect your normal work habits (and by this we don't mean working late and sleeping late!). For example, to set up a type-intensive workspace, you would open the Character and Paragraph panels and assign color labels to commands that you normally use when creating text. Or to create a painting workspace, open the Brush, Color, and Swatches panels, assign color labels to the brush preset commands, and maybe hide some unrelated commands.

## To save a custom workspace: ★

1. Do any or all of the following:

    Open and position all the panels in the desired locations, panel groups, and docks.

    Collapse the panels you use occasionally to icons and close the ones you rarely use. Or if you prefer to keep all your panels collapsed to icons or icons with names, set them up that way now.

    Resize any of the panels, as well as any of the pickers that open from the Options bar.

    Choose a thumbnail, swatch size, or other panel display options from any of the panel menus, or from any of the menus on the preset pickers that open from the Options bar.

    Choose Edit > Menus and use the dialog to assign color labels and/or visibility settings to menu commands. Save your changes to a new menu set. (To customize keyboard shortcuts, see "Keyboard Shortcuts" in Photoshop Help; to assign labels, see "Workspace.")

2. From the Workspace menu ➤➤ on the Application bar, choose New Workspace.

3. In the New Workspace dialog, enter a **Name** for the new workspace (include your own name, if desired). B

4. Under Capture, if you customized the **Keyboard Shortcuts** or the **Menus**, check those options.

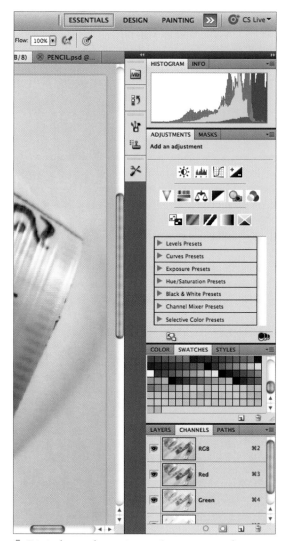

**A** *This is the panel setup in one of our custom workspaces.*

**B** *In the New Workspace dialog, enter a Name for your workspace and check either or both of the optional features.*

**5.** Click Save. Your workspace will appear in three locations: the Application bar, the Workspace menu,A and the Window > Workspace submenu.

➤ To edit an existing workspace, choose the workspace to be edited, make the desired changes to the Photoshop interface, then save the workspace under the same name; click Yes in the alert dialog.

➤ On a computer with dual displays, you can distribute freestanding panel groups or stacks between them and save that arrangement as a workspace.

➤ All panels that are open when you exit/quit Photoshop will reappear in the same location upon relaunch. There is no longer a preference option that lets you turn this feature on or off. ★

A *Our new workspace (named "Elaine's Workspace") appears on the Application bar and on the Workspace menu.*

## To delete a saved custom workspace:

**1.** On the Application bar, click any workspace *except* the one to be deleted.

**2.** From the Workspace menu on the Application bar, choose **Delete Workspace**.

**3.** In the Delete Workspace dialog, choose the name of the user workspace you want to get rid of,**B** click Delete, then click Yes in the alert dialog.

# Resetting workspaces

Say you chose a workspace and then rearranged some panels manually. If you were to switch to another workspace and then back to the first one, your manual changes would remain (be "sticky"). Follow the first set of instructions below to restore the original settings to an individual workspace, or the second set of instructions to restore the default settings to all the predefined Adobe workspaces.

## To reset one workspace: ★

**1.** On the Application bar or from the Workspace menu on the Application bar, choose the workspace to be reset.

**2.** Right-click the name of the workspace to be reset on the Application bar and choose **Reset** [workspace name] from the menu.

## To reset all the Adobe workspaces: ★

**1.** To open the Interface preferences dialog, right-click a panel tab or icon and choose **Interface Options**.

**2.** Under Panels & Documents, click **Restore Default Workspaces**, click OK to exit the alert dialog, then click OK to exit the Preferences dialog.

B *In the Delete Workspace dialog, choose the user-created workspace you want to get rid of.*

# Using the Application bar ★

Use controls on the Application bar to go to Bridge, arrange and choose options for your document windows, and access and save workspaces for Photoshop.**A** In Windows, the main Photoshop menus also display on the Application bar. In the Mac OS, the Application bar is docked in the Application frame. When the Application frame is hidden, the Application bar is docked below the main menu bar; if you don't see the bar, choose Window > Application Bar.

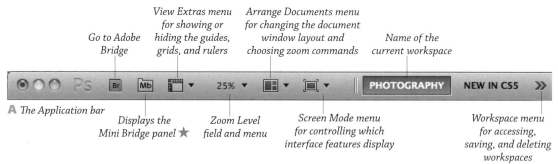

*Go to Adobe Bridge*

*View Extras menu for showing or hiding the guides, grids, and rulers*

*Arrange Documents menu for changing the document window layout and choosing zoom commands*

*Name of the current workspace*

**A** *The Application bar*

*Displays the Mini Bridge panel ★*

*Zoom Level field and menu*

*Screen Mode menu for controlling which interface features display*

*Workspace menu for accessing, saving, and deleting workspaces*

# Using the Options bar

You'll use the Options bar (Window > Options) to choose settings every time you switch tools — and sometimes to change settings while using a tool.**B** The Options bar is dynamic, meaning its features change depending on what tool is selected and how that tool is currently being used in the document. Your choices remain in effect for each tool until you change them. You can move the bar out of the Application frame by dragging its left edge.

*Tool Preset picker for choosing predefined tool settings*

*A preset picker (click the icon or arrowhead to open it)*

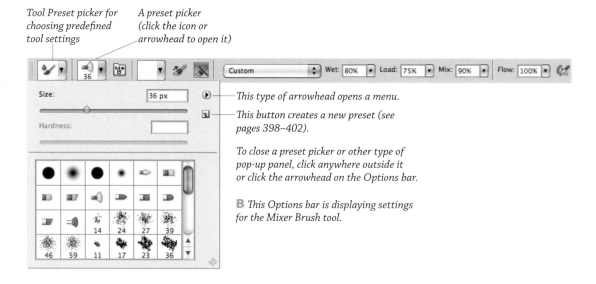

*This type of arrowhead opens a menu.*

*This button creates a new preset (see pages 398–402).*

*To close a preset picker or other type of pop-up panel, click anywhere outside it or click the arrowhead on the Options bar.*

**B** *This Options bar is displaying settings for the Mixer Brush tool.*

This chapter will help you become more acquainted with a feature of the Photoshop interface that you will be using constantly as you work: the panels. In the preceding chapter, you learned how to arrange the panels onscreen. Here you'll be introduced to the specific function of each one — from choosing color swatches (Swatches panel), to accessing and editing masks (Masks panel), to customizing brushes (Brush panel), to editing layers (the indispensable Layers panel). Step-by-step instructions for using most of the panels are amply provided in other chapters, such as how to monitor clone sources by using the Clone Source panel in Chapter 14, and how to style type by using the Character and Paragraph panels in Chapter 20. In some cases, a whole chapter is devoted to the mechanics of using a particular panel, such as the Layers panel in Chapter 8 and the History panel in Chapter 10.

You can read through this chapter with or without glancing at or fiddling with the panels onscreen, and also use it as a reference guide as you work. The panel icons are shown on the next page to help you identify them quickly. Following that, you'll find instructions for using the Tools panel and an illustration of the tools, followed by illustrations and descriptions of the other panels that are used in this book, in alphabetical order.

# PANELS

# 6

## IN THIS CHAPTER

---

### CHOOSING VALUES QUICKLY

➤ You can change numerical values quickly on the Options bar, on many panels (such as Adjustments, Masks, Layers, Character, and Paragraph), and in some dialogs by using a scrubby slider: Drag slightly to the left or right over the option name or icon, as shown below.

➤ To access a pop-up slider (e.g., to choose an Opacity percentage on the Layers panel) click the arrowhead. To close a slider, click anywhere outside it or press Enter/ Return. (If you click an arrowhead to open a slider, you can press Esc to close it and restore its last setting.)

➤ To change a value incrementally, click in a field in a panel or dialog, then press the up or down arrow key.

## The Photoshop panel icons

Each panel in Photoshop has a unique icon. **A** If you keep the panels collapsed to conserve screen space, you can identify them by their icons. You can also identify collapsed panels via tool tips. The panels are opened individually via the Window menu. (To learn how to configure the panels, see pages 95–97.)

*A When collapsed, each panel has a unique icon.*

### USING CONTEXT MENUS

When you right-click* in the document window—depending on where you click and which tool is selected—a menu of context-sensitive commands pops up temporarily onscreen. Many panel thumbnails, names, and other features also have context menus. If a command is available on a context menu (or can be executed quickly via a keyboard shortcut), we let you know in our instructions, to spare you from having to trudge up to the main menu bar.

*This is the context menu for a selection.*

*This is the context menu for a layer mask on the Layers panel.*

*If your mouse doesn't have a right-click button, hold down Control and click to open the context menu.*

# The Photoshop panels illustrated*

## Using the Tools panel

The Tools panel, which is illustrated on pages 104–106, contains 60 tools and a handful of buttons! Believe it or not, by the end of this book, you'll be marginally to intimately familiar with most of them.

To display the Tools panel if it's hidden, choose Window > **Tools**. To choose a tool, do one of the following:

➤ If the desired tool is visible on the Tools panel, click its icon.

➤ To cycle through related tools in the same slot, Alt-click/Option-click the one that's visible.

➤ To choose a hidden tool, click and hold on the visible tool, then click a tool on the menu.

➤ To select a tool quickly, press its designated letter shortcut (don't do this if your cursor is in type). The shortcuts are shown in the screen captures on the next three pages. The shortcut for each tool is also listed in its tool tip onscreen. If Use Shift Key for Tool Switch is unchecked in Edit/Photoshop > Preferences > General, simply press the designated letter to cycle through related tools in the same slot (for example, press L to cycle through the three Lasso tools). With the Use Shift Key for Tool Switch option checked, you have to press Shift plus the designated letter.

➤ To use (spring-load) a tool temporarily while another tool is selected, press and hold down its assigned letter key (see the sidebar at right).

To learn the function of a tool as you're using it, read the brief description (tool hint) at the bottom of the Info panel. If you don't see the tool hint, choose Panel Options from the Info panel menu, then check Show Tool Hints (see page 114).

Before using a tool that you've selected, you need to choose settings for it from the Options bar at the top of your screen. For example, for the Brush tool, you would choose a brush preset, and choose diameter, hardness, blending mode, opacity percentage, and other settings. If the Options bar is hidden, you can display it by choosing Window > Options (see page 100).

The current Options bar settings for each tool remain in effect until you change them, reset the tool, or reset all tools. To restore the default settings to a tool, right-click the thumbnail on the Tool Preset picker (located at the left end of the Options bar) and choose Reset Tool from the context menu. **A** Or to reset all tools, choose Reset All Tools from the menu, then click OK in the alert dialog.

In Edit/Photoshop > Preferences > Cursors, you can control whether the pointer displays as crosshairs or as the icon of the current tool or, for some tools, as a circle either the size or half the size of the current brush diameter, with or without the crosshairs inside it (see page 392).

**A** *To access these two commands, right-click the Tool Preset picker thumbnail, which is located at the left end of the Options bar.*

---

**SPRING-LOADING YOUR TOOLS**

➤ To quickly access a tool and its Options bar settings temporarily without having to actually click the tool on the Tools panel, hold down its letter shortcut key. For example, say the Brush tool happens to be selected but you want to move a layer, which requires using the Move tool. You would hold down the V key, drag in the document window, then release V. Or to access the Zoom tool temporarily, you would hold down the Z key.

➤ This process is slightly less efficient if you want to access a tool that shares a slot with other tools (as most tools do). In this case, the letter shortcut accesses whichever tool happens to be visible on the Tools panel. To make this work, you could plan ahead and select the tools that you want to switch back and forth among before using them.

---

*The 3D tools, and the 3D, Actions, Animation, Measurement Log, Notes, and Paths panels aren't illustrated in this chapter because they aren't covered in this book.

## Tools panel

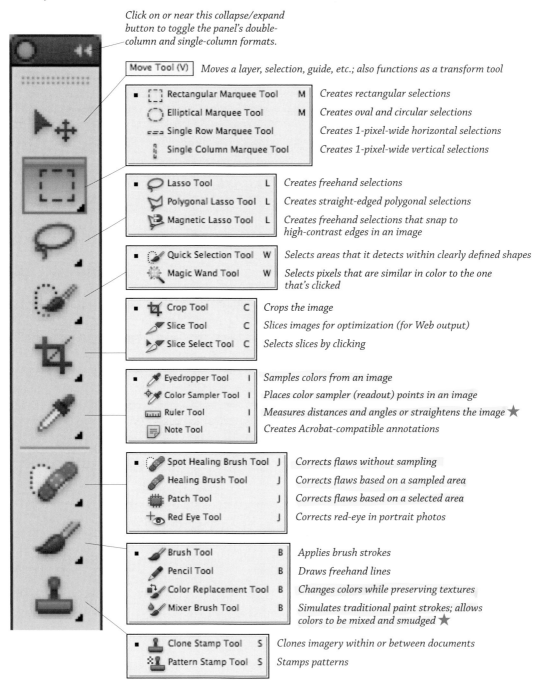

Click on or near this collapse/expand button to toggle the panel's double-column and single-column formats.

**Move Tool (V)** — *Moves a layer, selection, guide, etc.; also functions as a transform tool*

| | | |
|---|---|---|
| Rectangular Marquee Tool | M | *Creates rectangular selections* |
| Elliptical Marquee Tool | M | *Creates oval and circular selections* |
| Single Row Marquee Tool | | *Creates 1-pixel-wide horizontal selections* |
| Single Column Marquee Tool | | *Creates 1-pixel-wide vertical selections* |

| | | |
|---|---|---|
| Lasso Tool | L | *Creates freehand selections* |
| Polygonal Lasso Tool | L | *Creates straight-edged polygonal selections* |
| Magnetic Lasso Tool | L | *Creates freehand selections that snap to high-contrast edges in an image* |

| | | |
|---|---|---|
| Quick Selection Tool | W | *Selects areas that it detects within clearly defined shapes* |
| Magic Wand Tool | W | *Selects pixels that are similar in color to the one that's clicked* |

| | | |
|---|---|---|
| Crop Tool | C | *Crops the image* |
| Slice Tool | C | *Slices images for optimization (for Web output)* |
| Slice Select Tool | C | *Selects slices by clicking* |

| | | |
|---|---|---|
| Eyedropper Tool | I | *Samples colors from an image* |
| Color Sampler Tool | I | *Places color sampler (readout) points in an image* |
| Ruler Tool | I | *Measures distances and angles or straightens the image* ★ |
| Note Tool | I | *Creates Acrobat-compatible annotations* |

| | | |
|---|---|---|
| Spot Healing Brush Tool | J | *Corrects flaws without sampling* |
| Healing Brush Tool | J | *Corrects flaws based on a sampled area* |
| Patch Tool | J | *Corrects flaws based on a selected area* |
| Red Eye Tool | J | *Corrects red-eye in portrait photos* |

| | | |
|---|---|---|
| Brush Tool | B | *Applies brush strokes* |
| Pencil Tool | B | *Draws freehand lines* |
| Color Replacement Tool | B | *Changes colors while preserving textures* |
| Mixer Brush Tool | B | *Simulates traditional paint strokes; allows colors to be mixed and smudged* ★ |

| | | |
|---|---|---|
| Clone Stamp Tool | S | *Clones imagery within or between documents* |
| Pattern Stamp Tool | S | *Stamps patterns* |

**A** *The upper part of the Tools panel*

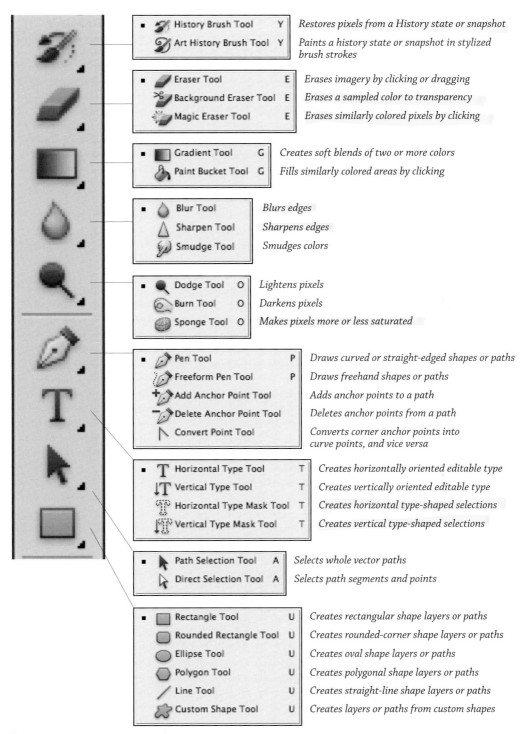

| | | | |
|---|---|---|---|
| ■ | History Brush Tool | Y | Restores pixels from a History state or snapshot |
| | Art History Brush Tool | Y | Paints a history state or snapshot in stylized brush strokes |

| | | | |
|---|---|---|---|
| ■ | Eraser Tool | E | Erases imagery by clicking or dragging |
| | Background Eraser Tool | E | Erases a sampled color to transparency |
| | Magic Eraser Tool | E | Erases similarly colored pixels by clicking |

| | | | |
|---|---|---|---|
| ■ | Gradient Tool | G | Creates soft blends of two or more colors |
| | Paint Bucket Tool | G | Fills similarly colored areas by clicking |

| | | | |
|---|---|---|---|
| ■ | Blur Tool | | Blurs edges |
| | Sharpen Tool | | Sharpens edges |
| | Smudge Tool | | Smudges colors |

| | | | |
|---|---|---|---|
| ■ | Dodge Tool | O | Lightens pixels |
| | Burn Tool | O | Darkens pixels |
| | Sponge Tool | O | Makes pixels more or less saturated |

| | | | |
|---|---|---|---|
| ■ | Pen Tool | P | Draws curved or straight-edged shapes or paths |
| | Freeform Pen Tool | P | Draws freehand shapes or paths |
| | Add Anchor Point Tool | | Adds anchor points to a path |
| | Delete Anchor Point Tool | | Deletes anchor points from a path |
| | Convert Point Tool | | Converts corner anchor points into curve points, and vice versa |

| | | | |
|---|---|---|---|
| ■ | Horizontal Type Tool | T | Creates horizontally oriented editable type |
| | Vertical Type Tool | T | Creates vertically oriented editable type |
| | Horizontal Type Mask Tool | T | Creates horizontal type-shaped selections |
| | Vertical Type Mask Tool | T | Creates vertical type-shaped selections |

| | | | |
|---|---|---|---|
| ■ | Path Selection Tool | A | Selects whole vector paths |
| | Direct Selection Tool | A | Selects path segments and points |

| | | | |
|---|---|---|---|
| ■ | Rectangle Tool | U | Creates rectangular shape layers or paths |
| | Rounded Rectangle Tool | U | Creates rounded-corner shape layers or paths |
| | Ellipse Tool | U | Creates oval shape layers or paths |
| | Polygon Tool | U | Creates polygonal shape layers or paths |
| | Line Tool | U | Creates straight-line shape layers or paths |
| | Custom Shape Tool | U | Creates layers or paths from custom shapes |

**A** The midsection of the Tools panel

Continued on the following page

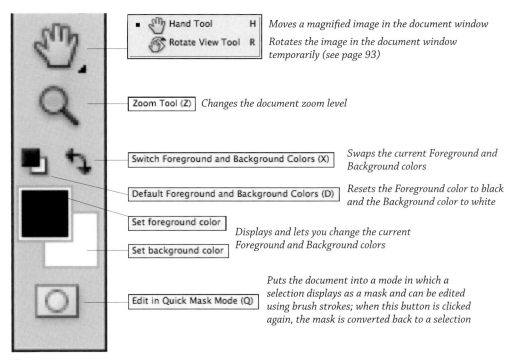

| | | | |
|---|---|---|---|
| ■ | Hand Tool | H | Moves a magnified image in the document window |
| | Rotate View Tool | R | Rotates the image in the document window temporarily (see page 93) |

Zoom Tool (Z)   *Changes the document zoom level*

Switch Foreground and Background Colors (X)   *Swaps the current Foreground and Background colors*

Default Foreground and Background Colors (D)   *Resets the Foreground color to black and the Background color to white*

Set foreground color

Set background color   *Displays and lets you change the current Foreground and Background colors*

Edit in Quick Mask Mode (Q)   *Puts the document into a mode in which a selection displays as a mask and can be edited using brush strokes; when this button is clicked again, the mask is converted back to a selection*

**A** *The lower part of the Tools panel*

---

**GETTING INFO ON PHOTOSHOP FEATURES**

► If you're unsure what an icon signifies, what a menu is called, or what a panel or dialog feature or tool does, you may get the information you need from the tool tip. Let the pointer hover on the feature in question without clicking the mouse button, and a tip pops up onscreen. (For this to work, Show Tool Tips must be checked in Edit/Photoshop > Preferences > Interface.)

► Some dialogs (such as Edit > Color Settings) have a Description area that contains information about the option your pointer is currently hovering over.

► Keep an eye on the Info panel for color breakdown readouts, document data (e.g. file size, color profile, dimensions, resolution), and tool hints (ways to use the currently selected tool). See page 114.

► Use the Histogram panel to monitor changes to the tonal ranges in an image as you apply color and tonal adjustments. See pages 203–204.

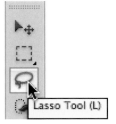

*Use the tool tip to learn a tool name or shortcut.*

## Adjustments panel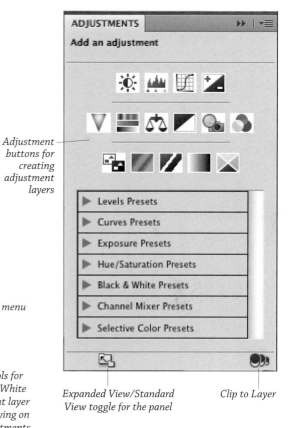

Unlike commands that are applied via the Image >
Adjustments submenu, adjustment layers don't alter
image pixels until you merge them with their underlying layers. They are a great mechanism for trying
out color and tonal adjustments, because you can
edit their settings and delete them at any time. Plus,
adjustment layers automatically have a layer mask.
By editing the mask, you can hide or reveal the
adjustment effect in specific areas of the image.

Using the Adjustments panel, you can easily
create and edit the settings for adjustment layers.
The panel also lets you restore the default settings to
any adjustment; hide and show the adjustment effect;
view the previous adjustment state; or, in a multi-
layered document, clip (limit) the adjustment effect
to just the underlying layer. See Chapters 12 and 13.

*Adjustment buttons for creating adjustment layers*

*Expanded View/Standard View toggle for the panel*  *Clip to Layer*

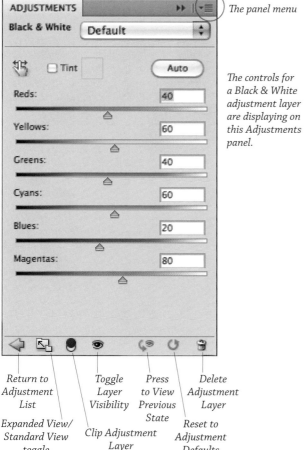

*The panel menu*

*The controls for a Black & White adjustment layer are displaying on this Adjustments panel.*

*Return to Adjustment List*

*Toggle Layer Visibility*

*Press to View Previous State*

*Delete Adjustment Layer*

*Expanded View/ Standard View toggle*

*Clip Adjustment Layer*

*Reset to Adjustment Defaults*

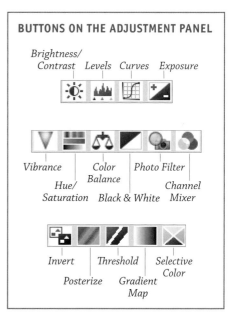

### BUTTONS ON THE ADJUSTMENT PANEL

*Brightness/ Contrast*  *Levels*  *Curves*  *Exposure*

*Vibrance*   *Color Balance*   *Photo Filter*

*Hue/ Saturation*   *Black & White*   *Channel Mixer*

*Invert*   *Threshold*   *Selective Color*

*Posterize*   *Gradient Map*

## Brush panel

You'll use the Brush panel to choose brush tips and create custom brushes for many tools, such as the Art History Brush, Blur, Brush, Burn, Clone Stamp, Dodge, Eraser, History Brush, Mixer Brush, Pattern Stamp, Pencil, Sharpen, or Smudge tool. Using this panel, you can also choose options for a graphics tablet and stylus.

Click an options set name on the left side of the panel to display settings on the right. At the bottom of the panel, the preview shows an example of a brush stroke made with the currently selected tip and settings. See Chapter 15.

➤ This panel can be opened from the Window menu; by clicking the Brush Panel button on the Brush Presets panel (see the following page); or when a tool that uses a brush is selected, by clicking the Toggle Brush Panel button on the Options bar. ★

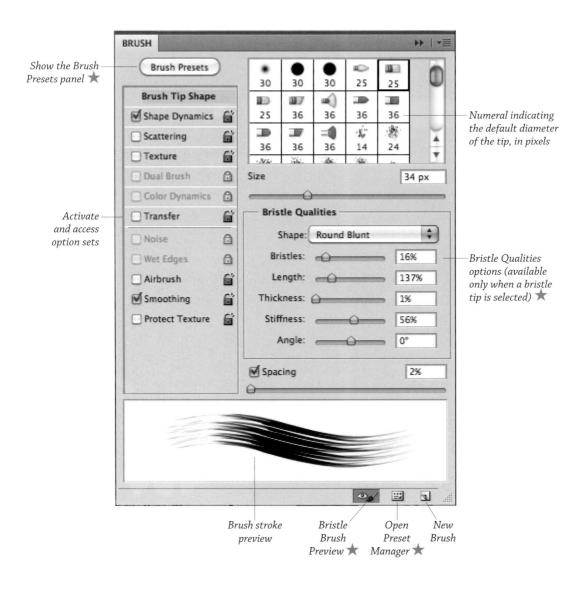

Show the Brush Presets panel ★

Activate and access option sets

Numeral indicating the default diameter of the tip, in pixels

Bristle Qualities options (available only when a bristle tip is selected) ★

Brush stroke preview

Bristle Brush Preview ★

Open Preset Manager ★

New Brush

## Brush Presets panel

Use the Brush Presets panel to store, display, and choose from an assortment of predefined and user-created brush presets. You can also use this panel to change the size of any brush preset temporarily, and to save a custom brush as a new preset.

Via buttons on the panel, you can turn the Bristle Brush preview on or off and quickly access the Preset Manager dialog. This panel can be opened from the Window menu or by clicking the Brush Presets button on the Brush panel. See page 260.

Brush Diameter · Open or close the Brush panel

BRUSH PRESETS
Size: 36 px

Brush presets

Bristle Brush Preview (on/off) · Open Preset Manager · New Brush · Delete Brush

### USING THE BRUSH PRESET PICKER

Brush presets can also be chosen from the Brush Preset picker, a pop-up panel that opens from the Options bar (shown below). Commands for loading, appending, and saving brushes and brush libraries are available on the Brush Presets panel menu and the Brush Preset picker menu.

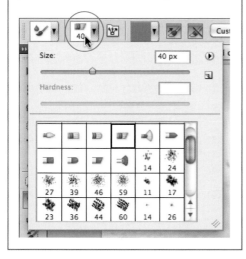

*The Bristle Brush preview displays a schematic of the current bristle tip and the settings you have chosen for it.*

## Channels panel

The Channels panel displays a list of, and the thumbnails for, all the color channels in an image. To show an individual channel in the document window, click the channel name or press the keystroke listed on the panel. To redisplay the composite image (all the channels), such as RGB or CMYK, click the topmost channel on the panel, or press Ctrl-2/Cmd-2. (See pages 2–3.)

You can also use this panel to save and load alpha channels (which are saved selections). See page 160. And you can use it to create and store spot color channels, which commercial print shops use to produce individual color plates for predefined ink colors, such as PANTONE inks.

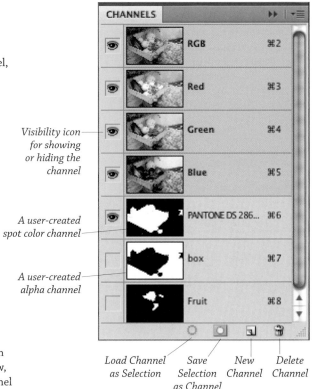

Visibility icon for showing or hiding the channel

A user-created spot color channel

A user-created alpha channel

Load Channel as Selection — Save Selection as Channel — New Channel — Delete Channel

## Character panel

You can choose attributes for the type tools from either the Character panel, which is shown below, or the Options bar (see page 100). Open this panel from the Window menu, or when a type tool is selected, by clicking the Toggle Character and Paragraph Panels button on the Options bar. See Chapter 20.

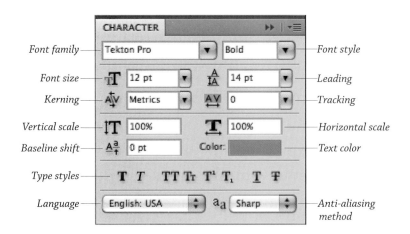

Font family — Tekton Pro — Bold — Font style
Font size — 12 pt — 14 pt — Leading
Kerning — Metrics — 0 — Tracking
Vertical scale — 100% — 100% — Horizontal scale
Baseline shift — 0 pt — Color: — Text color
Type styles
Language — English: USA — Sharp — Anti-aliasing method

## Clone Source panel

The Clone Source panel lets you keep track of up to five different sources (documents) when cloning pixels with the Clone Stamp tool. The sources are represented by a row of buttons at top of the panel. You can also use this panel to hide, show, and control the opacity and mode of the clone overlay, and flip, scale, rotate, invert, or reposition the source pixels before or while you clone them. See pages 248–249.

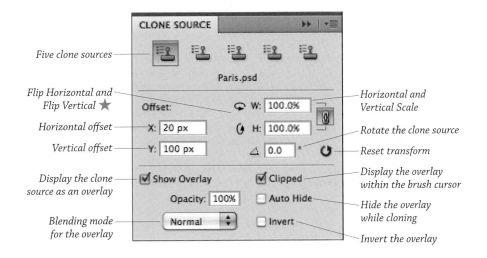

Five clone sources

Flip Horizontal and Flip Vertical

Horizontal offset

Vertical offset

Display the clone source as an overlay

Blending mode for the overlay

Horizontal and Vertical Scale

Rotate the clone source

Reset transform

Display the overlay within the brush cursor

Hide the overlay while cloning

Invert the overlay

## Color panel

The Color panel is one of several mechanisms that Photoshop provides for mixing colors. Choose a color model for the sliders or color ramp from the panel menu, then either mix a color using the sliders or quick-select a color by clicking the color ramp.

To open the Color Picker (or the Color Libraries dialog, from which you can also choose colors), click once on the Foreground or Background color square on the Color panel if it's already selected (has a black border), or double-click the square if it's not selected. Colors are applied by painting and editing tools, such as the Brush and Pencil tool, and by some commands, such as Edit > Fill and Image > Canvas Size. See page 188.

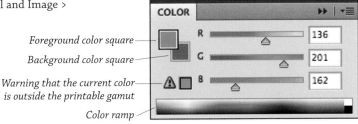

Foreground color square

Background color square

Warning that the current color is outside the printable gamut

Color ramp

## Histogram panel

While a file is being edited or while the Adjustments panel is being used, the Histogram panel provides valuable feedback in the form of a graph of either the current light and dark (tonal) values in the image or its current and modified tonal values.

Via the Channel menu, you can choose to have the panel display data about the composite channel (combined channels) or just a single channel. You can also expand the panel to display a separate histogram for each channel (as is shown at right). See pages 203–204.

*Source of the pixel data (all layers or just the currently selected layer)*

*Source channel for the graph*

*Displays the histogram using uncached data*

*Uncached Refresh*

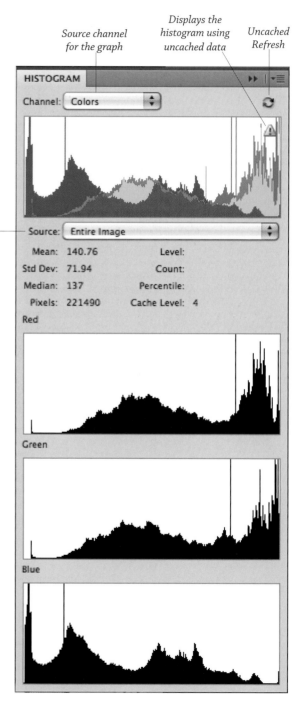

## History panel

Every image edit from the current work session — from the use of a filter or command to the creation of a selection, type, or a new layer — is listed as a separate state on the History panel. The most recent (last) edit is listed at the bottom. If you click a prior state, the document reverts to that stage of the editing process. In linear mode, the default mode for the panel, if you click an earlier state and then resume image editing from that state (or delete that state), all subsequent, dimmed states are discarded.

The oldest history states are deleted from the panel as new edits are made — that is, when the maximum number of history states is reached, as specified in Edit/Photoshop > Preferences > Performance, under History & Cache). All states are deleted when you close your document. The New Snapshot command creates states that stay on the panel until you close your document, regardless of the History States setting. See Chapter 10.

The History panel has two related tools. When you apply strokes with the History Brush tool, the areas under those strokes are restored to the state or snapshot you have designated as a source. The Art History Brush does the same thing, but in stylized strokes.

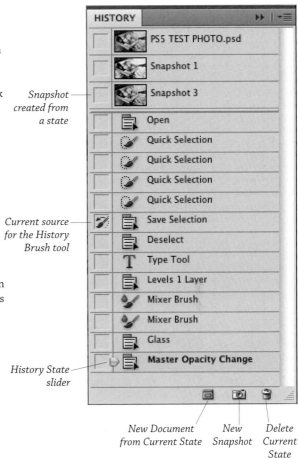

*Snapshot created from a state*

*Current source for the History Brush tool*

*History State slider*

*New Document from Current State*   *New Snapshot*   *Delete Current State*

---

### USING THE THREE UNDO COMMANDS

| | Windows | Mac OS |
|---|---|---|
| Undo the last Photoshop edit (not every edit can be undone) | Ctrl-Z (Edit > Undo) | Cmd-Z (Edit > Undo) |
| Undo multiple editing steps in reverse order (step backward) | Ctrl-Alt-Z | Cmd-Option-Z |
| Step forward through your editing steps (reinstate what you have undone) | Ctrl-Shift-Z | Cmd-Shift-Z |

## Info panel ⓘ

The Info panel displays a color breakdown of the pixel under the pointer at its current location in the document. While a color adjustment dialog is open or the Adjustments panel is being used, the panel displays before and after color readouts. The panel also lists the current location of the pointer on the x/y axes.

Other information may display on the Info panel, depending on which tool is being used, such as the distance between points when you move a selection or use the Ruler tool; the dimensions of a selection or crop marquee; or the width (W), height (H), angle (A), and horizontal skew (H) or vertical skew (V) of a layer or selection as you transform it. The panel also displays readouts for up to four color samplers that are placed in a document.

Press one of the mini arrowheads on the panel to choose a color model for that readout (this model can differ from the current document color mode). Or to choose color models via the Info Panel Options dialog (shown below), choose Panel Options from the panel menu, then change the Mode for the First Color Readout and Second Color Readout. In the same dialog, you can also change the Ruler Units for the panel (under Mouse Coordinates), check which Status Information you want displayed in the lower part of the panel, and check Show Tool Hints to display context-sensitive information about the current tool or edit.

➤ To choose a unit of measurement for the Info panel (and for the rulers in the document window), click the arrowhead on the panel for the X/Y readout.

*Color breakdown for the pixel currently under the pointer*

*Menu for choosing a color model for that readout*

INFO

| | | | | |
|---|---|---|---|---|
| R: | 197/ 197 | C: | 24/ | 24% |
| G: | 210/ 210 | M: | 8/ | 8% |
| B: | 203/ 203 | Y: | 19/ | 19% |
| | | K: | 0/ | 0% |
| 8-bit | | 8-bit | | |

| | | | |
|---|---|---|---|
| X: | 2.860 | W: | 1.600 |
| Y: | 3.040 | H: | 2.920 |

*Location of the pointer in the document*

*Width and height of the current selection*

Doc: 13.9M/30.3M
Adobe RGB (1998) (8bpc)
6 inches x 9 inches (300 ppi)
1 pixels = 1.0000 pixels
Scratch: 464.6M/1.67G
Efficiency: 100%*
0.7s (28%)
Rectangular Marquee

*Document (status) data*

Draw rectangular selection or move selection outline. Use Shift, Opt, and Cmd for additional options.

*A tool hint*

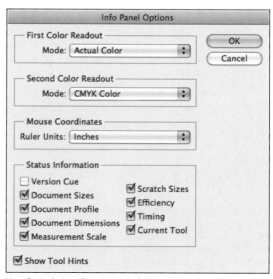

Info Panel Options

First Color Readout
Mode: Actual Color

Second Color Readout
Mode: CMYK Color

Mouse Coordinates
Ruler Units: Inches

Status Information
☐ Version Cue
☑ Document Sizes        ☑ Scratch Sizes
☑ Document Profile       ☑ Efficiency
☑ Document Dimensions    ☑ Timing
☑ Measurement Scale      ☑ Current Tool

☑ Show Tool Hints

OK
Cancel

*Use the Info Panel Options dialog to choose display preferences for the panel.*

## Kuler panel

Kuler (pronounced "cooler") is a free, Web-hosted Adobe application that lets users create and upload color groups, called color themes. By using the Kuler panel in Photoshop, you can access and browse through those themes. To open the Kuler panel, choose Window > Extensions > Kuler. (Also go to Edit/Photoshop > Preferences > Plug-Ins, and check Allow Extensions to Connect to the Internet.)

To use the Kuler panel efficiently, take advantage of its search field and menus. Enter a theme or creator name, or search by choosing ratings criteria from the menus. To add a selected theme to your Swatches panel, from the menu on the right side of that theme, choose Add to Swatches Panel. To save the current search parameters (e.g., for a search that you use frequently), choose Custom from the first menu, enter a search term or terms, then click Save. To learn more about Kuler, go to http://kuler.adobe.com.

## Layer Comps panel

When you create a layer comp (short for "composition"), it includes, collectively, any of the following document characteristics: the current layer Visibility (which layers are showing or hidden), Position (the location of imagery on each layer), and Appearance (layer styles, including layer blending modes, opacity settings, and layer effects). Via the Layer Comp Options dialog, you can decide which document attributes will be included in the comp, as well as add comments for the viewer.

Layer comps are useful if you're weighing the pros and cons of multiple versions of a document or need to present them to a client. For example, say you've created a few versions of a book cover. You could create a layer comp from each version, with or without lettering, or with lettering or a background image in two different colors, etc. When presenting the design to your client, instead of opening and closing separate files, you would simply display each version sequentially within the same file by clicking the Apply Layer Comp icon on and off for each comp on the panel.

Layer comps are automatically saved with the document in which they're created. (Whereas states on the History panel affect all editing done to an image but can't be saved, layer comps save with the document but let you display only layer options and settings.) See pages 382–384.

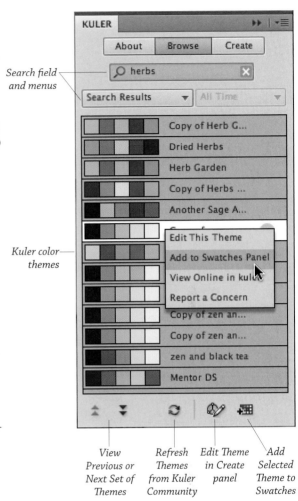

Search field and menus

Kuler color themes

View Previous or Next Set of Themes | Refresh Themes from Kuler Community | Edit Theme in Create panel | Add Selected Theme to Swatches

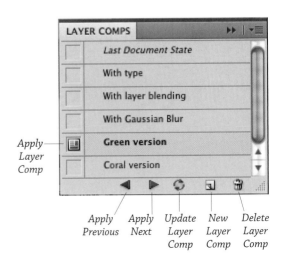

Apply Layer Comp

Apply Previous | Apply Next | Update Layer Comp | New Layer Comp | Delete Layer Comp

## Layers panel

Every new image starts out with either a solid-color Background or a transparent layer, depending on what Background Contents you choose in the New dialog or whether you opened a digital photo. On top of that, you can add layers of many types; some Photoshop features create layers automatically. Using the Layers panel, you can create, hide, show, duplicate, group, link, lock, unlock, merge, flatten, delete, and restack layers. You can also change the blending mode, opacity, or fill opacity for any layer; attach masks to them; and apply layer effects. The panel looks complex (Egads!), but you'll soon be accustomed to using it in all your work sessions. The following are the kinds of layers you'll encounter in this book:

➤ **Image** layers.

➤ **Editable type** layers, which are created by the Horizontal Type or Vertical Type tool.

➤ **Adjustment** layers, which apply editable adjustments to underlying layers, and **fill** layers, which apply editable tints to underlying layers.

➤ **Smart Object** layers, which are created manually when you convert one or more layers in a Photoshop image into a Smart Object, or automatically when you place an Illustrator or PDF file, another Photoshop file, or a Camera Raw file into a Photoshop document. Double-click a Smart Object layer and the object reopens in its original application for editing; save and close it, and the object updates in Photoshop. (See pages 308-311.)

To learn more about layers, see Chapter 8.

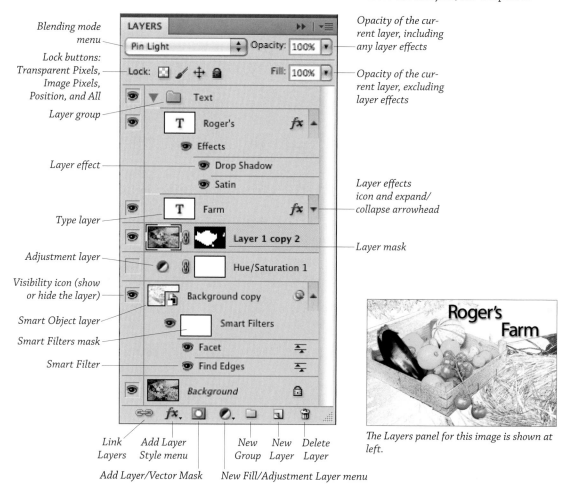

Blending mode menu

Lock buttons: Transparent Pixels, Image Pixels, Position, and All

Layer group

Layer effect

Type layer

Adjustment layer

Visibility icon (show or hide the layer)

Smart Object layer

Smart Filters mask

Smart Filter

Opacity of the current layer, including any layer effects

Opacity of the current layer, excluding layer effects

Layer effects icon and expand/collapse arrowhead

Layer mask

Link Layers

Add Layer Style menu

Add Layer/Vector Mask

New Group

New Layer

Delete Layer

New Fill/Adjustment Layer menu

The Layers panel for this image is shown at left.

## Masks panel

The Masks panel lets you add a pixel or vector mask to a layer, disable or enable an existing mask, or load a mask as a selection. When you're done using the mask, you can either apply its effect to your document or delete it. See pages 170–171 and 173.

Other controls on the panel include a Density slider for adjusting the opacity of a mask and a Feather slider for softening the edges between the white and black areas in a mask. These settings can be readjusted at any time without permanently altering the original mask.

The Mask Edge button opens the Refine Mask dialog (shown below), which offers the same controls for a mask as the Refine Edge dialog does for a selection (see page 239). The Color Range button gives you quick access to the Color Range dialog, for selecting areas to be masked, and the Invert button swaps the black and white areas in the mask.

*Add (or select) the Pixel Mask*    *Add a Vector Mask*

*Load Selection from Mask*    *Disable/ Enable Mask*    *Delete Mask*

*Apply Mask*

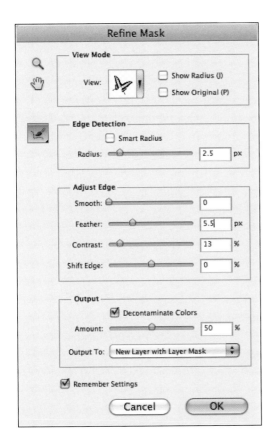

## Mini Bridge panel 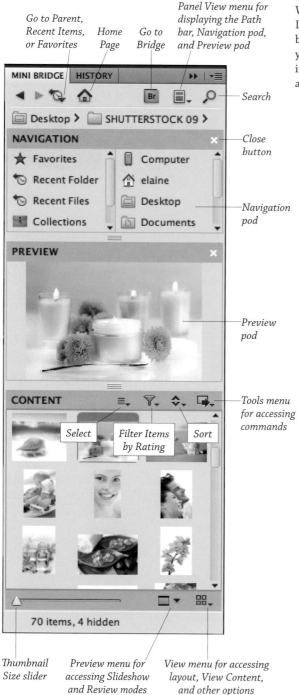 ★

To open the Mini Bridge panel, a miniature, convenient, panel-sized version of "big" Bridge, choose Window > Extensions > Mini Bridge or click the Launch Mini Bridge button Mb on the Application bar. Via Mini Bridge, you can do many of the things you can do in Bridge, such as locate and preview image thumbnails, open images, and apply ratings and labels. See pages 46–47.

Go to Parent, Recent Items, or Favorites

Home Page

Go to Bridge

Panel View menu for displaying the Path bar, Navigation pod, and Preview pod

Search

Close button

Navigation pod

Preview pod

Tools menu for accessing commands

Select

Filter Items by Rating

Sort

Thumbnail Size slider

Preview menu for accessing Slideshow and Review modes

View menu for accessing layout, View Content, and other options

## Navigator panel

You can use the Navigator panel to move a magnified image in the document window or to change the document zoom level (see page 92) — or if you prefer, you can accomplish the same tasks by using tools or keyboard shortcuts, as described in Chapter 5.

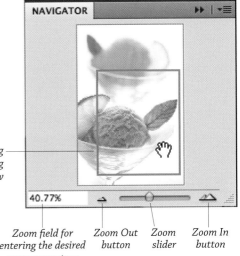

*View box for magnifying the image and for moving it in the document window*

*Zoom field for entering the desired zoom percentage*

*Zoom Out button*

*Zoom slider*

*Zoom In button*

## Paragraph panel

After creating paragraph type, you can use the Paragraph panel to apply or change such attributes as horizontal alignment, indentation, spacing before, spacing after, and auto hyphenation. From the panel menu, you can access additional type formatting commands (hanging punctuation and line-composer options) and the Justification and Hyphenation dialogs. See page 345.

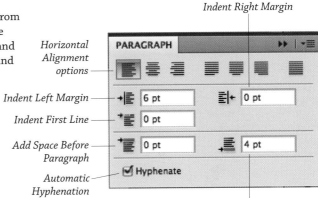

*Indent Right Margin*

*Horizontal Alignment options*

*Indent Left Margin*

*Indent First Line*

*Add Space Before Paragraph*

*Automatic Hyphenation*

*Add Space After Paragraph*

## Styles panel

Each style is a unique collection of layer settings that is saved to, stored in, and applied via the Styles panel. A style can include the settings for one or more layer effects (such as a Drop Shadow, an Outer Glow, or a Color Overlay) and/or blending options (such as the layer visibility, opacity, and blending mode settings). Like swatches on the Swatches panel, the styles on this panel are available for use in any document. Commands on the Styles panel menu let you save, load, and append style libraries, which are collections of styles. See pages 365–366.

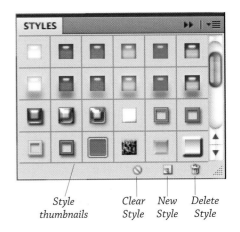

*Style thumbnails*

*Clear Style*

*New Style*

*Delete Style*

## Swatches panel

The Swatches panel stores predefined and user-created solid-color swatches, which are applied by various tools, filters, and commands. A wide assortment of predefined swatch libraries can be saved, loaded, and appended via commands on the panel menu. Color themes from the Kuler panel can also be added to this panel. See pages 189–190.

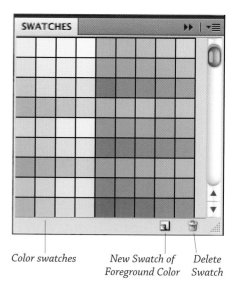

Color swatches     New Swatch of    Delete
Foreground Color    Swatch

## Tool Presets panel

A tool preset is a saved collection of settings for a particular tool. By using the Tool Presets panel, you can store settings for your favorite tools. This is a great way to customize and personalize the Photoshop interface, and the possibilities are infinite. The presets on this panel are available for all Photoshop documents.

Say, for example, you frequently resize and crop images to a particular set of dimensions with the Crop tool. By saving a preset for the tool with those width and height parameters, the next time you use the tool, instead of having to choose the same settings, all you would have to do is click that preset on either the Tool Presets panel or the Tool Preset picker, then click or drag in the document. (To open the picker, click the Tool Preset picker thumbnail on the left end of the Options bar.)

By using the Tool Presets panel or the Tool Preset picker, you can create, save, load, sort, rename, reset, and delete the presets for any Photoshop tool. To have the panel or picker list the presets for just the current tool (for a streamlined approach), check Current Tool Only, or uncheck that option to display the presets for all tools. See page 402.

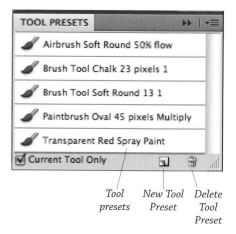

Tool    New Tool   Delete
presets    Preset     Tool
                       Preset

Before applying adjustment or image-editing commands, you need to make sure your document has the proper size and orientation and is cropped to your liking. In this chapter, you will learn how to change a document's resolution, dimensions, and canvas size, and how to crop, flip, rotate, and straighten it.

## Changing the document resolution and dimensions

In this section, you'll encounter three related terms:

➤ A file's pixel count (or pixel dimensions) is arrived at by multiplying its pixel height and width (as in 3000 x 2000 pixels).

➤ The resolution (or "res," for short), is the fineness of detail in a document, and is measured in pixels per inch (as in 250 or 300 ppi).

➤ The process of changing a file's pixel count (adding or deleting pixels) is known as resampling.

Some input devices (e.g., digital cameras that capture 8 megapixels of data or more and high-end scanners) produce files with a higher pixel count than is needed for most standard printing devices. In Photoshop, you can take advantage of a file's high pixel count to increase its print size or print resolution. You can keep the pixel count constant as you increase the print size (and thereby lower the resolution) or increase the resolution (and thereby lower the print size). No resampling occurs in either case, so the image quality isn't diminished.

You will need to resample a file if it contains too few or too many pixels to meet the resolution requirement of your target output device. If you resample a file as you increase its resolution, pixels will be added to it and its storage size will increase accordingly. Resample a file as you decrease its resolution (downsample it), and pixels will be deleted. The only way to get those pixels back is by clicking a prior state on the History panel before closing the file. Even more important, resampling reduces the image clarity. This can be a problem for print output, depending on the output resolution and how drastically the file is resampled, although it can be remedied somewhat by applying a sharpening filter afterward (see pages 296–300). Resampling isn't a problem for Web output.

We'll show you how to resize three common types of files for print output — low res/large dimensions, high res/small dimensions, and medium res/small dimensions — and how to resize a file for Web output.

PIXEL BASICS

7

**PIXELS**

Pixels, short for "picture elements," are the building blocks that make up a digital image — the tiny individual dots that a digital camera uses to capture a scene or that a computer uses to display images onscreen. When working in Photoshop and for Web output, you'll need to be aware of the pixel dimensions, or pixel count, of an image. For print output, you'll need to be aware of the resolution of your image — the number of pixels per unit of measure, which is normally per inch, or "ppi."

By default, photographs from a digital SLR camera have a low resolution (72 to 180 ppi) and very large width and height dimensions. They contain a sufficient number of pixels for high-quality output (prints as large as 8" x 12"), provided you increase their resolution to the proper value. You can do this via the Image Size command in Photoshop.

**To change the resolution of a digital photo for print output (low res/large dimensions):**

1. With the file open in Photoshop, choose Image > **Image Size** (Ctrl-Alt-I/Cmd-Option-I).

2. The Image Size dialog opens.**A** Because you need to increase the image resolution, uncheck **Resample Image**. When you lower the Width and Height in step 4, the resolution will increase automatically.

3. In the **Document Size** area, choose a unit of measure from the menu next to the Width field (we chose inches); the same unit will be chosen automatically for the Height.

4. Enter the **Width** or **Height** for the desired print size; the Resolution value increases.

5. If the resolution is now between 240 and 300 pixels per inch, you've achieved your goal — just click OK.**B** The pixel dimensions didn't change, so you won't need to resharpen the image (**A–B**, next page).

   If the resolution is greater than 300 ppi, check **Resample Image**, then enter a **Resolution** of 300. Also, from the menu at the bottom of the dialog, choose a resampling method for the way in which Photoshop reassigns color values based on the values of existing pixels. The **Bicubic** (Best for Smooth Gradients), **Bicubic Smoother** (Best for Enlargement), and **Bicubic Sharper** (Best for Reduction) options cause the least reduction in image quality. As a result of resampling, the pixel dimensions of the image will have changed.

6. Click OK. If the image was resampled, you should now resharpen it (see pages 296–300).

▶ To restore the settings that were in place when you opened the Image Size dialog, Alt-click/Option-click Reset (the Cancel button becomes a Reset button).

▶ To specify a default Image Interpolation method for Photoshop features, such as the Image Size dialog, see page 386.

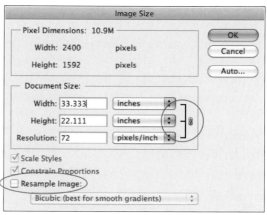

**A** In the Image Size dialog, uncheck Resample Image to make the Width, Height, and Resolution interdependent (as shown by the link icon).

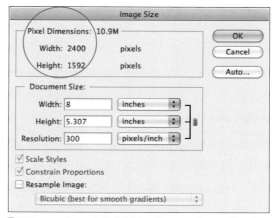

**B** When we changed the Width value to 8, the Height value changed automatically and the Resolution value increased to 300, but the Pixel Dimensions stayed the same.

**JPEGS FROM BRIDGE TO CAMERA RAW**

From Bridge, you can open JPEG files into Photoshop by way of the Camera Raw dialog. By default, Camera Raw assigns a resolution of 240 ppi to all files it opens into Photoshop. To achieve that 240 ppi resolution, Camera Raw preserves the pixel count but alters the Width and Height (Document Size). To increase the resolution of a JPEG file (say, to 300 ppi) or to reduce its Document Size dimensions, follow the steps on this page.

33.33%  |  25 inches x 35.556 inches (72 ppi)  ▶

33.33%  |  6 inches x 8.533 inches (300 ppi)  ▶

**A** *The original photo has dimensions of 25 x 35.556 inches (way too large for our printer) and a resolution of 72 ppi.*

**B** *When we reduced the photo size to 6 x 8.533 inches via the Image Size dialog, the resolution increased automatically to 300 ppi. Because the pixel count didn't change, the image size and quality were preserved.*

In many cases, scanned images have a high resolution and small dimensions and contain a sufficient number of pixels for large printouts.

### To resize a scanned image for print output (high res/small dimensions):

1. Choose Image > **Image Size** (Ctrl-Alt-I/Cmd-Option-I). The Image Size dialog opens.

2. Make sure **Resample Image** is unchecked.

3. Increase the **Width** or **Height** to the size needed for your printout. The Resolution will decrease.

   If the Resolution falls between 240 and 300 ppi, you're done; click OK. Because no resampling occurred, no resharpening is necessary.

   If the Resolution is still greater than 300 ppi, check **Resample Image,** **C** then lower the **Resolution** to 300. From the menu at the bottom of the dialog, choose **Bicubic Smoother** (Best for Enlargement) as the interpolation method. You've just resampled the image, so you should resharpen it after clicking OK (see pages 296–300).

4. Click OK.

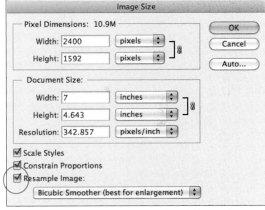

**C** *Our first attempt at resizing our photo left us with too high a resolution, so here we've checked Resample Image and will lower just the Resolution (not the Width and Height).*

---

**PERMITTING STYLES TO SCALE ... OR NOT**

When Resample Image and Constrain Proportions are checked in the Image Size dialog, you can check or uncheck Scale Styles to control whether any layer styles that were applied to the image will be scaled to fit the new size (to learn about styles, see Chapter 21).

---

Small files (with a resolution of, say, 180 to 200 ppi) lack a sufficient number of pixels to be enlarged without resampling, so they must be resampled to achieve the dimensions needed for print output. This is not an ideal scenario, as it reduces the image sharpness, and you'll certainly need to apply a sharpening filter afterward.

### To resize a scanned image for print output (medium res/small dimensions):

1. Choose Image > **Image Size** (Ctrl-Alt-I/Cmd-Option-I). The Image Size dialog opens.

2. Check both **Resample Image** and **Constrain Proportions**.

3. Enter the **Width** desired for your printout. The Height value will change proportionately and the file storage size and pixel dimensions will increase.

4. Click OK. Since the image was resampled, you should now use a sharpening filter to resharpen it (see pages 296–300).

Because Web images are viewed on computer displays, which are low-resolution devices, they should have a lower pixel count than images designed for print output. In most cases, you will need to downsample your files (discard image pixels) to make them the correct size for output.

### To change the pixel dimensions of an image for Web output:

1. Use File > Save As to make a copy of your file, then choose Image > **Image Size** (Ctrl-Alt-I/Cmd-Option-I). The Image Size dialog opens. 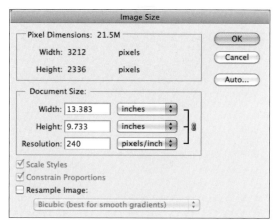A

2. Make sure **Resample Image** is checked.

3. To preserve the width-to-height ratio of the image, check **Constrain Proportions**.

4. From the menu at the bottom of the dialog, choose the **Bicubic Sharper** (Best for Reduction) resampling method, which will degrade the image the least.

5. Enter a **Resolution** of 72 ppi.

6. In the **Pixel Dimensions** area, choose pixels from the menu (the default unit), then enter the exact Width and/or Height dimensions needed.B

7. Click OK. On pages 421–426, you will learn how to optimize Photoshop files for output to the Web.

*A These are initial Image Size values of a typical digital photo. To prepare this photo for Web output, we will need to lower its pixel count.*

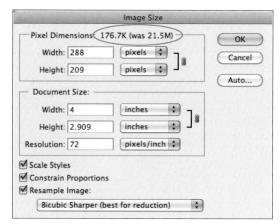

*B We checked Resample Image, changed the Resolution to 72, and set the Width (under Pixel Dimensions) to 288. The file size, which is listed at the top, is now smaller because we lowered the document's pixel count. The image now has an appropriate size for online viewing.*

---

**COPYCAT**

In some dialogs that have Width and Height fields, if you choose a unit of measure from the menu for the Width, the same unit is chosen automatically for the Height, and vice versa. If you want to prevent this from happening, hold down Shift while choosing a unit; the unit will change just for that dimension.

## PIXEL COUNTS, RESOLUTION, AND IMAGE SIZE COMPARED

The illustrations below explain the concept of resolution and how it affects image size. Figures **A–B** compare the same image at two different resolutions, and figures **C–D** compare the print sizes for those resolutions.

The moral here: Don't judge the output size of an image based on its onscreen size. Instead, consider these two factors: the current zoom level of the image in the document window and the image resolution.

**A** *This original image has a resolution of 300 ppi (the resolution value is listed on the Status bar when Document Dimensions is chosen for the bar).*

**B** *This is the same image with the same dimensions, except here the resolution is 150 ppi, which is half that of the image at left. When viewed at the same zoom level of 25%, the low-resolution image displays at only half its original size because it now contains fewer pixels (has a lower pixel count).*

**C** *For this 300 ppi image, we chose View > Print Size, which zoomed the image to an onscreen approximation of the printout size (that is, the Document Dimensions, as listed on the Status bar). Note the zoom level is 24%.*

**D** *We also chose View > Print Size for this low-res (150 ppi) version of the same image; note that the zoom level here is 48%. Although this image and the image shown at left will print at the same size, the print quality of this one will be lower because it has a lower pixel count.*

## Changing the canvas size

By using the Canvas Size command, you can enlarge or shrink a document's live, editable area. Pixels can be added to or removed from one, two, three, or all four sides of the image. This is useful, say, if you want to make room for type, as in the example shown on this page, or to accommodate imagery from other documents (see Chapter 14).

### To change the canvas size:

1. Choose Image > **Canvas Size** (Ctrl-Alt-C/Cmd-Option-C). The Canvas Size dialog opens.

2. *Optional:* Choose a different unit of measure from the Width menu.

3. Do either of the following:

   Enter new **Width** and/or **Height** values. The dimensions are independent of one another; changing one won't affect the other. **A–B**

   Check **Relative**, then in the **Width** and **Height** fields, enter positive values to increase those dimensions or negative values to decrease them.

4. *Optional:* The gray square in the center of the Anchor arrows represents the existing image area. Click an arrow to reposition the image relative to the canvas. The arrows point to where the new canvas area will be added.

5. From the **Canvas Extension Color** menu, choose a color for the added pixels. Or to choose a custom color, choose Other or click the color square next to the menu, then click a color in the Color Picker (see page 186) or in the document window. If the image doesn't have a Background (take a peek at the Layers panel), this menu won't be available.

6. Click OK. **C** Any added canvas area will automatically be filled with the color you chose in the preceding step, unless the image contains layers but not a Background, in which case the added canvas area will be transparent.

➤ You can also enlarge the canvas area manually by dragging with the Crop tool (see page 129).

**A** *This is the original image.*

**B** *To add canvas area to the top of the image, in the Canvas Size dialog, we increased the Height value, then clicked the bottom Anchor arrow to move the gray square downward.*

**C** *After adding pixels to the top of the canvas, we created some editable type.*

# Cropping an image

You can crop an image by using the Crop tool, the Crop command, or the Trim command. We'll show you how to use the Crop tool first.

## To crop an image using a marquee:

1. Choose the **Crop** tool 🔲 (C or Shift-C).

2. Drag a marquee over the part of the image you want to keep. **A**

3. On the Options bar, do the following:

   If the document contains image layers, click **Cropped Area**: **Delete** to have Photoshop delete the cropped-out areas, or click **Hide** to save them with the file (they will extend beyond the visible canvas area but can be moved back into view with the Move tool). Areas outside the crop marquee on the Background will be deleted, not hidden.

   Check **Shield** to darken the area outside the crop marquee temporarily (to help you see what will remain after cropping). If desired, you can change the shield color or Opacity value.

4. Perform any of these optional steps:

   To **resize** the marquee, drag any handle (double-arrow pointer). You can Shift-drag a corner handle to preserve the proportions of the marquee and/or hold down Alt/Option to resize the marquee from its center.

   To **reposition** the marquee, drag inside it.

   To **rotate** the marquee, position the cursor just outside it (🔄 pointer), then drag in a circular direction (you can straighten a crooked photo this way). To change the axis point around which the marquee rotates, drag the reference point away from the center of the marquee before rotating it. The image orientation will change after the next step.

5. To accept the crop, either press Enter/Return or double-click inside the marquee. **B**

➤ To cancel a crop marquee, press Esc, or right-click in the document and choose Cancel.

➤ To correct perspective problems, we recommend using the Lens Correction filter (which is discussed on pages 292–293) instead of the Perspective option for the Crop tool.

➤ To specify a default Image Interpolation method for Photoshop features, such as the Crop tool, see page 386.

**A** *With the Crop tool, drag a marquee over the portion of the image you want to keep, then accept the crop.*

**B** *The image is cropped.*

---

**REMEMBER TO RESHARPEN YOUR DOCUMENT AFTER CROPPING IT**

Cropping can make an image slightly blurry, so be sure to apply a sharpening filter afterward. See pages 296–300.

Next, we'll show you how to either crop an image to a specific size (such as a standard photo print) or crop it based on the dimensions of another image.

## To crop an image to a specific size or to the dimensions of another image:

1. Open an image, and choose the **Crop** tool 🔲 (C or Shift-C).

2. Do either of the following:

   On the Options bar, enter specific **Width** and **Height** values for the final image. You can click the Swap Width and Height button ⇄ to switch the current values.

   To crop using the Width, Height, and Resolution values from another image, open that document and click its tab. Click **Front Image** on the Options bar, then click the tab for the document to be cropped.

3. Drag a crop marquee on the image (without holding down any modifier keys).**A** You can drag inside the marquee to reposition it.

4. To accept the crop, either press Enter/Return or double-click inside the marquee.**B**

➤ To empty the Width, Height, and Resolution fields on the Options bar for the Crop tool, click Clear.

➤ To create presets for the Crop tool, see our instructions for creating tool presets on page 402.

### CROPPING BASED ON THE RULE OF THIRDS ★

The rule of thirds is a guideline that photographers sometimes follow for composing a composition, either when shooting a scene or when cropping it afterward. In Photoshop, draw a marquee with the Crop tool, then choose Crop Guide Overlay: Rule of Thirds from the Options bar. Grid lines will appear within the crop marquee. Drag the marquee or resize it, positioning the key features of the scene where the lines intersect. You can position those features at a pair of diagonal locations (see the colored circles we placed on the image below), or in a landscape, you could position the horizon along either one of the horizontal lines. Note: Although the rule of thirds often works like a charm, you don't have to adhere to it slavishly.

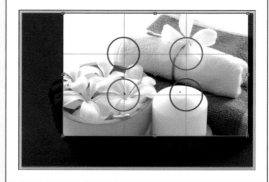

**A** *After choosing the Crop tool, we entered a Width of 6" and a Height of 4" on the Options bar, then dragged in the document to create a marquee.*

**B** *This image was cropped to a standard photo size of 6 x 4 inches, which you can verify by looking at the rulers.*

When you draw a crop marquee that is larger than the image, the canvas size is increased. Unlike the Canvas Size command, this technique gives you manual control over how much canvas area is added and where. Another use for this technique is to reveal imagery that extends beyond the live canvas area.

### To enlarge the canvas area with the Crop tool:

1. Choose a Background color (see Chapter 11).

2. To reveal more of the work canvas (gray area) around the image, either enlarge the document window or Application frame by dragging a side or corner, or lower the zoom level of your document.

3. Choose the **Crop** tool 🔲 (C or Shift-C).

4. Drag a crop marquee to the edges of the image.

5. Drag a corner or midpoint handle of the marquee into the work canvas (outside the live canvas area).**A**

6. To accept the crop, either press Enter/Return or double-click inside the marquee.**B**

   If the image has a Background (look on the Layers panel), the added canvas area will fill with the current Background color. If the image contains layers but no Background, the added canvas area will fill with transparent pixels.

   Note: Pixels on any layer that were formerly hidden outside the live canvas area may now fall within it, and will now be visible.

**A** *Drag any of the crop marquee handles outside the canvas area and into the work canvas. Here, we're dragging a midpoint handle to the right to add more canvas area to that side of the image.*

---

**OVERRIDING THE SNAP**

Normally, if you resize a crop marquee near the edge of the canvas area and View > Snap To > Document Bounds is on, the marquee snaps to the edge of the canvas area. If you want to crop slightly inside or outside the edge of the canvas, you'll need to override the snap function. Do either of the following: Turn the Snap To > Document Bounds feature off; or start dragging one of the handles of the marquee, then hold down Ctrl/Control and continue to drag.

---

**B** *When we accepted the crop, the added canvas pixels filled automatically with brown, which was the current Background color.*

Although the Crop command, discussed below, is simple and straightforward, it doesn't offer as many options as the Crop tool does.

**To crop an image using the Crop command:**

1. Choose the **Rectangular Marquee** tool ▢ (M or Shift-M).

2. Do one of the following:

   Drag a marquee over the part of the image you want to keep.**A**

   To constrain the proportions of the marquee to a width-to-height ratio, on the Options bar, choose **Style: Fixed Ratio**, enter **Width** to **Height** values (such as 1 to 2), then drag in the image.

   To draw a marquee of a specific size (such as a standard-size photo print), choose **Style: Fixed Size**, enter **Width** and **Height** values, then click in the document. You can move the marquee.

3. *Optional:* To scale the marquee, right-click in the document and choose Transform Selection, Shift-drag a corner handle, then double-click inside the marquee to accept the edit.

4. Choose Image > **Crop**, then deselect (Ctrl-D/Cmd-D).**B**

➤ If you chose the Fixed Ratio or Fixed Size style for the Rectangular Marquee tool, reset the tool by choosing Style: Normal from the Options bar.

The Trim command trims away any excess transparent or solid-color areas from the border of an image. Of course, the end result is still a rectangular image.

**To trim areas from around an image:**

1. Choose Image > **Trim**.

2. In the Trim dialog, click a **Based On** option:

   **Transparent Pixels** trims transparent pixels from the edges of the Background. If Photoshop doesn't detect any such areas in the image, this option isn't available.

   **Top Left Pixel Color** removes any border areas that match the color of the left uppermost pixel in the image.

   **Bottom Right Pixel Color** removes any border areas that match the color of the bottommost right pixel in the image.

3. Check which areas of the image you want the command to **Trim Away**: **Top**, **Bottom**, **Left**, and/or **Right**.

4. Click OK.

**A** *With the Rectangular Marquee tool, a marquee is drawn over the area of the image we want to keep.*

**B** *This is the result after we chose Image > Crop.*

Follow these instructions if you need to preserve the existing width-to-height ratio of an image as you crop it.

### To crop an image according to its existing aspect ratio:

1. With an image open, choose the **Crop** tool ![crop tool icon] (C or Shift-C).

2. Drag a marquee diagonally across the entire image, from one corner to the opposite corner.

3. Shift-drag a corner handle on the crop marquee to resize the marquee proportionately to the desired crop size.

4. *Optional:* Drag within the marquee to reposition it over the portion of the image you want to keep.**A**

5. To accept the crop, either press Enter/Return or double-click inside the marquee.**B**

## Flipping or rotating an image

You can flip all the layers in an image to create a mirror image, or flip just one layer at a time. (You'll learn all about layers in the next chapter.)

### To flip an image or a layer:

Do either of the following:

To flip all the layers, choose Image > Image Rotation > **Flip Canvas Horizontal** or **Flip Canvas Vertical**.**C**

To flip just one layer at a time, click that layer, then choose Edit > Transform > **Flip Horizontal** or **Flip Vertical**. Any layers that are linked to the selected layer or layers will also flip.

➤ If you've flipped a whole image that contains type, don't flip out! To make the type readable again, "unflip" the type layer by using the Flip Horizontal command.

**A** *After dragging a marquee across the entire image with the Crop tool, we Shift-dragged a handle, then moved the marquee over the area we want to keep.*

**B** *We accepted the crop. The original width-to-height ratio of the image was preserved.*

**C** *Here, we chose the Flip Canvas Horizontal command (compare this image with the original one in Figure **B**).*

The Image Rotation commands rotate all the layers in an image. (To rotate just one layer at a time, use a rotate command on the Edit > Transform submenu.)

## To rotate an image:

Do either of the following:

Choose Image > Image Rotation > **180°**, **90° CW** (clockwise), or **90° CCW** (counterclockwise).

Choose Image > Image Rotation > **Arbitrary**. Enter an **Angle** value, click **°CW** (clockwise) or **°CCW** (counterclockwise), then click OK.

# Straightening a crooked image

When used with its Straighten option, the Ruler tool squares off a crooked image based on a line you drag and also crops the image to remove any blank canvas areas that result around its borders.

## To straighten a crooked image: ★

1. Choose the **Ruler** tool ▭ (I or Shift-I).

2. Drag along a feature in the image that you want to orient horizontally or vertically.**A** If you need to adjust the line, move either endpoint. The current angle is listed as the **A** value on the Options bar.

3. On the Options bar, click **Straighten**.**B** Easy!

➤ To straighten an image without cropping it, hold down Alt/Option as you click Straighten and until the command is done processing.

**A** *This image is slightly askew. We dragged with the Ruler tool from top to bottom along one of the columns, then clicked Straighten on the Options bar.*

---

**IT CROPS! IT STRAIGHTENS!**

File > Automate > Crop and Straighten Photos locates rectangular areas in a document, rotates and crops those areas to square them off (if necessary), then opens each one as a new document. Note: This action isn't as smart as you are, so it can be fooled; see the suggestions and precautions below.

➤ Use the action to unrotate a Photoshop document that was previously rotated. Apply it to imagery that doesn't contain much white in the background, and click the Background on the Layers panel first.

➤ Scan multiple photos at a time and let the action sort them into individual documents. To help it do a proper job, don't let the photos overlap one another or hang off the side of the scanner.

➤ To control which area is cropped and straightened, select that area, including some extra pixels, then choose the command while holding down Alt/Option.

---

**B** *The command reoriented the image along the angle we defined and cropped away the blank canvas areas.*

The beauty of assigning various parts of a document to different layers is that they can be edited individually— maybe some text on one layer, a silhouetted shape on another layer, and a full image in the background. An image can contain only one Background (written with an initial cap "B"), but you can add multiple layers above it. Unlike the Background, which always remains fully opaque, a layer can contain partially or fully transparent areas. Onscreen, transparent areas of a layer are represented by a checkerboard pattern. **A**

You'll probably use the Layers panel  more than any other panel in Photoshop. It is so indispensable for image editing, it's either the star player or plays an important supporting role in many other chapters. In this chapter you'll learn basic techniques, such as how to create, duplicate, select, restack, group, delete, hide, show, move, merge, and flatten image layers. (Related topics, such as using layer masks, choosing layer blending options, and creating adjustment, editable type, and Smart Object layers, are covered in later chapters.)

## Creating layers

When creating a new document, if you choose Background Contents: White or Background Color in the File > New dialog, the bottommost tier of the image will be a Background; if you choose Background Contents: Transparent, the first tier will be a layer, and the document won't contain a Background.

*Continued on the following page*

**A** *This document contains a type layer and two image layers, which are listed above the Background. The Background, when present in a document, is always listed at the bottom.*

## LAYER BASICS

8

**GET A SNEAK PREVIEW**

To view a file that contains layers, open image No. 11 of the downloadable images. On the Layers panel, click any layer name, then click its visibility icon  on and off.

A new layer is created automatically when you perform some kinds of edits, such as when you paste a selection or create type with the Horizontal or Vertical Type tool. In these instructions, you will learn how to create new, blank image layers. To those layers, you can apply brush strokes, clone imagery, etc. You may add as many layers to a file as you like, depending on your computer's available memory and its storage capability.

## To create a layer:

1. Show the Layers panel.
2. Click a layer or the Background. The new layer is going to appear above the one you have clicked.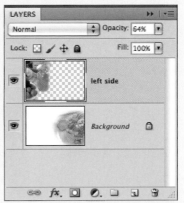
3. Click the **New Layer** button at the bottom of the panel. The new layer will have Opacity and Fill percentages of 100% and a blending mode of Normal.**B**
4. *Optional:* To rename the layer, double-click the existing name, type the desired one, then press Enter/Return.

➤ To choose options for a layer as you create it, Alt-click/Option-click the New Layer button on the Layers panel or press Ctrl-Shift-N/Cmd-Shift-N. In the New Layer dialog, you can change the layer Name or choose a nonprinting Color for the area on the Layers panel behind the visibility icon (see "To color-code a layer" on page 143). To learn about the layer blending mode and opacity controls, see page 142.

**A** *Click the layer above which you want the new one to appear.*

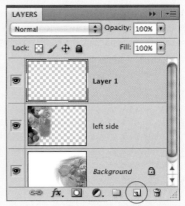

**B** *The New Layer button is clicked, and a new layer appears on the panel.*

---

### FLATTENING AND PRESERVING LAYERS

➤ Layers increase the file size considerably, so when you're completely done editing your document, consider using a merge or flatten command to shrink it back down (see pages 144–146).

➤ If you need to preserve layers, when saving your file via the File > Save As dialog, check Layers, and as the file Format, choose Photoshop, Photoshop PDF, Large Document Format (see the sidebar on page 22), or TIFF. The formats that don't preserve layers flatten them automatically and convert any transparency in the bottommost layer to opaque white.

➤ When switching document color modes (e.g., from RGB to CMYK), if you want to preserve layers, click Don't Flatten or Don't Merge in the alert dialog.

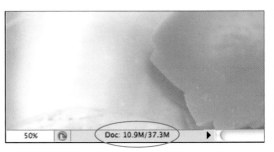

*After adding layers to your file, from the Status bar menu, choose Document Sizes. The value on the left is the file size without layers; the value on the right is its approximate file size with layers. This document contains three image layers in addition to the Background, which explains why the second value is more than three times greater than the first.*

Another method for creating a layer is to copy or cut imagery from an existing layer or the Background and put it on its own layer. This can be done easily with a simple command.

## To turn selected pixels into a layer:

1. On the Layers panel, click an image layer or the Background, then create a selection in the document.**A**

2. To create a new layer containing the selected pixels, do either of the following:

   To place a copy of the selected pixels on a new layer and leave the original layer intact, right-click in the document and choose **Layer via Copy** or press Ctrl-J/Cmd-J.**B**

   To place the selected pixels on a new layer and remove them from the original layer, right-click in the document and choose **Layer via Cut** or press Ctrl-Shift-J/Cmd-Shift-J. If you cut pixels from a layer, the exposed area on the original layer will be filled with transparency; if you cut pixels from the Background, the exposed area will be filled with the current Background color (see pages 185 and 233).

## Duplicating layers

Follow these instructions to duplicate a layer or layer group, or to turn a copy of the Background into a layer. (To learn about layer groups, see pages 138–140.)

## To duplicate a layer or layer group:

Do one of the following:

Click a layer, then press Ctrl-J/Cmd-J.

Drag a layer, layer group, or the Background over the **New Layer** button 🔲 at the bottom of the Layers panel. The duplicate will appear above the one you dragged.

To name the layer as you create it, right-click a layer, layer group, or the Background and choose **Duplicate Layer** or **Duplicate Group**. In the dialog, change the name in the "As" field (ignore the Destination fields), then click OK.

➤ To control whether the word "copy" is added to a duplicate layer name automatically, choose Panel Options from the Layers panel menu, then check or uncheck the Add "Copy" to Copied Layers and Groups command. ★

➤ When you duplicate a layer, any layer mask and/or effects on that layer are also duplicated. Similarly, when you duplicate a Smart Object layer, any Smart Filters contained on that layer are also duplicated (see pages 320–322).

**A** *An area of the Background is selected on the right side of this document.*

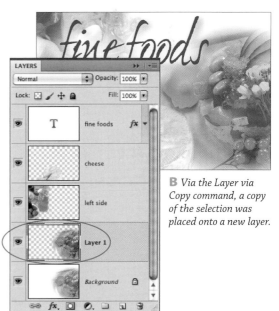

**B** *Via the Layer via Copy command, a copy of the selection was placed onto a new layer.*

## Converting the Background

There are many things you can do to a layer that you can't do to the Background. For example, you can't move the Background upward in the layer stack; change its blending mode, Opacity percentage, or Fill percentage; attach a mask to it; or embellish it with layer effects. You can, however, convert the Background into a layer, at which time it will adopt all the functions of a normal layer.

### To convert the Background into a layer:

Do either of the following:

Alt-double-click/Option-double-click the Background on the Layers panel to turn it into a layer without choosing options.

Double-click the Background on the Layers panel A to open the New Layer dialog. B Type a new Name. If desired, choose a Color for the area behind the visibility icon 👁 on the panel, a Mode, and an Opacity percentage. Click OK. C

If you need to create a Background for a file that doesn't have one, you can convert any existing layer into the Background — the reverse of the preceding instructions.

### To convert a layer into the Background:

1. Click a layer.

2. Choose Layer > New > **Background from Layer**. The new Background will appear at the bottom of the stack on the Layers panel (its usual position).

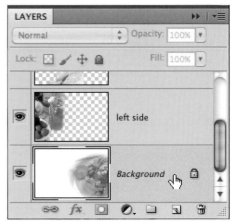

A *Double-click the Background.*

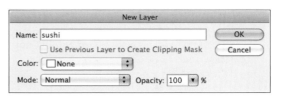

B *Enter a Name and choose options for the layer-to-be.*

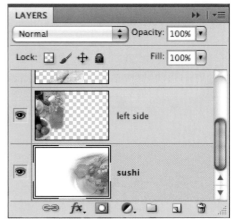

C *The former Background is now a normal, full-fledged layer.*

# Selecting layers

Always remember to select the layer or layers you want to work on before editing your document! This signals to Photoshop which part of your document you want to change. When a layer or layer group is selected, it becomes highlighted **A** and the layer or group name is listed in the title bar of the document window. (To learn about layer groups, see pages 138–140.)

## To select layers via the Layers panel:

Do one of the following:

To select a layer or layer group, click either the layer thumbnail or the area to the right of the layer or group name.

To select multiple layers, click a layer, then Shift-click the last in a series of consecutively listed layers, or Ctrl-click/Cmd-click individual layers (not the layer thumbnails). If you need to deselect individual layers, Ctrl-click/Cmd-click them.

To select all the layers in your document (but not the Background), choose Select > All Layers or press Ctrl-Alt-A/Cmd-Option-A.

To select all layers of a similar kind, such as all image layers, shape layers, or adjustment layers, right-click one of those layers and choose Select Similar Layers from the context menu.

## To select a layer or layer group by clicking in the document:

1. Choose the **Move** tool ►⊕ (V).
2. Do either of the following:

   To select the first layer that contains nontransparent pixels below the pointer, right-click in the document window and choose a layer or layer group name from the context menu.**B** (Or Ctrl-right-click/Cmd-Control-click with any other tool selected.)

   Check **Auto-Select** on the Options bar, choose **Group** or **Layer**, then click a visible pixel area in the document. The Background can't be selected with this method.

➤ If the Move tool is selected and Show Transform Controls is checked on the Options bar, the bounding box for the currently selected layer displays onscreen. Uncheck this option if you find the box to be distracting. To transform a layer via its bounding box, see pages 312–313.

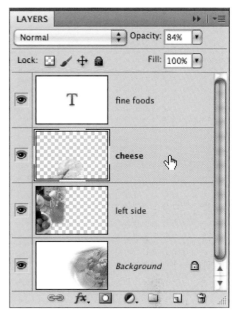

**A** *Simply click a layer to select it.*

**B** *On the context menu, choose the name of the layer you want to select.*

# Restacking layers

When you restack a layer upward or downward, the content of that layer shifts forward or backward in the document.

## To restack layers:

Drag a layer or group name upward or downward on the panel, and release the mouse when a double horizontal line appears in the desired location. **A–B**

➤ To move the Background upward on the list, you must convert it to a layer first (see page 136). Layers can't be stacked below the Background.

➤ You can also restack a selected layer via the commands (or via the shortcuts listed) on the Layer > Arrange submenu.

# Working with layer groups

The layers in a document can be gathered into groups and labeled by kind. In addition to helping to organize and streamline your Layers panel (so you won't need to scroll up and down as much), by putting layers into groups, you will be able to move, rotate, scale, duplicate, restack, lock, unlock, change the blending mode or opacity for, or hide or show multiple layers simultaneously. When you add a layer mask to a layer group, the mask applies to all the layers in the group (see page 168). Groups can be nested inside other groups.*

## To create a layer group:

### Method 1 (from existing layers)

1. Click a layer, then Shift-click or Ctrl-click/ Cmd-click one or more other layers (they can be nonconsecutive).

2. Do either of the following:

   Press Ctrl-G/Cmd-G. **C**

   From the Layers panel menu, choose **New Group from Layers**. In the dialog, change the Name, if desired, then click OK.

3. *Optional:* To add more layers to the group, drag them over the group listing, and release the mouse when the dark drop zone border appears. Or click the arrowhead to expand the group list, then drag layers into the group, releasing where you want them to be stacked.

➤ The default blending mode for a group is Pass Through, and we suggest you don't change it.

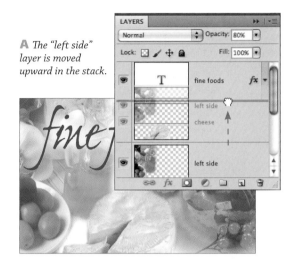

**A** *The "left side" layer is moved upward in the stack.*

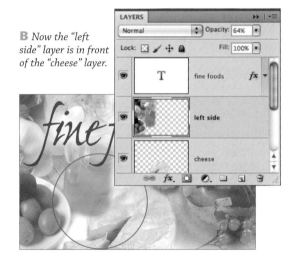

**B** *Now the "left side" layer is in front of the "cheese" layer.*

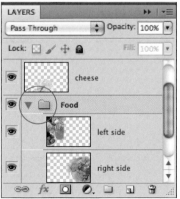

**C** *The "left side" and "right side" layers are now members of a group.*

*In Photoshop CS5, unlike in older versions of the program, you can nest layer groups more than five levels deep.*

**Method 2 (create a group, then add layers)**

1. Do either of the following:

   To create a group without choosing settings for it, click the layer above which you want the group to appear, then click the **New Group** button at the bottom of the panel.

   To choose settings for a group as you create it, Alt-click/Option-click the New Group button or choose **New Group** from the panel menu. In the dialog, change the Name, Color, or Opacity setting for the group, if desired, then click OK.

2. Do either of the following:

   Drag layers into the new group listing, releasing the mouse when the dark drop zone border appears around it.

   Click the arrowhead to expand the group list, then drag layers into the group, releasing the mouse where you want them to be stacked. **A**

➤ To expand or collapse a group and all the groups within it, Alt-click/Option-click the arrowhead.

➤ To rename a layer or layer group, double-click a layer or layer group name on the Layers panel. Type a new name, then press Enter/Return or click outside the name field.

**A** *A layer is moved into a group.*

**MOVING LAYERS OUT OF A GROUP**

➤ To move a layer out of a group, drag the layer outside the group stack.

➤ To move a layer from one group to another, drag it over the group name or icon, or over an existing layer in the group.

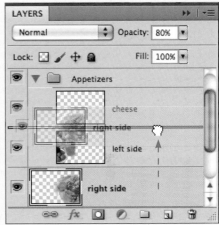

## USING CONTEXT MENUS WITH THE LAYERS PANEL

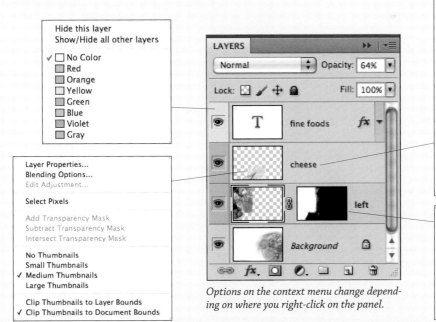

Hide this layer
Show/Hide all other layers

✓ ☐ No Color
  ☐ Red
  ☐ Orange
  ☐ Yellow
  ☐ Green
  ☐ Blue
  ☐ Violet
  ☐ Gray

Layer Properties...
Blending Options...
Edit Adjustment...

Select Pixels

Add Transparency Mask
Subtract Transparency Mask
Intersect Transparency Mask

No Thumbnails
Small Thumbnails
✓ Medium Thumbnails
Large Thumbnails

Clip Thumbnails to Layer Bounds
✓ Clip Thumbnails to Document Bounds

Layer Properties...
Blending Options...
Edit Adjustment...

Duplicate Layer...
Delete Layer

Convert to Smart Object

Rasterize Layer

Disable Layer Mask
Enable Vector Mask
Create Clipping Mask

Link Layers
Select Linked Layers

Select Similar Layers

Copy Layer Style
Paste Layer Style
Clear Layer Style

Merge Layers
Merge Visible
Flatten Image

Disable Layer Mask

Delete Layer Mask
Apply Layer Mask

Add Mask To Selection
Subtract Mask From Selection
Intersect Mask With Selection

Refine Mask...

Mask Options...

*Options on the context menu change depending on where you right-click on the panel.*

You can delete a layer group and its layers or merely disband the group while preserving the layers.

### To delete or disband a layer group:

On the Layers panel, do one of the following:

Click a group to be deleted, click the **Delete Layer** button, 🗑 then in the alert dialog, click **Group Only** or **Group and Contents**. Or to quickly delete a group and its contents, click the group, then press Backspace/Delete.

Right-click a group and choose **Delete Group** from the context menu, then click either **Group Only** or **Group and Contents**.

To disband a layer group without deleting the layers it contains, click the group, then press Ctrl-Shift-G/Cmd-Shift-G. The group icon disappears from the panel and the layer listings are no longer indented.

## Deleting individual layers

### To delete a layer:

1. Deselect (press Ctrl-D/Cmd-D).

2. Click the layer to be deleted, then press Backspace/Delete.

➤ Change your mind? Choose Edit > Undo or click the prior state on the History panel.

➤ Another way to delete a layer: Click the layer, click the Delete Layer button, 🗑 then click Yes in the alert dialog; or to bypass the alert, simply Alt-click/Option-click the Delete Layer button.

## Hiding and showing layers

By hiding the layers you're not currently working on, you eliminate them as a visual distraction. Hidden layers don't print. The instructions below apply to layers and the Background.

### To hide or show layers:

On the Layers panel, do one of the following:

To hide or show one layer or layer group, click in the visibility column. 👁 **A–B** The icon disappears.

To hide or show multiple layers, drag upward or downward in the visibility column.

To hide or show all layers and layer groups except one, Alt-click/Option-click the visibility column for the layer or layer group that you want to hide or show.

**A** *Click in the visibility column to show or hide a layer.*

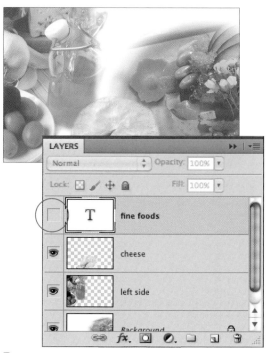

**B** *The type layer is now hidden.*

## Moving layer content

Follow these instructions to reposition a selected layer or group of layers with the Move tool. Note: To link layers first so they will move as a unit, see page 307.

### To move layers manually:

1. On the Layers panel, do one of the following:

   Click a layer.

   Shift-click or Ctrl-click/Cmd-click multiple layers.

   Click a layer group.

2. Choose the **Move** tool ▶⊕ or hold down V to spring-load the tool.

3. Drag in the document window.**A–B** If you move part of the layer or layers outside the canvas area, don't worry—those pixels will save with the document and can be moved back into view at any time. (See "Working with pixels outside the canvas area" on page 235.)

➤ To nudge a selected layer by one pixel at a time, choose the Move tool, then press an arrow key. Or press Shift-arrow to move a layer by 10 screen pixels at a time. (Don't press Alt-arrow/Option-arrow—unless your intention is to duplicate the layer.)

➤ For a more precise approach to repositioning layers, use the align buttons on the Options bar. See page 247.

**A** *The type layer is being moved with the Move tool.*

**B** *The type layer was moved downward.*

---

### USING SMART GUIDES TO ALIGN IMAGERY

You can use Smart Guides to align the edge of a layer you're moving with the edge or center of other layers. Turn on View > Show > Smart Guides, then with the Move tool, start moving a layer or layer group. Temporary magnetic guide lines will appear onscreen when the edge of the layer imagery you're moving encounters the edge or center of nontransparent pixels, type, or a shape on another layer. To learn more about Smart Guides, see page 252.

# Choosing Layers panel options

You can dramatically change the appearance of a layer and the layers below it by using the blending mode and/or opacity controls.**A** The layer opacity control makes the layer content (e.g., imagery, brush strokes, type, shape, Smart Object, adjustments, layer effects) more or less opaque, whereas the blending mode affects how the layer content blends with underlying layers.

Note: The following is a brief introduction to these two features. The blending modes are illustrated fully on pages 192–196, and instructions for using them are given on pages 302–303. The Opacity and Fill options are compared on page 301.

## To change the blending mode or opacity of a layer or layer group:

1. Select one or more layers or a layer group. Note: In order to see the results of the next step, the contents of the selected layer must overlap some contents of the underlying layer.

2. Choose a **blending mode** from the menu in the upper left corner of the Layers panel and/or change the **Opacity** percentage (use the scrubby slider).

The Lock Transparent Pixels button on the Layers panel prevents or allows the editing of transparent pixels by any command or tool. In the following instructions, you'll see how this option affects strokes that are applied with the Brush tool, but remember that this button also affects other edits. By default, transparent pixels on a layer are represented by a gray and white checkerboard pattern.

## To limit edits by locking transparent pixels:

1. Click an image layer (not an editable type layer).

2. Choose the **Brush** tool ✎ (B or Shift-B). To change the brush diameter, press [ or ].

3. Show the Swatches panel, ⊞ then click a color.

4. On the Layers panel, click the **Lock Transparent Pixels** button, ⊠ then draw brush strokes in the document.**B** Only nontransparent pixels can be recolored.

5. To deactivate the Lock Transparent Pixels button, click again or press /.

6. Paint on the layer again. Notice that now all the layer pixels are fair game for editing, whether they're transparent or not.**C**

**A** *We chose Color Burn mode for the type layer and lowered the Opacity of the "cheese" layer to 40% (compare this image with the one on the preceding page).*

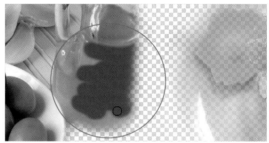

**B** *With the Lock Transparent Pixels option on, our brush strokes are affecting only nontransparent pixels.*

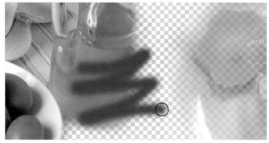

**C** *With the Lock Transparent Pixels option off, brush strokes can be applied anywhere on the layer.*

---

**CUSTOMIZING THE CHECKERBOARD**

In the Transparency Settings area of Edit/Photoshop > Preferences > Transparency & Gamut, you can change the size or color of the checkerboard pattern that represents transparent pixels (or you can hide it from view by choosing None from the Grid Size menu).

Use the lock options for layers to prevent inadvertent edits as you work on other layers.

## To lock a layer or layer group:

1. Click a layer or layer group.

2. Click any of the following:

   The **Lock Image Pixels** button 🖌 to prevent all layer pixels from being edited. You can still move the layer, as well as choose options for it, such as a blending mode, opacity level, layer effects, etc.

   The **Lock Position** button ✛ to lock only the location of the layer. The layer content (e.g., pixels, type characters, or styling) can be edited as usual.

   The **Lock All** button 🔒 to prevent the layer from being moved or edited (both of the above). Unlike the other lock options, this button is also available for layer groups.

   When a lock button is activated for a layer, a padlock icon displays next to the layer name.**A**

## To choose thumbnail options for the Layers panel:

Right-click a layer thumbnail and choose any of the following:

**Small Thumbnails**, **Medium Thumbnails**, or **Large Thumbnails**. Note: Turning off thumbnails by choosing No Thumbnails can help boost Photoshop's performance, but frankly, we find it pretty darn hard to work without them.

**Clip Thumbnails to Layer Bounds** to show, in the panel thumbnails, only the area that encompasses the opaque pixels on the layer (a useful option if your layers contain many silhouetted shapes or pixels outside the canvas area),**B** or **Clip Thumbnails to Document Bounds** to display the whole layer in the thumbnails, including any surrounding transparent pixels that lie within the canvas area.

You can assign a color to the area behind the visibility icon on each layer to help categorize them, make them easier to identify — and make the panel look pretty, too!

## To color-code a layer:

Click a layer, then right-click the visibility column 👁 and choose a color label.**C**

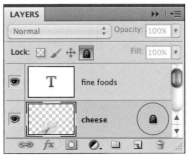

**A** When the Lock All button option is activated for a layer, the padlock icon is black.

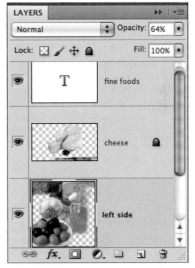

**B** For this Layers panel, we chose the Large Thumbnails and Clip Thumbnails to Layer Bounds options.

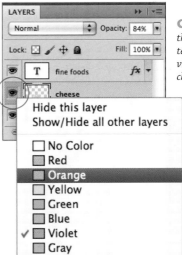

**C** Click a layer, then from the context menu for the visibility column, choose a color.

# Merging layers

The merge commands — Merge Down, Merge Layers, and Merge Visible — merge two or more selected layers into one layer (the bottommost of the selected layers). You can apply any of these commands periodically during the editing process to reduce the file size of your document or to reduce unnecessary clutter on the Layers panel.

Note: The Flatten Image command, which is discussed on page 146, is normally applied to a copy of a file as a step before final output.

## To merge selected layers:

1. Do one of the following:

   Click the upper layer of two layers to be merged. **A** The bottom one must be an image layer or the Background, and cannot be a group.

   Ctrl-click/Cmd-click nonconsecutive layers. The layers can be solo, within a group, or a combination thereof.

   Click a group. (All the layers in the group will be merged — but just with one another.)

   Note: You can merge an adjustment layer into an image layer, but you can't merge adjustment layers into one another. You can also merge an editable type layer downward, but be aware that it will become rasterized.

2. Do either of the following:

   Right-click the selected layer and choose **Merge Down**, or choose **Merge Layers** if multiple layers are selected, or choose **Merge Group** if you selected a group.

   Press Ctrl-E/Cmd-E. **B**

   If the underlying layer contains a layer mask, an alert dialog will appear. Click Preserve to keep the mask editable, or click Apply to apply the mask effect to the newly merged layer and delete the mask.

   If you merged the layers in a group, the group icon will disappear from the panel.

➤ If you want to merge layers while preserving access to a copy of the original, separate layers, see "To copy and merge layers" on the next page.

➤ The Merge Down command won't be accessible if the Lock All button is enabled for the currently selected layer.

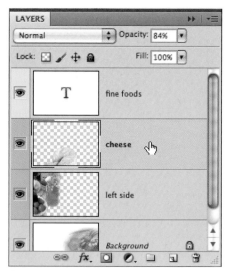

**A** We clicked the "cheese" layer.

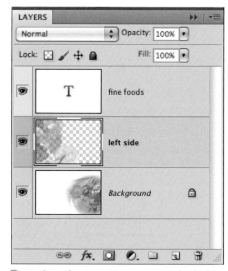

**B** We chose the Merge Down command, which merged the "cheese" layer into the "left side" layer.

---

**SMART OBJECT INSTEAD OF MERGE OR FLATTEN**

Instead of merging or flattening layers, consider grouping them into a Smart Object layer instead. You'll achieve the same reduction of layers, plus you'll gain the ability to edit the original layers individually by double-clicking the Smart Object layer thumbnail. See the first task on page 308.

The Merge Visible command merges all the currently visible layers while preserving any hidden layers as separate layers. By hiding the layers you don't want to merge before choosing this command, you can control which ones will be merged.

## To merge all visible layers:

1. Make sure only the layers you want to merge are visible (have eye icons), and hide any layers (including the Background, if desired) that you don't want to merge.

2. Right-click one of the visible layers (not a type layer) and choose **Merge Visible** (Ctrl-Shift-E/ Cmd-Shift-E).**A–B**

   Note: This sort of goes without saying, but if you merge an editable type layer or adjustment layer, the specific features of that kind of layer (such as the settings from an adjustment layer) will no longer be editable.

The commands in the following instructions will copy and merge ("stamp") two or more selected layers into a new layer in a single easy step, while preserving the original, separate layers. This might come in handy, say, if you want to test some edits (such as filters or transformations) on multiple layers. You would use one of these commands first, then apply your edits to the new layer. Note: For an alternative to using these commands, see the sidebar on the preceding page.

## To copy and merge layers:

Do either of the following:

Ctrl-click/Cmd-click the layers (not the Background) to be copied or merged into a new layer, then press Ctrl-Alt-E/Cmd-Option-E.

To copy and merge all the currently visible layers into a new layer, including the Background (if visible), click any visible layer, then press Ctrl-Alt-Shift-E/Cmd-Option-Shift-E.

➤ If layers and the Background are selected when you use the first shortcut listed above, content from the selected layers will be stamped into the Background, and no new layer will be created.

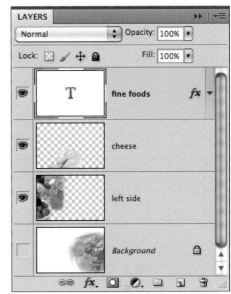

**A** In this document, we hid the Background because we don't want our layers to merge into it.

**B** The Merge Visible command merged all the layers except the Background, which remains hidden.

# Flattening layers

Two reasons to flatten all the layers in a file are to conserve storage space or to prepare it for output or export. At the present time, the only file formats that support multiple layers are Photoshop PDF, Photoshop, Large Document Format, and TIFF. If the application to which you're planning to export your file can't read or accept layered files, you'll have to either flatten it or save a flattened copy of it by using File > Save As. The latter method (which is the one we normally use) preserves the layered version so you can overwork it to death at a later time.

### To save a flattened copy of a file:

1. Choose File > **Save As** (Ctrl-Shift-S/Cmd-Shift-S).The Save As dialog opens.

2. Do all of the following:

   Change the file name.

   Choose a location.

   Uncheck Layers (the As a Copy option becomes checked automatically; keep it that way).

   Choose a file format from the Format menu.

   Click Save.

   Note: The layered version remains open; the flattened version is saved to disk.

If you're confident that your image is totally complete, *finis,* you can use the Flatten Image command instead of saving a flattened copy. This command merges the currently visible layers into the bottommost visible layer — but be aware that it also discards hidden layers!

### To flatten the layers in a document:

1. Make sure all the layers and layer groups you intend to flatten are visible (have eye icons). It doesn't matter which layer is selected.

2. Right-click any layer name (not a type layer) and choose **Flatten Image**. If the file contains any hidden layers, an alert dialog will appear; click OK. Any formerly transparent areas in the bottommost layer are now white.

   The Layers panel shown in figure **A** contains a type layer, layer styles, image layers, layer masks, and an adjustment layer. The Flatten Image command will rasterize all of the above, apply the masks, and flatten all the layers.**B**

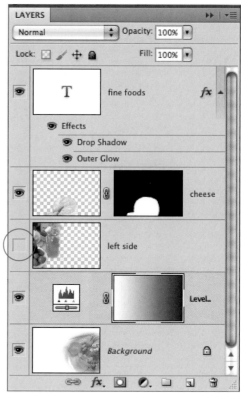

**A** When you choose the Flatten Image command, it doesn't matter which layer is selected. In this document, the "left side" layer is hidden.

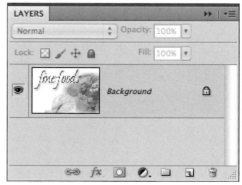

**B** The Flatten Image command flattened all the visible layers into the Background and discarded the hidden layer ("left side").

When you select part of a layer, only that area can be edited, and the rest of the layer is protected. If you were to apply a filter, for example, only pixels within the selection area on the currently selected layer would be affected. In this chapter, you'll learn how to create and modify selections using a wide assortment of methods, refine their edges, and store them for future use. You will also learn how to use layer masks to hide layer pixels from view — an essential Photoshop skill that you will practice again in other chapters.

Each of the mechanisms discussed in this chapter represents the isolation of image areas in a unique way. A selection is displayed as a marquee of "marching ants," a channel or mask is displayed as black and white areas, and a Quick Mask is displayed as red and clear areas. (For a comparison of the selection methods in Photoshop, see page 174.)

## Creating layer-based selections

### To select pixels on a layer:

On the Layers panel, 🖤 do either of the following:

Click a layer or the Background, then choose Select > **All** or press Ctrl-A/Cmd-A. A marquee of "marching ants" will surround the entire layer.

To select only the nontransparent areas on a layer, Ctrl-click/Cmd-click the layer thumbnail, **A–B** or right-click the layer thumbnail and choose **Select Pixels**.

SELECTIONS & MASKS

**A** *Ctrl-click/Cmd-click a layer thumbnail…*

**B** *…to select only nontransparent pixels on that layer.*

### IN THIS CHAPTER

## Using the Rectangular and Elliptical Marquee tools

### To create a rectangular or elliptical selection:

1. Click a layer.

2. Choose the **Rectangular Marquee** ⬚ or **Elliptical Marquee** ⬭ tool (M or Shift-M).

3. *Optional:* For a smoother edge on an elliptical selection, check Anti-alias on the Options bar (see the sidebar on page 155), and keep the Feather value at 0 px.

4. Drag diagonally, A or Shift-drag to create a perfect square or circle. A marquee appears.

5. *Optional:* To add to the selection, Shift-drag again; to subtract from it, Alt-drag/Option-drag.

➤ To move the marquee while drawing it, keep the mouse button down, then hold down the Spacebar and continue to drag. To move the marquee after releasing the mouse, drag inside it with any selection tool.

➤ As you draw a marquee, its dimensions are listed in the W and H areas on the Info panel.

➤ To draw a marquee from the center, hold down Alt/Option while dragging.

➤ To create the thinnest possible selection, choose the Single Row Marquee or Single Column Marquee tool, then click in the image.

### To create a selection with a fixed ratio or specific dimensions:

1. Click a layer.

2. Choose the **Rectangular Marquee** ⬚ or **Elliptical Marquee** ⬭ tool (M or Shift-M).

3. On the Options bar, set the Feather value to 0, then do either of the following:

   From the Style menu, choose **Fixed Ratio**, enter **Width** and **Height** values to be used as the ratio of the selection (e.g., 5 to 7), B then drag in the image diagonally to make a marquee appear. C

   From the Style menu, choose **Fixed Size**, enter exact **Width** and **Height** values, then click in the image. D

➤ Click the Swap Height and Width ⇄ button on the Options bar to swap the current values.

A *Drag diagonally with the Rectangular Marquee tool.*

B *We chose Fixed Ratio for the Rectangular Marquee tool and entered a Width to Height ratio of 5 to 7.*

C *With the Fixed Ratio option chosen, any size selection marquee you draw will have that ratio.*

D *Choose Fixed Size, enter values, then click in the image: The marquee appears. You can drag the marquee to reposition it, as we are doing here.*

## Using two of the lasso tools

We like to use the Lasso tool to select an area loosely, say, to limit subtle color adjustments to a general area. We also use this tool to clean up selections we have made with other tools, such as the Magic Wand or Quick Selection tool.

### To create a free-form selection:

1. Click a layer.

2. Choose the **Lasso** tool 🔲 (L or Shift-L).

3. *Optional:* For a smoother edge on an elliptical selection, check Anti-alias on the Options bar. (Keep the Feather value at 0 px.)

4. Drag around an area on the layer. This initial selection doesn't have to be precise, as you will be able to refine it easily in the next step. When you release the mouse, the open ends of the selection will be joined automatically.

5. To add to the selection, position the pointer inside it, then Shift-drag around the area to be added.**B** To subtract from the selection, position the pointer outside it, then Alt-drag/Option-drag around the area to be removed.**C–D**

➤ To feather an existing selection, see pages 161 and 237.

➤ To create a straight side with the Lasso tool, with the mouse button still down, hold down Alt/Option and click to create corners. To resume creating free-form edges, press the mouse button, release Alt/Option, then continue to drag.

### To create a straight-edged selection:

1. Click a layer.

2. Choose the **Polygonal Lasso** tool 🔲 (L or Shift-L).

3. Click to create points.**E** To create a selection edge at a multiple of 45°, hold down Shift while clicking.

4. To **join** the open ends of the selection, do either of the following:

   Click the starting point (make sure you see a small circle next to the pointer).

   Ctrl-click/Cmd-click or double-click anywhere in the document.

➤ To create a free-form segment while creating a polygonal selection, Alt-drag/Option-drag. Release Alt/Option and click to resume creating straight sides.

➤ To erase the last corner while using the Polygonal Lasso tool, press Backspace/Delete.

**A** *With the Lasso tool, we are selecting the left part of the ice cream.*

**B** *Using Shift, we are adding to the selection, to complete the shape.*

**C** *We want to remove the pistachio nut from the selection.*

**D** *We Alt-drag/Option-drag with the Lasso tool to remove the nut.*

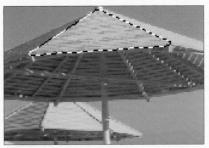

**E** *We created this straight-edged selection with the Polygonal Lasso tool.*

## Deselecting and reselecting selections

If you don't like having to retrace your steps (we sure don't), deselect your selections only when you're sure you're finished using them. Selections register as states on the History panel, but histories are short-lived. To preserve a selection for future access and use, save it in an alpha channel (see page 160) or convert it to a layer mask (see page 168).

### To deselect a selection:

Do one of the following:

Choose the **Lasso,** **Rectangular Marquee,** or **Elliptical Marquee** tool, then click inside or outside the selection. **A**

Press Ctrl-D/Cmd-D.

Right-click anywhere in the document and choose **Deselect**.

### To reselect the last selection:

Do one of the following:

Press Ctrl-Shift-D/Cmd-Shift-D.

With any selection tool except the Magic Wand chosen, right-click in the document and choose **Reselect**.

On the History panel, click the state that bears the name of the tool or command that was used to create the selection.

## Deleting selected pixels

When you delete a selection of pixels from a layer, **B** that area is filled automatically with transparent pixels. **C** When you delete a selection of pixels from the Background, that area is filled with the current Background color. **D**

### To delete selected pixels:

1. On the Layers panel, click a layer or the Background. If you click the Background, also choose a Background color (see Chapter 11).

2. Do one of the following:

   If a layer is active, press Backspace/Delete; if the Background is active, press Ctrl-Backspace/Cmd-Delete. ★

   Choose Edit > **Cut** (Ctrl-X/Cmd-X) to put the selection on the Clipboard. (To learn about the Clipboard, see pages 233–236.)

   Choose Edit > **Clear**.

**A** *Click inside a selection to deselect it.*

**B** *We selected the blue sky, then pressed Backspace/Delete.*

**C** *Because the pixels we deleted were on a selected layer, they were replaced by transparent pixels.*

**D** *Here, we deleted pixels from the Background instead of from a layer, so they were replaced with the current Background color (which in this case is red).*

## Moving a selection marquee

You can move a selection marquee to a different area of the image without moving its contents.

### To move a selection marquee:

1. Choose any selection tool except the Quick Selection tool, and make sure the **New Selection** button ▣ is activated on the Options bar (you can also hold down M, L, or W to spring-load a selection tool).

2. Do either of the following:

   Drag inside an existing selection. To constrain the movement to a multiple of 45°, start dragging, then hold down Shift and continue to drag.

   Press any arrow key to nudge the marquee by one pixel at a time, or press Shift-arrow to nudge the marquee by 10 pixels at a time.

▶ With a selection tool, you can drag a selection marquee from one image window into another.

▶ To transform a selection marquee (but not its contents), choose any selection tool except the Magic Wand. Right-click the image and choose Transform Selection. Drag a handle on the transform box to scale, rotate, skew, or distort the selection (see pages 312–313).

---

**REMEMBER TO USE THE LAYERS PANEL!**

Before editing the pixels within a selection area, always remember to let Photoshop know which part of your document you want to edit by clicking a layer or the Background.

---

## Moving selection contents

In these steps, you will move a selection and its contents on a layer.

### To move the contents of a selection:

1. Create a selection.

2. *Optional:* To help you position the selection precisely at a specific location in the document, display the rulers (Ctrl-R/Cmd-R), drag a guide from the horizontal or vertical ruler, and turn on View > Snap To > Guides.

3. Do either of the following:

   On the Layers panel, click the **Background**, then choose a Background color (see Chapter 11). The area that becomes exposed when you move the selection will fill with this color.

   Click a **layer**. The area you expose when you move the selection will fill with transparent pixels.

4. Choose the **Move** tool ▶⊕ (or hold down V to spring-load the Move tool).

5. Position the pointer over the selection, then drag. Let the edge of the selection snap to a ruler guide, if you created one.

6. Deselect (Ctrl-D/Cmd-D).

▶ In Chapter 14, Combining Images, you will learn how to copy the contents of a selection within the same file and between files, and to use alignment aids, such as ruler guides and Smart Guides.

▶ With the Move tool chosen, you can press an arrow key to nudge a selection and its contents by one pixel at a time, or press Shift-arrow to nudge the marquee by 10 pixels at a time.

**A** *A selection marquee is moved with a selection tool.*

**B** *Selection contents are moved on a layer with the Move tool.*

## Using the Quick Selection tool

The Photoshop features we're going to discuss next
— the Quick Selection tool, Magic Wand tool, and
Color Range command — create selections in a
more automatic way than the marquee and lasso
tools. With these tools, the work of detecting the
color boundaries is done for you, and the resulting
selections tend to be very precise.

If the area you want to select has well-defined borders, instead of using a lasso tool, try using the
Quick Selection tool. Rather than tediously tracing
a precise contour, with this tool, you merely drag
across a shape and stand by as it detects and selects
the shape's color boundary. You can push the resulting selection outward to include an adjacent color
boundary or inward to make it smaller.

### To use the Quick Selection tool:

1. Click a layer.

2. Choose the **Quick Selection** tool 🖌️ (W or
   Shift-W).

3. On the Options bar:

   Click the **New Selection** button 🖌️ to replace
   any existing selections with the one you're about
   to create (or press Ctrl-D/Cmd-D to deselect).

   Use the **Sample All Layers** check box to control
   whether you want the tool to detect color boundaries on just the current layer or on all layers.

   Check **Auto-Enhance** for a smoother, more
   refined selection edge.

4. To choose a brush diameter, Alt-right-click-drag/
   Control-Option-drag to the left or right or
   press ] or [, then drag within the area to be
   selected. **A** The selection will expand to the first
   significant color or shade boundary that the tool
   detects. The selection will preview as you drag,
   and will become more precise when you release
   the mouse.

5. Do any of the following optional steps:

   To **enlarge** the selection, click or drag in an
   adjoining area; the selection will expand to
   include it. **B–C**

   To **shrink** the selection, Alt-drag/Option-drag
   along the edge of the area to be subtracted (this
   is a temporary Subtract From button) (**A–B**,
   next page).

   Note: To block an adjacent area from becoming selected by the Quick Selection tool as you

**A** *We selected the kumquat in the center of this image
by dragging the Quick Selection tool across it.*

**B** *After enlarging the brush diameter, we clicked the
kumquat on the right to add it to the selection.*

**C** *Next, we dragged across the green leaf above the
kumquats. The selection spread beyond the edge of the
leaf to include some of the background area, which
wasn't our intention.*

enlarge an existing selection, Alt-click/Option-click or drag in that area, release Alt/Option, then drag to enlarge the selection area. The block will remain in effect until you click the blocked area again with the Quick Selection tool. **C–E**

➤ To undo the last click or drag of the Quick Selection tool, press Ctrl-Z/Cmd-Z.

➤ To save any kind of selection to an alpha channel, see page 160.

➤ To clean up a Quick Selection, you can use another selection tool, such as the Lasso. To refine the selection, see page 161.

**A** *We Alt-dragged/Option-dragged below the leaf to subtract the background area from the selection...*

**B** *...and did the same thing to subtract the area below the kumquats.*

**C** *We zoomed in, reduced the brush diameter, then Alt-clicked/Option-clicked areas around the stems to prevent them from becoming selected.*

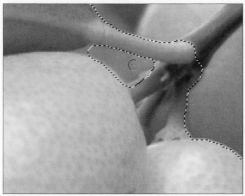

**D** *We dragged along the stems to select them, then Alt-clicked/Option-clicked the background areas between the stems to remove them from the selection.*

**E** *To finalize our selection, we cleaned up the selection of the stems.*

## Using the Magic Wand tool

With the Magic Wand tool, you simply click a color in the image and the tool selects all adjacent pixels of the same (or a similar) shade or color. Like the Color Range command, which is discussed on pages 156–157, the Magic Wand lets you control the range of pixels the tool selects, but unlike Color Range, this tool lets you add nonsimilar colors to the selection.

### To select color areas with the Magic Wand tool:

1. Click a layer or the Background.

2. Choose the **Magic Wand** tool ✎ (W or Shift-W).

3. On the Options bar:

   Choose a **Tolerance** value (use the scrubby slider) to control the range of colors the tool selects (for a starting value, try between 30 and 40).

   Check **Anti-alias** to allow the tool to add semitransparent pixels along the edges of the color areas it detects. This will produce smoother edge transitions for your image edits.

   Check **Contiguous** to limit the selection to areas that are connected to the first pixel you click, or uncheck this option to allow the tool to select similarly colored, noncontiguous (unconnected) areas throughout the image with the same click.

   To select possible occurrences of a similar color on all visible layers, check **Sample All Layers**, or uncheck this option to select colors on just the current layer.

4. Click a color in the image.

5. Unless your image contains nothing but totally flat color areas (which is unlikely), you'll have to do some extra work to refine the selection. Do any of the following:

   To **add** to the selection, Shift-click any unselected areas.

   To **subtract** any areas from the selection, hold down Alt/Option and click them. Or choose the Quick Selection tool, then with the Alt/Option key held down, drag short strokes across the areas to be subtracted.

   To select additional, noncontiguous areas of a similar color or shade based on the current Tolerance value, right-click in the document and choose **Similar**. (This command works the same whether the Contiguous option is checked or not.)

**A** *To select the sky in this image layer, we clicked on the right side with the Magic Wand tool (Tolerance 38; Contiguous checked), then Shift-clicked more sky areas to add them to the selection (as shown above).*

**B** *Some areas of the keys became selected, so we are using the Quick Selection tool with Alt/Option held down to remove them from the selection.*

6. *Optional:* If you have selected a background
   area that you want to remove and you clicked
   a layer in step 1, press Backspace/Delete;  or
   if you clicked the Background in step 1, press
   Ctrl-Backspace/Cmd-Delete. ★ Deselect (Ctrl-D/
   Cmd-D).

➤ You can change the Tolerance value for the
   Magic Wand tool between clicks. For example,
   for more control when adding unselected shades
   or colors along the edges of a selection, lower
   the Tolerance value incrementally: Click with a
   Tolerance of 30–40 first, lower the value to 15–20
   and click again, then finally lower it to 5–10 and
   click once more. To select just one color or shade,
   use a Tolerance of 0 or 1.

➤ To undo the results of the last click made with
   the Magic Wand tool or to undo the last use of
   the Similar command, press Ctrl-Z/Cmd-Z.

## To expand a selection using a command:

With any selection tool chosen, choose Select >
**Grow** or **Similar**. These commands use the
current Tolerance setting of the Magic Wand
tool. You can repeat either command to further
expand the selection.

➤ When the Magic Wand tool is selected, you can
   access the Grow and Similar commands via the
   context menu.

*A Finally, we pressed Backspace/Delete to get rid of the
selected pixels (in this document, the Background is hidden).*

*B We clicked the blue
sky area with the Magic
Wand tool (Tolerance of
35), Shift-clicked once
on the clouds...*

*C ...then chose Select >
Similar. The Tolerance setting
controlled which pixel range
was added to the selection.*

---

**TO ANTI-ALIAS OR NOT?**

Before using a selection tool, check Anti-alias (if available) on the
Options bar to fade the edge of the selection to transparency, or
uncheck this option to produce a crisp, hard-edged selection. The effect
of anti-aliasing won't be visible until you edit the selected pixels.

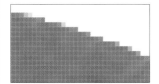

*The Anti-alias option was on
when this selection was created.*

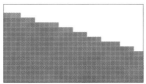

*The Anti-alias option was off
when this selection was created.*

# Using the Color Range command

To create a selection with the Color Range command, you click a color area in the document window or in the preview area of the dialog, and depending on the parameters you have chosen, all occurrences of just one color or a range of related colors become selected. The dialog also provides controls for widening or narrowing the range. After closing the dialog, you can further refine the selection with any selection tool. The more solid the color areas in an image, the more effectively this command works.

## To create a selection using the Color Range command:

1. Click a layer. The command will sample colors from all the currently visible layers, but of course only the current layer can be edited.

2. *Optional:* Create a selection to limit where the command can select colors.

3. Choose Select > **Color Range**, or if a selection tool is in hand, right-click in the document and choose Color Range.

4. In the Color Range dialog, choose from the **Select** menu to limit the selection to Sampled Colors (shades or colors you'll click with the Color Range eyedropper); to a specific preset color range (e.g., Reds, Yellows); or to a luminosity range (Highlights, Midtones, or Shadows).

5. If you chose Sampled Colors in the preceding step, with the Eyedropper tool from the dialog, click in either the dialog preview or the document window to sample a color in the image. **A–B**

6. To **add** more colors or shades to the selection, Shift-click in the document or preview window; or to remove colors or shades from the selection, Alt-click/Option-click.

   To expand or reduce the range of selected colors and to control the number of partially selected pixels, adjust the **Fuzziness** value. **C**

7. Choose a **Selection Preview** option for viewing the selection in the document window: None for no preview, Grayscale to see a larger version of the dialog preview, Black Matte to view the selection against a black background, or White Matte to view the selection against a white background. Choose one of the latter two options when you need to see if the edges are properly selected.

**A** *We chose the Color Range command, then with the Eyedropper, clicked the blue sky at the top of the image.*

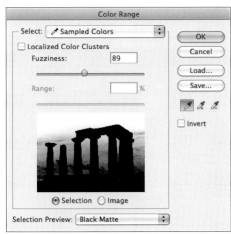

**B** *In the preview, the white areas represent fully selected pixels, the gray represent partially selected pixels, and the black areas represent unselected pixels.*

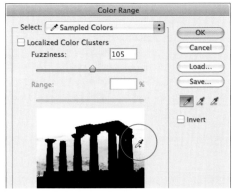

**C** *To fully select the sky and background, we Shift-clicked a lower section of the sky in the preview and increased the Fuzziness value to 105.*

8. Click OK. A Note: If you chose a preset color range and the image contains only minimal levels of that color, an alert dialog will inform you that the selection marquee will be active but invisible.

➤ Press Ctrl/Cmd to toggle between the Selection and Image previews in the dialog.

*A In the final Color Range selection, the entire blue sky and distant background are selected, including the noncontiguous areas between the columns.*

## USING THE LOCALIZED COLOR CLUSTERS OPTION IN THE COLOR RANGE DIALOG

The Localized Color Clusters option in the Color Range dialog creates a more accurate selection of colors based on their proximity to the sampled color. Click a layer, open the Color Range dialog, choose Select: Sampled Colors, then with the Eyedropper tool, click in the document window to sample a color. B Check Localized Color Clusters, then use the Range slider to control the distance from the sampled color (or colors, if you Shift-clicked) within which similar colors may become selected. C You can Shift-drag in the preview or document to add more color areas to the selection, within the current range, D or Alt-drag/ Option-drag to remove color areas. E

*B We chose the Color Range command, then with the Eyedropper, clicked the grapefruit in the image.*

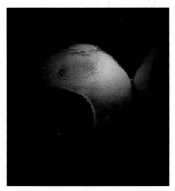

*C We checked Localized Color Clusters and lowered the Range value to 15 to shrink the selection area.*

*D Next, we Shift-dragged to select more grapefruit colors, within the current Range.*

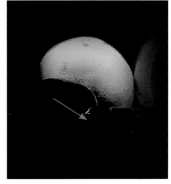

*E Finally, we dragged with Alt/ Option held down to remove some color areas from the selection.*

## Hiding and showing selection edges

If your selection edges (those "marching ants") become distracting or annoying, you can hide them from view. If you do so, remember that the selection remains in effect even when you can't see it!

### To hide or show the edges of a selection:

Press Ctrl-H/Cmd-H or choose View > Extras. If this command doesn't work, make sure View > Show > **Selection Edges** has a check mark. **A–B**

Note: The Ctrl-H/Cmd-H shortcut hides or shows all the options that are currently checked on the Show submenu.

➤ Mac OS users: The first time you press Cmd-H after installing Photoshop and then opening or creating your first document, an alert dialog will appear. ★ If you click Hide Photoshop, the Cmd-H shortcut will be assigned to the Photoshop > Hide Photoshop command; if you click Hide Extras (as we do and recommend), the shortcut will be assigned to the View > Extras command. The alert won't reappear unless you reset all warning dialogs (see page 386).

➤ If an option is unchecked in the View > Show > Show Extras Options dialog, you can turn it on or off only via the Show submenu, not by using the Ctrl-H/Cmd-H shortcut. For this reason, we like to keep all the options checked in that dialog.

➤ To verify that there is an active selection in your document, click the Select menu. If most of the commands on the menu are available, you know that there is an active selection.

➤ You can hide or show selection edges via the shortcut while using the Adjustments panel and while any of the Image > Adjustments dialogs are open.

## Swapping the selected and unselected areas

### To swap the selected and unselected areas:

Do either of the following:

With any tool chosen, press Ctrl-Shift-I/Cmd-Shift-I (or choose Select > Inverse). **C–D**

With any selection tool chosen, right-click in the document and choose **Select Inverse**.

(Repeat either step above to switch back to the original selection.)

**A** *We applied the Texture > Grain filter (Grain Type: Speckle) to this selection…*

**B** *…then we hid the selection edges to gauge the results.*

**C** *This is the original selection.*

**D** *And this is the inverse of the same selection.*

# Creating a frame-shaped selection

With the Rectangular Marquee or Elliptical Marquee tool, you can create a selection in the shape of a frame, either at the edge of the canvas area or floating somewhere within it. You can then apply filters or adjustment settings to the frame-shaped selection or turn it into an adjustment layer mask (don't worry, you'll learn those tricks later in this book). Your edits will affect only pixels within the frame-shaped border.

## To create a selection in the shape of a frame:

### Method 1 (at the edge of the canvas area)

1. Click a layer.

2. Choose the **Rectangular Marquee** ⬚ (M or Shift-M).

3. In the document window, drag a marquee to define the inner edge of the frame selection.

4. *Optional:* To soften the edges of the selection, click Refine Edge on the Options bar, choose On White (W) from the View menu, ★ zero out all the sliders, adjust the Feather value to achieve the desired degree of softness, then click OK.

5. Right-click in the document and choose **Select Inverse.A–B**

### Method 2 (within the image)

1. Click a layer.

2. Choose the **Rectangular Marquee** or **Elliptical Marquee** tool (M or Shift-M), then drag to define the outer edge of the selection.

3. Alt-drag/Option-drag inside the first selection to create the inner edge of the frame selection.**C** Reposition the inner selection, if needed.

**C** *Alt-drag/Option-drag to create one rectangular selection within another.*

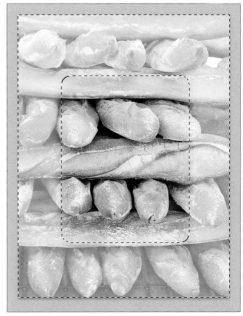

**A** *We created an inner selection with the Rectangular Marquee tool on this 300 ppi image, applied a Feather value of 25 px via Refine Edge, then chose Select > Inverse. Next, we used a Levels adjustment layer to lighten the area within the frame selection (see pages 206–207).*

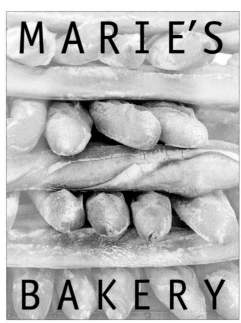

**B** *Finally, we added an editable type layer. The type is easy to read because we lightened the background.*

# Saving and loading selections

Creating a selection can be tedious, but fortunately, it can be saved either as an alpha channel or as a layer mask. Once saved, a selection can be loaded onto the document at any time, and can be reshaped, if needed.

## To save a selection to an alpha channel:

1. Create a selection. A

2. Display the Channels panel, then click the **Save Selection as Channel** button on the panel. Press Ctrl-D/Cmd-D to deselect. A new alpha channel appears on the panel. B

➤ To reverse the masked and unmasked areas in an alpha channel, click the alpha channel on the Channels panel, then press Ctrl-I/Cmd-I.

➤ To rename an alpha channel, double-click the name, type a new one, then press Enter/Return.

➤ To delete an alpha channel, right-click the listing and choose Delete Channel.

➤ Alpha channels can be saved with files in several formats, such as Photoshop, JPEG 2000, TIFF, and Photoshop PDF. In the File > Save As dialog, check Alpha Channels.

## To load an alpha channel as a selection:

On the Channels panel, do either of the following:

Ctrl-click/Cmd-click the alpha channel thumbnail or listing. Your selection will reappear in the document window.

Drag the channel name to the **Load Channel as Selection** button at the bottom of the panel.

➤ To learn more about saving and loading alpha channels, see Photoshop Help.

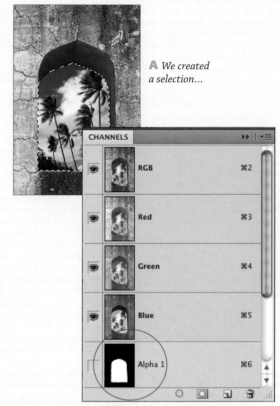

A *We created a selection...*

B *...then clicked the Save Selection as Channel button on the Channels panel. This alpha channel listing appeared.*

---

**RESHAPING AN ALPHA CHANNEL**

➤ To reshape an alpha channel, click the channel, then with the Brush tool, paint with white to expand the selection area or with black to remove areas from it. When you're done, click the topmost channel.

➤ If you prefer to display an alpha channel as a ruby-lith (a red tint), click the alpha channel, then click the visibility icon for the topmost channel. To restore the normal display after reshaping the channel, hide the alpha channel by clicking its visibility icon (then click the topmost channel).

**SAVING A SELECTION AS A MASK**

If you save a selection as a layer mask, not only is it stored with the document, but you can also reshape it easily by editing the mask (see pages 169–170), and redisplay it as a selection at any time (see page 172).

# Refining selection edges

Use the improved Refine Edge dialog to apply refinements, such as feathering, to your selections. Practical uses for this dialog are illustrated on pages 162–165 and 237.

## To refine the edges of a selection: ★

1. Create a selection. With your selection tool still chosen, click **Refine Edge** on the Options bar or press Ctrl-Alt-R/Cmd-Option-R.

2. Set the zoom level to 100% or 200% by pressing Ctrl-+/Cmd-+.

3. To control how the selection previews in the document, choose from the **View** menu. A You can also choose a view by pressing the letter shortcut that's listed on the menu, or cycle through them by pressing F. We're partial to these views:

   **Overlay** (V) to view the selection as a Quick Mask (useful for viewing areas beyond the selection).

   **On Black** (B) to view the selection against a black background (useful if you're going to copy the selection to a dark background or if the background areas are light).

   **On White** (W) to view the selection against a white background (useful if you're going to copy the selection to a light background).

   **On Layers** (L) to view the selection on top of the layer immediately below it (useful for judging the selection edge against an underlying layer, if there is one).

4. Check **Smart Radius** to allow the Radius to adapt to hard and soft edges in the imagery.

   If you want to widen the refinement area to include pixels just outside the selection edge, increase the **Radius** value (use the scrubby slider).

   To view the current refinement area, check **Show Radius** (J), then uncheck it before proceeding.

   ➤ At any time, press P to toggle between the original selection and the refined one.

5. In the Adjust Edge area, move any of the following sliders, if desired:

   To smooth out small bumps or jagged edges, raise the **Smooth** value slightly.

   To soften the transition between selected and unselected pixels, raise the **Feather** value.

   To heighten the contrast between pixels within the refinement area to remove noise from a high

Radius value and produce a crisper selection edge, increase the **Contrast** value.

To shrink the selection edge inward (to eliminate background pixels) or expand it outward from the edge, adjust the **Shift Edge** value slightly.

6. In the Output area:

   If you want to replace background pixels along the edges of the selection with colors from within the selection, check **Decontaminate Colors**, then raise the **Amount** value.

   Choose **Output To: Selection** to refine the selection without putting its contents on a new layer. Or to copy the selection contents to a new layer, choose **New Layer** (no mask) or **New Layer with Layer Mask** (the shape of the selection appears in a layer mask). If Decontaminate Colors is checked, only new layer options will be available.

7. *Optional:* Check Remember Settings to have the current settings become the new default values for the dialog.

8. Click OK.

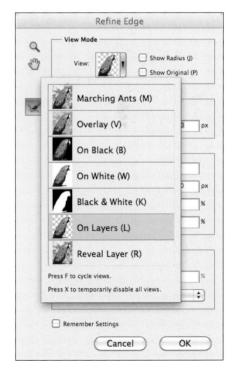

A *To quickly switch among the View options in the Refine Edge dialog, press the letter shortcuts.*

## REFINE A SELECTION EDGE AND CREATE A SILHOUETTE — ALL IN ONE DIALOG! ★

**A** *We duplicated the Background of a 300 ppi photo, created a solid-color layer below it, then selected the parrot with the Quick Selection tool.*

**B** *In the Refine Edge dialog, we chose On White (W) view and zoomed in to 100%. With no refinement applied, the edges of the selection of the feathers and beak are imprecise.*

**C** *We checked Smart Radius to allow the Radius to adapt to the hard and soft edges in the image, and we increased the Radius to 55 px\* to include more of the fine feathers — this also softened the edges.*

\**Use a lower Radius value for a low-resolution image.*

**D** *We increased the Contrast value to 8% to sharpen the border edges temporarily and create a more accurate selection. To judge our results against the solid-color layer, we chose On Layers from the View menu.*

**E** *We increased the Shift Edge value (to +20%) to expand the selection edge. More of the soft feathers are now included, but more of the original blue background color is, too.*

**F** *We checked Decontaminate Colors and set the Amount value to 45% to remove any color fringe from the selection edge. Decontamination results can be judged in On Layers, On Black, or On White view.*

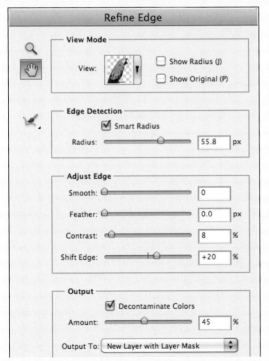

**G** *These are our final Refine Edge settings. To create a silhouette using the current selection, we chose Output To: New Layer with Layer Mask. This option duplicated the Background copy and turned our selection into a layer mask.*

**H** *The new layer and layer mask appeared on the Layers panel. The final image is shown above.*

Using the Refine Radius tool in the Refine Edge dialog, along with the sliders, you can extend a selection border into specific areas manually. Here we'll use these features to refine a selection of hair. Although these steps won't work magically on every image, it's a timesaver when they do.

## To refine a selection of hair via the Refine Edge dialog: ★

1. *Optional:* Duplicate the Background, then create a solid-color layer between the Background and the duplicate image layer.

2. In a photo that contains fine hair strands, use the Quick Selection or Magic Wand tool to create a selection.**A**

3. Click **Refine Edge** to open the Refine Edge dialog. Set all the sliders to zero and uncheck Decontaminate Colors.

4. Choose **On White** or **On Black** view. (Or if you created a solid-color layer below the duplicate layer, choose **On Layers** view.) Check **Smart Radius** and set the **Radius** value to 20–30 px.**B**

5. Click the **Refine Radius** tool, ✎ and press **X** to view the original image layer. Press ] or [ to change the brush to a medium size, then drag over the fine hair strands. Your brush work will display as green strokes (**A–B**, next page).

6. Press X to return to your View choice. Raise or lower the **Radius** value to better define the hair strands. Also try increasing the **Shift Edge** value slightly to reveal more strands. (Keep the Contrast, Smooth, and Feather values at 0 so they don't hinder the Refine Radius tool effect.)

7. Check **Decontaminate Colors**, then raise the **Amount** value until any background colors are removed (**C–D**, next page).

8. Choose Output To: **New Layer with Layer Mask**, then click OK. Now, wasn't that easy?

**A** *With a few clicks of the Magic Wand tool on this 300 ppi photo, we selected the sky, then chose Select > Inverse.*

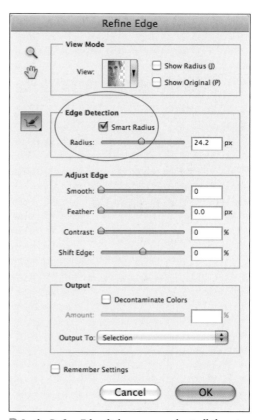

**B** *In the Refine Edge dialog, we zeroed out all the settings first. To widen the refinement area to include more hair strands, we checked Smart Radius, then increased the Radius value. The Smart Radius option produced a more accurate selection edge.*

**A** *We clicked the Refine Radius tool, pressed X to preview the original image, then applied strokes over the fine hair strands and neck to control how much the radius extends locally. Our goal is to pick up more details along the edge.*

➤ *If you need to shrink the radius to remove details from the selection, apply strokes with the Erase Refinements tool.* ✎

**B** *We pressed X to restore the preview to On White view, then checked Show Radius to view the results of the expanded radius.*

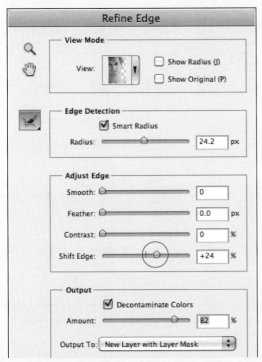

**Refine Edge**

View Mode

View:

☐ Show Radius (J)
☐ Show Original (P)

Edge Detection

☑ Smart Radius

Radius: ———————○——————— 24.2 px

Adjust Edge

Smooth: ○———————————— 0

Feather: ○———————————— 0.0 px

Contrast: ○———————————— 0 %

Shift Edge: ————————○———— +24 %

Output

☑ Decontaminate Colors

Amount: ——————————○—— 82 %

Output To: New Layer with Layer Mask ⬍

**C** *For our final Refine Edge settings, we checked Decontaminate Colors, set the Amount value to 82%, and increased the Shift Edge value just enough to include more fine hair strands without including any of the background.*

**D** *To produce this result, we placed a white background layer below the silhouetted image layer.*

## Using Quick Masks

With your document in Quick Mask mode, you can paint a mask onto the parts of your image that need protection, and reshape (add to or remove areas from) the mask with the Brush or Pencil tool. If you create a selection first, the mask will cover just the unselected areas. By default, the mask is semitransparent red, as in a traditional rubylith. The Quick Mask itself can't be saved, but when you put your document back into Standard (non-Quick Mask) mode, the mask will turn into a selection automatically, at which point it can either be saved as an alpha channel or turned into a layer mask.

### To reshape a selection using a Quick Mask:

1. Select an area of a layer. **A**

2. Click the **Edit in Quick Mask Mode** button [O] at the bottom of the Tools panel, or press Q. A mask should cover the unselected areas of the image. **B** (If it doesn't, double-click the same button, click Color Indicates: Masked Areas, then click OK.)

3. Choose the **Brush** tool 🖌 (B or Shift-B).

4. On the Options bar, click the **Brush Preset** picker arrowhead, then click a Hard Round brush; choose **Mode:** Normal, and set the **Opacity** and **Flow** to 100%.

5. Zoom in on the mask area to be reshaped, then do any of the following:

   Apply strokes with black as the Foreground color to enlarge the masked (protected) area.

   Press X to swap the Foreground and Background colors (make the Foreground color white), then apply strokes in the document to enlarge the unmasked area. **C**

   ➤ To create a partial mask, lower the brush opacity via the Options bar before applying strokes. When you edit pixels within the selection, that area will be only partially affected by your edits.

6. To restore the normal document mode, click the **Edit in Standard Mode** button [O] on the Tools panel or press Q. The unmasked areas turn into a selection.

7. *Optional:* To preserve the selection, save it as an alpha channel (see page 160) or as a layer mask (see page 168).

**A** *An area of a layer is selected.*

**B** *The unselected area is covered with a red Quick Mask.*

**C** *With our document in Quick Mask mode, we're unmasking the helmet by applying strokes with the Brush tool.*

In these steps, you'll paint the mask directly in a document without creating a selection first. When you put the document back into Standard mode, the mask will turn into a selection. You can use this technique to select areas for retouching, such as the eyes or teeth in a portrait photo (see page 274).

## To paint a Quick Mask in a document:

1. Choose the **Brush** tool, and choose tool options as described in step 4 on the preceding page.

2. Double-click the **Edit in Quick Mask Mode** button on the Tools panel.

3. Click Color Indicates: **Selected Areas,** then click OK.

4. Zoom in, then with black as the Foreground color, apply strokes to create a mask. **A**

   If you need to remove any areas of the mask, press X to switch the Foreground color to white.

   ➤ You can start by painting with a medium-sized brush, then refine the mask with a smaller brush (press [ to shrink the brush).

5. Press Q to put the document back into Standard mode. **B** The mask turns into a selection.

   ➤ To store the selection as a mask on the current layer, **C** see the next page. Or to save it as an alpha channel, see page 160.

Via the Quick Mask Options dialog, you can control whether a mask covers the protected or unprotected areas of an image, and also change its color and opacity.

## To choose Quick Mask options:

1. Double-click the **Edit in Quick Mask Mode** button on the Tools panel. The Quick Mask Options dialog opens.

2. Do any of the following:

   Click Color Indicates: **Masked Areas** or **Selected Areas**.

   Click the **Color** swatch, then choose a new color for the Quick Mask.

   Change the **Opacity** of the mask color.

3. Click OK.

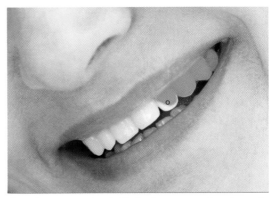

*A In this image, a Quick Mask is being painted on the teeth.*

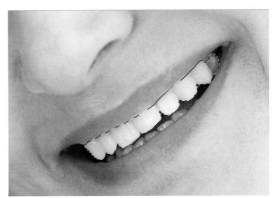

*B When we put the image back into Standard mode, the mask turned into a selection. Note: To soften the edges of the selection slightly before applying image edits, we could use the Feather slider in the Refine Edge dialog.*

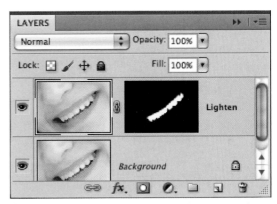

*C The selection that is shown in the preceding figure is being stored in this document as a layer mask.*

# Creating layer masks

A layer mask is an editable (and removable) 8-bit grayscale channel that hides all or some of the pixels on a layer. White areas in a layer mask permit pixels to be seen, black areas hide pixels, and gray areas hide pixels partially. With the layer mask thumbnail selected, you can edit or deactivate the mask, or move or copy it to other layers. At any time, you can either apply the mask to make its effect permanent or discard it to undo its effect. The Masks panel provides access to most of the masking controls in Photoshop.

**A** *The original image contains a photo of an archway on the Background below a photo of tile on a layer. We selected the archway, then clicked the tile layer.*

## To create a layer mask:

1. *Optional:* Create a selection, which is to become a shape in the mask.

2. On the Layers panel, click a layer or layer group. **A**

3. To create a white mask in which all the layer pixels are visible or, if you created a selection, to reveal the layer contents only within the selection area, do one of the following:

   Display the Masks panel, 🔲 then click the **Add Pixel Mask button** 🔲 at the top of the panel. **B–D**

   At the bottom of the Layers panel, click the **Add Layer Mask** button. 🔲

   Click **Refine Edge** on the Options bar, and use the dialog to make any desired refinements to the edge of the selection (see page 161). From the Output To menu, choose **Layer Mask**, ★ then click OK.

   A mask thumbnail appears on the Layers panel.

➤ To swap the black and white areas in a selected mask and thereby reverse its effect, click Invert on the Masks panel.

➤ To create a black mask in which all the layer pixels are hidden or in which just the pixels within the selection are hidden, Alt-click/Option-click either the Add Pixel Mask button on the Masks panel or the Add Layer Mask button on the Layers panel.

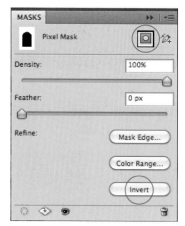 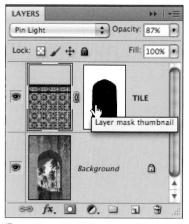 

**B** *We clicked the Add Pixel Mask button on the Masks panel to add a layer mask to the tile layer, then clicked Invert to swap the black and white areas in the mask.*

**C** *Finally, to blend the mosaic layer with the stone wall, on the Layers panel, we chose Pin Light blending mode and lowered the layer opacity.*

**D** *The center of the tile layer is hidden by the arch-shaped layer mask.*

# Editing layer masks

In these instructions, you'll edit a layer mask by applying strokes with the Brush tool. In the instructions on the next two pages, you'll edit a mask by using controls on the Masks panel. These are very important skills to learn.

## To reshape a layer mask:

1. Choose the **Brush** tool ![brush icon] (B or Shift-B).

2. On the Options bar, click a brush on the Brush Preset picker, choose Mode: Normal, and choose an Opacity of 100% to hide layer pixels fully or a lower opacity to hide them partially.

3. Do either of the following:

   To display the mask as a colored overlay on top of the image, Alt-Shift-click/Option-Shift-click the layer mask thumbnail on the Layers panel.**A–B**

   To display the mask in black and white with the image hidden, Alt-click/Option-click the layer mask thumbnail on the Layers panel.

4. Do either or both of the following:

   Paint with white as the Foreground color to reduce the mask and reveal pixels on the layer.**C**

   Paint with black as the Foreground color to enlarge the mask and hide pixels on the layer.**D**

   ➤ You can change brush settings, such as the size or hardness, between strokes. Right-click in the image to display a temporary brush preset picker.

5. When you're done editing the layer mask, click the layer thumbnail to restore the normal display.

If it's hard to see the overlay because it's too similar to the image color, you can change the overlay color or opacity.

## To choose layer mask display options:

1. Double-click a layer mask thumbnail on the Layers panel (or click the mask thumbnail, then choose Mask Options from the Masks panel menu).

2. In the Layer Mask Display Options dialog, do either or both of the following: **E**

   Click the **Color** square, choose a different overlay color from the Color Picker, then click OK.

   Change the **Opacity** percentage.

3. Click OK.

4. To view the change in the document, Alt-Shift-click/Option-Shift-click the layer mask thumbnail.

**A** *We're painting out (removing) areas of the mask, which is displayed as a red overlay on top of the image.*

**B** *The mask is reshaped.*

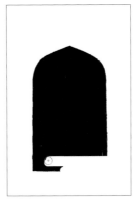

**C** *Only the mask is displayed in the document window. We're eliminating areas from it by painting with white.*

**D** *We're enlarging the mask by painting with black chosen as the Foreground color.*

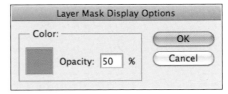

**E** *By using the Layer Mask Display Options dialog, you can change the Color and/or Opacity of the mask overlay.*

The Density control on the Masks panel affects the opacity of the overall mask, whereas the Feather control affects the opacity of its edge. Both of these useful controls are nondestructive, meaning they don't alter the original mask and can be readjusted at any time.

## To adjust the density or feather value of a layer mask:

1. Click a layer that contains a layer mask, and display the Masks panel. **A**

2. Click the **Select Pixel Mask** button, then do either or both of the following:

   Reduce the **Density** value to lighten the black part of the mask and partially reveal layer pixels. **B–C** The lower the density, the more transparent the mask.

   Increase the **Feather** value to soften the edge of the mask, for a more gradual transition between the masked and unmasked areas (**A**, next page).

## To refine the edges of a layer mask:

1. Click a layer that contains a layer mask, and display the Masks panel. Zoom to around 100%.

2. Click **Mask Edge**; the Refine Mask dialog opens.

3. Use the Refine Mask controls to adjust the softness or sharpness of the edge of the mask, as you would for a selection in the Refine Edge dialog (see page 161). We've found the following settings to be helpful for cleaning up the edge of a mask: a low Radius value (1–2), a low Contrast value (5–7), and a slightly negative Contract/Expand value to shrink the mask inward (to hide more background pixels).

➤ We recommend keeping the Feather slider in the Refine Mask dialog at 0 because it's destructive, and using the nondestructive Feather slider on the Masks panel instead.

## To swap the black and white areas in a layer mask:

Do either of the following:

Click a layer that contains a layer mask, display the Masks panel, then click the **Invert** button.

Click a layer mask thumbnail on the Layers panel, then press Ctrl-I/Cmd-I.

➤ Repeat either method above to restore the original state of the mask.

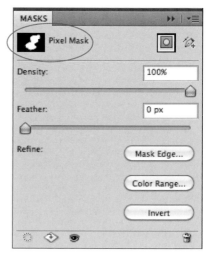

**A** *By looking at the upper left area of the Masks panel, we know that a Pixel Mask is selected.*

**B** *A mask is hiding all but the two flowers on an image layer, which is stacked above a solid white Background.*

**C** *We reduced the Density of the mask to 77%, to allow it to partially reveal the surrounding layer pixels.*

**A** *We increased the Feather value of the mask to 96 px, to make the transition between the masked and unmasked areas more gradual.*

## USING THE MASKS PANEL TO DRAW ATTENTION TO PART OF AN IMAGE

**B** *The original hard-edged mask is hiding everything but the car on an image layer, which is stacked above a solid white Background.*

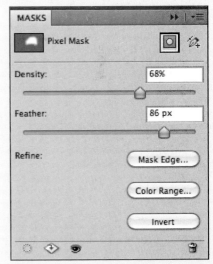

**C** *We reduced the Density value and increased the Feather value for the layer mask to make the transition between the masked and unmasked areas more gradual. The car is still the star of the show, but the soft imagery around it provides a complementary setting.*

# Working with layer masks

By default, a layer and its layer mask are linked and, when moved, travel as a unit. If you want to move either component separately, you have to unlink them first.

## To move the layer content or mask independently:

1. On the Layers panel, click the **Link** icon 🔗 between the layer and layer mask thumbnails. **A–B** The icon disappears.

2. Click either the layer thumbnail or the layer mask thumbnail, depending on which one you want to move.

3. Choose the **Move** tool ▶⊕ (or hold down V to spring-load the tool), then drag in the document window. **C**

4. Click between the layer and layer mask thumbnails to make the link icon reappear.

## To duplicate a layer mask or move it to another layer:

Do either of the following:

To move a mask, drag its thumbnail to another layer (you can't move it to the Background).

To duplicate a mask, Alt-drag/Option-drag its thumbnail to another layer.

When you load a mask as a selection, it displays in the document as a marquee of "marching ants."

## To load a mask as a selection:

1. Do either of the following:

On the Layers panel, Ctrl-click/Cmd-click a layer mask thumbnail.

On the Layers panel, click a layer mask thumbnail, then on the Masks panel, click the **Load Selection from Mask** button. 🔲

**A** *A layer mask is hiding the center of the tile layer and revealing part of the underlying Background image.*

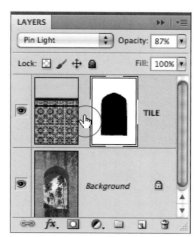

**B** *We clicked the Link icon to disengage the layer image from the mask, and also clicked the layer mask thumbnail.*

**C** *With the Move tool, we dragged the mask in the document window to reveal a different part of the Background. (If you want to move the layer imagery instead, click the layer thumbnail before dragging.)*

## To deactivate a layer mask temporarily:

Do either of the following:

On the Layers panel, Shift-click the layer mask thumbnail **A** (the thumbnail won't become selected).

On the Layers panel, click a layer mask thumbnail, then at the bottom of the Masks panel, click the **Disable/Enable Mask** button. ⬭ **B**

A red X appears over the thumbnail on both the Layers and Masks panels, and the entire layer is now visible. To reactivate the mask at any time, repeat either method above.

One disadvantage of using layer masks is that they occupy some storage space (albeit a small amount), so when you're done using them, consider applying those whose effects you're pleased with to make them permanent and deleting those you don't need. When you apply or delete a mask, its thumbnail disappears from the Layers panel.

Note: Before applying or deleting any masks — a permanent change — use the File > Save As command to copy the file, and preserve the original file that contains the layer masks for future editing.

## To apply or delete a layer mask:

Do either of the following:

On the Layers panel, click a layer mask thumbnail, then on the Masks panel, click the **Apply Mask** button ⬭ to apply the mask or the **Delete Mask** button 🗑 to delete it.

On the Layers panel, right-click a layer mask thumbnail and choose **Apply Layer Mask** or **Delete Layer Mask**.

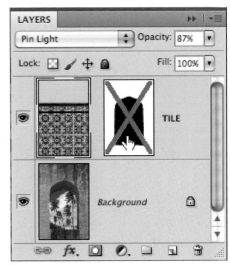

**A** *To deactivate or activate a layer mask via the Layers panel, Shift-click the layer mask thumbnail. A red X appears in the thumbnail.*

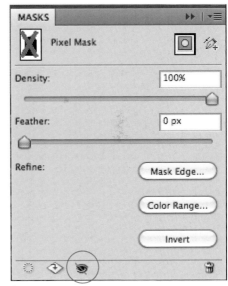

**B** *To deactivate or activate a layer mask via the Masks panel, click the layer mask thumbnail on the Layers panel, then click the Disable/Enable Mask button on the Masks panel.*

---

**SOME MASK TOPICS IN OTHER CHAPTERS**

➤ "Editing the adjustment layer mask" on page 202

➤ "Fading the edge of a layer via a gradient in a layer mask" on pages 244–246

➤ "Working with the Smart Filter mask" on page 322

➤ "To use type shapes as a layer mask" on page 349

## Comparing the selection methods

Now that you're acquainted with most of the selection methods in Photoshop, you can use the following summary to shop and compare.

| SELECTION METHOD | WHAT IT'S BEST FOR SELECTING |
|---|---|
| Rectangular and Elliptical Marquee tools | Rectangular and round shapes; you can specify a width-to-height ratio or dimensions (page 148) |
| Lasso tool | Irregular areas; very useful for cleaning up selections created with other tools or commands (page 149) |
| Polygonal Lasso tool | Straight-edged shapes (page 149) |
| Quick Mask mode | Paint a mask onto a document in Quick Mask mode (and remove areas of the mask where necessary); it converts to a selection automatically when the document is returned to Standard mode (pages 166–167) |
| Magnetic Lasso tool | Objects or figures that are clearly delineated from their background in tonality or color (see Photoshop Help) |
| Quick Selection tool | Well-defined shapes, including irregular areas; creates selections by detecting color boundaries (pages 152–153) |
| Magic Wand tool | Color areas based on a Tolerance range; good for selecting a background area, such as sky or water; use the Lasso or Quick Selection tool afterward to add areas or remove stray areas from the selection (pages 154–155) |
| Color Range command | Discrete color areas; via a dialog, lets you select all occurrences of one color or a specific tonal range (pages 156–157) |

| MODIFY SELECTIONS | HOW IT WORKS |
|---|---|
| Add or subtract with a selection tool | Shift to add; Alt/Option to remove; Alt-Shift/Option-Shift to select the intersection of the existing and new selections |
| Refine Edge command | Refine the smoothness, sharpness, or precision of a selection edge; preview the selection on different backgrounds (pages 161–165) |
| Grow and Similar commands | Enlarge a selection based on the current Tolerance setting of the Magic Wand tool; the Similar command selects noncontiguous, similar areas |
| Convert a selection to a path | Convert a selection to a path, reshape it by manipulating its anchor points, then convert it back to a selection; or to create a smooth, precise path, trace a shape with the Pen tool, then convert it to a selection |

| PRESERVE SELECTIONS | METHOD |
|---|---|
| Save a selection as a layer mask; refine the mask; load the mask as a selection | Save a selection as a layer mask (page 168); refine a selection before saving it as a layer mask via the New Layer with Layer Mask option in the Refine Edge dialog (page 161); change the mask density or feather value using the Masks panel (page 170); refine the mask edges using the Refine Mask dialog (page 170); load a layer mask as a selection (page 172) |
| Save a selection as an alpha channel | Save a selection as an alpha channel to the Channels panel (page 160) |

Using the History panel, you can selectively undo or restore previous stages (called "states") of the current work session. In this chapter, you will choose default settings for the History panel; restore, delete, and clear history states; preserve states by using snapshots; create a new document from a state or snapshot; and restore areas of an image to a prior state by using the History Brush tool or by filling a selection or layer with a history state.

## Choosing History panel options

The History panel displays a list of states (edits) that you have made to the currently open document. The most recent state is listed at the bottom. When you click a prior state, the document is restored to that stage of the editing process. What happens to the panel when you do this depends on whether it's in linear or nonlinear mode, **A** so you need to learn how the two modes differ.

*Continued on the following page*

HISTORY

10

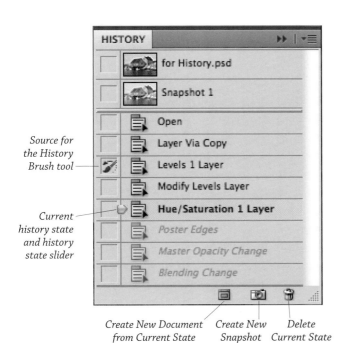

*Source for the History Brush tool*

*Current history state and history state slider*

*Create New Document from Current State*    *Create New Snapshot*    *Delete Current State*

**A** *This History panel is in linear mode. When we clicked an earlier state, the subsequent states became dimmed.*

## Choosing a mode for the History panel

To choose a mode for the panel, choose History Options from the panel menu, then in the History Options dialog, check or uncheck **Allow Non-Linear History**. We recommend keeping the History panel in **linear mode** (unchecking the Allow Non-Linear History option), especially if you're new to Photoshop.**A** With the panel in this mode, if you click an earlier state and resume image editing from that state or delete it, all the subsequent (dimmed) states are discarded. This way, the document can be restored to an earlier state with a nice, clean break.

In **nonlinear mode**, if you click on or delete an earlier state, subsequent states aren't deleted or dimmed. If you resume image editing when an earlier state is selected, your next edit will show up as the latest state on the panel, and all the states in between will be preserved. That is, the latest state will incorporate the earlier stage of the image plus your newest edit. If you change your mind, you can click any in-between state whenever you like and resume editing from there.**B** Nonlinear is the more flexible of the two modes, but it can be confusing or disorienting.

## Choosing other options for the History panel

The last option in the History Options dialog, **Make Layer Visibility Changes Undoable**, controls whether clicking the visibility icon on the Layers panel is listed as a state on the History panel. We prefer to keep this option off. (For other options in this dialog, see page 179.)

To specify the number of states that can be listed on the panel at a time, go to Edit/Photoshop > Preferences (Ctrl-K/Cmd-K) > Performance and, under History & Cache, enter a **History States** value (the default value is 20). If the maximum number of history states is exceeded during an editing session, the oldest steps are removed to make room for new ones. The maximum number of states may be limited by various factors, including the image size, the kind of edits made to the image, and currently available system memory. Each open document has its own list of states. Note: Regardless of the preference setting, when you close a document, all history states (and all snapshots) are deleted from the panel!

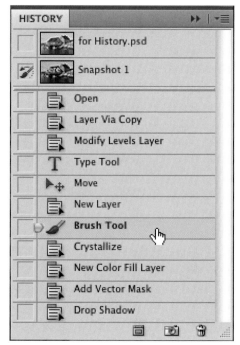

**A** *In the History Options dialog, uncheck Allow Non-Linear History for linear mode, or check it for nonlinear mode.*

**B** *This History panel is in nonlinear mode. When we clicked an earlier state, all the states remained available, even those listed below the one we clicked.*

## Changing history states

To summarize the two modes for the History panel, if the panel is in linear mode (the Allow Non-Linear History option is off) and you click an earlier state, all the states below the one you click will become dimmed. If you then delete the state you clicked or continue editing the image with that earlier state still selected, all the dimmed states are deleted. (If you change your mind, you can choose Undo immediately to restore the deleted states.) If the panel is in nonlinear mode and you click an earlier state, then perform another edit, the new edit will become the latest state, but the prior states won't be deleted.

### To change history states:

1. Perform some edits on an image.

2. Do any of the following:

   Click a **state** on the History panel. **A**

   On the left side of the panel, drag the **History State** slider upward or downward to the desired state.

   To **Step Forward** one state, press Ctrl-Shift-Z/Cmd-Shift-Z; or to **Step Backward** one state, press Ctrl-Alt-Z/Cmd-Option-Z.

➤ When you choose File > Revert, it becomes a state on the History panel, and like other states, all the states preceding it are preserved. You can restore the image to a state prior to or after the Revert state.

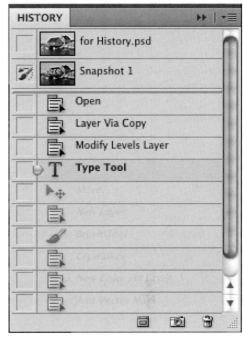

**A** *This is after we clicked a prior state, with the History panel in linear mode.*

# Deleting and clearing history states

We will presume you followed our advice and put your History panel in linear mode (you unchecked the Allow Non-Linear History option). With the panel in linear mode, if you delete a state and then resume editing your document, that state and all the subsequent ones will be discarded from the panel.

## To delete a history state:

Do one of the following:

Right-click a state on the History panel, choose **Delete** from the context menu, **A** then click Yes in the alert dialog. **B**

To bypass the alert, drag the state to be deleted over the **Delete Current State** button 🗑 on the History panel.

To delete previous states sequentially without an alert appearing, click a state, then Alt-click/ Option-click the **Delete Current State** button as many times as needed.

Note: The Undo command will restore only the last deleted state.

## To clear the History panel:

To clear all states (but not snapshots) from your History panel for all the currently open documents to free up memory, choose Edit > Purge > **Histories**, then click OK in the alert dialog. This command cannot be undone!

To clear all states (but not snapshots) from the History panel for just the current document, right-click any state and choose **Clear History**. This command doesn't free up memory for Photoshop, but it can be undone.

**A** *Right-click a state and choose Delete from the context menu, then click Yes in the alert dialog.*

**B** *Because our History panel was in linear mode (Allow Non-Linear History was unchecked) when we deleted a state, all subsequent states were also deleted.*

# Using snapshots

States are deleted from the History panel if any of the following occur: the specified maximum number of history states is exceeded; you clear or purge the panel; or the panel is in linear mode, you click an earlier state, and then resume editing the document. A snapshot, which is created from a history state, remains on the panel even if any of the above occur. When you click a snapshot, the document is restored to the state it represents. Both snapshots and history states are deleted when you close your document.

In these instructions, you'll choose snapshot options, which affect all Photoshop files; on the next page, you'll learn how to create snapshots for a specific document.

## To choose snapshot options:

1. Choose **History Options** from the History panel menu. The History Options dialog opens.**A**

2. Check or uncheck any of the following options that pertain to snapshots:

   **Automatically Create First Snapshot** to have Photoshop create a snapshot every time a file is opened (this option is checked by default and we keep it on).

   **Automatically Create New Snapshot When Saving** to have Photoshop create a snapshot every time a file is saved. The snapshot will be named by the time of day it was created.

   **Show New Snapshot Dialog by Default** to have the New Snapshot dialog appear whenever you click the New Snapshot button, enabling you to choose options.

3. Click OK.

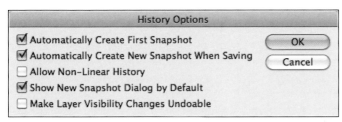

**A** *The History Options dialog contains three snapshot options.*

If the Automatically Create New Snapshot When Saving option is turned off for your History panel, you should get in the habit of creating snapshots periodically as you work and before running any actions on your document. If you use the New Snapshot dialog (the second method below), you'll be able to choose whether the snapshot is made from all the layers in the document, from all the layers at a particular state, or from just the current layer.

## To create a snapshot of a state:

### Method 1 (without choosing options)

1. Edit your document so it contains the changes that you want to capture as a snapshot.

2. If the Show New Snapshot Dialog by Default option is off in the History Options dialog, click the **New Snapshot** button. If that option is on, Alt-click/Option-click the New Snapshot button. A new snapshot thumbnail appears below the last one, in the upper section of the panel.

### Method 2 (choosing options)

1. On the History panel, right-click the state that you want to create a snapshot of and choose **New Snapshot.** The layer associated with that history state becomes selected and the New Snapshot dialog opens.

2. Type a **Name** for the snapshot.

3. Choose an option from the **From** menu:

   **Full Document** to include in the snapshot all the layers the document contained at the chosen state.

   **Merged Layers** to merge into the Background all the layers that were visible at the chosen state.

   **Current Layer** to create a snapshot of the layer that became selected when you right-clicked a history state.

4. Click OK.

➤ To rename a snapshot, double-click the existing name.

**A** *Right-click a state and choose New Snapshot from the context menu.*

**B** *In the New Snapshot dialog, enter a name and choose which part of the image you want the snapshot to be created from.*

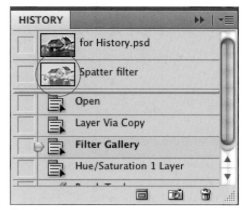

**C** *A thumbnail for the new snapshot appears on the History panel.*

Having snapshots on your History panel not only adds flexibility to your workflow by letting you keep document stages in reserve — it can save the day if, say, a state that you were hoping to revert a document to becomes deleted from the History panel.

### To make a snapshot become the current state:

Do either of the following:

Click a snapshot name or thumbnail. If the History panel is in linear mode (as we recommend), the document will revert to the snapshot stage of editing, and all the states will be dimmed. If you now resume editing, all the dimmed states will be deleted.

Alt-click/Option-click a snapshot name or thumbnail to keep earlier states available and have that snapshot become the latest state. Use this approach if you need to preserve access to prior edits.

➤ To delete a snapshot, drag it to the Delete Current State button. Remember that all snapshots disappear from the panel when a document is closed anyway.

## Creating documents from states

By using the New Document command, you can spin off versions of your current document (and the state of the Layers panel) from any state or snapshot.

### To create a new document from a history state or snapshot:

Do either of the following:

Right-click a snapshot or a state, then choose **New Document** from the context menu.**A**

Click a snapshot or a state, then click the **New Document from Current State** button.

A new document appears onscreen, bearing the title of the snapshot or state from which it was created. The starting state for the new document will be named "Duplicate State." **B** Save the new document.

**A** *Right-click a snapshot or state and choose New Document.*

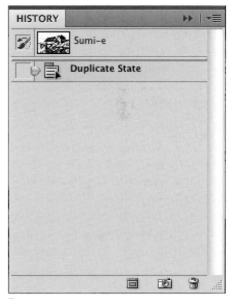

**B** *This is the History panel for the new document.*

## Using the History Brush tool

When you apply strokes to a document with the History Brush tool, pixels below the pointer are restored from whichever state or snapshot you have designated as the history source.

Note: The History Brush tool can't be used if certain kinds of edits were made after the document was opened, such as cropping, changing the document color mode or canvas size, or adding or deleting layers. Furthermore, the tool can't restore deleted or modified layer effects, vector data (type or shapes), pixels from a deleted layer, or the effects of an adjustment layer. Moral: Keep the layers in your document for as long as possible!

**To use the History Brush tool:**

1. Open an image, and make some edits. (For the image shown at right, we duplicated an image layer via Ctrl-J/Cmd-J, renamed the duplicate, and applied a filter to it.) **A–C**

2. Choose the **History Brush** tool 🖌 (Y or Shift-Y).

3. On the Options bar:

   Click the Brush Preset picker arrowhead, then click a brush on the picker.

   Choose a blending Mode, Opacity percentage, and Flow percentage.

4. On the History panel, click in the leftmost column for a state or for a snapshot that was created with the Full Document option, to designate it as the source for the History Brush tool. The history source icon 🖌 moves to that slot. **D**

5. On the Layers panel, click the layer that you want to restore pixels to, and make sure the Lock Transparent Pixels button ⊠ is deactivated.

**A** *This is the original image.*

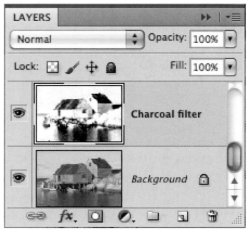

**B** *We duplicated the image layer, then applied the Charcoal filter to the duplicate layer.*

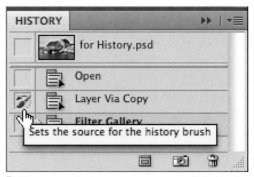

**D** *Next, to set the history source icon, we clicked in the leftmost column for a state prior to "Filter Gallery," but after the layer addition (in this case, at a state called "Layer Via Copy").*

**C** *This is how the image looks after we applied the Charcoal filter to a duplicate image layer.*

**6.** Apply strokes to the image. Pixel data from the prior state of that layer will replace the current data where you apply strokes.**A–C**

➤ Say you apply some brush strokes to a layer (and your History panel is in linear mode), then decide a few editing steps later that you want to remove them. If you click the state above the one labeled "Brush Tool" and then resume editing, the states that you want to keep will be deleted from the panel. Instead, set the source for the History Brush tool to the state above "Brush Tool," click the layer on the Layers panel that you applied the brush strokes to, then with the History Brush tool, paint out the strokes from the document. (This will make more sense when you actually do it.)

**A** *On the duplicate layer that we applied the filter to, we applied strokes with the History Brush tool (the tool Opacity was 55%, and we used a big, scratchy-looking Spatter brush).*

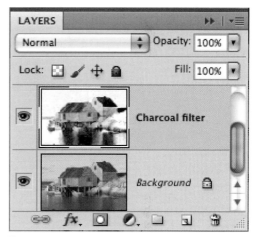

**B** *In the Layers panel for the final image (which is shown below), you can see that we restored the original color to some areas of the duplicate layer.*

**C** *Some of the original color is visible in this final image.*

# Filling an area with a history state or snapshot

The Fill command, when used with the History option, fills a layer or selection with pixels from a designated history state or snapshot. Our Note on page 182 also applies to this command.

## To fill a selection or layer with a history state or snapshot:

1. Edit your document, and click an image layer. **A**

2. *Optional:* Create a selection. You can either leave the selection edges sharp or use the Refine Edge dialog to feather them. **B**

3. On the History panel, click in the leftmost column for the state or snapshot to be used as the fill data. The history source icon will appear where you click.

4. Choose Edit > **Fill** (Shift-Backspace/Shift-Delete).

5. In the Fill dialog, do the following:

   Choose **Use**: **History**. **C**

   Choose a **Blending Mode** and an **Opacity** percentage.

   Check **Preserve Transparency** to replace only existing pixels, or leave it unchecked to allow pixels to appear anywhere on the current layer. This option is available only if the current layer contains transparent pixels.

   Click OK. **D**

**A** *This is the original image.*

**B** *We applied the Conté Crayon filter to a duplicate image layer, selected the bottom part of that layer, then feathered the selection via the Refine Edge command.*

**C** *In the Fill dialog, we chose Use: History.*

**D** *The selection filled with the unedited imagery at an Opacity of 75%.*

In the first part of this chapter, you'll learn how to choose the colors that are applied with various tools and commands. The second part of this chapter is a reference guide to the blending modes, which are available for tools, layers, and commands. In other chapters, you'll learn how colors are actually applied.

## Choosing colors

The current Foreground color is applied by some tools, such as the Brush, Pencil, and Mixer Brush. It is also applied when you create type, and by some commands, such as Canvas Size. The current Background color is applied by other procedures, such as when you apply a transform command to, or move a selection on, the Background. One or both of these colors are also used by some of the Photoshop filters.

These two colors are displayed in the Foreground and Background color squares on the Tools panel **A** and on the Color panel.**B** (Written with an uppercase "F" or "B," these terms refer to the two colors, not to the foreground or background areas of a picture.) On the following pages, you will choose Foreground and Background colors via these methods:

➤ Use the controls in the **Color Picker** dialog or in the onscreen color picker.

➤ Choose a premixed color from a matching system via the **Color Libraries** dialog.

➤ Use the controls on the **Color** panel.

➤ Click a swatch on the **Swatches** panel.

➤ Pluck a color from an image with the **Eyedropper** tool.

**COLORS & BLENDING MODES**

# 11

*The Default Foreground and Background Colors button (D) makes the Foreground color black and the Background color white.*

*The Switch Colors button (X) swaps the current Foreground and Background colors.*

*The currently selected square has a black border.*

*Foreground color square*

*Background color square*

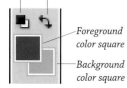

*Foreground color square*

*Background color square*

**A** *These color controls are on the Tools panel.*

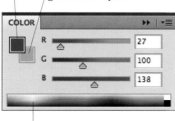

*Color ramp*

**B** *Use the Color panel to mix colors.*

# Using the Color Picker

## To choose a color using the Color Picker:

**1.** Do either of the following:

On the Tools panel, click the Foreground or Background color square.

On the Color panel, click the Foreground or Background color square if it's already selected (has a black border), or double-click the square if it's not yet selected.

Note: If the square you click contains a custom color from a matching system, the Color Libraries dialog will open instead of the picker. Click the **Picker** button to get to the Color Picker dialog.

**2.** Do one of the following:

Click a color on the vertical color slider or drag the slider to choose a **hue**, then click a brightness and saturation value of that hue in the large square.**A** (You can also click or drag in the document while the Color Picker dialog is open.)

To mix a process color for print output, enter **C**, **M**, **Y**, and **K** percentages for that color from a printed fan deck for a color matching system (you can use the scrubby sliders).

For onscreen output, enter **R**, **G**, and **B** values (0 to 255).

In the # field, enter the number for a hexadecimal color.

**3.** Click OK. The color will appear in the Foreground or Background color square on the Tools and Color panels. To preserve the color by adding it to the Swatches panel, see page 189.

➤ To change the color picker interface, go to Edit/Photoshop > Preferences (Ctrl-K/Cmd-K) > General, then from the Color Picker menu, choose either Windows/Apple (the picker for your system) or Adobe (the default Photoshop picker).

➤ You can also enter numbers in the H, S, and B or L, a, and b fields in the Color Picker. For an explanation of HSB, see the sidebar on page 188.

➤ Because modern computer video systems display millions of colors, you don't need to restrict yourself to Web-safe colors for Web graphics. Ignore the non-Web-safe icon 🔲 if it appears in the Color Picker, and keep Only Web Colors unchecked. To learn about the out-of-gamut icon,⚠ which also may display on the Color Picker, see the last tip on page 188.

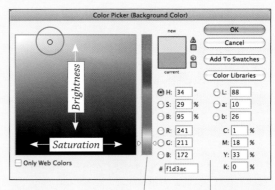

*A Click a hue on the color slider or drag the slider, then click a color in the large square...*

*...or enter percentages in the fields for one of the color models.*

## USING THE HUD COLOR PICKER ★

➤ To access color picker controls quickly without opening that dialog, choose a tool that uses colors, Alt-Shift-right-click/Cmd-Option-Control-click in the image to display the picker, drag to choose a hue from the hue bar or wheel, then drag to choose a brightness and saturation value in the large square. If you want to change the hue without changing the current brightness and saturation values, when the picker displays, release the keys but keep the mouse button down, hold down the Spacebar and drag to the hue bar or wheel, release the Spacebar, then drag to the desired hue (practice, practice).

➤ The default interface for the HUD color picker is Hue Strip (shown below). From the HUD Color Picker menu in Edit/Photoshop > Preferences > General, you can choose a different wheel or strip design and size.

# Choosing colors from a library

To help you pick colors from the many libraries and color matching systems that are accessible in Photoshop, such as PANTONE and FOCOLTONE, you can purchase and refer to a printed fan guide from a third-party supplier. For Web publishing or small-scale desktop printing, you don't need to do this, but it is imperative that you do so for commercial printing. If you pick colors willy-nilly based on whether they look appealing onscreen, you may be in for a surprise when you see the printed result, because even when carefully calibrated, a display can only simulate CMYK colors.

Before choosing specific colors in Photoshop for print output, the first step is to ask your commercial printer which brand of ink they're planning to use. Get the printed fan guide for that system, and flip through it to decide which colors you're going to use. To access those colors in Photoshop, use the Color Libraries dialog, as described below.

## To choose a color from a library:

1. Do either of the following:

   On the Tools panel, click the Foreground or Background color square.

   On the Color panel, click the Foreground or Background color square if it's already selected (has a black border), or double-click the square if it's not yet selected.

2. If the color square you clicked isn't a custom color, the Color Picker dialog will open. Click **Color Libraries** to get to the Color Libraries dialog.

3. From the **Book** menu, choose the matching system that your commercial printer has recommended you use.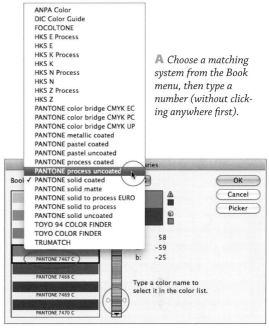A

4. Do either of the following:

   Without clicking anywhere, type the number that is assigned to the desired color (refer to your fan guide); that swatch will become selected.

   Click a color on the vertical color slider, then click the desired swatch on the left side of the dialog.**B**

5. Click OK. To add the color to the Swatches panel, see page 189.

   ➤ To load a library of matching system colors onto the Swatches panel, see the second task on page 190.

*A Choose a matching system from the Book menu, then type a number (without clicking anywhere first).*

*B Another option is to click a color on the vertical color slider, then click a swatch on the scroll list.*

---

**COLOR LIBRARIES FOR PRINT OUTPUT**

➤ ANPA colors are used in the newspaper industry.

➤ DIC Color Guide and TOYO Color Finder colors are used in Japan.

➤ FOCOLTONE is a process color system that was developed to help prevent registration problems. It can be used in North America.

➤ HKS process colors and HKS spot colors (without "Process" in the name) are used primarily in Europe.

➤ PANTONE process colors and PANTONE spot colors (without "Process" in the name) are widely used in North America.

➤ TRUMATCH is a process color system, organized in a different way from PANTONE. It is used worldwide.

**SPOT OR PROCESS?**

By default, when color-separating an image for printing, Photoshop separates all colors — both process and spot — into the C, M, Y, and K process colors. If you want to output a spot color to a separate plate from Photoshop, you have to create a separate spot color channel for it (see page 352).

# Using the Color panel

For Web output, another option is to mix RGB or HSB colors directly on the Color panel by using the color ramp, sliders, or fields.

## To choose an RGB or HSB color using the Color panel:

1. Click the Foreground or Background color square on the Color panel, ■ if the desired square isn't already selected. A

2. From the top of the Color panel menu, choose a color model for the sliders. B For Web output, choose RGB Sliders or HSB Sliders (hue, saturation, and brightness). For output to an inkjet printer, choose RGB Sliders.

3. Do any of the following: C

   Move any of the sliders.

   Click on or drag in the color ramp.

   Enter values in the fields.

4. *Optional:* To add the new color to the Swatches panel, see the instructions on the next page.

➤ To choose a different style for the color ramp, right-click the color ramp.

➤ Alt-click/Option-click the color ramp to choose a color for whichever color square (Foreground or Background) isn't currently selected.

➤ If Dynamic Color Sliders is checked in Preferences (Ctrl-K/Cmd-K) > General, colors in the bars above the sliders will update interactively as you mix or choose a color.

➤ An out-of-gamut alert icon ⚠ on the Color Picker or Color panel indicates that the current color isn't printable (has no ink equivalent). If you click the icon, Photoshop will substitute the closest printable color, as shown in the swatch next to or below the icon. Note that when your image is converted to CMYK mode or printed on an inkjet device, all the image colors are brought into the printable gamut anyway, so you really don't have to worry about converting any colors individually. The out-of-gamut range is defined by the CMYK output profile, which is chosen via the Working Spaces: CMYK menu in Edit > Color Settings. Similarly, if the color currently under the pointer is outside the printable gamut, exclamation points will display on the Info panel.

A *Click the Foreground or Background color square.*

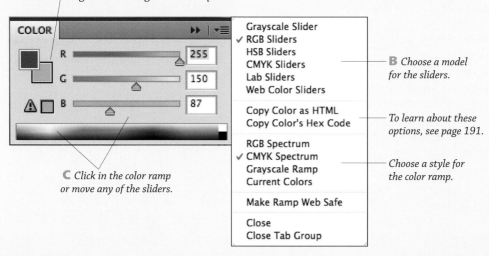

B *Choose a model for the sliders.*

*To learn about these options, see page 191.*

*Choose a style for the color ramp.*

C *Click in the color ramp or move any of the sliders.*

# Using the Swatches panel

Note: For easy access, detach the Swatches panel from the Color panel group by dragging its tab.

## To choose a color from the Swatches panel:

1. Display the Swatches panel.
2. Do either of the following:

   To choose a Foreground or Background color if that color square is selected on the Tools and Color panels, click a swatch.

   To choose a Foreground or Background color if that color square isn't selected on the Tools and Color panels, Ctrl-click/Cmd-click a swatch.

➤ To access other libraries of swatches, see "To replace or append a library of swatches" on the next page.

➤ To access a wide assortment of process color swatches, use the Kuler panel. See page 115.

Colors that you add to the Swatches panel will remain there until the swatches are deleted, replaced, or reset, and are available for use in all documents. (To save swatches as a permanent library, see "To save the current swatches as a library" on the next page.)

## To add a color to the Swatches panel:

1. Mix or choose a Foreground color by using the Color panel or the Color Picker.
2. On the Swatches panel, do either of the following:

   Click the blank area below the swatches on the panel (paint bucket pointer), **A–B** or right-click any existing swatch and choose **New Swatch**. Name the swatch in the dialog, then click OK.

   To create a new swatch without assigning it a name, click the **New Swatch of Foreground Color** button at the bottom of the Swatches panel.

   Regardless of the method used, the new swatch will be displayed (or listed) last on the panel.

➤ To rename a swatch, double-click it, change the name, then click OK. To learn a swatch name, either use the tool tip or choose Small List or Large List from the panel menu.

## To delete a color from the Swatches panel:

Alt-click/Option-click the swatch to be deleted (scissors pointer); or right-click a swatch and choose **Delete Swatch**, then click OK. **C** You can't undo the deletion of a swatch.

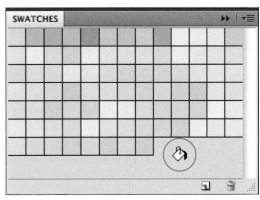

**A** *To add a color to the Swatches panel, click the blank area below the swatches.*

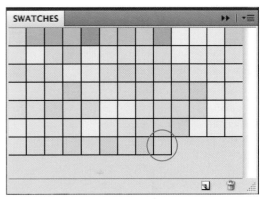

**B** *The new swatch appears on the panel.*

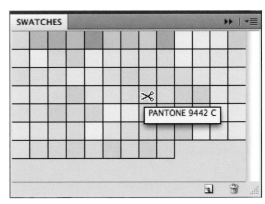

**C** *Alt-click/Option-click a swatch to delete it.*

If you save the current swatches as a permanent library, you'll be able to load that library onto the Swatches panel at any time for use in any document.

## To save the current swatches as a library:

1. Make sure all the colors you want to save in the new library are on the Swatches panel, ▦ then choose **Save Swatches** from the panel menu.

2. In the **File Name/Save As** field, enter a name for the library (keep the .aco extension and the default location), then click Save.

➤ In the Mac OS, the default location for storing swatches is Users/[user name]/Library/Application Support/Adobe/Adobe Photoshop CS5/Presets/Color Swatches.

➤ To replace an existing user-created library, after following step 1 above, click the existing library in the scroll window, click Save, then click Replace in the alert dialog.

➤ If the library you want to load isn't in the default location, from the Swatches panel menu, choose Load Swatches. Locate and click the desired library, then click Load.

You can load any user-created library or any of the preset swatch libraries that ship with Photoshop into the Swatches panel. You can either replace the existing swatches with the new ones or add the additional swatches to the existing ones on the panel.

## To replace or append a library of swatches:

1. From the lower portion of the Swatches panel menu, choose the desired library name.

2. Do either of the following:

   Click Append to add the new library of swatches to the current ones.

   Click OK to replace the current swatches with the new ones. A prompt may appear, giving you the option to save the existing swatches on the panel as a library. **A**

➤ If you want to use your current swatches in another Creative Suite application, save them via the Save Swatches for Exchange command on the Swatches panel menu.

➤ If you do interior design work, you may already know that some paint companies let you download swatches from their website (such

as on benjaminmoore.com, under Select an Option > Architects and Designers > Color Direction, click Download Color Palettes). Install the files in the default location for storing swatches (Macintosh users, see the first tip at left), relaunch Photoshop, then load them from the Swatches panel menu.

➤ The Paint Color Swatches library is new. ★

## To restore the default swatches:

Choose **Reset Swatches** from the Swatches panel menu, then click OK. A prompt may appear, offering you the option to save the existing swatches as a library.

**A** *This prompt will appear in the Mac OS if the Swatches panel contains unsaved swatches and you try to replace them. (In Windows, the buttons are Yes, No, and Cancel.)*

---

### DESIGNING FOR THE COLOR-BLIND

At some point in your career, you may be hired to design graphics, such as signage, that are fully accessible to color-blind viewers. In fact, some countries require graphics in public spaces to comply with the Color Universal Design (CUD) guidelines. The View > Proof Setup > Color Blindness – Protanopia-Type and Color Blindness – Deuteranopia-Type commands in Photoshop simulate how your document will look to viewers with common forms of color blindness.

In case you're not familiar with those two terms, for a protanope, the brightness of red, orange, and yellow is dimmed, making it hard for such a person to distinguish red from black or dark gray. Protanopes also have trouble distinguishing violet, lavender, and purple from blue because the reddish components of those colors look dimmed. Deuteranopes are unable to distinguish between colors in the green-yellow-red part of the spectrum and experience color blindness similar to that of protanopes, without the problem of dimming. For color and design suggestions, search for "Soft-proof for color blindness" in Photoshop Help.

## Using the Eyedropper tool

**To sample a color from an image using the Eyedropper:**

1. Choose the **Eyedropper** tool ✎ (or hold down I to spring-load the tool).

2. On the Options bar, do the following:

   Choose a **Sample Size** (see the sidebar on this page).

   Choose **Sample: Current Layer** (then click a layer) or choose **All Layers**.

   *Optional:* Check Show Sampling Ring. ★

3. When you do either of the following, the sampled color will appear in the currently active square on the Tools and Color panels. If Show Sampling Ring is checked, the sampled color will also preview on the top part of a large ring and the current Foreground or Background color will preview on the bottom part.

   **Click** a color in any open document. **A**

   **Drag** in any document (the current color square changes dynamically), and release the mouse when the pointer is over the desired color.

➤ Alt-click/Option-click or drag in the document window with the Eyedropper tool to choose a Background color when the Foreground color square is selected, or vice versa.

## Copying colors as hexadecimals

For Web output, you can copy colors as hexadecimal values from a file in Photoshop and then paste them into an HTML file.

**To copy a color as a hexadecimal value:**

1. To copy a color to the Clipboard as a hexadecimal value, do either of the following:

   Choose the **Eyedropper** tool ✎ (I or Shift-I) and choose Options bar settings for the tool. Right-click a color in the document window, then choose **Copy Color as HTML** (HTML color tag) or **Copy Color's Hex Code** ★ (HEX number).

   Choose a Foreground color via the Color panel, Color Picker, or Swatches panel. From the Color panel menu, choose **Copy Color as HTML** or **Copy Color's Hex Code.** ★

2. To paste the color into an HTML file, display the HTML file in your HTML-editing application, then choose Edit > Paste (Ctrl-V/Cmd-V).

**A** *We checked Show Sampling Ring for the Eyedropper tool on the Options bar, then clicked a color in the image.*

---

**CHOOSING A SAMPLE SIZE**

➤ To change the size of the area from which the Eyedropper tool samples, on the Options bar, choose Sample Size: Point Sample (to sample the exact pixel you'll click on) or one of the Average options (e.g., to sample an average value from a 5-by-5-pixel square area).

➤ You can also right-click in the document with the Eyedropper tool and choose a sample size from the context menu.

➤ The 3 by 3 Average and 5 by 5 Average options are useful for sampling continuous tones, such as skin tones in a portrait photo or the background area in a landscape (we usually use 3 by 3 Average). The 11 by 11 Average through 101 by 101 Average options are suitable for very high-resolution files.

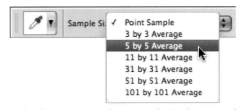

*We're choosing a Sample Size for the Eyedropper tool from the Options bar.*

# Choosing a blending mode

The blending mode **A** that you choose for a tool or layer affects how that tool or layer interacts with underlying pixels. You can choose from a menu of blending modes in many locations in Photoshop, such as the Options bar (for most painting and editing tools), the Layers panel, and the Layer Style and Fill dialogs.

In the text that accompanies the figures in this section, the colors of existing underlying pixels are called the **base** colors; the color in the upper layer or that you apply with a tool (such as the Brush), and that you choose a mode for, is called the **blend** color. In all the images, we used the same three color squares, as shown in the first figure below (Normal mode). To avoid confusion, we kept the blend layer opacity at 100% (except for Dissolve mode).

➤ For most blending modes, Photoshop compares the colors of the two layers (or the layer and the paint color being applied by a tool) on a channel-by-channel basis. For example, the lightness of a pixel in the Red channel of the blend layer is compared to the lightness of a corresponding pixel in the Red channel of the base layer.

➤ When choosing an Opacity percentage for a tool (via the Options bar), keep in mind that the impact of the tool is also affected by the opacity of the layer that strokes are applied to. For example, strokes applied with a Brush tool of 50% opacity on a layer opacity of 50% will appear lighter than the same strokes applied to a layer that has an opacity of 100%.

**CYCLING THROUGH THE MODES**

To cycle through the blending modes for the current painting or editing tool, or for the currently selected layer if a nonediting tool (such as the Move tool or a selection tool) is being used, press Shift - + (plus) or Shift - – (minus).

| | |
|---|---|
| ✓ Normal | |
| Dissolve | *Basic* |
| Darken | |
| Multiply | |
| Color Burn | *Darken* |
| Linear Burn | |
| Darker Color | |
| Lighten | |
| Screen | |
| Color Dodge | *Lighten* |
| Linear Dodge (Add) | |
| Lighter Color | |
| Overlay | |
| Soft Light | |
| Hard Light | |
| Vivid Light | *Contrast* |
| Linear Light | |
| Pin Light | |
| Hard Mix | |
| Difference | |
| Exclusion | |
| Subtract | *Comparative* |
| Divide | |
| Hue | |
| Saturation | |
| Color | *Component* |
| Luminosity | |

**A** *The blending modes are grouped according to their function and effect.*

## THE BASIC BLENDING MODES REPLACE THE BASE COLORS

**Normal**
All the base colors are modified. (When an image is in Bitmap or Indexed Color mode, this mode is called Threshold.)

**Dissolve (50% Opacity)**
Creates a chalky, dry-brush texture using the blend color. The higher the pressure or opacity of the tool (and the higher the opacity of the layer), the more solid the color.

## THE DARKEN BLENDING MODES DARKEN THE BASE COLORS

**Darken**
The blend color tints the base color.

**Multiply**
A dark blend color produces darker base colors; a light blend color merely tints the base colors. Good for creating semitransparent shadows.

**Color Burn**
Increases contrast in the base color by darkening the shadow areas and lightening the highlight areas.

**Linear Burn**
Uses the blend color to darken the base colors by decreasing brightness.

**Darker Color**
The blend color replaces base colors lighter than itself without affecting darker base colors. The blend color is fully opaque. Could be used to "paint out" light colors on an underlying layer without having to use a selection.

*The light blue strokes were applied to a blank layer above the image layer. The layer that contains the brush strokes has a blending mode of Darker Color.*

*Continued on the following page*

## THE LIGHTEN BLENDING MODES LIGHTEN THE BASE COLORS

### Lighten
Modifies only base colors that are darker than the blend color, not base colors that are lighter than the blend color.

### Screen
A light blend color produces lighter, bleached base colors; a dark blend color lightens the base colors less.

### Color Dodge
A light blend color lightens the base colors by decreasing the layer's contrast; a dark blend color tints the base colors slightly.

### Linear Dodge (Add)
A light blend color lightens the base colors by increasing the layer's brightness; a dark blend color tints the base colors slightly.

### Lighter Color
The blend color replaces base colors darker than itself without affecting lighter base colors. The blend color will be fully opaque. Could be used to "paint out" dark colors on an underlying layer without having to use a selection.

*The light blue strokes were applied to a blank layer above the image layer. Lighter Color blending mode is chosen for the layer that contains the brush strokes.*

# THE CONTRAST BLENDING MODES INCREASE OR DECREASE THE OVERALL CONTRAST

### Overlay
Multiplies (darkens) dark base colors and screens (lightens) light base colors while preserving luminosity (light and dark) values. Black and white pixels aren't changed, so details are preserved.

### Soft Light
Softens the base color by applying a light tint. Preserves luminosity values in the base colors.

### Hard Light
Screens (lightens) the base colors if the blend color is light; multiplies (darkens) the base colors if the blend color is dark. Increases contrast in the blend color. Good for composite effects or for painting glowing highlights.

### Vivid Light
Burns (darkens) the base colors by increasing contrast if the blend color is dark; dodges (lightens) the base colors by decreasing contrast if the blend color is light.

### Linear Light
Burns (darkens) the base colors by decreasing their brightness if the blend color is dark; dodges (lightens) the base colors by increasing their brightness if the blend color is light.

### Pin Light
A light blend color replaces the base colors; a dark blend color merely tints the base colors.

*Continued on the following page*

*Contrast blending modes (continued)*

### Hard Mix
Posterizes (reduces) the base colors to approximately 5–8 flat colors. A dark blend color produces more black in the base colors; a light blend color produces more white in the base colors.

## THE COMPARATIVE BLENDING MODES INVERT THE BASE COLORS

**Difference**
Inverts the base and blend colors. The lighter the blend color, the more saturated the resulting color.

**Exclusion**
Grays out the base colors where the blend color is dark; inverts the base colors where the blend color is light. Lowers contrast.

**Subtract** ★
A light blend color darkens the base colors; a dark blend color tints the base colors with the invert value of the blend color.

**Divide** ★
A light blend color tints the base colors; a dark blend color preserves dark tonal values in the base color and whites out all other colors.

## THE COMPONENT BLENDING MODES APPLY A SPECIFIC COLOR COMPONENT

**Hue** applies just the hue of the blend color; saturation and luminosity values (and whites and blacks) in the base colors are preserved.

**Saturation** applies the saturation of the blend color without changing hue and luminosity values in the base colors.

**Color** applies the saturation and hue of the blend color but preserves luminosity values (details) in the base colors. This a good mode to use for tinting.

**Luminosity** replaces luminosity values in the base colors with luminosity values from the blend color; hue and saturation values in the base colors are unchanged.

You're happy with the composition of a photo, but it looks a bit dull or the contrast is too strong? Or perhaps the shadows or highlights lack detail? Enter the digital darkroom. Photoshop offers a wide assortment of commands for adjusting images, most of which are accessible from the Adjustments panel. In addition to letting you create and edit 15 types of adjustment layers, this panel also provides buttons for viewing, clipping, and restoring your settings. This chapter is devoted primarily to the mechanics of using the Adjustments panel. It also includes an overview of the Histogram panel. Specific adjustment controls are covered in the next chapter.

## Creating adjustment layers

The effects of a command that is applied to a layer via the Image > Adjustments submenu are permanent, whereas the effects of an adjustment layer (applied via the Adjustments panel) become permanent only when you merge it downward into the underlying layer or flatten your document. We recommend using adjustment layers whenever possible because they're flexible, meaning you can change the settings for them whenever you like — plus you can restack, hide, show, or delete them, and even drag-copy them between files. Furthermore, adjustment layers don't increase the file size, so you can create and keep as many as you need.

Note: The last six commands on the Image > Adjustments submenu, including the valuable Shadows/Highlights command, can be applied only via their respective dialogs, not via an adjustment layer.

For some of the kinds of adjustment layers that you can create via the Adjustments panel, you can choose a settings preset; for all of them, you can choose individual settings (you can also modify the settings for a preset). Via the presets, you can apply basic adjustments quickly, such as to increase the image contrast using three progressively stronger Levels presets, or to increase the image saturation using progressively stronger Hue/Saturation presets.

### To create an adjustment layer:

1. Click an image layer. The adjustment layer is going to appear above the layer you have selected.

2. *Optional:* To restrict the adjustment effect to a specific area of the image, create a selection.

*Continued on the following page*

ADJUSTMENT LAYER BASICS

12

**3.** Display the Adjustments panel. The **Add an Adjustment** buttons and scroll list display. **A**

**4.** Do either of the following:

Click the button for the desired adjustment type. They are arranged as follows: tonal adjustments in the top row, color adjustments in the middle row, and miscellaneous adjustments in the bottom row.

Click an expand/collapse arrow on the scroll list to expand a category of presets, then click a preset (not all of the adjustment types have presets).

**5.** Controls for the adjustment layer display on the Adjustments panel, and a new adjustment layer and layer mask appear on the Layers panel. **B**

**6.** If you clicked a preset, the controls are already set for you. If you didn't click a preset or you want to alter the preset settings, choose the desired settings **C** (and **A–B**, next page).

➤ To redisplay the Add an Adjustment list when the controls for an adjustment layer are displaying, click the Return to Adjustment List button at the bottom of the panel.

➤ To enlarge the Adjustments panel, click the Switch Panel to Expand View button at the bottom of the panel. Click the button again to shrink the panel.

➤ You can also create an adjustment layer by choosing one of the same adjustment types from the New Fill/Adjustment Layer menu . at the bottom of the Layers panel.

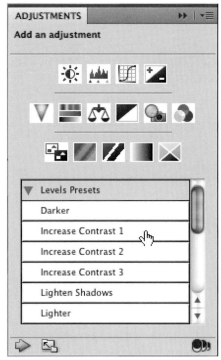

**A** *On the Add an Adjustment list of the Adjustments panel, either click a button to display controls for that adjustment type, or click a preset, if available on the scroll list, to display its predefined settings.*

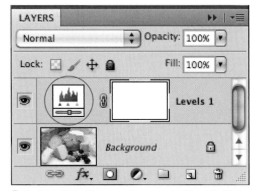

**B** *Each kind of adjustment layer can be identified by its unique icon, which displays in the layer thumbnail.*

**C** *This image lacks contrast.*

**A** *Via the Adjustments panel, we applied the Increase Contrast 1 preset, found in the Levels Presets category.*

**B** *To darken the midtones and add tonal depth to the photo, we fine-tuned the Levels preset adjustment by dragging the midtones (gray) Input Levels slider slightly to the right.*

## Editing the settings for an adjustment layer

### To change the settings for an adjustment layer:

1. On the Layers panel, double-click the thumbnail (icon) for an adjustment layer. The layer becomes selected and the current settings display on the Adjustments panel. (Alternatively, you could also click an adjustment layer, then show the Adjustments panel, in two separate steps.)

2. Do either or both of the following:

   Edit the settings.

   For a Levels, Curves, Exposure, Hue/Saturation, Black & White, or Channel Mixer adjustment type, choose a preset from the menu at the top of the panel.

➤ To undo the last individual slider, check box, or other adjustment edit, press Ctrl-Z/Cmd-Z.

➤ To lessen the overall impact of an adjustment layer, lower its opacity via the Layers panel.

➤ To expand or collapse the list of presets for all the available adjustment types, Alt-click/Option-click one of the expand/collapse arrows.

➤ Each time you select and edit an existing adjustment layer, those edits are listed collectively on the History panel as one state (e.g., "Modify Levels Layer").

By holding down the View Previous State button, you can display the image temporarily without the new settings you have chosen for the currently selected adjustment layer.

### To view the image without the latest adjustment changes:

1. On the Layers panel, double-click an adjustment layer thumbnail to select the layer and show the Adjustments panel, then edit the settings.

2. To toggle the latest edits off, press and hold down the **View Previous State** button 💬 or the \ key. To toggle the edits back on, release the button or key.

The Reset button on the Adjustments panel either undoes the most recent changes made (if any) to the current adjustment layer since the document was opened, or restores the default settings. The button icon changes depending on whether the settings for the adjustment layer were edited. Run through the following steps, just to see how the button works.

### To reset an adjustment layer:

1. Double-click an adjustment layer thumbnail to display its settings on the Adjustments panel.

2. Edit the settings.

3. Click the **Reset to Previous State** button 🔄 to cancel the current changes and restore the last settings.

4. Click the **Reset to Adjustment Defaults** button ⟳ (same button, different icon) to restore the default settings.

### To hide the effect of an adjustment layer:

Click the visibility icon 👁 on the Adjustments panel or Layers panel; click it again to redisplay.

Normally, an adjustment layer affects all the layers below it, but you can clip (restrict) its effect to just the layer directly below it.

### To restrict the effect of an adjustment layer to the layer directly below it:

1. On the Layers panel, click an adjustment layer.**A**

2. On the Adjustments panel, click the **Clip to Layer** button. 🔘 (Click it again to "unclip.") **B**

## Saving adjustment presets

Regardless of how you arrive at custom settings (whether by choosing a preset first or not), you can save those settings for future use.

### To save custom adjustment settings as a preset:

1. Create and choose settings for an adjustment layer. Note that presets can be saved only for Levels, Curves, Exposure, Hue/Saturation, Black & White, Channel Mixer, and Selective Color.

2. From the Adjustments panel menu, choose **Save** [adjustment type] **Preset**. In the Save dialog, enter a name, keep the default location and extension, then click Save. Your user preset is now available for any document via the Add an Adjustment list on the Adjustments panel, and also via the preset menu at the top of the panel when the controls for that adjustment type (e.g., Levels or Curves) are displaying.

➤ To delete a user preset, choose that preset, choose Delete Current Preset from the panel menu, then click Yes in the alert dialog.

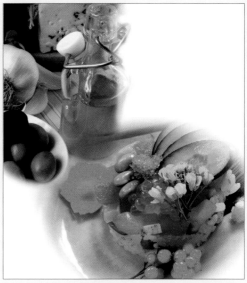

**A** *A Levels adjustment layer is being used to intensify the overall contrast in this image.*

**B** *We clipped the effect of the adjustment layer to just the layer directly below it (the layer that contains the photo of olive oil).*

# Merging and deleting adjustment layers

When you merge an adjustment layer downward, the adjustments are applied permanently to the underlying image layer. If you change your mind, either choose Edit > Undo (right away!) or click the prior state on the History panel.

## To merge an adjustment layer:

Do either of the following:

Click the adjustment layer to be merged downward,**A** then press Ctrl-E/Cmd-E.**B**

Right-click on or near the adjustment layer name and choose **Merge Down**.

Note: Adjustment layers don't contain pixels, so you can't merge them with one another. However, you can merge multiple adjustment layers into an image layer (or layers) by using the Merge Visible command (see page 145) or the Flatten Image command (see page 146).

Adjustment layers are as easy to delete as they are to create.

## To delete an adjustment layer:

Do either of the following:

Click the icon for an adjustment layer on the Layers panel, then click the **Delete Layer** button 🗑 on the same panel or the **Delete Adjustment Layer** button 🗑 on the Adjustments panel. Click Yes if an alert appears. *Optional:* Click Don't Show Again to prevent the alert from reappearing.

Click the icon or layer mask thumbnail for an adjustment layer on the Layers panel, then press Backspace/Delete. (See also the sidebar at right.)

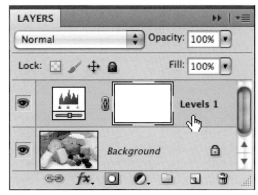

**A** *Click the adjustment layer to be merged downward.*

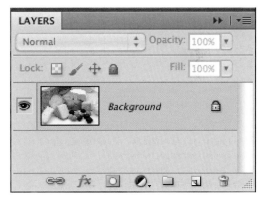

**B** *The Merge Down command applied the Levels values from the adjustment layer to the underlying image layer, which in this case is the Background.*

---

**BYPASSING THE AUTO-SELECT PARAMETER OPTION** ★

The new Auto-Select Parameter option (on the Adjustments panel menu) causes the first entry field on the panel to become highlighted automatically when you create an adjustment layer or when you double-click the icon for an existing adjustment layer on the Layers panel. Although this option enables you to quickly enter or change values, it can be an annoyance because it prevents some shortcuts from working (e.g., selecting a tool via its letter shortcut or deleting a layer by pressing Backspace/Delete). If this option is on and you want to shift the focus from the Adjustments panel to the Layers panel, click either the icon or the layer mask thumbnail for the adjustment layer.

# Editing the adjustment layer mask

By default, every adjustment layer has a blank white layer mask. To limit which area of the image the adjustment affects, you can add black areas to the mask, either by filling a selection or by applying brush strokes, as we show you in the steps below.

## To edit the adjustment layer mask:

1. Click the mask thumbnail on an adjustment layer.

2. Press D to choose the default colors, then press X to switch to black as the Foreground color.

3. To partially mask the adjustment layer effect, do either or both of the following:

   Create a selection with any selection tool (e.g., Rectangular Marquee or Lasso), choose Edit > **Fill** (Shift-Backspace/Shift-Delete), choose Use: **Foreground Color**, click OK, then deselect.

   Choose the **Brush** tool ✐ (B or Shift-B). On the Options bar, choose a Soft Round brush, Mode: Normal, and an Opacity of 100% (or a lower opacity to create a partial mask), adjust the brush diameter by pressing [ or ], then apply brush strokes to the image. **A–C**

4. *Optional:* To reverse the effect of the mask in specific areas, press X to switch colors (make the Foreground color white), then with the Brush tool, apply strokes to remove the mask.

➤ To remove all black areas from the mask, deselect, click the adjustment layer mask, choose Edit > Fill, then choose Use: White in the dialog.

➤ To confine the effect of an adjustment layer to a small area, start with a fully black mask (click Invert on the Masks panel or apply Edit > Fill, Use: Black), then apply strokes with white.

➤ To create a gradual mask by applying a gradient, see pages 244–245. To refine the edge or density of the mask, see pages 170–171.

**A** *This original photo looks too pink.*

**B** *We used Curves to correct the color, then with the mask for that adjustment layer selected, we applied brush strokes to the top part of the image. Now the adjustment is visible in only the bottom half of the photo.*

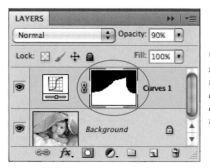

**C** *Our brush strokes are represented by black areas in the adjustment layer mask thumbnail.*

## SHORTCUTS FOR LAYER MASKS

| | |
|---|---|
| View the mask by itself in the document window | Alt/Option click the layer mask thumbnail (repeat to restore the normal view) |
| View the mask over the image as a Quick Mask (the default color is red) | Alt-Shift/Option-Shift click the layer mask thumbnail (repeat to restore the normal view) |
| Deactivate or activate the mask | Shift-click the layer mask thumbnail (Layers panel) or click the Disable/Enable button 👁 (Masks panel) |
| Convert the unmasked area into a selection | Ctrl/Cmd click the layer mask thumbnail (Layers panel) or click the Load Selection from Mask button ⬚ (Masks panel) |

# Using the Histogram panel

The **Histogram** panel displays a graph of the current tonal (light and dark) values in an image, which updates dynamically as the document is edited. The panel is always accessible, even while the Adjustments panel is being used or an adjustment dialog is open. You can better judge how adjustment edits are affecting your document if you monitor the changes in its histogram.

After opening a photo into Photoshop — but before you begin editing it — study the histogram to evaluate the existing distribution of tonal values in the image. The horizontal axis on the graph represents the grayscale or color levels between 0 and 255, the vertical bars represent the number of pixels at specific color or tonal levels, and the contour of the graph represents the overall tonal range.

## To choose a view for the Histogram panel:

From the Histogram panel menu, choose one of the following: **Compact View** (just the histogram), **A** **Expanded View** (the histogram plus data and access to individual channels), **B** or **All Channels View** (all the features of Expanded View, plus separate histograms for each channel). To display document data in the latter two views, check Show Statistics.

For Expanded or All Channels view, choose an option from the **Channel** menu: RGB, **C** a specific channel, Luminosity, or Colors. To display the individual channels in color, check Show Channels in Color on the panel menu.

While a large file is being edited, Photoshop maintains the redraw speed of the Histogram panel by reading the data from the histogram cache — not from the actual image. When this is occurring, a Cached Data Warning icon ⚠ appears on the panel. Remember to keep updating the panel, as we instruct you here (even while editing the settings for an adjustment layer), so it will continue to reflect the current tonal values of the image.

## To update the Histogram panel:

Do one of the following:

Double-click anywhere on the histogram.

Click the **Cached Data Warning** icon. ⚠

Click the **Uncached Refresh** button. 

➤ To specify a Cache Levels value in the Preferences dialog, see page 391.

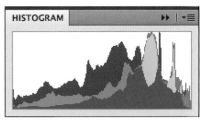

**A** *This Histogram panel is in Compact View.*

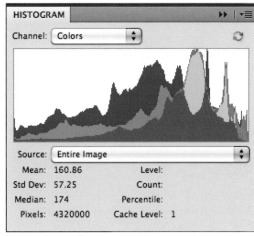

**B** *Here the panel is in Expanded View. By default, the Channel menu is set to Colors.*

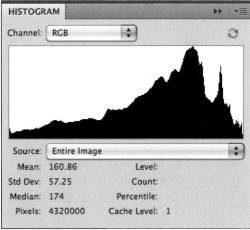

**C** *With RGB chosen on the Channel menu, the current tonal values in the image are represented by black areas on the graph.*

## Interpreting the Histogram panel

To focus on tonal values when using the Histogram panel, choose Expanded View from the panel menu and choose RGB from the Channel menu. Pixels are represented by vertical bars in the graph, with shadows on the left, midtones in the middle, and highlights on the right. For a dark, low-key image (such as a night scene), the bars will be clustered primarily on the left side of the graph; for an average-key image with more balanced lights and darks, the bars will be more uniformly distributed across the graph; and for a very light, high-key image containing few or no shadow areas, the bars will be clustered primarily on the right side.

If an image has a wide tonal range, the bars will be more uniformly distributed in all the tonal zones, and will stretch fully from one end of the graph to the other. Also, the graph will be mostly solid and will have a relatively smooth contour rather than a spiky one. **A** If an image lacks detail in a particular tonal range, on the other hand, the graph will contain gaps and spikes, like teeth on a comb. The following are some graph profiles that you might encounter:

➤ For an average-key but underexposed image that lacks details in the highlights, pixels will be clustered primarily on the left side of the histogram. **B**

➤ For an overexposed image that lacks details in the shadows, pixels will be clustered mostly on the right side of the histogram. **C**

➤ For an image in which pixels were clipped (details discarded) from the extreme shadow or highlight areas, a line or cluster of pixels will rise sharply at the left or right edge, respectively, of the histogram. **D**

➤ If an image has lost details as a result of editing (such as from filters or adjustments), the histogram will have gaps and spikes. **E** The gaps indicate a loss of specific tonal or color levels, whereas the spikes indicate that pixels from different levels have been averaged together and assigned the same value (the bar becomes taller at that level). A few gaps and spikes are an acceptable result of editing, whereas large gaps signify that posterization has occurred and too many continuous tonal values have been discarded. On the other hand, a lousy-looking histogram doesn't always signify failure — the graph can be thrown off by something as simple as adding a white border. If you like the way the image looks, ignore the histogram!

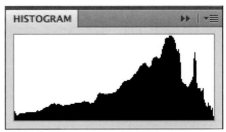

**A** *The tonal ranges in this image are well balanced.*

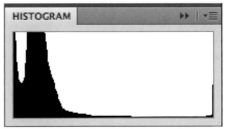

**B** *The histogram shows this image is underexposed.*

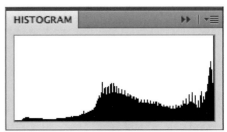

**C** *This image is overexposed.*

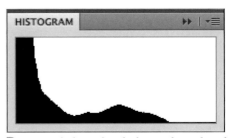

**D** *This graph shows that shadow pixels are clipped.*

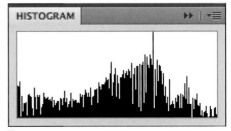

**E** *This graph contains gaps and spikes.*

Upon opening a photograph into Photoshop, take a few minutes to study it and see if it has any tonal or color defects. Is it over- or under-exposed? Does it have a color cast (does it look ghostly blue or sickly green)? To some extent, the subject matter of the photo will dictate what kind of adjustments it needs. For instance, we might rebalance the skin tones in a portrait to make it look more natural, but apply a tint or photo filter to a photo of an abstract texture or to an extreme closeup for an artistic effect.

If you capture your photo as raw files or in the JPEG or TIFF format, you will be able to rectify many of their defects in Camera Raw. If you can't use Camera Raw for your files or they need further correction, not to worry: Photoshop offers a smorgasbord of adjustment controls. Each adjustment type has a specialized function (see the icons below). Some are easy to get the hang of, and others may take longer to master but offer more power or more nuanced controls.

In the preceding chapter, we stepped you through the mechanics of creating and working with adjustment layers. In this chapter, we delve into their specific features. The good news is that by the end of this chapter, you will have mastered most of the key Photoshop commands!

*Continued on the following page*

ADJUSTMENTS IN DEPTH

**13**

## IN THIS CHAPTER

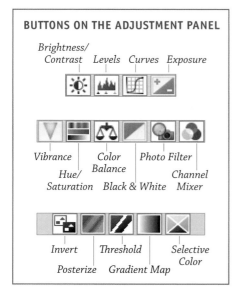

**BUTTONS ON THE ADJUSTMENT PANEL**

*Brightness/*
*Contrast*  *Levels*  *Curves*  *Exposure*

*Vibrance*  *Color*  *Photo Filter*
          *Balance*
   *Hue/*              *Channel*
*Saturation*  *Black & White*  *Mixer*

*Invert*  *Threshold*  *Selective*
                      *Color*
   *Posterize*  *Gradient Map*

When performing adjustments, please consider these suggestions:

➤ Make sure your monitor is properly calibrated first (see pages 7–9). Also learn how to create a soft proof of your document so you can get an inkling of how it will look when printed (see pages 404–405.

➤ Digital photos are captured in RGB Color mode automatically. Keep them in this mode for adjustments. Should you need to adjust an image for a specific CMYK output device, do so on a copy of the file, not on the original. (The document color mode of high-resolution CMYK scans shouldn't be changed, either.)

➤ Put your document into Standard Screen mode (choose that option from the Screen Mode menu 🖿 on the Application bar); Mac OS users should also display the Application frame. The gray area around the image will provide a good neutral backdrop for judging your color and tonal corrections.

## Correcting tonal values using a Levels adjustment layer

Now that you know how a read a histogram (see pages 203–204), you're ready to create a Levels adjustment layer. Levels has a histogram of its own. We usually use Levels when we first bring a photo into Photoshop, then sometimes use it again during the course of editing. In the following steps, you will use Levels to correct tonal values (Levels is also used on pages 220–221 and page 232).

### To correct tonal values using Levels:

1. Click a layer that needs a contrast adjustment, **A** then on the Adjustments panel, ⬭ click the **Levels** button. 🔛 The Levels controls display.

2. Do any of the following: **B**

   To intensify the contrast, brighten the highlights by moving the white Input Levels highlights slider to the left and darken the shadows by moving the black Input Levels shadows slider to the right. Any pixels located to the left of the black slider will become black; any pixels located to the right of the white slider will become white. (This shifting of tonal values is called "clipping.")

   Another way to figure out where to position the highlights and shadows sliders is to activate Threshold mode, a temporary, high-contrast

**A** *The original image lacks contrast (looks dull).*

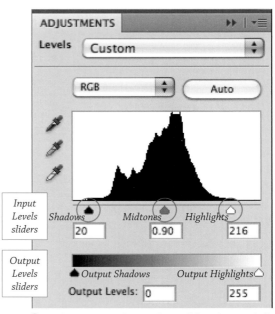

**B** *The histogram in this Levels panel doesn't extend all the way to the edges, an indication that the tonal range of this photo is narrow. To expand the range, we moved the shadows and highlights Input Levels sliders inward to align with the outer edges of the histogram, and moved the midtones slider to the right to darken the midtones.*

display of clipping. Alt-drag/Option-drag the highlights slider, and release the mouse when only a few areas of color or white display;**A** these pixels will become the lightest tonal value. Also Alt-drag/Option-drag the shadows slider, releasing the mouse when only a few areas of color or black appear;**B** these pixels will become the darkest tonal value.

3. With the shadows and highlights sliders now in their proper positions, move the gray **Input Levels** midtones slider to lighten or darken the midtones separately from the shadows or highlights.**C–D**

➤ To apply the current Levels settings to other open images (perhaps images that were taken under similar lighting conditions, that require the same adjustments), choose Save Levels Preset from the Adjustments panel menu. Enter a name for the preset (keep the default location), then click Save. Click another document tab, and click an image layer in that document. Expand the Levels Presets list on the Adjustments panel, then click your new preset at the bottom of the list. A Levels adjustment layer will be created, using your saved settings.

**A** *This is Threshold mode as we Alt-drag/ Option-drag the white Input Levels (highlights) slider.*

**B** *This is Threshold mode as we Alt-drag/ Option-drag the black Input Levels (shadows) slider.*

**C** *Our Levels adjustments improved the contrast (the shadows and highlights are intensified).*

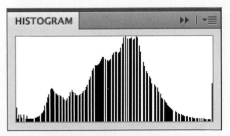

**D** *The Levels adjustments expanded the tonal range of the image; now the bars extend from one end of the graph to the other.*

# Applying a Brightness/Contrast adjustment

To subtly tweak the brightness or contrast in an image, try using the simple but powerful Brightness/Contrast controls.

## To apply a Brightness/Contrast adjustment:

1. Click a layer or the Background.
2. On the Adjustments panel, click the **Brightness/Contrast** button. The Brightness/Contrast controls display.
3. Move the **Brightness** and/or **Contrast** sliders. **A–D**

➤ Keep the Use Legacy option for Brightness/Contrast unchecked, as it would permit tonal levels to be eliminated from the image. With this option off, pixel data from the entire tonal range is preserved; after adjustment, you'll see evidence in the histogram of only a minor redistribution in tonal values.

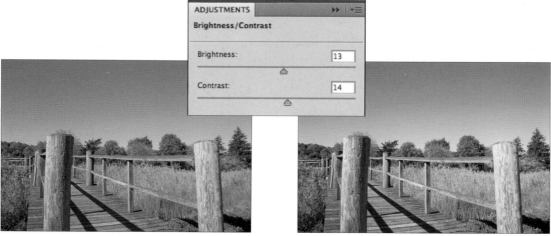

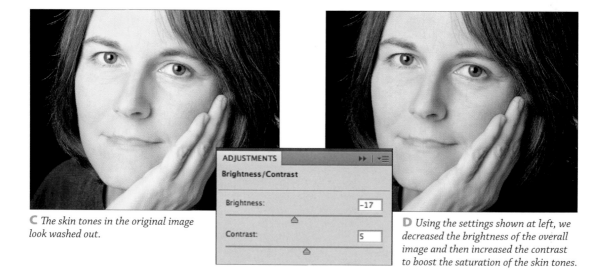

**A** *The original image looks a bit dull (it lacks contrast and the color is undersaturated).*

**B** *Using the Brightness/Contrast settings shown above, we increased the brightness of the overall image and increased the contrast to make the colors more saturated.*

**C** *The skin tones in the original image look washed out.*

**D** *Using the settings shown at left, we decreased the brightness of the overall image and then increased the contrast to boost the saturation of the skin tones.*

# Applying a Photo Filter adjustment

To change the color temperature of a scene (make it look warmer or cooler), photographers use colored lens filters at the time of the shoot. In Photoshop, you can simulate the effect of a camera filter by using a Photo Filter adjustment layer, to neutralize a color cast or to apply a tint (as a special effect). You can choose from 20 preset tints or choose a custom color. When using this feature, go for subtle or extreme, but not in between.

## To apply a Photo Filter adjustment:

1. Click a layer or the Background. **A**

2. On the Adjustments panel, click the **Photo Filter** button. The Photo Filter controls display. **B**

A *The original image has a magenta cast.*

3. Do either of the following:

   Click **Filter**, then from the menu, choose a preset warming or cooling filter or a filter color. The filter color displays in the swatch.

   Click the **Color** swatch, choose a color for the filter from the Color Picker (note the change in the image), then click OK.

   ➤ For a subtle change, pick a related color; for a more obvious change, pick a complementary color (opposite on the color wheel).

4. Using the **Density** slider or scrubby slider, choose an opacity percentage for the tint. Try a modest value between 10% and 25%, or a higher value for a dramatic change. **C** You can also lower the opacity of the adjustment layer.

5. Check **Preserve Luminosity** to preserve the overall brightness and contrast of the image. With this option unchecked, the contrast will be softer in the highlights, but the resulting colorization effect may be too pronounced. For a portrait, you may prefer the results with this option off.

6. To compare the original and adjusted images, click the Layer Visibility button 👁 on the Adjustments panel off and then on again (or do likewise with the visibility button for the adjustment layer on the Layers panel).

C *The Photo Filter adjustment removed the magenta cast but preserved the warm tones from the afternoon sun.*

B *For our Photo Filter adjustment layer, we chose Cyan from the Filter menu and left the Density at 25%.*

# A quick and dirty method for correcting over- or underexposure

For a quick and dirty way to correct an over- or underexposed photo, create an adjustment layer, choose a blending mode for the layer that has a lightening or darkening effect, then duplicate it a few times. It's not the most precise method in the world, but if it works, it works (and if it makes your art director happy, maybe you can go home early!).

## To correct the exposure via the Layers panel:

1. Open an over- or underexposed photo,**A** and click the Background or a layer.

2. On the Adjustments panel,◍ click the **Levels** button.◍ Leave the settings as they are.

3. On the Layers panel, click the new adjustment layer, then choose a **blending mode** that produces a lightening or darkening effect. For example, to darken an overexposed image, you could try Multiply mode, or to lighten an underexposed image, try Screen or Lighten mode.

4. If the image is still too light or dark, duplicate the adjustment layer by pressing Ctrl-J/Cmd-J.**B** Repeat the shortcut until you reach a point where the image is slightly overcorrected and you need to step it back a bit.

5. Lower the opacity of the topmost adjustment layer until the exposure looks just right.**C**

**A** *The original image is underexposed.*

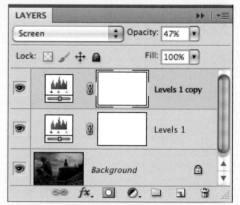

**B** *We created an adjustment layer, chose Screen blending mode, duplicated the layer, then lowered the opacity of the duplicate adjustment layer to 47%.*

**C** *The two Levels adjustment layers produced this result.*

# Dodging and burning small areas

To lighten or darken pixels by hand in small areas, you might instinctively reach for the Dodge and Burn tools. However, those tools, even with their new enhancements, permanently alter layer pixels. A better method is to dodge and burn areas with the Brush tool on a removable, editable neutral color layer, as in the steps below.

## To dodge and burn areas via a neutral color layer:

1. If the document isn't in RGB Color mode, convert it by choosing Image > Mode > **RGB Color**.

2. Click an image layer or the Background,**A** then Alt-click/Option-click the **New Layer** button. The New Layer dialog opens.

3. Choose Mode: **Overlay**, check **Fill with Overlay-Neutral Color (50% gray)**, then click OK.

4. Choose the **Brush** tool (B or Shift-B). From the Options bar, choose a Soft Round brush and an Opacity of 20%. Press [ or ] to set the brush diameter.

5. Press D to make the Foreground color black, then apply brush strokes to areas that you want to darken. To lighten areas, press X to swap the Foreground and Background colors (make the Foreground color white), then apply strokes.**B–C**

6. *Optional:* To remove any unwanted dodge or burn strokes, hide the image layer. Alt-click/Option-click to sample the gray value in an untouched area, then with a brush opacity of 100%, paint over those strokes. Redisplay the image layer.

➤ To lessen the whole dodge or burn effect, click the neutral gray layer on the Layers panel, then lower the layer opacity or choose Soft Light as the layer blending mode.

**A** *The central figure in this image, where the focal point should be, lacks contrast. We'll adjust the reflected light on the cobblestones to draw more attention to that area.*

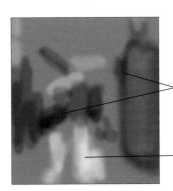

**B** *When displayed by itself, a neutral gray layer looks like this.*

*We applied black strokes to darken the shadows on the sides of the buildings,...*

*...then applied white strokes to lighten the cobblestones around the figure.*

**C** *We applied strokes to the neutral gray layer to dodge the road and burn the houses, then lowered the layer opacity to 78% to soften the effect.*

# Converting layers to grayscale via a Black & White adjustment

Next, we'll show you several ways to strip color from a layer without changing the document color mode. Our favorite way (described here), is to use a Black & White adjustment layer because it enables us to control how the individual R, G, B and C, M, Y color channels are converted to grayscale values.

## To convert a layer to grayscale via a Black & White adjustment:

1. In an RGB image, click a layer or the Background. **A**

2. On the Adjustments panel, ◔ click the **Black & White** button.◼ The Black & White controls appear on the panel.

3. Do any of the following:

   Click **Auto** to have the program choose the settings for you (**A**, next page) or choose a preset from the **Preset** menu. You can customize the settings, as described in the remaining steps.

   Adjust the sliders to control how each color is converted to a particular gray level. A lower value produces a darker gray equivalent for a color; a higher value produces a lighter gray equivalent.

Click the **Targeted Adjustment** tool 👆 on the panel, then drag horizontally over an area in the image to lighten or darken it. The slider corresponding to the predominant color in that area will shift accordingly.

4. To further adjust the grayscale conversion, move the sliders, starting with **Reds, Yellows, Cyans**, or **Blues**. For example, you could try using the Yellows slider to lighten or darken a portrait or to correct a landscape image that contains a lot of green (**B–C**, next page).

5. *Optional:* To apply a tint to the whole image, check Tint, click the color swatch, choose a color from the Color Picker, then click OK.

6. *Optional:* To restore some original color to the whole layer uniformly, lower the opacity of the adjustment layer. Or to restore color to select areas, click the adjustment layer mask thumbnail, choose black as the Foreground color, then with the Brush tool, apply strokes to the image (for a subtle effect, lower the tool opacity first).

**A** *In this image, the color differences between the skin tones and water naturally help us to distinguish between them.*

A *To produce this grayscale version of the image, we chose the Auto setting for a Black & White adjustment layer. We think the contrast between the figure and background needs improvement.*

## AUTO-SELECTING THE TARGETED ADJUSTMENT TOOL ★

To have the Targeted Adjustment tool become selected automatically on the Adjustments panel when you create a Curves, Hue/Saturation, or Black & White adjustment layer, display the controls for one of those adjustment types, then choose Auto-Select Targeted Adjustment Tool from the panel menu.

## ORCHESTRATING A SCENE

In our environment, as in fine art and photography, colors help to define spatial and shape relationships and draw our attention to specific parts of a scene. When converting an image to grayscale, think about how you want to reinterpret the composition. To orchestrate visual movement with lights and darks instead of color, choose gray levels based on which areas you want to draw the viewer's attention to. For example, say a bright red shape is located in the center of the original composition. Using the Black & White controls, you could lighten or darken that shape to make it stand out from the surrounding grays.

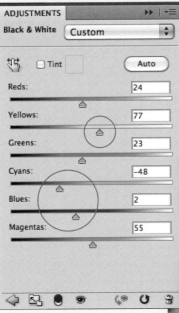

B *To improve the contrast, we reduced the Cyans and Blues values to darken the water, and increased the Yellows value to lighten the woman's neck and cheek.*

C *Now that the contrast between the figure and background has been improved, the figure stands out better.*

## Applying a Vibrance adjustment

Using a Vibrance adjustment layer, you can either strip the color completely from a layer or desaturate a layer partially and then adjust the Vibrance to control the color intensity.

### To desaturate a layer using a Vibrance adjustment:

1. Click a layer or the Background in an RGB image.**A**

2. On the Adjustments panel,⬤ click the **Vibrance** button.☑

3. Do either of the following:

   For a simple, full desaturation, reduce the **Saturation** to its lowest value (to –100).

   To adjust the color vibrance as you desaturate the layer, reduce the **Saturation** to between –60 and –80, then to control the color intensity in the now almost grayscale layer, increase or reduce the **Vibrance** value.**B–D** The Vibrance option boosts the intensity of the least saturated colors the most.

**A** *This is the original image.*

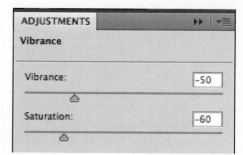

**B** *To desaturate the color partially, we lowered the Saturation value for the Vibrance adjustment layer to –60 and set the Vibrance to –50.*

**C** *This is the image after we applied the Vibrance adjustment layer settings shown in the preceding figure.*

**D** *Here the image has the same Saturation value of –60 but a higher Vibrance value of +100.*

## To desaturate a color layer and restore color selectively using Vibrance:

1. Click a layer or the Background in an RGB image.

2. On the Adjustments panel, click the **Vibrance** button.

3. Click the mask thumbnail on the adjustment layer.

4. Reduce the **Saturation** all the way to –100. **A**

5. Choose the **Brush** tool, and on the Options bar, choose a Soft Round brush, Normal mode, and an Opacity of 50% or less. Choose black as the Foreground color.

6. Adjust the brush diameter, then apply strokes where you want to restore the original colors. **B–C** You can change the brush opacity and diameter between strokes. To restore grayscale areas, press X and paint with white.

**A** *To strip the color from this image, we lowered the Saturation value for a Vibrance adjustment layer to –100.*

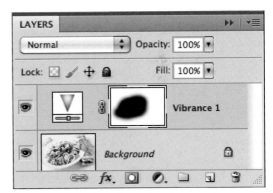

**B** *We applied brush strokes to the adjustment layer mask to restore color to the salad, where we want to draw the viewer's attention.*

**C** *Now the color is visible only in the center of the image.*

You can also use the Vibrance controls to adjust the saturation of a full color layer. To guard against oversaturation and clipping, the Vibrance slider boosts the intensity of less saturated colors more than that of highly saturated colors. For this reason, this slider is useful for reviving skin tones. The Saturation slider, on the other hand, applies the same change to all colors regardless of their original saturation levels.

### To adjust the vibrance of a color layer:

1. Click a layer or the Background in an RGB image. **A**

2. On the Adjustments panel, ✐ click the **Vibrance** button. **V**

3. Do either of the following:

   Increase the Vibrance value, then reduce the Saturation value slightly. **B**

   Reduce the Vibrance value, then increase the Saturation value slightly. **C**

**A** *The color in this portrait is oversaturated.*

**B** *For the Vibrance adjustment layer, we set the Saturation value to −25 and the Vibrance value to +40. Now the color and the contrast are less intense.*

**C** *For a subtle variation, we set the Saturation value to +25 and the Vibrance value to −40. The colors are also less intense here, but the contrast is slightly stronger.*

## Applying a Color Balance adjustment

A Color Balance adjustment layer can be used to apply a warm or cool cast to an image or, conversely, to neutralize an unwanted cast. The three Tone choices of Shadows, Midtones, and Highlights let you restrict the adjustments to a specific tonal range, and each slider affects a pair of cool and warm colors. Note: If you need to pinpoint color adjustments to an even narrower range, use Curves or Hue/Saturation.

### To make an image cooler or warmer using a Color Balance adjustment layer:

1. Click a layer or the Background. **A**

2. On the Adjustments panel, ⊘ click the **Color Balance** button. ⚙

3. For **Tone**, click the range to be adjusted: **Shadows, Midtones,** or **Highlights**.

   *Optional:* Keep Preserve Luminosity checked to preserve the tonal values of the layer as you make corrections. Or uncheck this option to

apply soft color adjustments to highlights, such as to skin tones.

4. Each slider pairs a cool color with a warm one. Move a slider toward any color you want to add more of or away from any color you want to reduce **B–C** (also **A–B**, next page). For example, you would move a slider toward green to subtract magenta, or toward yellow to reduce blue. Watch how the overall image changes as you add or reduce a particular color.

   ► To make the image warmer or cooler, move multiple sliders toward similar colors. For example, to add a cool cast, you could move the first slider toward Cyan and the third one toward Blue. Or to make an image warmer, move the first slider toward Red and the third one toward Yellow.

5. Click any other Tone button, then adjust the color sliders for that range. You can click the visibility icon ● to compare the adjusted image with the original.

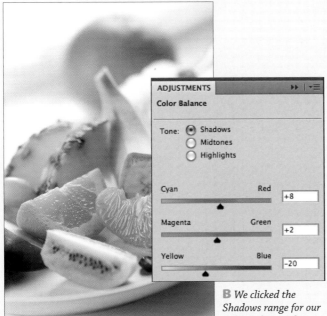

**A** *This image has a cool blue cast.*

**B** *We clicked the Shadows range for our Color Balance adjustment layer, then moved the sliders toward Red, Green, and Yellow to neutralize the shadows.*

**C** *The shadow areas look more neutral than before, but further corrections are needed.*

*See also the figures on the following page*

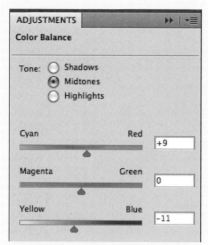

**A** *To neutralize the blue cast in the midtones, we clicked Tone: Midtones, then moved the sliders toward Red and Yellow. A blue cast in the highlights remains to be fixed.*

**B** *To warm the highlights and neutralize the remaining traces of the blue cast, we clicked Tone: Highlights, then moved the sliders toward Red and Yellow (and also slightly toward Magenta). Now the food and the plate look warmer (and more appetizing!) and the shadows are more neutral.*

# Applying a Hue/Saturation adjustment

For making precise hue and saturation corrections without having to make a selection, try using a Hue/Saturation adjustment layer. With the Hue/Saturation controls, you can target specific colors, then shift just those colors to a different hue or adjust their saturation or lightness. This is a useful way to swap out colors in a product or fashion shot.

## To use a Hue/Saturation adjustment layer for color correction:

1. Click a layer. **A**

2. On the Adjustments panel, 🖋 click the **Hue/Saturation** button. ▦

3. Do any of the following:

   To correct all the colors in the image, keep **Master** as the choice on the second menu. Move the **Hue** slider to adjust all the hues, the **Saturation** slider to adjust their color intensity, or the **Lightness** slider to lighten or darken them. After adjusting the Lightness, you may need to increase the Saturation to revive any colors that became too light or dark.

   To change the hue of a specific color, **B** click the **Targeted Adjustment** tool 🖑 on the panel, then Ctrl-drag/Cmd-drag horizontally over that color in the image. **C** The color range you drag over is now listed on the menu, and the adjustment slider shifts to that color on the color bar. Or to change the saturation of a specific color, drag horizontally with the Targeted Adjustment tool over that color in the image without holding down Ctrl/Cmd.

**A** We will change the blue napkin on the right side of this image to yellow, to coordinate better with the lemons on the left.

**ADJUSTMENTS**

Hue/Saturation — Custom

🖑 Blues

Hue: +180

Saturation: +8

Lightness: -7

☐ Colorize

183°/220°

*Changes to the sliders are reflected in the lower color bar*

**B** We created a Hue/Saturation adjustment layer, then clicked the Targeted Adjustment tool. Holding down Ctrl/Cmd, we dragged over the blue of the napkin until the hue shifted into the yellow range. Finally, we increased the Saturation and reduced the Lightness for the adjusted colors.

**C** Now the napkin is yellow.

# Applying an Auto Color Correction

The Auto Color Correction Options dialog offers a choice of three preset algorithms (formulas) for adjusting the color and contrast in an image, and in addition, it lets you correct the luminosity and color temperature of the midtones.

## To apply an Auto Color Correction:

1. Open an image.**A**

2. On the Adjustments panel,✎ click the **Levels** button,⊞ then hold down Alt/Option and click **Options** (the Auto button becomes Options).

3. The Auto Color Correction Options dialog opens.**B** Move it, if necessary, so it's not blocking the Levels histogram, which you should monitor as you choose options.

4. Click the **Find Dark & Light Colors** algorithm (see the sidebar on the next page).

5. Check **Snap Neutral Midtones**. Any colors that are close to neutral will be adjusted to match the Midtones target color swatch in the dialog.

6. To adjust the color temperature of the image, you can assign a subtle color tint to the midtones. Click the **Midtones** swatch. The Select Target Midtone Color picker opens.**C**

   Click the **H** button in the **HSB** group, then drag the circle in the large square slightly to the right (keep the **S** value around 10–30). Next, on the vertical Hue bar, click a reddish-yellow hue to make the overall temperature of your image warmer, or a greenish-blue hue to cool it down. To adjust the brightness of the midtones, drag the circle slightly upward or downward (keep the **B** value around 45–55).

**A** *The midtones in the original image have a magenta cast, which is noticeable in the sand.*

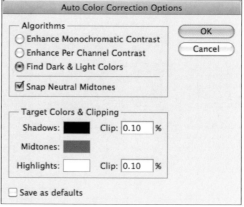

**B** *In the Auto Color Correction Options dialog, we clicked Find Dark & Light Colors and checked Snap Neutral Midtones.*

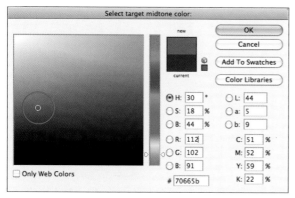

**C** *We clicked the Midtones swatch to open this dialog, then chose a medium brown to neutralize the color temperature of the sand.*

Note: Midtones is the only swatch you need to change; the other two swatches will be adjusted automatically when the file is prepared for printing.

7. Click OK to exit the Select Target Midtone Color dialog, then again to exit the Auto Color Correction Options dialog.**A**

When the alert dialog appears, offering you the option to save the new target colors as defaults, click No (we would rather choose settings on a case-by-case basis than establish global default settings).

➤ The Auto Color Correction Options dialog also opens when you Alt-click/Option-click the Auto button for a Curves adjustment layer.

➤ You could also adjust the midtones by clicking a neutral gray area in the image with the gray point (middle) eyedropper in Levels or Curves, but this method is less reliable because it only works if you click in the right spot, which isn't as easy as it sounds.**B**

**A** *The adjustments made to the midtones via the Snap Neutral Midtones and Target Colors options in the Auto Color Correction Options dialog successfully removed the magenta cast.*

### THE AUTO COLOR CORRECTION ALGORITHMS

➤ Enhance Monochromatic Contrast moves the black and white Input Levels sliders inward to enhance contrast. The sliders are moved the same amount for each channel, to preserve color relationships. (The Image > Auto Contrast command also uses this algorithm.)

➤ Enhance Per Channel Contrast moves the Input Levels sliders inward by a different amount for each channel, and produces more noticeable color shifts and changes in contrast than the other algorithms. (The Image > Auto Tone command also uses this algorithm.)

➤ Find Dark & Light Colors (our favorite algorithm) positions the black and white Input Levels sliders in each channel based on the average darkest and lightest pixels in the image, and enhances the contrast. (The Image > Auto Color command also uses this algorithm.)

**B** *By comparison, clicking in the original image with the gray eyedropper in Levels (in the location shown above) failed to remove the magenta cast from the midtones.*

# Correcting the color using Curves

By using a Curves adjustment layer, you can adjust the values in a narrow tonal range, such as the highlights, quarter tones, midtones, three-quarter tones, or shadows. Precise corrections can be applied to the composite channel (all the channels in the image combined) or to individual color channels. In these steps, you will make tonal corrections first, then adjust the color.

## To correct color and tonal values using a Curves adjustment layer:

**Part 1: Apply tonal adjustments**

1. Open an RGB image that needs a color adjustment.**A**

2. On the Adjustments panel,⬤ click the **Curves** button.⬚ Choose Curves Display Options from the Adjustments panel menu, check all four of the Show options (described in the sidebar at right), leave Show Amount Of on the default setting of Light (0-255), then click OK.

3. If the contrast in the image needs improvement, do either of the following:

   The **Input** sliders affect the lightest and darkest tonal values in the image. To increase the contrast (darken the shadows and brighten the highlights), drag the black shadow Input slider and white highlight Input slider inward so they align with the ends of the histogram. The steeper the curve, the greater the contrast.

   To increase the contrast by establishing the lightest and darkest values in a high-contrast display of clipping called **Threshold** mode, Alt-drag/ Option-drag the black slider until a few areas of black appear, and the white slider until a mere smidgen of white appears. (Note that this can also be done in Levels.)

4. For more targeted adjustments, do any of the following:

   Drag part of the curve; a point will appear on it. For example, to lighten the midtones, drag the middle of the curve upward, or to darken the midtones, drag the middle of the curve downward.

   ➤ When a tonal value is lightened, its Output value (after adjustment) becomes higher than its Input value (the original brightness value). When a tonal value is darkened, its Output value becomes lower than its Input value.

**A** *This image is underexposed (too dark) and has a blue cast.*

---

**USING THE DISPLAY OPTIONS IN CURVES**

The four Show options in the Curves Display Options dialog are as follows:

| Channel Overlays | Color channel curves |
|---|---|
| Histogram | Static histogram for the image |
| Baseline | Straight diagonal line representing no adjustments, for comparison |
| Intersection Line | Axis guides that appear as you move a point on the curve |

In the same dialog, you can click the larger grid button ⊞ to display quarter-tone grid lines or the smaller grid button ⊞ for a finer grid.

Click the **Targeted Adjustment** tool on the panel, then move the pointer over the image; a small circle appears on the curve. Drag upward in the image to lighten the tonal value under the pointer, or downward to darken it. A point corresponding to that value appears on the curve.**A–B**

To cycle through the points on the curve, press the + (plus) key. To nudge a selected point, press an arrow key. (To remove a selected point, press Backspace/Delete.)

Keep the Curves controls showing on the panel. To correct the color, follow the steps on the next page.

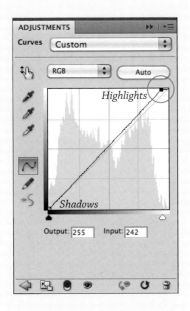

**A** *To lighten the highlights, we moved the white slider to the left.*

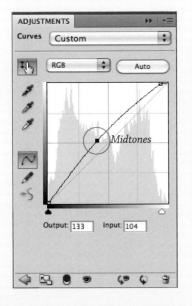

**B** *To lighten the midtones, we clicked the Targeted Adjustment tool, then dragged upward slightly on the grass. Although our adjustments improved the tonal balance, the image still has a blue color cast. We'll work on that next.*

## Part 2: Correct the color

1. With the Curves adjustment layer still selected, from the second menu, choose **Red** to adjust that channel separately, then do any of the following:

   Drag the middle of the curve upward to add red to the midtones or downward to subtract red (to a lesser extent, this adjustment will also affect the reds in the shadows and highlights). This midtone adjustment is often all that's required.

   You can also add or subtract red in the shadows by dragging the lower part of the curve, or in the highlights by dragging the upper part of the curve.**A**

   Click the Targeted Adjustment tool on the panel, 🖑 then drag in the image to adjust the part of the curve that corresponds to that color value.**B**

2. Choose the **Green** channel, then the **Blue** channel, adding or subtracting that color from the image, as in the preceding step. You can switch back and forth between the color channels, and readjust them if needed (**A–D**, next page).

3. *Optional:* To lessen the impact of the Curves adjustment layer, lower the layer opacity; or click the adjustment layer mask, then with the Brush tool and the Foreground color set to black, apply brush strokes to the image.

➤ To save your adjustment settings as a preset for future use, see page 200.

---

**APPLYING CURVES TO A CMYK IMAGE**

The Curves options work the opposite way for a CMYK image than for an RGB image:

➤ Readouts from the Curves graph refer to percentages of ink. Black equals 100% and white equals 0%.

➤ Shadow values are represented by the upper right part of the curve, and highlights are represented by the lower left part of the curve. Drag the curve downward to lighten a tonal value or upward to darken it. For an individual color channel, you can drag the curve upward to add more of that color or downward to subtract it.

➤ Colors work in tandem. For example, reducing cyan adds red, reducing magenta adds green, and reducing yellow adds blue.

---

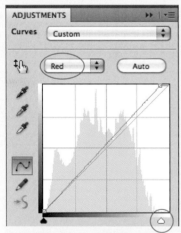

**A** *To add red to the highlight areas (such as in the clouds), with the Red channel selected, we moved the white slider slightly inward.*

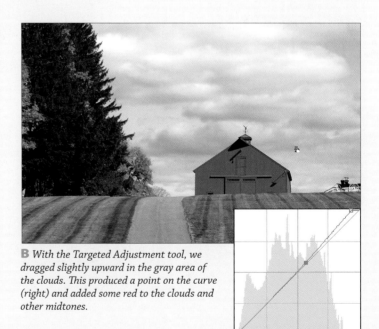

**B** *With the Targeted Adjustment tool, we dragged slightly upward in the gray area of the clouds. This produced a point on the curve (right) and added some red to the clouds and other midtones.*

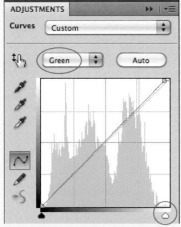

**A** *To remove red and blue from the highlights, with the Green channel selected, we dragged the white slider slightly inward.*

**B** *To reduce green in the image, we dragged downward with the Targeted Adjustment tool on the gray clouds and on the grass below the barn. Two points appeared on the curve.*

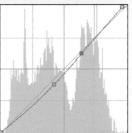

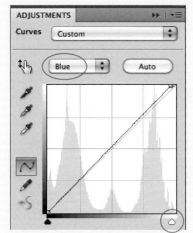

**C** *And finally, to remove green from the highlights, with the Blue channel selected, we dragged the white slider slightly inward.*

**D** *To reduce blue in the midtones, we dragged downward slightly with the Targeted Adjustment tool on the road. A point appeared on the curve. This is the cumulative result of all our Curves adjustments.*

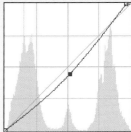

## APPLYING THE SAME ADJUSTMENT SETTINGS TO MULTIPLE IMAGES

Open a series of photos that were shot under the same lighting conditions, have the same color profile, and require the same color correction. Adjust one photo via a Levels, Curves, Exposure, Hue/Saturation, Black & White, Channel Mixer, or Selective Color adjustment layer, then save your settings as a preset via the Save [preset name] Preset command on the panel menu.**A** Click another document tab, then for the same type of adjustment layer, choose your saved preset from the preset menu.**B** Note: To copy adjustment settings for controls that can't be saved as a preset, on the Arrange Documents menu on the Application bar, click an appropriate "Up" button to tile the documents. Drag and drop the adjustment layer from the Layers panel of the corrected document into each of the other document windows.

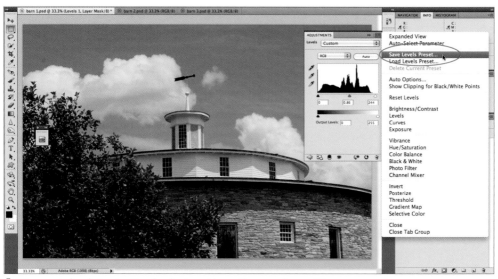

**A** We corrected a photo via a Levels adjustment layer, then saved our settings as a preset.

**B** We clicked the tab for another photo in the same series, created a Levels adjustment layer, then chose our preset of saved settings from the preset menu.

# Applying the Shadows/Highlights command

Shadows/Highlights **A** is one of our favorite tonal adjustment commands because it provides very targeted controls. It adjusts the luminance of each individual pixel depending on the darkness or lightness of neighboring pixels, and lets you apply corrections to a specific tonal range without overadjusting other areas of the image. The command does a good job of recovering details in the shadows and highlights, making it invaluable for correcting overexposed and underexposed areas, such as subjects that are in shadow due to strong side or back lighting.

Shadows/Highlights preserves more pixels in each tonal range than Levels and Curves, which can be confirmed by studying the Histogram panel before and after applying the command to an image.**B** And because Shadows/Highlights lets you pinpoint the tonal ranges to be corrected, you won't have to use multiple adjustment layers and layer masks to limit the area of adjustment, as you do when using Levels and Curves.

*Continued on the following page*

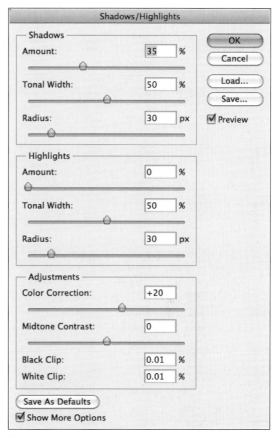

**A** *We checked Show More Options at the bottom of the Shadows/Highlights dialog to display the Shadows, Highlights, and Adjustments sliders. The sliders will give us extra control over which image areas are affected by the adjustment.*

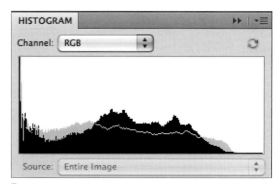

**B** *No gaps or spikes appear on the Histogram panel when you apply Shadows/Highlights because the command preserves an adequate number of pixels in each tonal range.*

## To apply the Shadows/Highlights command:

1. Click a layer or the Background, **A** and display the Histogram panel  so you'll be able to monitor the tonal adjustments.

   *Optional:* The Shadows/Highlights command can't be applied via an editable adjustment layer. To keep the Shadows/Highlights settings accessible and editable, convert the layer to be adjusted to a Smart Object layer.

2. Choose Image > Adjustments > **Shadows/Highlights**. The Shadows/Highlights dialog opens and the image is adjusted automatically using preliminary settings. Check **Show More Options** to display all the available options.

3. For the **Shadows:**

   Adjust the **Amount** value. **B** To lighten the shadows in order to recover details in those areas, start with the default Amount of 35%. If your photo needs a stronger correction, increase this value to 70%.

   Change the **Tonal Width** value to control the range of midtones that are included in the

   adjustment. For example, to limit the adjustment to only the very dark shadows, keep the Tonal Width value low (**A–B**, next page). Note: If halos appear along dark or light edges, lower the Tonal Width value.

   Raise or lower the **Radius** value to allow more or fewer neighboring pixels to be compared to a specific pixel in each shadow area in order to produce the adjustment. Don't raise this value too much, as allowing too many pixels to be compared could diminish the contrast and counteract the desired adjustment.

   Note: After adjusting the Tonal Width or Radius value, you may need to readjust the Amount value.

4. For the **Highlights:**

   Adjust the **Amount** value. Increase this value to darken and recover details in the highlight areas. By lowering the brightness of the highlights, you are allowing the midtones to stand out more.

*Instructions continue on page 230*

**A** *The shadow areas in this original image lack detail.*

**B** *In the Shadows/Highlights dialog, our Shadows setting of Amount 57 successfully lightened the shadows but also lightened too many of the midtones.*

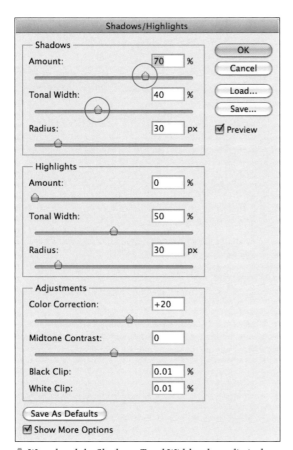

**B** *Our choice of increased Shadows: Amount and reduced Shadows: Tonal Width values (shown at left) successfully restored details to the shadows and midtones.*

*Continued on the following page*

**A** *We reduced the Shadows: Tonal Width value to limit the adjustment to just the lower midtones and shadows, and with that new tonal restriction in place, increased the Shadows: Amount value (slightly) to further lighten the shadows.*

Adjust the **Tonal Width** and/or **Radius** sliders to control the range of midtones that are included in the Highlights adjustment.**A–C** If needed, readjust the Highlights: Amount value.

5. To compare the original and adjusted images, press P to toggle the Preview on and off.

6. Under **Adjustments**, use the **Color Correction** slider to adjust the saturation, which may have been thrown off by the other adjustments.

7. Use the **Midtone Contrast** slider to increase or decrease the contrast in the midtones.

8. *Optional:* To save your Shadows/Highlights settings as a preset for use with other images, click Save, enter a descriptive name (keep the .shh extension), choose a location for the preset file, then click Save again. To load a saved settings preset in the dialog, click Load.

9. Click OK.

➤ To restore the default settings to the dialog, hold down Alt/Option and click Reset (Cancel becomes Reset).

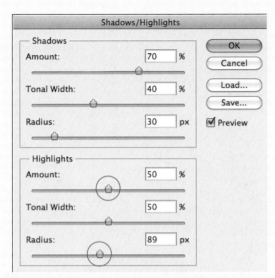

*A Next, we increased the Highlights: Amount value to subdue the sky. This had the unintended result of making the lower part of the sky too dark. To lighten just the upper midtones, we increased the Radius value (instead of changing the Highlights: Tonal Width value).*

**B** *This is the original photo, for comparison with the final corrected image at right.*

**C** *Using the Shadows/Highlights controls, we lightened the shadows and midtones in this photo and improved the overall balance between the midtones, shadows, and highlights.*

# Applying a tint via a Solid Color fill layer

If you apply a color to a layer (or to a selection on a layer) via a Solid Color fill layer, you will be able to edit or remove it at any time. This is a simple but effective way to correct a color cast or apply a color tint — typically, to a selected area of an image.

**To apply a tint via a Solid Color fill layer:**

1. *Optional:* To restrict the tint to part of an image, create a selection.**A**

2. From the **New Fill/Adjustment Layer** menu ⊘. on the Layers panel, choose **Solid Color**.

3. In the Color Picker dialog, choose a color for the tint.**B** Don't sweat over this; you can change the color later if you wish. Click OK.

4. The fill layer is fully opaque. Lower the layer opacity to make it semitransparent and/or change its blending mode (press Shift- + or Shift- –) to make it interact differently with underlying layers.**C**

➤ To change the tint for a color fill layer, double-click the adjustment layer thumbnail; this reopens the Color Picker.

➤ You can limit the effect of a Solid Color, Gradient, or Pattern fill layer by clicking the layer mask thumbnail, then applying black strokes to areas in the document. (This couldn't be done for the Color Overlay, Gradient Overlay, or Pattern Overlay layer effect.) Note: Keep the Use Default Mask on Fill Layers option checked in the Panel Options dialog, which opens from the Layers panel menu, to ensure that all new fill layers that you create will automatically have a mask.

**A** *The sky in this image looks washed out. To select that area before applying a tint, we chose the Quick Selection tool, , then dragged across the sky. Next, we clicked the sky area below each arm, then Alt/Option dragged to deselect any selected areas of snow.*

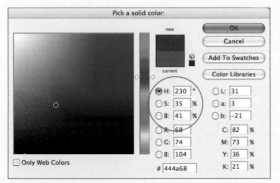

**B** *In the Color Picker, the color we chose has values of H: 230, S: 35, and B: 41.*

**C** *The blue tint that we applied via a Solid Color fill layer enlivened the sky. In addition, we chose Vivid Light as the blending mode for the adjustment layer to restore some definition to the clouds.*

## Screening back a layer using Levels

Printing dark text on top of a photo can be tricky. The picture has to be light enough to allow the text to be readable, yet visible enough to be interpreted as an image. Screening back an image is yet another great use for a Levels adjustment layer.

### To screen back a layer using Levels:

1. Open an image.

2. *Optional:* To limit the screened-back effect to a specific area of the image, create a selection.

3. Click an image layer or the Background,**A** then on the Adjustments panel, click the **Levels** button. The Levels controls display.

4. To reduce contrast in the image, move the **Output Levels** shadows (black) slider to the right.**B**

5. To lighten the midtone values in the image, move the **Input Levels** midtones (gray) slider to the left.**C**

6. *Optional:* Hold down the View Previous State button to view the original state of the image temporarily, then release.

**A** *The original document contains an editable type layer above an image layer.*

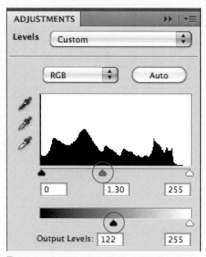

**B** *We used these settings for a Levels adjustment layer to lighten the image.*

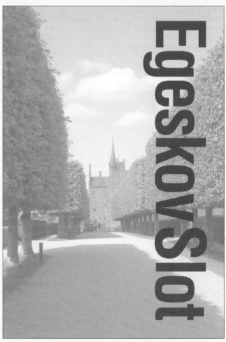

**C** *With the image screened back, now the type is more eye-catching and easier to read.*

If we had to pick one chapter that represents the heart and soul of Photoshop, this would be it. Here you will learn various ways to copy selections and layers within the same document and between documents, and fade the edges of a layer using a layer mask. You will also use the Clone Stamp tool and Clone Source panel to clone imagery, use the Photomerge command to create a panorama from multiple images, and use Smart Guides and other Photoshop features to position and align multiple layers. You'll be amazed at how easy (and how much fun) it is to create composite images!

## Using the Clipboard

One way to get a selection of imagery from one layer or document to another is by using the Clipboard commands, which are found on the Edit menu. First you choose the Cut, Copy, or Copy Merged command to put the current selection into a temporary storage area in memory, called the Clipboard. Then you choose a paste command, such as Paste or Paste in Place, to paste the Clipboard contents as a new layer in the same document or another document. Or if there is an active selection in the target document, another option is to use the Paste Into or Paste Outside command ★ to paste the Clipboard contents inside or outside of that selection, respectively.

If you cut (remove) a selection from the Background via the Cut command, the exposed area fills automatically with the current Background color.**A** If you cut a selection from a layer, the area left behind is replaced with transparent pixels.**B** (These are the same results that you get when you move pixels on a layer.)

The same Clipboard contents can be pasted as many times as needed. Only one selection can be stored on the Clipboard at a time, however, and it is replaced by new contents when you use the Cut, Copy, or Copy Merged command. With Export Clipboard checked

*Continued on the following page*

**COMBINING IMAGES**

# 14

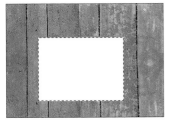

**A** *A selection is cut from the Background.*

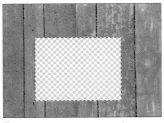

**B** *A selection is cut from a layer.*

in Edit/Photoshop > Preferences > General, the Clipboard contents will remain in temporary system memory even when you exit/quit Photoshop (but only until you shut down your computer).

➤ To empty the Clipboard at any time to reclaim system memory, choose Edit > Purge > Clipboard, then click OK.

➤ Unlike the Cut command, the Edit > Clear command empties a selection area without putting the selection contents onto the Clipboard.

When you use a paste command, the contents of the Clipboard appear on a new layer.

## To copy and paste a selection:

1. Read the sidebar on this page, and change the resolution of the source document, if necessary.

2. Click a layer in the source document, then create a selection. *Optional:* Refine the selection edge via the Refine Edge dialog (see page 161).

3. Choose one of the following commands:

   Edit > **Copy**  (Ctrl-C/Cmd-C) to copy pixels from the current layer within the selection area.

   Edit > **Copy Merged** (Ctrl-Shift-C/Cmd-Shift-C) to copy all the pixels that are visible within the selection area, from any layers.

   Edit > **Cut** (Ctrl-X/Cmd-X) to cut the selection out of the current layer.

4. Click in the same document or in another document.

5. Do either of the following:

   To have the Clipboard contents land in the center of a new layer, choose Edit > **Paste** (Ctrl-V/Cmd-V).

   To have the Clipboard contents land in the same *x/y* location as in the source layer or document, choose Edit > Paste Special > **Paste in Place** (Ctrl-Shift-V/Cmd-Shift-V). ★

6. If the source document has a different color profile than the target document, the Paste Profile Mismatch alert dialog will appear. Click Convert or Don't Convert, then click OK.

7. The pasted pixels will appear on a new layer.**B** You can restack the layer or reposition it in the image with the Move tool (see the next page).

**A** *We created a selection, then pressed Ctrl-C/Cmd-C to copy its contents.*

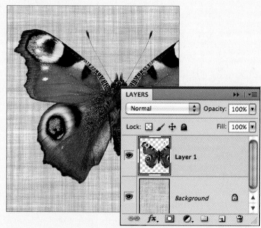

**B** *In another document, we pressed Ctrl-V/Cmd-V to paste the contents of the Clipboard, which arrived on a new layer.*

---

### HEY! MY PICTURE SHRANK!

When you paste or drag and drop a selection between documents, the copied imagery is rendered in the resolution of the target document. If the resolution of the target document is higher than that of the source one, the copy will look smaller relative to imagery on other layers; if the resolution of the target document is lower than that of the source document, the copy will look larger. To prevent a size discrepancy when copying imagery between files, before creating the copy, change the resolution of the source document via Image > Image Size to match that of the target document, and then resharpen the image.

➤ To compare the relative sizes of the source and target documents, use the Arrange Documents menu to arrange them side by side, and choose the same zoom level for both.

If the dimensions of the Clipboard contents that you paste are larger than those of the target document, some of the pasted pixels will be hidden from view outside the canvas area (they will be preserved and will save with the document). Here are some suggested ways to work with those pixels.

## Working with pixels outside the canvas area

➤ To bring hidden pixels into view, click the layer, then drag in the image with the Move tool. **A**

➤ To enlarge the canvas area to include all hidden pixels, choose Image > Reveal All.

➤ To select all the nontransparent pixels on a layer, including any pixels outside the live canvas area (or that are hidden by a layer mask), Ctrl-click/ Cmd-click the layer thumbnail on the Layers panel. (Select > All selects only the canvas area.)

➤ If you apply an image-editing command (such as a filter) to a layer, it will alter the entire layer, including any pixels outside the canvas area.

➤ To remove pixels that are outside the canvas area on all layers, choose Select > All, then choose Image > Crop. This can help reduce the file size.

➤ If a layer contains pixels outside the canvas area and you merge it with the Background (not with another layer), the hidden pixels will be discarded.

➤ To shrink the contents of a selected layer, choose the Move tool, ▸✛ check Show Transform Controls on the Options bar, Shift-drag a corner handle on the bounding box inward, then press Enter/Return to accept the new size.

### SHRINKING YOUR SELECTION EDGES

You can shrink or soften the edges of a selection before you move, drag-copy, or paste it (and you can also clean up the edges afterward). To remove edge pixels from an active selection before copying it, click Refine Edge on the Options bar, then lower the Contract/Expand value. To use the Feather slider to soften the edges of a selection, see the sidebar on page 237.

### COPYING THE LAYER SETTINGS, TOO

To copy layer settings (e.g., blending mode, opacity, and layer effects) along with imagery when creating composite documents, use the method described on page 238 or pages 242–243 instead of the Clipboard.

### COPYING IMAGERY TO A NEW LAYER

As an alternative method to the copy and paste commands, you can quickly get imagery onto a new layer within the same file using an easy one-step command. Click a layer or the Background, and create a selection. To put a copy of the selected pixels on a new layer, press Ctrl-J/Cmd-J or right-click within the selection and choose Layer via Copy. To remove the selected pixels from the original layer and put them on a new layer, press Ctrl-Shift-J/ Cmd-Shift-J or right-click within the selection and choose Layer via Cut. See also page 135.

**A** *A layer is dragged from left to right to reveal some of its hidden pixels.*

When you use the Paste Into command to paste the contents of the Clipboard into a selection, in addition to creating a new layer, the selection is converted to a layer mask. The pasted imagery can be repositioned within the mask, and the mask can be reshaped or modified via the Masks panel to reveal more or less of the imagery that it is hiding.

### To paste into a selection:

1. Select an area of a layer or the Background. **A**

2. Choose Edit > **Copy** (Ctrl-C/Cmd-C) to copy pixels from only the currently selected layer, or choose Edit > **Copy Merged** (Ctrl-Shift-C/Cmd-Shift-C) to copy all the pixels that you can see within the selection area, from any and all layers.

3. Click a layer in the same document or in another document.

4. Select the area (or areas) that you want to paste the Clipboard contents into. **B** *Optional:* Click Refine Edge and use the controls to adjust the selection edge.

5. Choose Edit > **Paste Special** > **Paste Into** or press Ctrl-Alt-Shift-V/Cmd-Option-Shift-V. ★ **C** A new layer and layer mask are created.

6. Do any of these optional steps:

   Although the entire contents of the Clipboard were pasted onto the layer, the layer mask may be hiding some of the imagery. Choose the **Move** tool or hold down V. To move the layer contents within the mask, click the layer thumbnail (on the left), then drag in the document. Or to move the layer mask, click the layer mask thumbnail (on the right), then drag in the image.

   To reshape the mask, click the mask thumbnail. With the **Brush** tool (B or Shift-B), a Soft Round brush, and with white chosen as the Foreground color, paint on the layer mask in the document to expose more of the pasted image. To hide more of the image, paint with black.

   To move the layer and layer mask as a unit, click between the layer and layer mask thumbnails to make the **Link** icon appear, choose the Move tool (V), then drag in the document.

➤ The dimensions in the File > New dialog automatically display the dimensions of the current contents of the Clipboard, if any.

➤ To paste Illustrator artwork into a Photoshop document, see the last task on page 308.

**A** *We used the Rectangular Marquee tool to select an area of this image layer, then chose the Copy command.*

**B** *Next, we used the Quick Selection tool to select the sky in this document.*

**C** *Finally, we used the Paste Into command to paste the contents of the Clipboard into the selection.*

# Drag-copying a selection in the same document

## To drag-copy a selection in the same document:

1. Select an area of a layer or the Background.

2. Do either of the following:

   Choose the **Move** tool ▸⊕ (V), then Alt-drag/
   Option-drag the selection. A The duplicate pixels
   will remain selected. B

   With a tool other than the Move tool chosen,
   Ctrl-Alt-drag/Cmd-Option-drag the selection.

3. Deselect.

➤ Include Shift with either shortcut listed above
   to move the selection by increments of 45°.

**A** *Create a selection on a layer or the Background (we
selected the window area with the Rectangular Marquee
tool), then Alt-drag/Option-drag it with the Move tool.*

**B** *A copy of the window is made.*

## REFINE EDGE IN ACTION

The Feather option in the Refine Edge dialog fades a
selection edge by a specified number of pixels. With a
selection tool chosen and a selection active, right-click
in the document window and choose Refine Edge, or
click Refine Edge on the Options bar. Choose View: On
White (W), then choose a Feather value. The higher
the document resolution, the higher the Feather value
needed. The feather will become evident in the document
when you move, drag-copy, copy and paste, or edit
(e.g., apply brush strokes or filters to) the selection.

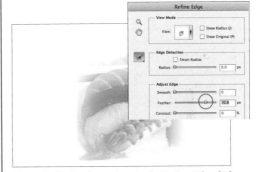

*We created a selection.*

*We applied a Feather value via the Refine Edge dialog.*

*We drag-copied the selection.*

# Drag-copying a selection or layer between files with the Move tool

When you drag and drop a selection of pixels from one document to another, presto, a duplicate of those pixels appears on a new layer in the target document. Pixels that land outside the canvas area can be moved into view at any time. An advantage of this method, as opposed to using the Clipboard, is that the layer style settings (blending mode, opacity, etc.) of the layer that you drag and drop are also copied. If the layer contains a layer mask, it will be copied, too.

## To drag and drop a selection or layer between documents with the Move tool:

1. Open the source and target documents. Read the sidebar on page 234 and change the resolution of the source document, if necessary.

2. Click in the source document, then click a layer or the Background on the Layers panel.

   *Optional:* Select part of the layer or Background.

3. Choose the **Move** tool ▶︎⊹ (V). On the Options bar, check **Auto Select** and choose **Layer** from that menu.

4. Drag from inside the selection or layer in the source document to the tab of the target document,**A** pause until the target document displays, then release the mouse where you want the copied imagery to appear.**B**

5. If the source document has a different color profile than the target document, the Paste Profile Mismatch alert dialog will appear. Click Convert or Don't Convert, then click OK.

   An alert will also appear if the source and target documents have a different bits-per-channel setting. Click Yes to accept the change in image quality (or click No to call the whole thing off).

6. The duplicate imagery will appear on a new layer.**C** You can reposition it with the Move tool.

➤ Hold down Shift as you drag and drop a selection or layer to have it appear in the center of the target document, regardless of where you release the mouse.

➤ To drag and drop a selection or layer between floating (not tabbed) documents, position them so they're both visible. Drag the selection or layer image from one document into the other, and release the mouse where you want the pixels to be dropped.

**A** *Drag a selection from inside a tabbed window over the tab of another document.*

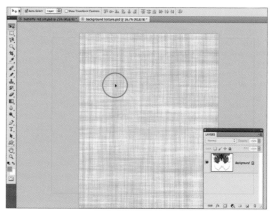

**B** *When the target image displays, drag the selection into the image, then release.*

**C** *The selection appears as a new layer in the target image.*

## REFINING THE EDGE OF A LAYER THAT YOU DRAG-COPY OR PASTE ★

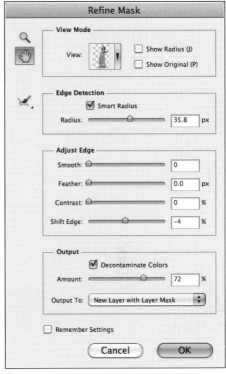

**A** *We drag-copied a layer containing a silhouetted image of a hula girl from a source document into this one. To convert the transparent areas into a layer mask (shown above), we chose Layer > Layer Mask > From Transparency. We're not happy with the white fringe along the edges of the layer, which is especially noticeable on the skirt (it's the wrong kind of fringe!).*

**B** *On the Masks panel, we clicked Mask Edge to open this dialog, then used the settings shown above to mask the fringe. We chose Output To: New Layer with Layer Mask before clicking OK.*

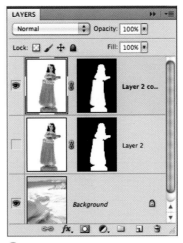

**C** *Because of the Output To setting we chose, a duplicate layer was created.*

# Creating new layers or documents from file thumbnails

This new, ultra-easy method for drag-copying a file may very well become a new standard.

## To drag-copy a file thumbnail into an existing Photoshop document: ★

1. Open a target Photoshop document.

2. *Optional:* To have the new object become a Smart Object layer in the target document, go to Edit/Photoshop > Preferences > General and make sure the Place or Drag Raster Images as Smart Objects option is checked.

3. From Bridge, Mini Bridge, or the Desktop, drag a file thumbnail into the target document window.  In our testing, this worked for files in all the popular file formats.

The image will appear in a transform box in the target document, with an X across it (**A**, next page).

4. *Optional:* Scale the image object by Shift-dragging a handle on the transform box.

5. To accept the new layer, double-click inside it or press Enter/Return (**B**, next page). If you checked the preference in step 2, the imagery will become a Smart Object layer.

➤ To learn how to edit a Smart Object layer, see page 310.

**A** *We dragged an image thumbnail from Mini Bridge into a Photoshop document.*

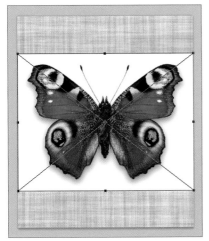

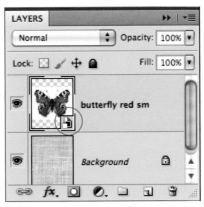

**B** *When we double-clicked inside the "X", the new layer became a Smart Object layer.*

**A** *The image appeared in the target document.*

This is another way to quickly get file thumbnails to arrive as layers in a new Photoshop document.

### To create a new document from thumbnails via a command:

1. In Bridge or Mini Bridge, select the thumbnail for one or more files that you want to create Photoshop layers from.

2. In Bridge, choose Tools > Photoshop > **Load Files into Photoshop Layers;C** or in Mini Bridge, choose that command from the Tools menu.

3. Stand by as the thumbnails are processed into standard (non-Smart Object) layers in a new Photoshop document.**D**

4. Save the new file. If you want to create a Background for it, see page 136.

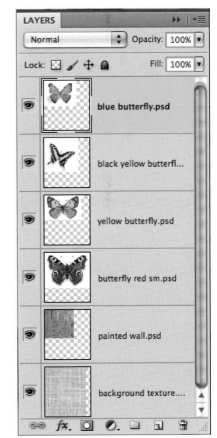

**C** *In Bridge, we selected six image thumbnails, and are choosing the Load Files into Photoshop Layers command.*

**D** *The selected thumbnails became layers in a new Photoshop document.*

# Drag-copying layers between files via the Layers panel

So far, you have learned how to drag and drop layers with the Move tool and create layers from file thumbnails. Here you will drag and drop a layer, multiple layers, or a layer group from the Layers panel of a source document into a target document. An advantage of this method is that if the source file contains multiple layers, you can control which ones are copied. Here, as with the Move tool method, pixels that lie outside the live canvas area are included.

### To drag-copy a layer between files via the Layers panel:

1. Open the source and target documents. On the Arrange Documents menu ▦ on the Application bar, click one of the 2 Up icons.**A**

2. Click in the source document window, then on the Layers panel, click the layer, Background, or layer group that you want to duplicate, or Ctrl-click/Cmd-click multiple layers.

3. Drag your selection from the Layers panel of the source document into the target document **B**

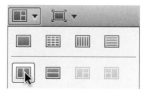

**A** *On the Arrange Documents menu on the Application bar, click a 2 Up icon.*

---

**SELECTING A LAYER UNDER THE POINTER**

To quickly select a layer that contains nontransparent pixels below the pointer, choose the Move tool.▶⊕ Check Auto-Select on the Options bar, choose Group or Layer from the menu, then click an image area in the document.

---

**B** *After clicking in the source document window, we are Shift-dragging a layer group from the Layers panel of that document into the target document window.*

(or Shift-drag the selection to make the new imagery appear in the center of the target document). The new layer(s) will be stacked above the previously selected one.**A**

4. If the source document has a different color profile than the target document, the Paste Profile Mismatch alert dialog will appear. Click Convert or Don't Convert, then click OK.

   An alert will also appear if the source and target documents have a different bits-per-channel setting. Click Yes to accept the change in image quality (or click No to call the whole thing off).

5. Either close the source document or click the Consolidate All (first) icon on the Arrange Documents menu.

6. *Optional:* With the Move tool (V), reposition the new layer.

   Or to scale the new layer, choose the Move tool and check Show Transform Controls on the Options bar. If you can't see all the handles, press Ctrl-0/Cmd-0 to change the document zoom level. Shift-drag a corner handle on the bounding box, then press Enter/Return to accept the new size.

---

**CREATING A NEW DOCUMENT FROM A LAYER**

To quickly create a new document from a layer, click the layer, then from the Layers panel menu, choose Duplicate Layer. The Duplicate Layer dialog opens. From the Document menu, choose New, enter a name for the new document in the Name field, then click OK. Save the new file.

---

**A** *When we released the mouse, the duplicate layer group appeared in the center of the target document.*

# Fading the edge of a layer via a gradient in a layer mask

One effective way to create a composite image is by adding layers to a target file that contains a white or solid-color Background, a photograph of a texture, or a screened-back image. You can scale or move the image layers individually to create a pleasing composition, and fade the side of any layer by applying a gradient to its layer mask, as we show you here.

## To fade the edge of a layer using a gradient in a layer mask:

1. Open several documents, one of which is to be used as a background (target) image for the whole composition.**A** The target image should be the largest of the bunch. To prevent any scale discrepancies, make sure all the images have the same resolution.

2. Follow the instructions on pages 238–239, page 240, or pages 242–243 to drag and drop the source imagery into the target document, including scaling the new image layers with the Move tool, if necessary.**B**

3. Save the target image and close the others.

4. Click one of the new image layers, then click the **Add Layer Mask** button ◻ at the bottom of the Layers panel (**A**, next page). Keep the layer mask thumbnail selected.

5. Choose the **Gradient** tool ◼ (G or Shift-G). Click the Gradient picker arrowhead on the Options bar, then click the "Black, White" gradient. (If you don't see this preset, choose Reset Gradients from the picker menu, then click OK in the alert dialog.) Also click the Linear Gradient button ◼ on the Options bar.

6. In the document window, start dragging horizontally or diagonally from where you want the complete fadeout to be, and stop dragging where you want the image to remain fully opaque (**B**, next page). Hold down Shift while dragging to constrain the angle to an increment of 45°. The gradient will fill the layer mask, and the imagery on that layer will be partially hidden (**C–D**, next page).

   ▶ To redo the fade effect, make sure the layer mask thumbnail is still selected, then drag in the document again with the Gradient tool (drag in a new direction or start dragging from a new position).

7. Repeat steps 4–6 for other layers you want to partially mask.

**A** We began by opening some theme-related images, just to see how they would look together and to get our creative juices flowing. We decided to use the photo of a burlap texture as the background for a montage.

**B** We dragged layers from some other documents onto our target image, which contains a photo of burlap. We resized and repositioned the new layers, and also rotated two of them.

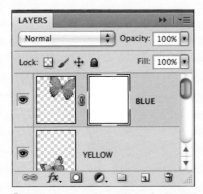

**A** *Next, we created a mask for the "BLUE" layer, and kept the layer mask thumbnail selected.*

**B** *We chose the Gradient tool and the "Black, White" preset. To hide the edge of the imagery on the "BLUE" layer, we dragged a short distance to the left, starting from outside the canvas area. (The black areas in a mask hide layer pixels. Note the black areas in Figure* **D**, *below.)*

**C** *We also created a layer mask for the "WALL" layer, then dragged in the document with the Gradient tool, in a different direction.*

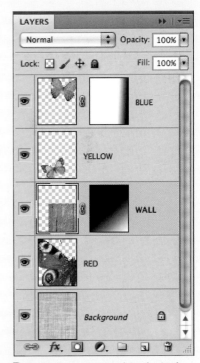

**D** *This is the Layers panel for the final image, which is shown at left.*

## HIDING A SEAM WITH A BRUSH

You can edit a layer mask using the Brush tool, a basic Photoshop technique that is described on page 169.

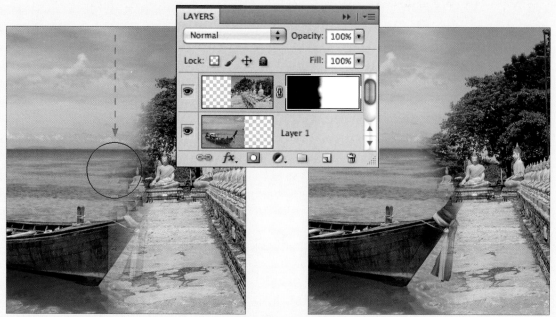

**A** *The edge of an image layer in this document is partially hidden by a gradient that we applied to the layer mask. We want to eliminate the noticeable seam. We chose the Brush tool, a Soft Round brush, an Opacity value of 100%, and black as the Foreground color. We made the brush very large, clicked the layer mask thumbnail, and are dragging downward in the image (above left). With a couple of quick swipes of the brush, the seam is gone (above right).*

## REMOVING AREAS OF A MASK WITH A BRUSH

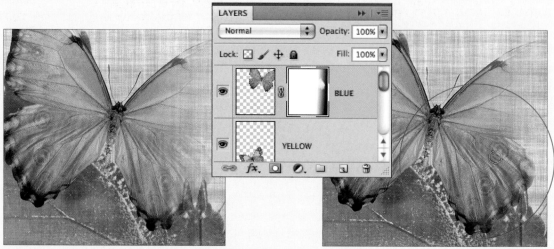

**B** *The right edge of the "BLUE" layer is partially hidden by a gradient that we applied to the layer mask (above left). To reveal more of the texture of the blue butterfly, we chose a Soft Round brush and an Opacity of 55% for the Brush tool, and are painting with white as the Foreground color to partially remove the mask (above right).*

# Aligning and distributing layers

Similar to the way you might align objects in a drawing program, via buttons on the Options bar, you can align the visible parts of one layer to another layer, or align multiple layers to one another.

## To align layers to one another:

1. Choose the **Move** tool ⊕ (V), then check **Auto Select** and choose **Layer** on the Options bar.

2. Click one image or type layer, then Ctrl-click/Cmd-click one or more additional layers.**A**

3. Click one of the six **align** buttons on the Options bar (use tool tips to identify them).**B–C**

➤ To align layers to the edges of a selection, create the selection before following the steps above.

The distribute buttons equalize the spacing among multiple selected or linked layers. You must select three or more layers first.

## To equalize the spacing among layers:

1. Choose the **Move** tool ⊕ (V), then check **Auto Select** and choose **Layer** on the Options bar.

2. Click a layer, then Ctrl-click/Cmd-click at least two other layers.

3. Click one of the six **distribute** buttons on the Options bar.**D–E**

➤ Oops! You clicked the wrong button? Choose the Undo command before applying a different one.

**A** *We chose the Move tool and we selected four layers.*

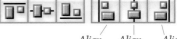

Align Top Edges  Align Vertical Centers  Align Bottom Edges

Align Left Edges  Align Horizontal Centers  Align Right Edges

**B** *These are the align buttons on the Options bar.*

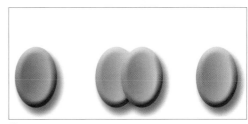

**C** *We clicked Align Bottom Edges.*

Distribute Top Edges  Distribute Vertical Centers  Distribute Bottom Edges  Auto-Align Layers

Distribute Left Edges  Distribute Horizontal Centers  Distribute Right Edges

**D** *These are the distribute buttons on the Options bar.*

**E** *We clicked Distribute Horizontal Centers.*

# Using the Clone Stamp tool and the Clone Source panel

By dragging with the Clone Stamp tool, you can clone all or part of an image from one layer to another in the same document or between documents. This tool is useful for creative montaging, commercial retouching, and video editing. The Clone Source panel lets you keep track of up to five different source documents (represented by a row of buttons at the top of the panel); reassign new sources; clone repeatedly from the same source; and transform the source pixels before or as you clone them.

## To use the Clone Stamp tool and the Clone Source panel:

1. Open one or more RGB documents to be used as source imagery, and create or open a target document.

2. Choose the **Clone Stamp** tool (S or Shift-S). From the Options bar, choose a Soft Round brush, a Mode, an Opacity of 100% (to start with), and a Flow percentage, and check Aligned.

   *Optional:* If you have a stylus and tablet, you can activate the Tablet Pressure Controls Opacity button and/or the Tablet Pressure Controls Size button on the Options bar. ★

   *Optional:* If the source file contains adjustment layers and you want the Clone Stamp tool to ignore their effects when sampling, activate the Ignore Adjustment Layers When Cloning button.

3. Display the Clone Source panel. **A** By default, the first source button is selected. Check **Show Overlay** and **Auto Hide**, then set the **Opacity** to around 35–50% so you'll be able to preview the source as an overlay (a faint version of the source layer). If you want the overlay to display only within the brush cursor, check **Clipped**.

4. In the target document, create a new blank layer.

5. Click the source document tab. From the **Sample** menu on the Options bar, choose which part of the document is to be cloned: **Current Layer**, **Current & Below**, or **All Layers**. For either of the first two options, also click a layer.

6. Alt-click/Option-click an area in the image to set the source point. **B** The source file and layer will be assigned to, and will be listed below, the first source button on the Clone Source panel.

7. Click the target document tab.

8. To position the clone, move the pointer over the image without clicking. Adjust the tool diameter by pressing [ or ], then start dragging to make the cloned pixels appear (**A**, next page). The overlay will disappear temporarily (because you checked Auto Hide), then will reappear when you release the mouse. (For other ways to transform the overlay, see the next page.)

9. To clone from another document, click the second source button at the top of the Clone Source panel, then repeat steps 4–8. Or to switch to a different clone source, click its button.

   *Beware!* The Clone Source panel keeps the links active only while the source documents are open. If you close a source document, its link to the Clone Source panel is broken!

► To use the Clone Stamp tool to retouch imagery within the same document, see pages 276–277.

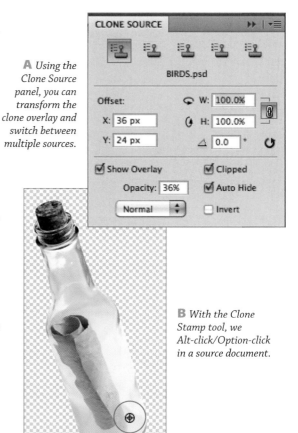

**A** *Using the Clone Source panel, you can transform the clone overlay and switch between multiple sources.*

**B** *With the Clone Stamp tool, we Alt-click/Option-click in a source document.*

A *We're dragging with the Clone Stamp tool on a new blank layer in our target document to brush in some pixels from the source document.*

B *This time, before we began cloning the bottle, we clicked the Flip Horizontal button on the Clone Source panel and changed the Offset values (see the panel at right).*

Once you start cloning with the Clone Stamp tool, the position and orientation of the source overlay becomes fixed. Well...not permanently. You can reposition, scale, flip, or rotate it by changing values on the Clone Source panel or by using keyboard shortcuts before you resume cloning. Note: The new values will apply only to the currently selected source.

## To reposition, scale, flip, or rotate the clone source overlay:

With the Clone Stamp tool 🖊 selected and an overlay displaying in your document, do any of the following (if you use the Clone Source panel, you can use the scrubby sliders):

To reposition the source overlay, change the **Offset X** and/or **Y** values on the panel; or Alt-Shift-drag/Option-Shift-drag the overlay.

To scale the source overlay, change the **W** or **H** values on the panel; or hold down Alt-Shift/ Option-Shift and press (and keep pressing) [ or ]. Activate the Maintain Aspect Ratio button 🔳 to preserve the current aspect ratio as you change the W or H value. Try not to scale the source more than 120 or –120%.

To flip the source, click the **Flip Horizontal** 🔄 and/or **Flip Vertical** 🔄 button.B ★

To rotate the overlay, change the **Rotate** value,◿ or hold down Alt-Shift/Option-Shift and press (and keep pressing) < or >. Drag to clone at the chosen angle.

➤ To restore the default scale, flip, and rotation values to the current clone source, click the Reset Transform button.↺

➤ To display the Clone Source panel when the Clone Stamp tool is selected, click the Toggle Clone Source panel button 🔳 on the Options bar.

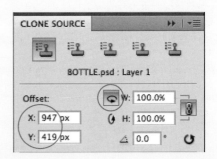

# Using the Photomerge command

The Photomerge command combines two or more photos of the same scene into a single panoramic image. It creates a layer from each photo and adds a layer mask to each one to control the transitions between them. Photoshop does the work for you!

## To merge photos into one document via the Photomerge command:

1. In Bridge, arrange the photos in the correct sequence for the panorama (this will help Photomerge work faster), then multiple-select them. PSD files are processed more quickly than raw files.

2. Choose Tools > Photoshop > **Photomerge**. The Photomerge dialog opens.**A**

3. Click a **Layout** option: **Auto** (Photoshop picks the best layout), **Perspective**, **Cylindrical**, **Spherical** (best for a 360° panorama), **Collage** (photos are combined by stretching and rotating), or **Reposition** (no stretching or rotating occurs) (**A–C**, next page). Unfortunately, the layout can't be previewed.

4. Check any of the following correction options, if they're available for your Layout choice:

   **Blend Images Together** uses color matching and layer masks to create seamless transitions between the photos. By default, this option is checked for all the Layout options.

   **Vignette Removal** lightens any dark areas that the camera lens produced around the perimeter of the photos.

   **Geometric Distortion Correction** corrects lens distortion, such as pincushioning (pinching), barreling (bulging), or extreme wide angles.

5. Click OK, then sit back while Photoshop opens the source files, aligns and blends them into a panorama, and opens a new document onscreen.

6. To eliminate any unwanted transparent areas from the edges, use the Crop tool.

7. Save the new document.

➤ The Tools > Photoshop > Process Collections in Photoshop command (in Bridge) locates a series of photos within the current folder that contain similar exposure settings and capture times, creates a panorama, saves the file to the current folder in the PSD format, then closes it.

---

**SHOOTING PHOTOS FOR A PANORAMA**

To get good results from the Photomerge command, Adobe makes the following recommendations:

➤ For the most precise alignment among multiple photos, and to help prevent distortion, use a tripod and shoot all the photos from the exact same spot, in the sequence needed for the panorama.

➤ Choose the same focal length (zoom) setting for all the photos.

➤ Overlap the viewing area from one shot to the next by approximately 40%.

➤ For optimal results, choose the same exposure or aperture setting for all the shots. You don't have to fuss over matching the exposures perfectly, because as Photomerge processes the files, it will even out exposure discrepancies.

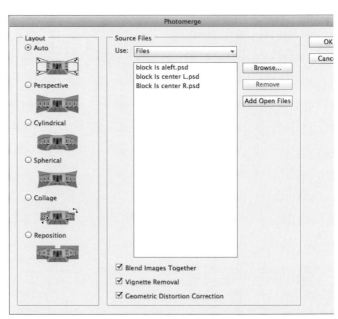

**A** Choose a Layout and correction options in the Photomerge dialog.

## THREE OF THE LAYOUT OPTIONS IN PHOTOMERGE

*We chose these three source photos for our panorama.*

**A** *The Perspective Layout option in Photomerge shrank the images in the center to add depth but also produced some distortion on the left side (flattened the roadway). This option would be better suited for creating a narrower panorama from just two photos, preferably ones that don't show obvious lens distortion.*

**B** *The Cylindrical option enlarged the images at the center. This option is good for a wide panorama like this one (a panorama made from three or more photos).*

**C** *The Reposition Only option simply places the images in a row without transforming them. For our photos, this option produced results similar to the Cylindrical option, except here the horizon became slightly arched in the center.*

# Using Smart Guides, ruler guides, and the grid

Sometimes successful composite images come together in a serendipitous way without a lot of forethought or careful alignment. At other times, you may need to plan ahead or position objects more precisely — perhaps if your Photoshop image needs to fit perfectly within the confines of a Web or print page layout. To accomplish this, such layout features as grids, rulers, and guides come in handy.

Our favorite precision alignment feature in Photoshop is Smart Guides. If this feature is on and you move an item (such as an image or type layer) in a multilayer document, temporary guide lines will appear onscreen when it nears the top, middle, or bottom of another layer.

## To use Smart Guides while moving a layer:

1. Make sure both the View > **Extras** and View > Show > **Smart Guides** commands have check marks.

2. Click a layer in a multilayer document.

3. With the **Move** tool ⊹ (V), drag the layer. Magenta (the default color) lines will appear when the layer nears the top, middle, or bottom of imagery or type on other layers.**A–B** Let the layer snap to a guide or to a pair of intersecting guides.

➤ In the Guides, Grid & Slices panel of the Edit/ Photoshop > Preferences dialog, you can change the color of guides, Smart Guides, and the grid, and choose other related options (see page 394). Your preference settings will apply to all Photoshop documents.

---

**VIEWING EXTRAS**

The View > Extras command (Ctrl-H/Cmd-H) shows or hides whichever features are currently enabled on the View > Show submenu. Among the Show submenu features that you can show and hide are Layer Edges, Selection Edges, the Grid, (ruler) Guides, and Smart Guides. These choices affect the current document and any documents that you subsequently open.

Mac OS users: If a dialog opens when you choose the Extras command for the first time, see the first tip on page 158.

---

**A** *With the help of a Smart Guide, we are aligning the top of the blue butterfly layer to the top of the yellow butterfly layer.*

**B** *Here, we are aligning the bottom of the blue butterfly layer to the center of the yellow butterfly layer.*

The rulers display on the top and left sides of the document window. They are useful for positioning objects (as we show you in this task) and for creating guides (as in the next task).

### To show or hide the rulers:

Do either of the following:

Choose **Show Rulers** from the **View Extras** menu ![icon] on the Application bar (and make sure Show Guides is also checked).

Choose View > **Rulers** or press Ctrl-R/Cmd-R.

The current location of the pointer on the image is indicated by a dotted marker on each ruler. Move the pointer, and you'll see what we mean. If you drag a layer with the Move tool, you can note its position using the markers on the rulers.**A**

➤ To change the units for both rulers quickly, right-click either ruler and choose a unit from the context menu. Or to get to the Units & Rulers panel in the Preferences dialog quickly, where you can also change the units, double-click either ruler.

➤ To change the ruler origin (to measure distances from a specific location), starting from the upper left corner where the two rulers meet, drag diagonally into the image. To restore the default origin, double-click in the upper left corner.

You can place ruler guides where you need them and remove them individually at any time. Like Smart Guides, they have magnetism (see "To use the Snap To feature" on the next page), but unlike Smart Guides, they linger onscreen and save with your file.

### To create ruler guides:

Show the rulers, then drag from the horizontal or vertical ruler into the image,**B–C** releasing the mouse where you want the guide to appear.

As you create guides, you can do the following:

Snap a guide to a selection, to the edge of imagery on a selected layer, or to the grid, if displayed (see the next page).

Make sure View > Snap is checked, then Shift-drag slowly to snap a guide to a ruler increment.

➤ You can move any existing guide with the Move tool (the pointer becomes a double arrow), provided the guides aren't locked (see the next page).

➤ Alt-drag/Option-drag as you create a guide to switch its orientation from vertical to horizontal, or vice versa.

**A** *As we move a layer, the current location of the pointer is indicated by a dotted line on each ruler.*

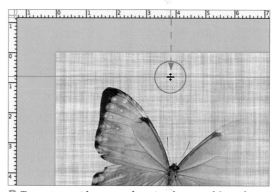

**B** *To create a guide, we are dragging downward from the horizontal ruler.*

**C** *We snapped the new guide to the top edge of the butterfly layer. (Via the Guides, Grid & Slices panel of the Preferences dialog, we changed the color of our guides to light red.)*

When the View > Snap command is on (and depending on which options are checked on the View > Snap To submenu), as you move a selection border or layer near a ruler guide, grid line, the edge of layer imagery, or the canvas area, the pointer or item will snap (to the item) with a subtle tug. (Personally, we prefer to use Smart Guides... but here it is, for what it's worth.)

### To use the Snap To feature:

1. Choose View > Snap To > **Guides**, **Grid**, **Layers**, **Slices**, **Document Bounds**, or **All** (of the above). Note: For the Snap To > Guides, Grid, or Slices option to be available, that feature must also have a check mark on the View > Show submenu.

2. Make sure View > **Snap** has a check mark (Ctrl-Shift-;/Cmd-Shift-;). This command enables whichever options are currently checked on the Snap To submenu.

To reposition ruler guides (Move tool), they must be unlocked first. Conversely, to prevent guides from being moved unintentionally, lock 'em up.

### To lock or unlock all ruler guides:

Choose View > **Lock Guides** (Ctrl-Alt-;/Cmd-Option-;). Rechoose the command to unlock.

➤ If guides aren't locked and you change your document size via the Image Size command, the guides will maintain their relative positions in proportion to the image.

### To create a ruler guide at a specific location:

1. Choose View > **New Guide**.

2. In the New Guide dialog, click **Orientation: Horizontal** or **Vertical**, enter a **Position** value relative to the 0 (zero) point on that axis in any measurement unit that is used in Photoshop, then click OK. A guide appears in the document.

### To remove ruler guides:

Do either of the following:

To remove one guide at a time, make sure guides aren't locked, hold down V to spring-load the Move tool, then drag the guide out of the document window. *Beware!* Don't press Delete, or you could delete the current layer.

To remove all the guides from the document, choose View > **Clear Guides**.

The grid is a nonprinting framework that you can snap a layer or selection to. It can be displayed or hidden as needed, and can be turned on or off for individual documents.

### To show or hide the document grid:

To show or hide the grid, A choose **Show Grids** from the **View Extras** menu on the Application bar or press Ctrl-'/Cmd-'.

If the View > Snap To > Grid option is on, a selection, layer, or ruler guide will snap to a grid line if it is moved within 8 screen pixels of the line.

### To measure the distance and angle between two points:

1. Choose the **Ruler** tool (I or Shift-I).

2. Drag in the document window. The angle (A) and length (L1) of the measure line will be listed on the Options bar and the Info panel. Shift-drag to constrain the angle to a multiple of 45°.

3. *Optional:* You can drag the measure line to a new location. Or to change the angle of the line, drag either of its endpoints.

4. To hide the measure line, choose another tool.

➤ To redisplay the measure line, hold down I for a temporary Ruler tool. To remove the line, click Clear on the Options bar. A document can contain only one measure line at time.

**A** *The grid is displayed in this document.*

Brush settings apply to many Photoshop tools, such as the Brush, Mixer Brush, Pencil, History Brush, Healing Brush, Spot Healing Brush, Dodge, Burn, Sharpen, Clone Stamp, and Eraser. In this chapter, you will paint with the Brush tool, choose and customize brushes using the Brush panel, and manage brush presets using the Brush Presets panel. You will create bristle brushes for the new Mixer Brush tool, use that tool to transform a photo into a painting, smudge colors with the Smudge tool, then finally zap out parts of an image with the Eraser and Magic Eraser tools.

## Using the Brush tool

Before delving into the complexities of the Brush panel, take a few minutes to get acquainted with the Brush tool. In these instructions, you'll choose a brush preset for the tool and choose Options bar settings to control its behavior.

### To use the Brush tool:

1. Click an image layer or create a new layer.

   *Optional:* If you want to confine your brush strokes to a specific area, create a selection.

2. Choose the **Brush** tool ✦ (B or Shift-B).

3. Choose a Foreground color.

4. On the Options bar, do the following:

   Click the Brush Preset picker arrowhead or thumbnail, then click a preset.**A**

   Choose a blending Mode (see pages 192–196).

   Choose an Opacity percentage. At 100%, the stroke will completely cover underlying pixels.

*Continued on the following page*

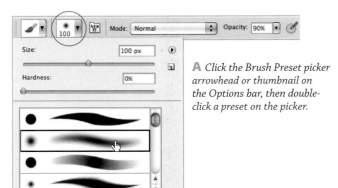

**A** *Click the Brush Preset picker arrowhead or thumbnail on the Options bar, then double-click a preset on the picker.*

# BRUSHES

# 15

Choose a Flow percentage for the rate at which paint is applied (for thick or thin coverage).

Click the Airbrush button,  if desired, to allow the paint to spread and build up when you hold down the mouse, as in traditional airbrushing.

5. *Optional:* If you have a stylus and tablet, you can activate the Tablet Pressure Controls Opacity button and/or the Tablet Pressure Controls Size button on the Options bar. ★

6. Draw strokes in the document window. If the Airbrush option is on and you press and hold in one spot, the paint drop will gradually widen (up to the maximum diameter of the brush) and become more dense and opaque. **A–B** Feel free to change Options bar settings between strokes.

➤ On the Layers panel, click the Lock Transparent Pixels button for the current layer to allow the tool to recolor only nontransparent pixels.

➤ To draw a straight stroke, hold down Shift while dragging with the Brush tool.

➤ To sample colors with a temporary Eyedropper, Alt-click/Option-click in the document.

**A** *This stroke was created with the Airbrush option off.*

**B** *This stroke was created with the Airbrush option on.*

**C** *You can make a temporary change to the Size or Hardness of a preset quickly via the context menu.*

## Choosing temporary brush settings

There are a gazillion ways to customize a brush. An easy way to start is by changing the Size and Hardness settings. The settings will remain in effect until you choose a different preset.

### To choose temporary settings for a brush preset:

1. Choose any tool that uses brush presets, such as the Brush, Mixer Brush, Pencil, or Eraser tool.

2. Do one of the following:

   Right-click in the document, then change the **Size** and/or, if available, the **Hardness** value (you can use the scrubby sliders), then press Enter/Return. **C** These settings can also be changed on the Brush Preset picker, which opens from the Options bar (see the preceding page), and the Size can also be changed via the Brush panel (see page 257) or Brush Presets panel (see page 260).

   To resize the brush via the keyboard, press [ or ].

   To resize the brush interactively, Alt-right-click-drag/Control-Option-drag horizontally in the document. If OpenGL was on in Edit/Photoshop > Preferences > Performance when Photoshop was launched and a round or elliptical brush is selected, a color (representing the current hardness value) displays in the brush cursor as it's scaled. To change the hardness, drag vertically using the same shortcut. ★

---

**SHORTCUTS FOR CHANGING TOOL SETTINGS**

With the Blur, Brush, Burn, Clone Stamp, Color Replacement, Dodge, Healing Brush, Paint Bucket, Pencil, Sharpen, or Smudge tool, some or all of these shortcuts can be used:

| Cycle through blending modes for the tool | Shift- + (plus) or Shift- - (minus) |
|---|---|
| Change the opacity, exposure, or strength percentage* (Shift-press a number to change the Flow level) | On the row of number keys or the keypad, press a digit between 0 and 9 (e.g., 2 = 20%) or quickly type a percentage (e.g., "38"); 0 = 100% |

*If the Airbrush option is on, press a number to change the Flow percentage or Shift-press a number to change the Opacity percentage.*

# Customizing a brush

Via a wealth of features on the Brush panel, you can customize the characteristics of any brush for use with the Brush, Mixer Brush, Smudge, or Eraser tool (all of which are featured in this chapter), and for the Pencil, History Brush, Art History Brush, Clone Stamp, Pattern Stamp, Blur, Sharpen, Dodge, Burn, and Sponge tools.

On the Brush panel, most of the settings for customizing brushes are organized into option sets; a few solo options simply get switched on or off. Many of the options are dynamic, meaning they add randomness or variation to the stroke, such as to its shape, texture, or color. The availability of options varies depending on the currently chosen tool and tip, and some features apply only to a graphics tablet and stylus. The choices are vast, but we'll boil them down to the ones we gravitate to. With practice, you'll learn which options and settings suit your painting style.

## To customize a brush via the Brush panel: ★

1. Choose a tool from the list at the top of this page. To see the greatest differences among the settings, select the Brush or Mixer Brush tool.

2. To show the Brush panel, click the panel tab or icon 🖌 or click the Toggle Brush Panel button 🖌 on the Options bar. Click **Brush Tip Shape** on the left side of the panel, and for now, click a non-bristle tip (a tip that doesn't look like a drawing of a brush).**A**

3. As you adjust settings for the tip, keep an eye on the stroke preview at the bottom of the panel:

   To change the brush **Size** (diameter), use the slider or scrubby slider. (To restore the original size to a non-Round or nonbristle preset at any time, click the Restore Original Size button.🔄)

   To change the **Angle** (slant) of an elliptical tip, use the scrubby slider, or drag the arrowhead around the circle, or enter a specific angle.

   To change the **Roundness** of the tip (make it more oval or more circular),**B** use the scrubby slider (0–100%) or drag either of the two tiny dark circles on the ellipse inward or outward.

   To change the **Hardness** of the tip (feather or sharpen its edge),**C** move the slider or enter a percentage. This option isn't available for all the brush tips.

*Continued on the following page*

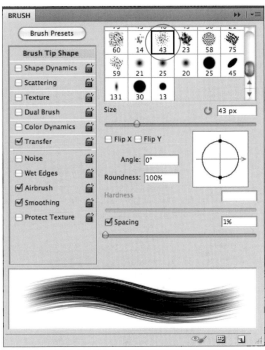

**A** *The Brush panel lets you choose a brush tip, customize it via a wide assortment of options, and save it as a preset. The preview at the bottom of the Brush panel updates dynamically as you change the settings.*

**B** *100% Roundness*

*20% Roundness*

**C** *100% Hardness*

*3% Hardness*

---

**WHERE THE BRUSH TIPS COME FROM**

When you load a library onto the Brush Presets panel (see page 260), the tips that are used by those presets also load onto the Brush panel, and display in the scroll window on that panel when you click the Brush Tip Shape button. Eight or nine standard tips also display below the other tips in the scroll window.

To control the distance between marks within the stroke, check **Spacing**, then move the slider (1–1000%),**A**–**B** or turn this option off to let the speed of your brush stroke control the spacing.

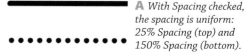

*A With Spacing checked, the spacing is uniform: 25% Spacing (top) and 150% Spacing (bottom).*

4. Next, you'll customize the behavior variations for the chosen brush, using three of the option sets on the panel. Checking the box for an option set, such as Scattering, activates the current settings for that set; clicking the set name both activates the current settings and displays the set options. If an option set isn't available for the current tool, the set name is dimmed.

*B With Spacing unchecked, the spacing is uneven: A slow stroke (top) and a fast stroke (bottom).*

To control the amount of allowable variation in the brush tip shape, click **Shape Dynamics**, then do any of the following:

*100% Size Jitter, 25% spacing*

Choose **Size Jitter,C Angle Jitter**, and **Roundness Jitter** values to establish an allowable amount of random variation for those attributes. The variations are more noticeable when the Spacing value (in the Brush Tip Shape option set) is greater than 10%.

*C 0% Size Jitter*

► To have the angle of the brush tip reflect the direction of your strokes, under Angle Jitter, choose Control: Initial Direction.

If you have a stylus, from each of the **Control** menus, choose which stylus feature is to control the variation for that option. Note that variations will occur even when this setting is Off.

*0% Scatter, 100% Spacing*

Choose **Minimum Diameter** and **Roundness** percentages.

5. To control the placement of pigment in the stroke, click **Scattering**, then do any of the following:

*500% Scatter, Both Axes option checked*

Check **Both Axes** to scatter pigment along and perpendicular to the stroke you draw, or uncheck this option to scatter pigment perpendicular to, but not along, the stroke.**D** Also choose a Control option, if desired.

*D 500% Scatter, Both Axes option unchecked*

Choose a **Scatter** percentage (1–1000%) to control how far the pigment can stray from the stroke. The lower the Scatter percentage, the more solid the stroke.

Choose a **Count** value (1–16) to control the number of marks in the stroke (also increase the Spacing value).

*0% Count Jitter, 100% Spacing*

Choose a **Count Jitter** percentage (0–100%) to control the amount of variation in the Count.**E**

*E 100% Count Jitter: The Count varies randomly from 1% to 100% of the Count value.*

6. To control how randomly the overall stroke opacity can vary as you use the tool, click **Transfer**, then do any of the following:

Choose an **Opacity Jitter** percentage (0–100%) for the amount the opacity can vary.**A–D** Choose a Control option to control the fading.

Choose a **Flow Jitter** percentage (0–100%) to control the rate at which paint is applied. A high Flow Jitter will make the stroke blotchy, but that may be the look you're after. Choose a Control option.

7. And last but not least (you're almost done!), check any of these options on or off:

**Noise** to add random grain to your brush strokes to make them look more rough.

**Wet Edges** to simulate the buildup of pigment that occurs at the edges of brush strokes in traditional watercoloring.**E–F**

**Airbrush** to allow strokes to build up for as long as the mouse button is held down in one spot. Activating the Airbrush 🖌 button on the Options bar does the same thing. This effect is noticeable only when the Spacing value is greater than 6.

**Smoothing** for smoother curves.

**Protect Texture** to apply the same texture pattern and scale to other brushes for which the Texture option is enabled, to create a uniform surface texture across the entire canvas.

8. *Optional:* Click the open lock icon 🔓 next to the name of any option set (the icon becomes a closed lock) to prevent the current settings in that set from being edited, even if you change presets. Locked settings are applied, but not saved, to any other preset you choose. To make those settings editable again, click the closed lock icon.

9. *Beware!* The custom settings that you have chosen are only temporary. To save them as a brush preset for future use, click the **Create New Brush** button 🔲 at the bottom of the Brush panel. Change the name in the Brush Name dialog (include some settings in the name for easy identification), check **Capture Brush Size in Preset** ★ (if desired), then click OK. Your saved preset will appear at the bottom of the Brush Presets panel (see the following page) and on the Brush Preset picker.

Now you can paint with your customized brush!

**A** *0% Opacity Jitter*

**B** *100% Opacity Jitter*

**C** *100% Opacity Jitter, Control off: The Opacity varies randomly from 1% to 100%.*

**D** *0% Opacity Jitter, Control set to Pen Pressure: The Opacity is controlled by the amount of pressure that is exerted on the tablet by the stylus.*

**E** *This stroke was drawn with Wet Edges unchecked.*

**F** *This stroke was drawn with Wet Edges checked.*

# Managing brush presets

The new Brush Presets panel stores and displays presets, as the Brush Preset picker does, and it offers several additional features (but doesn't have a Hardness slider). Via the panel, you can save and choose brush presets, change the size of the currently chosen preset, save and load brush preset libraries, and access the Preset Manager. Unlike the Brush Preset picker, the Brush Presets panel can be kept open onscreen.

## To use the Brush Presets panel: ★

1. Choose a tool that uses brushes, such as the Brush, Mixer Brush, or Pencil.

2. To show the Brush Presets panel, **A** click the panel tab or icon ; or click the Brush Presets button on the Brush panel; or choose Window > Brush Presets.

3. On the panel, do any of the following:

   Click a **tip** to be used with the current tool.

   Change the brush **Size** (diameter). (To restore the original size to a preset that lists a size value, click the Restore Original Size button.)

   To **load** different presets onto the panel, choose a library name from the panel menu, then click Append or OK (see also page 401).

   To save the current brush and its settings as a preset, click the **Create New Brush** button, add to or change the name in the Brush Name dialog (be descriptive), then click OK.

   To save all the presets that are currently on the panel as a new library, choose **Save Brushes** from the panel menu, type a name for the library, then click Save (see also page 401).

   To access the Preset Manager dialog, from which you can organize, append, replace, and reset which items load onto the Brush Preset picker and Brush Presets panel at startup, click the **Open Preset Manager** button, then see "Using the Preset Manager" on pages 398–399. This button is also available on the Brush panel.

   To delete the currently selected preset from the panel (but not from its library), click the **Delete Brush** button, then click OK.

   (For the Bristle Brush Preview button, see step 4 on the next page.)

➤ From the panel menu, choose a thumbnail or list option as the display type for the panel.

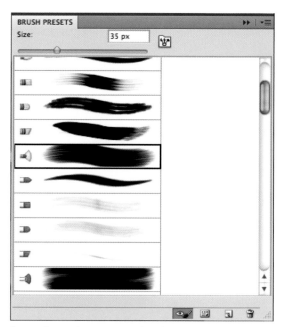

**A** *Use the Brush Presets panel to choose from the current library of presets, change the brush size, load in a different library, create a new library, and access the Preset Manager dialog.*

**OPENING THE PANELS QUICKLY** ★

➤ From the Brush panel, you can open the Brush Presets panel by clicking this button: [ Brush Presets ].

➤ From the Brush Presets panel, you can open the Brush panel by clicking the Toggle Brush panel button.

**RESETTING THE PRESETS**

To restore the Size and other saved Brush panel settings to an individual brush preset (but not the settings in the option sets), simply click the preset again. To restore the whole library of default presets to the Brush Presets panel, see page 401.

**GOING ONE STEP FURTHER BY USING TOOL PRESETS**

Brush presets contain only settings from the Brush panel, not from the Options bar. When you save settings as a tool preset via the Tool Presets panel or picker (such as for the Brush or Mixer Brush tool), the preset will contain the Brush panel settings, Options bar settings, and optionally for some tools, the current Foreground color, too (see page 402).

# Creating bristle brushes for the Mixer Brush tool

With the new Mixer Brush tool, you can create more painterly strokes than was previously possible in Photoshop. Brush characteristics can be modified to mimic different types of natural bristle brushes. You can also control the wetness of the paint, the paint flow, and the degree to which existing colors mix with new strokes. Although Photoshop paint lacks the viscosity of traditional oils, you can achieve some nice effects with it.

## To build a bristle brush: ★

1. Choose the **Mixer Brush** tool (B or Shift-B).

2. Display the Brush panel. If the bristle tips (they look like a drawing of a brush) aren't displaying on the panel, as they are in **A**, click Brush Presets, choose Reset Brushes from the panel menu, then click OK. Redisplay the Brush panel by clicking the **Toggle Brush Panel** button.

3. Click **Brush Tip Shape**, then click a bristle tip in the scroll window. **B** The tip shape is listed on the Shape menu.

4. Activate the **Bristle Brush Preview** button to display a schematic of the current tip and settings. **C** (To reposition the preview, move the pointer over the top left corner, then drag the black bar.) To view the current brush tip at different angles, keep clicking in the preview.

5. To pare down the number of options that will affect your brush, uncheck all the options on the left side of the panel except Smoothing or choose **Clear Brush Controls** from the panel menu.

6. Note the changes in the preview as you use the **Bristle Qualities** sliders to choose these physical characteristics for the tip:

   **Bristles** to control the number of bristles.

   **Length** to control the length of the bristles.

   **Thickness** to control the thickness of the bristles (and therefore the density of the stroke).

   **Stiffness** to control how easily the bristles bend. Choose a low value for smooth, fluid strokes or a high value for "dry" bristle marks.

   **Angle** to control the brush angle when a mouse is used. Angle variations are most noticeable when a Flat shape is chosen for the tip.

7. Continue with the steps on the next page to choose paint options for the Mixer Brush tool.

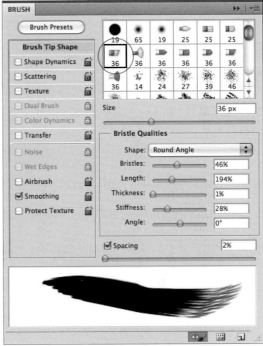

**A** When the Mixer Brush tool and a bristle tip are selected, the Bristle Qualities controls display on the Brush panel.

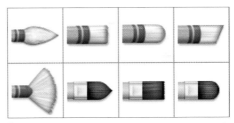

**B** Among the bristle tips, the light ones are Round shapes and the dark ones are Flat shapes.

**C** The Bristle Brush preview is a schematic and dynamic display of the Bristle Qualities settings that you have chosen for the currently selected brush tip.

Before using the bristle brush that you have created, you should choose Options bar settings to control how it will apply paint.

## To choose paint options for a bristle brush: ★

1. Follow the instructions on the preceding page, and with the **Mixer Brush** tool still selected, on the Options bar, do both of the following:

   Activate the **Load Brush After Each Stroke** button 🖌 to have the current Foreground color reload onto the brush after each stroke.

   Activate the **Clean Brush After Each Use** button ✖ to have a clean Foreground color reload after each stroke, or deactivate it to allow the last color that was in the brush to mix with the current Foreground color.

2. Choose a preset combination of settings from the **Useful Blending Brush Combinations** menu. The **Dry** presets are good for defining object details and edges, the **Moist** presets allow for moderate paint mixing, and the **Wet** and **Very Wet** presets work well for blending new strokes with existing paint.

   If you prefer to choose custom options (or to customize a preset), do any of the following:

   Choose a **Wet** value to control the dryness of the existing paint and the extent to which your brush will be able to pick it up in the stroke.**A–B**

   Choose a **Load** value to control how much paint is supplied to the brush (how quickly the brush runs out of paint).

   Choose a **Mix** value to control how much mixing and smearing can occur between the existing paint (including any white from the Background) and the new strokes.**C–D**

   Choose a **Flow** value to control the rate at which paint is applied (the amount of coverage).

   Check **Sample All Layers** to allow the brush to mix paint from all layers.

3. Create a new, blank layer (it can be above an image layer), then apply brush strokes. See also "To wipe a bristle brush clean," above right.

   ➤ For a quick way to get started or just to see some examples of tool presets, load the Mixer Brush Tool library onto the Tool Presets panel via the panel menu.

Use this method if you want to wipe a brush clean manually before applying more color, that is, override an activated Clean Brush After Each Stroke ✖ or Load Brush After Each Stroke 🖌 button.

## To wipe a bristle brush clean: ★

With the Mixer Brush tool selected, click the **Current Brush Load** menu ▤▾ on the Options bar and click **Clean Brush**, then click **Load Brush**.

> **PICKING UP COLORS FROM AN IMAGE**
>
> With the Mixer Brush tool, Alt-click/Option-click an area of an image layer. Pixel data from the sampled area will appear in the Current Brush Load thumbnail on the Options bar.

**A** *Wet 10 and Mix 10 paint options: The stroke hardly blended at all with the existing color.*

**B** *Wet 90 and Mix 10 paint options: The stroke blended somewhat with the existing color.*

**C** *Wet 10 and Mix 90 paint options: The stroke blended and smeared more with the existing color.*

**D** *Wet 90 and Mix 90 paint options: The stroke blended and smeared almost completely with the existing color.*

Follow these steps to reinterpret the shapes in a photo as a painting with the Mixer Brush tool.

## To transform a photo into a painting: ★

1. Open a photo. Create one or more blank layers to contain your brush strokes, so it will be easier to erase any unwanted marks.

2. Choose the **Mixer Brush** tool ![icon] (B or Shift-B).

3. On the Brush panel, ![icon] click **Brush Tip Shape**, then click a bristle tip. For variety in your brush strokes, try switching among these bristle tips: Round Fan to fill in large areas, Round Curve for medium-sized areas, or Round Point for small areas or lines.

   Choose **Bristle Qualities** settings, focusing on the Thickness and Stiffness controls. Choose low Thickness and Stiffness values for smooth strokes, a higher Thickness value for denser strokes, or a higher Stiffness value for dry, bristly strokes. See also page 261.

4. On the Options bar, do the following:

   To create a "clean" brush to be used to reinterpret the photo, deactivate the **Load Brush After Each Stroke** button ![icon] and activate the **Clean Brush After Each Stroke** button. ![icon] The current Load setting will now have no effect.

   From the **Useful Blending Brush Combinations** menu, choose a preset to control the character of the paint. The Wet and Very Wet presets are good for painting areas of minimal detail, such as backgrounds, and for picking up color from a photo, whereas the Moist presets are better for defining object details and edges. (For this task, don't use any of the Dry presets; their Wet value of 0 would prohibit the brush from interacting with colors in the photo.)

   Check **Sample All Layers** to allow the brush to pick up colors from the photo layer. Your strokes will appear on the new, blank layer.

5. As you apply strokes with the tool, try to mimic the direction of the shapes in the photo. Also remember to start each stroke with the pointer over the desired starting color, since the brush will be picking up colors from the photo **A–B** (and **A–C**, next page).

6. *Optional:* To remove any unwanted brush strokes, use the Eraser tool (see page 266).

*Illustrations continue on the following page*

**A** *This is the original, undoctored photo.*

**B** *We created a new layer, then with a Round Fan bristle tip and the Moist blending preset chosen, we applied some long brush strokes, brushing outward from the stem of the flower to convey a sense of movement.*

**A** *We created another blank layer, then drew brush strokes across the top of the image. Next, we created a third blank layer, then with a Wet preset chosen (and switching between Round Curve and Round Flat brushes), we defined the petals in quick strokes.*

**B** *On a fourth and final blank layer, we painted over the petals in broad strokes with a Round Flat brush, and defined the fine edges of the petals with a Round Point brush. Because we continued to use a Wet preset, a lot of blending occurred between the petals and the colors in the background.*

**C** *We converted this photo to a painting using the Mixer Brush tool, with assorted Useful Blending Brush Combinations presets chosen for our bristle brush.*

## Smudging colors

If all you want to do is merely smudge colors, you can use the Smudge tool instead of the Mixer Brush.

### To smudge colors:

1. Click an image layer.

2. Choose the **Smudge** tool ![icon] (you'll find it on the Blur tool pop-out menu).

3. On the Options bar, do the following:

   Click a brush on the **Brush Preset** picker.

   Choose a blending **Mode**. Normal smudges all shades or colors; Darken pushes only dark colors into lighter ones; Lighten pushes only light colors into darker ones; Hue, Saturation, and Color smudge only that color attribute without changing the tonal (light and dark) values; and Luminosity smudges tonal values without changing the hue or saturation.

   Choose a **Strength** percentage to control how forcefully the stroke smudges pixels.

   Check **Sample All Layers** to smudge colors from all visible layers and send the results to the active layer.

   Keep Finger Painting unchecked to allow each brush stroke to begin with the color under the pointer.

   If you're using a stylus and tablet, activate the **Tablet Pressure Controls Size** button. ![icon] ★

4. Create a new, blank layer.

5. To adjust the brush diameter, either press [ or ] or Alt-right-click-drag/Control-Option-drag to the left or right, then drag across any area of the image. **A–D** Your smudges may redraw slowly — even on a fast machine — so pause between strokes and be patient while Photoshop runs through its calculations.

➤ With the Finger Painting option checked on the Options bar, the Smudge tool will begin each stroke with the current Foreground color. To toggle this option on or off, hold down Alt/Option while dragging.

**A** *This is the original image.*

**B** *With Normal mode chosen for the Smudge tool, all the image colors were smudgeable.*

**C** *With the tool in Lighten mode, only light colors could be smudged.*

**D** *With the tool in Color mode, we were able to smudge hues but not luminosity values.*

# Using two of the eraser tools

The Eraser tool is handy for quickly removing stray pixels or isolated shapes from an image. The "magic" aspect of the Magic Eraser is that it erases only pixels that are similar in color to the one you click, within the tool's current Tolerance range. Be sure to use these tools on a duplicate image layer, because they remove pixels permanently.

## To use the Eraser tool:

1. Choose the **Eraser** tool ![eraser icon] (E or Shift-E).

2. On the Options bar, do the following:

   Click a Soft Round brush on the **Brush Preset** picker.

   Choose a **Mode** of **Brush**, **Pencil**, or **Block**.

   For Brush or Pencil mode, choose an **Opacity** percentage and deactivate the **Airbrush** button; for Brush mode, keep the **Flow** setting at 100%.

   If you're using a stylus and tablet, activate the **Tablet Pressure Controls Opacity** ![icon] and/or **Tablet Pressure Controls Size** buttons.![icon] ★

3. Duplicate the layer (or Background) that contains the area to be erased. Hide the original, and keep the duplicate selected. To allow pixels to be erased to transparency, deactivate the Lock Transparent Pixels button.![icon]

4. To adjust the brush diameter, either press [ or ] or Alt-right-click-drag/Control-Option-drag sideways. Drag across the areas to be erased.**A–B**

➤ Instead of erasing pixels permanently, hide them with an editable layer mask (see pages 168–169).

## To use the Magic Eraser tool:

1. Choose the **Magic Eraser** tool ![icon] (E or Shift-E).

2. On the Options bar, do the following:

   Choose a **Tolerance** value to control the range of colors the tool may erase. Try a value of around 30, or for a very narrow range, enter 3 or 4. You can change this value between clicks.

   Check **Anti-alias**. Check **Contiguous** to permit only pixels that are adjacent to one another to be erased, or uncheck this option to erase similarly colored pixels anywhere on the layer.

   Uncheck **Sample All Layers** and choose an **Opacity** of 100%.

3. Duplicate a layer or the Background, hide the original, and keep the duplicate selected. Click the areas to be erased.**C**

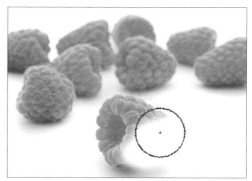

**A** *For the Eraser tool, we chose Brush mode, an Opacity of 100% (to allow the tool to remove pixels completely), and a Soft Round tip. Here, we're dragging across the raspberry in the foreground (on a duplicate image layer).*

**B** *With the raspberry removed from the foreground, the solid white Background beneath it is visible.*

**C** *One click of the Magic Eraser tool removed most of the sky from this photo (one more click and it will be gone). Our tool settings were Tolerance 38, Contiguous on, and Opacity 100%.*

Photoshop has tools for correcting many kinds of imperfections, from smoothing pores and wrinkles to removing unsightly power lines. It also has commands for retouching colors, from whitening teeth to swapping out colors in a product shot.

In this chapter, you will change colors by using the Match Color command, the Replace Color command, and the Color Replacement tool; clone areas with the Clone Stamp tool; smooth textures, such as skin, with the Surface Blur filter; smooth wrinkles or remove blemishes with the Healing Brush, Spot Healing Brush, and Patch tools; remove unwanted objects with the Spot Healing Brush tool and its new Content-Aware option;**A–B** and correct red-eye in a portrait with the Red Eye tool.

# RETOUCHING

## 16

**A** *We want to remove the red boat from the background of this image.*

**B** *We chose the Content-Aware option for the Spot Healing Brush tool, then brushed across the boat in the background. The boat was replaced with shapes from neighboring areas.*

# Using the Match Color command

You can use the Match Color command to match the color saturation and brightness of one layer or document to those of another layer or document, and to remove color casts. This would be useful, say, for unifying a series of related product photos that were shot with slightly different camera settings or lighting conditions. For the best results, use this command on images of the same or very similar content (e.g., beach scenes, indoor fashion or product shots).

## To correct color by using the Match Color command:

1. Open an RGB document to be used as the source for color and tonal values, and an RGB document to become the target of the color match. **A–B**

2. *Optional:* Display the Histogram panel 📊 so you will be able to monitor tonal changes in the file.

3. With the target document active, on the Layers panel, click the Background, press Ctrl-J/Cmd-J to duplicate it, and keep the duplicate selected.

4. Choose Image > Adjustments > **Match Color**. In the dialog, check Preview (**A**, next page).

5. From the **Source** menu, choose the name of the source document that you opened in step 1. The target document will instantly adopt color values from the source document. Note: If the source document contains multiple layers, choose a source layer (or Merged) from the Layer menu.

6. Under **Image Options**, do any of the following:

   Move the **Luminance** slider to adjust the overall brightness of the image (the default value is 100).

   Move the **Color Intensity** slider to adjust the color saturation (the default value is 100).

   Move the **Fade** slider to restore some of the original color to the image, if you want to blend the old with the new.

   Check **Neutralize** to remove any color casts from the target document. If this causes too great a color shift, lessen the effect via the Fade slider.

7. Readjust any of the sliders as needed, then click OK (**B**, next page).

➤ To limit the range of colors that are used as source data (and to help prevent odd color shifts), create a selection in the source document before opening the Match Color dialog, then in the dialog, check Use Selection in Source to Calculate Colors.

**A** *We will correct the orange cast in this photo…*

**B** *…by matching it to the more balanced color and tonal values of this photo.*

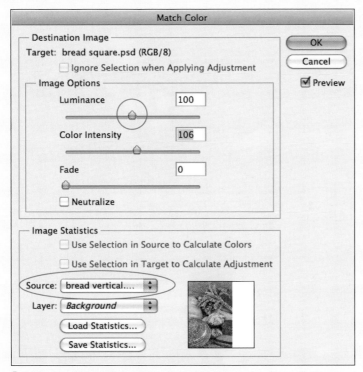

**Match Color**

Destination Image

Target: bread square.psd (RGB/8)

☐ Ignore Selection when Applying Adjustment

Image Options

Luminance                    100

Color Intensity              106

Fade                         0

☐ Neutralize

Image Statistics

☐ Use Selection in Source to Calculate Colors

☐ Use Selection in Target to Calculate Adjustment

Source:  bread vertical....

Layer:  *Background*

Load Statistics...

Save Statistics...

OK

Cancel

☑ Preview

**A** *In the Match Color dialog, from the Source menu, we've chosen the image that contains the desired color values.*

### REMOVING A COLOR CAST IN THE SAME DOCUMENT

► To correct the color in a document without using another document as source data, choose None as the Source image in the Match Color dialog and check Neutralize. Use the Luminance, Color Intensity, and Fade sliders, as needed. This method doesn't work in every case, but when it does, it's a good quick fix.

► To reuse your Match Color settings, click Save Statistics and use the Save dialog to choose a location for the data file. To load your saved settings, click Load Statistics.

**B** *Now the color and tonal values in this image are similar to those in figure* **B** *on the preceding page. If we were to import them into the same layout document, they would look harmonious together.*

# Using the Replace Color command

By using the Replace Color command, you can adjust the hue, saturation, or lightness of colors in specific areas of an image using selection and color controls in a dialog. This command works best for recoloring discrete areas that are easy to isolate.

## To use the Replace Color command:

1. *Optional:* For an RGB document that you're going to send to a commercial printer, choose View > Proof Setup > Working CMYK to view a soft proof of the image in simulated CMYK color.

   Once you've made a choice from the Proof Setup submenu, you can toggle the proof on and off while the Replace Color dialog is open by pressing Ctrl-Y/Cmd-Y. Regardless of whether the proof is on or off, the Color and Result swatches in the Replace Color dialog always display in RGB.

2. Click a layer (not a Smart Object layer) or the Background.

3. *Optional:* Create a selection to confine the color replacement to a specific area. **A**

4. Choose Image > Adjustments > **Replace Color**. The Replace Color dialog opens.

5. In the document, click the color to be replaced. The color you clicked appears in the Color swatch at the top of the dialog. **B**

6. Do any of the following:

   To add more color areas to the selection, click the Eyedropper tool 🖊 in the dialog, then Shift-click or drag in the preview or document window.

   Increase the **Fuzziness** value to add similar colors to the selection, or reduce it to narrow the range of selected colors.

   Check **Localized Color Clusters** to limit the selection to similar, contiguous colors. (We sometimes get similar or better results by lowering the Fuzziness value instead.)

7. If you added colors to the selection that you now want to subtract, with the Eyedropper tool, 🖊 Alt-click/Option-click or drag in the preview or document window (this is a temporary Subtract from Sample Eyedropper tool).

   ➤ For the preview window, click Selection to view the current selection, or Image to display the entire document. To toggle between the two display modes, press Ctrl/Cmd, then release.

**A** *We want to recolor the purple eyeshadow in this image. We loosely selected that area first.*

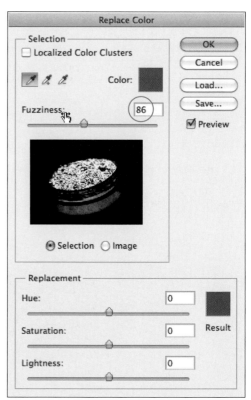

**B** *We opened the Replace Color dialog, then clicked the pot of eyeshadow. Areas matching that color displayed as a selection in the preview window. Our next step was to choose a Fuzziness value of 86.*

**8.** To replace the colors you have selected, do either of the following:

In the **Replacement** area, choose replacement **Hue**, **Saturation**, and **Lightness** values (you can use the scrubby sliders). The Result swatch will update as you do this.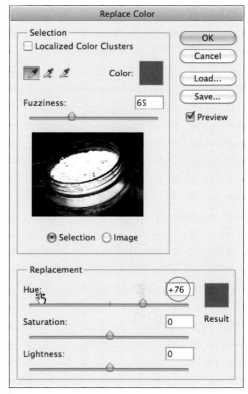 Note: A Saturation value greater than +25 may produce a non-printable color.

Click the **Result** swatch, choose a color from the Color Picker, then click OK. The sliders will shift to reflect the values of the new color.

Note: The Replacement sliders will stay put, even if you click a different area of the image or add to or subtract from the selection.

**9.** Click OK.**B** (For another use of this command, see page 274.)

➤ The Replacement sliders won't change the amount of Black (K) in a color for a CMYK document. That component is established by the CMYK Working Space, which is chosen in Edit > Color Settings.

➤ To restore the original dialog settings, hold down Alt/Option and click Reset (Cancel becomes Reset).

**A** *We lowered the Fuzziness value to 65, Shift-clicked more areas on the pot to add them to the selection, then changed the Hue.*

**B** *The original purple eyeshadow is now reddish brown.*

# Using the Color Replacement tool

The Color Replacement tool lets you change color, hue, saturation, and luminosity values, except instead of using a dialog as you do with Replace Color, you apply changes manually with a brush. You can also specify mode, sampling, limits, and tolerance parameters for the tool. And unlike the Brush tool, which applies flat colors, the Color Replacement tool tries to preserve the original texture as it changes colors. This tool, like the Replace Color and Match Color commands, is especially useful to advertising and catalog designers.

## To use the Color Replacement tool:

1. Open an RGB image.

2. Choose the **Color Replacement** tool 🖌 (B or Shift-B).

3. To choose a replacement color, do either of the following:

   Choose a **Foreground** color from the Color or Swatches panel, or sample a Foreground color by Alt/Option clicking in the document.

   If you're going to choose Background Swatch as the Sampling option in step 5, choose a **Background** color now.

4. If the color you chose isn't on the Swatches panel, 🎨 add it to the panel by clicking the **New Swatch of Foreground Color** button. 🔲

5. From the Options bar, choose parameters for the tool: **A**

   From the Brush Preset picker, choose a high **Hardness** value and a low **Spacing** value.

   To control which color characteristics the tool applies to the image, choose a **Mode** of **Hue**, **Saturation**, **Color**, or **Luminosity**. We've been pleased with the results we've gotten with Color mode.

   Click a **Sampling** button: **Continuous** 🖉 to apply the current Foreground color to all pixels the brush passes over (we prefer this option because it lets us replace both light and dark

colors); or **Once** ⊕🖋 to sample the first pixel the brush crosshairs click on and apply the Foreground color only to pixels that match that initial sampled color (since this option confines the sampling to just one color, if you need to replace, say, different shades of a particular color, you would have to sample each one separately); or **Background Swatch** 🖋 to replace only colors that match or are similar to the current Background color.

From the **Limits** menu, choose **Discontiguous** to recolor only pixels under the pointer; or **Contiguous** to recolor pixels under the pointer plus adjacent pixels; or **Find Edges** (our favorite option) to recolor pixels under the pointer while keeping the color replacement within discrete shapes. Note: Remember that in addition to the Limits choice, the tool is also controlled by the current Sampling and Tolerance choices.

Choose a **Tolerance** value (1–100%) for the range of colors to be recolored. A high Tolerance value permits a wide range of colors to be recolored; a low value allows only pixels that closely match the sampled color to be recolored.

*Optional:* Check Anti-alias for smoother transitions between the original and replacement colors.

If you're using a stylus and tablet, click the **Tablet Pressure Controls Size** 🖉 button and from the **Size** menu on the Brush Preset picker, choose Pen Pressure or Stylus Wheel. ★

6. Click a layer, adjust the brush diameter by pressing [ or ], then drag across the areas to be recolored (**A–D**, next page). Only pixels that fall within the chosen Mode, Sampling, Limits, and Tolerance parameters will be recolored.

➤ For precise control when using the Color Replacement tool, you can change Options bar settings or brush diameter between strokes.

---

| | | Mode: Color ⬧ | | Limits: Find Edges ⬧ | Tolerance: 20% ▾ | ☑ Anti-alias | 🖉 |

**A** *Choose settings for the Color Replacement tool from the Options bar.*

**A** *We want to change the light green stripes on the woman's sweater to aqua blue.*

**B** *With the Color Replacement tool and the tool settings shown in the figure on the preceding page, we're painting aqua blue (our current Foreground color) over the light green on the woman's sweater.*

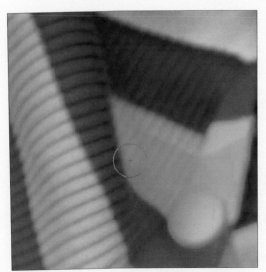

**C** *Next, we zoomed in to recolor smaller areas. At a Tolerance of 40%, we were able to replace the color of both the highlight and shadow areas within a stripe. When replacing the colors along the edges of the stripe, we used a lower Tolerance of 15%.*

**D** *We unintentionally recolored some dark stripes, which was possible even when Find Edges was the Limits setting for the tool. To repair the error, we Alt/Option click to sample the original color in the darker stripe (as shown above), then will apply strokes with that sampled color.*

# Whitening teeth or eyes

Another use for the Replace Color command is to whiten teeth or the whites of the eyes in a portrait photo. You will select those problem areas in the document before using the dialog to correct the discoloration.

## To whiten the teeth or eyes in a portrait photo:

1. Open a portrait photo, and duplicate the Background. Zoom in on the area to be corrected, then do either of the following:

   Choose the **Quick Selection** tool, then drag to create a tight selection of the teeth **A** or of the white areas of both eyes.

   Paint a **Quick Mask** on the teeth, then restore the document to Standard mode (Q). The mask will be converted to a selection (see page 167).

   *Optional:* Save the selection to an alpha channel (see page 160).

2. With a selection tool chosen, click **Refine Edge** on the Options bar. In the Refine Edge dialog, click View: On White, increase the **Feather** value to soften the edge of the selection slightly, then click OK.

3. Choose Image > Adjustments > **Replace Color.**

4. Click the Eyedropper tool in the Replace Color dialog, **B** then click the selection in the document window.

5. To add more white areas to the selection, move the **Fuzziness** slider, or Shift-click or drag across those areas.

6. *Optional:* Check Localized Color Clusters to limit the selection to contiguous colors.

7. To desaturate the selected area and remove the off-white tinge, reduce the **Saturation** (you can use the scrubby slider); and to brighten the selected area, increase the **Lightness** slightly.

8. Click OK. Deselect the selection.**C**

➤ To remove facial "hot spots" (shiny areas), as in the photo at right, see page 280.

➤ To save your Replace Color settings for use in other documents, click Save.

**A** *We used the Quick Selection tool to select the teeth.*

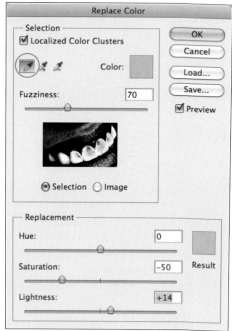

**B** *We refined the selection using the Eyedropper tool in the Replace Color dialog.*

**C** *The teeth were whitened using the settings shown in the dialog above — no whitening strips were needed!*

# Using the Surface Blur filter

Using the Surface Blur filter, you can easily smooth out skin pores or mottled surfaces on objects.

## To smooth skin or other surfaces:

1. Press Ctrl-J/Cmd-J to duplicate the Background in an image that needs some surface smoothing.**A**

2. Choose Filter > Blur > **Surface Blur**. The Surface Blur dialog opens. Check Preview.

3. Choose a low **Threshold** value (try 3–6) to blur only low-contrast areas, such as the cheeks and forehead in a portrait, while preserving the contrast in key details, such as the facial features.

4. To soften skin (cheeks, forehead again), choose a **Radius** of around 6–12, or just to the point that the desired degree of smoothing is reached. If the Radius is too low, the posterizing effect of the filter may make the skin look blotchy.

5. Readjust the **Threshold** to increase or decrease the amount of blurring in low-contrast areas. Too much smoothing could make a face look artificial — but then again, this whole task is a lesson in artifice!

6. Click OK.**B**

7. *Optional:* To restore details from the original image, either lower the opacity of the duplicate layer slightly or follow the next instructions.

➤ We don't recommend applying the Surface Blur filter as a Smart Filter (to a Smart Object), because if further retouching were needed, you wouldn't be able see the smoothing effect onscreen.

You can selectively restore details that were blurred from the Surface Blur filter by applying strokes to a layer mask.

## To restore details selectively after using the Surface Blur filter:

1. With the duplicate layer selected, click the **Add Layer Mask** button 🔲 on the Layers panel.

2. Choose the **Brush** tool ✍ (B or Shift-B).

3. On the Options bar, choose a small Soft Round brush and an Opacity of 80–90%.

4. With black as the Foreground color, draw strokes on any areas you want to restore sharpness to, such as the lips, eyes, eyebrows, or hair in a portrait.**C** To restore the blur effect to areas that you mask unintentionally, paint with white.

**A** *The pores on this woman's skin look too prominent.*

**B** *The Surface Blur filter successfully smoothed the skin texture while keeping the facial features crisp (we chose a Radius setting of 9 pixels and a Threshold setting of 5 levels for our 300 ppi file). Compare the cheeks and under-eye areas in this image with those in figure* **A**.

**C** *We painted with black on a layer mask to restore facial details from the underlying layer.*

# Retouching by cloning imagery

You can use the Clone Stamp tool to clone imagery within the same document or between documents.

## To retouch a photo by cloning imagery:

1. Open an RGB document.**A**

2. Choose the **Clone Stamp** tool 🔧 (S or Shift-S).

3. On the Options bar,**B** do the following:

    Click the **Brush Preset** picker arrowhead, then click a Soft Round brush.

    Choose a blending **Mode**.

    Choose an **Opacity** percentage.

    Choose a **Flow** percentage to control the rate of application.

    Check **Aligned** to maintain the same distance between the source point and the area that you drag across, even if you release the mouse, switch modes, or switch brushes between strokes (to clone a large area seamlessly); or uncheck Aligned to resample from the original source point each time you release the mouse (to produce repetitive clones of a smaller area).

From the **Sample** menu, choose **All Layers** to sample pixels from all the visible layers that are directly below the pointer where you Alt-click/ Option-click (see the sidebar on the next page).

*Optional:* If the document contains adjustment layers and you want the Clone Stamp tool to ignore their effects when sampling, activate the Ignore Adjustment Layers When Cloning button.🗙

*Optional:* If you have a stylus and tablet, you can activate the Tablet Pressure Controls Opacity button 🖉 and/or the Tablet Pressure Controls Size button.🖉 ★

4. Press [ or ] to scale the brush to suit the area to be cloned.

5. Create a new, blank layer in the target document, and keep it selected.

6. In the source document (which can be a different document or the same one), Alt-click/Option-click the area to be cloned to establish a source point.**C**

7. Drag the Clone Stamp tool back and forth to make the cloned pixels appear. You will see two pointers onscreen: crosshairs over the source point and

**A** *We want to remove the metal pipes from the side of the building and add more leaves to fill in the front of the trellis.*

**C** *We Alt-clicked/Option-clicked with the Clone Stamp tool to sample a blank area of the wall.*

**B** *We chose these Options bar settings for the Clone Stamp tool.*

the brush pointer where you drag the mouse.**A** Imagery from the source point will display inside the brush cursor.**B** Note: If the whole layer displays in the overlay as you clone, show the Clone Source panel, 🔁 then check Clipped.

8. *Optional:* To establish a new source point to clone from, Alt-click/Option-click a different area in the source document.**C–D** You can also change Options bar settings for the Clone Stamp tool between strokes.

➤ To create a "double-exposure" effect, with underlying pixels partially showing through the cloned ones, choose a low Opacity percentage for the Clone Stamp tool.

➤ To keep track of multiple source documents while using the Clone Stamp tool, use the Clone Source panel (see pages 248–249).

---

**SAMPLING LAYERS**

With Sample: All Layers checked/chosen on the Options bar for the current editing tool, the tool will sample pixels from all the visible layers (and send the results to the current layer). If the currently selected layer is a new, blank layer (as in step 5 on the preceding page), you'll be able to show and hide the results of your edits — or erase any unwanted edits — at any time.

---

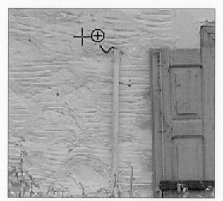

**A** *We're dragging with the Clone Stamp tool to replace the wire and pipe with pixels from the blank wall.*

**B** *We're continuing to sample the wall and clone away the pipe. Multiple sampling prevents a noticeable (tacky!) repetition of the texture.*

**C** *We're sampling the vine leaves because we want to add more leaves to the front of the trellis.*

**D** *Compare this final image with the original one on the preceding page.*

Unlike the Clone Stamp tool, which merely copies a source color without blending it into the target area, the three tools discussed next sample a texture, apply it to the target area, and blend the texture into the existing color and brightness values. With these tools, it's easy to fix imperfections such as facial blemishes or paper creases in a vintage photo, and the results are usually seamless.

With the Healing Brush tool, you Alt-click/ Option-click to sample from an unblemished area, then apply strokes to repair the blemish.**A** The blemish pixels are replaced with the sampled pixels.

With the Patch tool, you select the blemish area first, then drag the selection marquee over an unblemished area to sample it. Here again, the blemish pixels are replaced with the sampled ones.

And with the Spot Healing Brush tool, you simply stroke over blemishes without sampling. Pixels are replaced almost magically based on data from neighboring pixels.

## Using the Healing Brush tool
### To use the Healing Brush tool:

1. Choose the **Healing Brush** tool 🖉 (J or Shift-J).

2. Create a new, blank layer.

3. *Optional:* To confine the repair to a specific area and to prevent the Healing Brush from picking up colors from neighboring areas, create a selection with the Lasso tool.

4. On the Options bar,**B** do all of the following:

   Click the Brush picker arrowhead, and choose a high **Hardness** value. (Also, in Edit/Photoshop > Preferences > Cursors, click Full Size Brush Tip.)

   Choose **Mode**: Normal to preserve the grain, texture, and noise of the area surrounding the target; or if you don't need to preserve those attributes, choose a different mode, such as Lighten for subtle retouching or to correct wrinkles or creases that are very close together, to prevent them from cloning onto one another.

   Click **Source**: Sampled.

   Because you will be working on a new, blank layer, from the **Sample** menu, you should choose

**All Layers** to sample pixels from all the layers below the pointer.

Check **Aligned** to maintain the same distance between the source point and the area that you drag across, even if you release the mouse between strokes, or uncheck this option to resample from the original source point each time you release the mouse.

If you're using a stylus and tablet, click the **Tablet Pressure Controls Size** 🖉 button and from the **Size** menu on the Brush Preset picker, choose Pen Pressure or Stylus Wheel. ★

Click the **Toggle Clone Source** panel button, 🔲 then check **Show Overlay** and **Clipped** on the panel.

5. Press [ or ] to scale the brush to suit the area to be cloned.

6. Alt-click/Option-click an area to sample it as the source texture (**A**, next page). The sampled area displays inside the brush cursor.

**A** *We will soften the crow's feet around the eyes in this portrait photo.*

**B** *We chose these Options bar settings for the Healing Brush tool.*

**7.** With the new, blank layer still selected, drag across the area to be repaired.**B** When you release the mouse, the source texture will be applied to the target area and will be blended with neighboring pixels. It will render in two stages, so be patient.**C–D**

**8.** To establish a new source point for further repairs, Alt-click/Option-click a different area, then apply more strokes (you can change the diameter of the brush tip).

**9.** *Optional:* To make the results more subtle, lower the opacity of the new layer slightly to blend it with the original image layer.

➤ To correct mistakes made with the Healing Brush tool, hide the image layers below the new layer that you applied strokes to so you'll be able to see your strokes more easily, then with the Eraser tool, erase the unwanted strokes. This is easier than stepping back through states on the History panel.

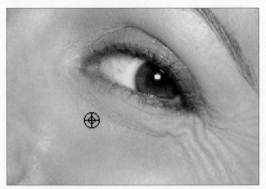

**A** *With the Healing Brush tool, we held down Alt/Option and clicked the area to be used as replacement pixels...*

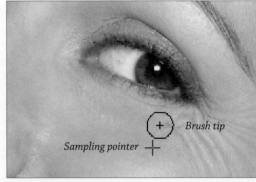

**B** *...then dragged across the area to be repaired. Note that the brush tip is separate from the sampling pointer.*

**C** *The area around the eye on the right now looks smoother.*

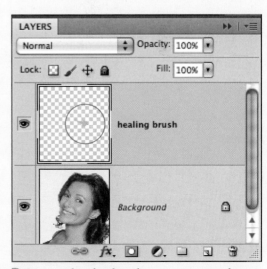

**D** *Our retouching brush strokes are on a separate layer that we named "healing brush."*

## REMOVING FACIAL HOT SPOTS

**A** *The Healing Brush tool is also handy for removing shiny hot spots from a portrait, which are caused by harsh, uneven lighting. Choose Mode: Darken on the Options bar for the tool, then Alt-click/Option-click to sample a medium-tone area of skin.*

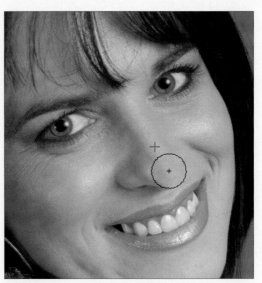

**B** *Drag once or twice over a hot spot, letting your stroke(s) follow the natural contours of the face.*

**C** *With Darken chosen as its Mode, the tool repaired only the light areas of skin. Now her nose looks less shiny.*

---

**PUPPET WARP**

To apply reshaping to areas of an image (perhaps to slim a neck or chin in a portrait), try using the Puppet Warp command (see pages 314–315).

# Using the Spot Healing Brush tool

Sampling an area correctly for a repair can be difficult in tight areas, such as folds of skin, which tend to be close together and have highlights and shadows. With the Spot Healing Brush tool, no sampling is required. It's an effective blemish and wrinkle remover (and it's cheaper than Botox!).

## To use the Spot Healing Brush tool:

1. Do either of the following:

   Duplicate the Background by pressing Ctrl-J/Cmd-J, and keep the duplicate layer selected.

   Create a new, blank layer to contain your correction strokes, and keep it selected.

2. Choose the **Spot Healing Brush** tool 🖌 (J or Shift-J), and zoom the document to 100%.

3. In Edit/Photoshop > Preferences > Cursors, under Painting Cursors, click Full Size Brush Tip and check Show Crosshair in Brush Tip.

4. On the Options bar, do the following:

   Choose a **Mode**. For preserving skin tones, we've achieved good results with Normal and Lighten modes. When used with Replace mode,

the tool may pick up unwanted facial details in the stroke, such as hair or eyelashes.

To help preserve the existing tonal values, such as in skin tones, click **Type: Create Texture**. (For the Content-Aware option, see the next three pages.)

To allow the brush to sample pixels from all the layers below the pointer, check **Sample All Layers** (check this option if you created a new, blank layer in step 1), or uncheck this option if you're working directly on an image layer.

5. Make the brush slightly wider than the area to be repaired (such as a crease) by pressing [ or ], then drag once along it. **A–B** Repeat to repair other areas. **C** We've found that a small brush produces the most seamless repairs.

6. *Optional:* To make the results look more subtle, lower the opacity of the new layer slightly to blend it with the original image layer.

➤ If you applied the Spot Healing strokes to a separate layer, you can erase any unwanted strokes from that layer.

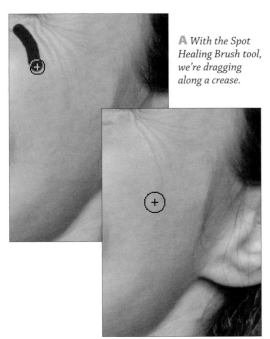

**A** *With the Spot Healing Brush tool, we're dragging along a crease.*

**B** *The creases we dragged over are smoothed out.*

**C** *The creases are removed.*

## USING THE CONTENT-AWARE OPTION WITH THE SPOT HEALING BRUSH TOOL ★

In the right scenario, the Spot Healing Brush tool, used with its Content-Aware option, can be quick, easy, and powerful. When used to remove an object from a photo, it works better if the object being removed has small random shapes around it (such as foliage, water, or clouds in a landscape) **A–C** than if the surrounding area contains isolated, distinct objects. This tool and option also work well for repairing tears or scratches in a vintage photo.

**A** *We want to remove the hydrant from this image.*

**B** *For the Spot Healing Brush tool, we chose a brush Hardness of 100% and Normal mode, and clicked the Content-Aware option. We made the brush a medium size, then with one continuous stroke, we covered the hydrant and its shadow.*

**C** *Poof! To supply the replacement pixels, the Spot Healing Brush tool analyzed and sampled pixels from neighboring areas. This is as easy as retouching gets.*

## USING THE CONTENT-AWARE OPTION FOR THE FILL COMMAND ★

On this page, you'll see an unsuccessful use of the Content-Aware option with the Spot Healing Brush tool, **A–C** and on the next page, you'll see a successful alternative solution (**A–C**, next page).

**A** *We want to zap the barn from this photo.*

**B** *For the Spot Healing Brush tool, we chose a brush Hardness of 100% and Normal mode, and clicked the Content-Aware option. We made the brush a medium size, then covered the barn with one continuous stroke.*

**C** *On this photo, we ran into a glitch: The automatic healing process that the tool performed left behind a red tint from the original object. To see how we were able to apply a successful content-aware repair without healing, see the following page.*

*Continued on the following page*

**A** *Via Undo, we removed the Spot Healing Brush edit from the photo so we could try a different approach. Our first step was to create a loose selection of the barn with the Lasso tool.*

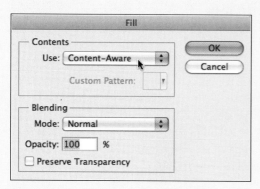

**B** *Next, we chose Edit > Fill. In the dialog, we chose Use: Content-Aware, Mode: Normal, and Opacity: 100%, then clicked OK.*

**C** *The content-aware fill successfully removed the barn without leaving behind a reddish tint, because no healing was involved.*

➤ *To achieve a similar result with the Spot Healing Brush tool, use it with Replace mode chosen and the Content-Aware option clicked on the Options bar.*

## Using the Patch tool

The Patch tool is a good choice for retouching bagginess or wrinkles below the eyes in a portrait photo and for repairing rips, stains, or dust marks in vintage photos. With this tool, you select an area before applying the repair.

### To retouch a photo using the Patch tool:

1. Choose the **Patch** tool ▥ (J or Shift-J).

2. On the Options bar, click **Patch: Source.**

3. Press Ctrl-J/Cmd-J to duplicate the Background, and keep the duplicate layer selected.

4. Drag a marquee around the area to be repaired. **A**

5. *Optional:* Shift-drag to add to the selection or Alt-drag/Option-drag to subtract from it.

6. Drag from inside the selection to the area to be sampled from. **B** Release the mouse, and imagery from the sampled area will appear within the original selection. Deselect (Ctrl-D/Cmd-D). **C**

➤ To hide the selection marquee temporarily (and then to redisplay it), press Ctrl-H/Cmd-H.

➤ When retouching a portrait, if you notice a color change in the patched skin, try changing the blending mode of the duplicate "Patch" layer to Lighten.

➤ If you're not satisfied with the Patch tool results but you want to reuse the Patch selection, click the "Patch Tool" state on the History panel, then drag to sample pixels from a different area.

➤ For a more precise selection, select a small area to be repaired with any selection tool or by using a Quick Mask. Click the Patch tool, then drag the selection to the area to be sampled from.

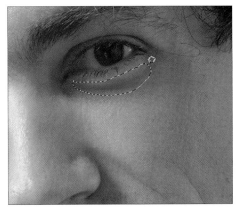

**A** *With the Patch tool, we selected the area that needs to be repaired.*

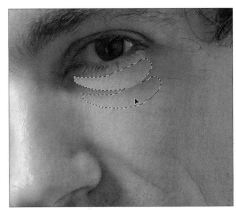

**B** *We dragged from the selected area to the area we want to sample pixels from. To best preserve the skin texture, we're sampling an area near the eye.*

**C** *The sampled pixels were applied instantly to the selection.*

# Using the Red Eye tool

Red-eye (red areas in the pupils) is produced when a person situated in a relatively dark room looks straight at the camera, and light emitted by a camera-mounted or built-in electronic flash reflects off their retina. You're less likely to run into this problem if your camera has a built-in red-eye control feature or if you use a flash bracket and an off-camera flash — and if the subject is looking away from the camera. To remove the red-eye from a photo taken without such controls, try using the simple Red Eye tool in Photoshop.

## To remove red-eye from a portrait:

1. Open a portrait photo, and zoom way in on the eye area (200%–300% view).

2. Choose the **Red Eye** tool 🔴 (J or Shift-J).

3. On the Options bar, do the following:

   Choose a **Pupil Size** for the size of the correction (try the default value of 50%). You don't want the pupil to be enlarged.

   Choose a **Darken Amount** to control how much the pupil will be darkened in order to remove the red (try the default value of 50%). This setting should be lower for light eyes than for dark eyes. If it's too high, the pupils will be darkened too much.

4. Click once on the red area on each pupil. The tool should remove all traces of red. **A–B** (See also the sidebar at right.)

   ▶ If the tool enlarged the pupil too much, undo the results, lower the Pupil Size value, then click again. Similarly, to try a different Darken Amount value, undo your initial click first.

   ▶ You don't need to drag across the eye with the Red Eye tool; the tool is clever enough to find the pupil area automatically from a simple click.

   ▶ The Camera Raw dialog has an equivalent tool called the Red Eye Removal tool.

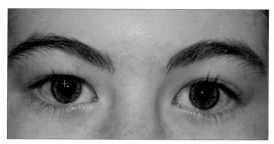

**A** *With the Red Eye tool, we clicked once on each eye.*

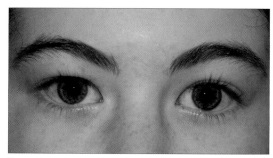

**B** *Poof! The red-eye is gone.*

---

**REMOVING THE REMAINING TRACES OF RED**

If the Red Eye tool fails to remove traces of red from the iris of the eyes (the area around the pupils), do the following: Zoom in on an eye (200%–300%), then choose the Color Replacement tool 🖌 (B or Shift-B). On the Options bar, choose Mode: Color, Sampling: Once, ⊕ Limits: Contiguous, and Tolerance: 30%. Make the brush tip very small, Alt-click/Option-click a color in the iris of an eye, then apply strokes over the remaining traces of red to recolor them with the sampled color.

Photographers use focusing techniques to orchestrate a scene, such as blurriness to convey motion or a shallow depth of field to contrast an in-focus subject with its background. In Photoshop, you can apply similar special effects, and also correct for defects produced by a camera lens. In this chapter, you'll apply the Lens Blur filter and use vignettes to create a focal point in a photo; apply the Lens Correction filter to correct for camera lens distortion; apply the Motion Blur filter to simulate motion; and use the Sharpen tool and the Smart Sharpen and Unsharp Mask filters to resharpen the image.

## Applying the Lens Blur filter

In a photograph, some parts of the scene are more in focus than others. If your camera lets you adjust the depth of field via the aperture, or f-stop setting (it's not a "point-and-shoot" type of camera), you can control how much of your subject matter stays in focus. Objects that are outside the depth of field — either in front of it or behind it — will be blurred. Other factors affecting the focus are the zoom setting and the camera lens.

The Lens Blur filter in Photoshop attempts to replicate this type of blurring. What formerly required the use of multiple channels, gradients, and editing steps can now be accomplished with a single filter. All of this number crunching does have a price, however: The filter may process slowly on a large image.

### To apply the Lens Blur filter:

1. Click an image layer (or duplicate the Background via Ctrl-J/Cmd-J), then click the **Add Layer Mask** button 🔲 on the Layers panel.

2. Keep the layer mask thumbnail selected. Choose the **Gradient** tool 🔳 (G or Shift-G), click the Gradient picker arrowhead on the Options bar, and click the "Black, White" preset. Shift-drag across the entire document window vertically or horizontally to apply the gradient. The Lens Blur filter is going to use this gradient "invisibly." Keep this in mind when you choose a Blur Focal Distance setting in step 5. (Don't concern yourself with where the white and black areas of the gradient land; you'll be able to swap them in the Lens Blur dialog.)

3. Shift-click the layer mask thumbnail to disable the layer mask (you don't want to mask the imagery).

*Continued on the following page*

# REFOCUSING

# 17

Click the layer thumbnail, then choose Filter > Blur > **Lens Blur**. The Lens Blur dialog opens. A

4. Check **Preview** and click a speed. For a large file (larger than 100 MB), click **Faster**, or for a smaller file, click **More Accurate**.

You can also change the zoom level for the preview via the zoom buttons or menu in the lower left corner of the preview window. We like to use the Fit in View setting.

5. To mimic the depth of field in a camera, you will specify that the grayscale values in the layer mask control where the blur is applied. In the **Depth Map** area, do the following:

From the **Source** menu, choose **Layer Mask** as the source for the depth map. The grayscale values in the source will control which areas

remain in focus. (A setting of None would allow the whole image to blur uniformly.)

To set the **Blur Focal Distance**, either specify which grayscale value (from 0, black, to 255, white) in your depth map will remain in full focus via the scrubby slider or, in the preview, click the area that you want to keep in focus. In either case, you are choosing a grayscale value from the gradient in the layer mask. Shades lighter or darker than this value will become progressively more blurry. You'll see the effect of this after moving the Radius slider, in the next step.

*Optional:* Check Invert to swap the white and black areas in the depth map, and thereby swap the areas in focus with those that are not.

**A** *After Shift-dragging upward in the document with the Gradient tool (starting from the bottom of the image), we opened the Lens Blur dialog.*

6. In the **Iris** area, use the **Radius** value to control the intensity of the blur. This produces the most pronounced effect of all the controls in the dialog. (The other Iris sliders are used for creating "photographic" highlights.) Keep the Shape setting on the default setting of Hexagon (6).

➤ At any time while choosing settings, you can uncheck, then recheck Preview to compare the original and blurred images.

7. Blurring averages the values of neighboring pixels and tends to gray out white specular highlights. In the **Specular Highlights** area, you can use the **Brightness** slider to brighten highlight areas that have become blurred and move the **Threshold** slider (slightly) to control which tonal range the Brightness setting affects. At 255, only pure white pixels will be affected, whereas at a low setting, most of the blurred areas will be brightened.

8. *Optional:* If the blurring smoothed out too much noise from the original photo, you can reintroduce noise by doing any of the following: Move the Noise: Amount slider slightly, click Distribution: Uniform or Gaussian, or check Monochromatic to limit the noise to just grayscale pixels instead of color pixels.

9. Click OK. **A–B**

**A** *In the original photo, both the foreground and background areas are in focus.*

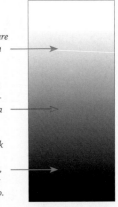

*Light grayscale values are allowing full blurring in this area of the photo.*

*Intermediate grayscale values are allowing partial blurring of this area of the photo.*

*Because we chose a dark grayscale value (47) as the Blur Focal Distance, no blurring is occurring in this area of the photo.*

**B** *We specified that a layer mask be used by the Lens Blur filter to blur the background of this photo, in order to draw the viewer's attention to the foreground (a detail of the mask is shown at right above). The dialog settings we chose are shown in the figure on the preceding page.*

## Changing the focus with a vignette

Next, you'll create an area of focus by using a Smart Filter and filter mask. An advantage of this method is that you can modify the filter settings and edit the mask to change which part of the image is in focus.

### To create an area of focus (a vignette) by using a mask:

1. Open an image in which you want to emphasize the center.**A**

2. On the Layers panel, click an image layer or the Background, then press Ctrl-J/Cmd-J to duplicate it.

3. Select the area of the image that you want to emphasize (keep in focus). For example, you could use the Elliptical Marquee tool (M or Shift-M) then Alt-drag/Option-drag to create an oval (as we did), or use the Lasso tool to create an irregular-shaped selection.

4. On the Options bar, click **Refine Edge**. From the View menu, choose On White (W), ★ increase the **Feather** value to soften the selection edge, then click OK.

5. Press Ctrl-Shift-I/Cmd-Shift-I (Select > Inverse) to swap the selected and unselected areas.**B**

6. Choose Filter > **Convert for Smart Filters**, then click OK if an alert dialog appears.

7. Choose Filter > Blur > **Gaussian Blur**. In the Gaussian Blur dialog, click the zoom out (–) button until you see all or most of the image in the preview window, increase the **Radius** for the desired amount of blurring, then click OK.**C–D**

➤ To change the Radius setting at any time, double-click the Gaussian Blur listing on the Layers panel.

**A** *In the original image, all the areas are in focus.*

**B** *We created an oval selection, used Refine Edge to feather it (a Feather value of 40 px for this 300 ppi photo), and chose Select > Inverse. Now the areas outside the oval marquee are selected.*

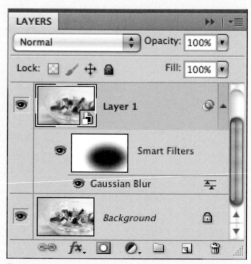

**D** *Our Smart Object layer (Layer 1), with its filter mask and Smart Filter, are shown in this Layers panel.*

**C** *For our vignette, we chose a Radius value of 5.7 pixels in the Gaussian Blur dialog.*

Another way to create a vignette is by manipulating light and dark values. Here you will use (and move) the layer mask on a Levels adjustment layer to control where the vignette is positioned in the image.

## To create a darkening vignette via Levels:

1. Open an image in which you want to emphasize an area at or near the center.

2. Follow steps 2–4 on the preceding page, and keep the duplicate layer selected.

3. On the Adjustments panel, ⬤ click the **Levels** button. 🏛 Ignore the Levels settings for the moment.

4. With the adjustment layer thumbnail selected, press Ctrl-I/Cmd-I to invert the mask.

5. On the Adjustments panel, move the white **Output Levels** slider to the left to darken all but the masked part of the image.

6. *Optional:* To change the location of the darkening vignette, on the Layers panel, click the Levels adjustment layer, click the Link Layer Mask icon 🔗 to unlink the mask from the adjustment layer, click the layer mask thumbnail, then with the Move tool ⤢ (V), drag the mask shape to the desired location in the document window — it's like shining a spotlight. **B–D** On the Layers panel, click again to restore the link icon.

*A We darkened the image via a Levels adjustment layer (we moved the white Output Levels slider to 180).*

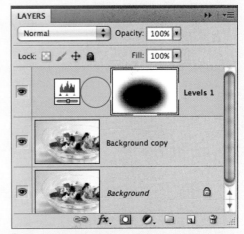

*B We unlinked the layer mask from the adjustment layer thumbnail (the link icon disappeared), then with the Move tool, moved the layer mask to the left.*

*C Because we moved the layer mask to the lower left, the light area (the area blocked by the mask) is now on that side.*

*D As an optional variation to make the lighting more dramatic, we changed the blending mode of the Levels adjustment layer to Difference and lowered its opacity to 80%.*

# Applying the Lens Correction filter

The Lens Correction filter lets you correct for many types of lens distortion, such as a building or column that tilts away from the camera (called "keystoning"), color fringes along high-contrast edges (chromatic aberration), or under- or overexposure at the edges (vignetting). The CS5 version of this filter offers many enhancements, such as the ability to correct for idiosyncrasies of a specific camera model and lens.

## To correct lens distortion: ★

1. Open an RGB photo (**A**, next page). On the Layers panel, click an image layer or the Background, then press Ctrl-J/Cmd-J to duplicate it.

2. Right-click the duplicate layer and choose **Convert to Smart Object**.

3. Choose Filter > **Lens Correction** (Ctrl-Shift-R/ Cmd-Shift-R). At the bottom of the dialog, check Preview and uncheck Show Grid.

4. To try an automatic correction, in the **Auto Correction** tab, from the menus under Search Criteria, choose your **Camera Make** and **Camera Model**; or if your model isn't listed, choose All. From the **Lens Model** menu, choose All, then under **Lens Profiles**, click the nearest match to your camera lens (**B**, next page).

   To further customize the profile, right-click the Lens Profile that you have chosen and pick a camera setting, such as "28mm, f/4.5, 1 m." Note that if this data is in the camera's EXIF metadata, the correct setting is chosen automatically.

5. Under Correction, check which problem in the photo needs correction: **Geometric Distortion, Chromatic Aberration**, or **Vignette**.

6. If the automatic correction wasn't fully successful, click the **Custom** tab, then do one of the following, depending on what needs correction:

   Under Geometric Distortion, lower the **Remove Distortion** value to spread the image out (to fix pincushion distortion), or raise this value to pinch the image inward (to fix barrel distortion).

   Use the **Chromatic Aberration** sliders to correct any color fringes along high-contrast edges (the Fix Green/Magenta Fringe slider is new).

   Use the **Vignette** sliders to help correct for under- or overexposure at the edges of the image.

7. To evaluate the correction of geometric distortion relative to a grid, check **Show Grid** (located below the preview window). You can change the grid size via the Size slider or change the grid color by clicking the Color swatch.

8. To further correct geometric distortion, under **Transform**, do any of the following:

   Lower the **Vertical Perspective** value to widen the top of the image (**C**, next page), or raise it to widen the bottom. After doing this, you may need to readjust the Remove Distortion value to level the horizontal shapes.

   Lower the **Horizontal Perspective** value to widen the left edge of the image, or raise it to widen the right edge of the image.

   To rotate the image, change the **Angle** via the scrubby slider (it's easier to control than the dial).

   ➤ Press P to toggle the preview off and on.

9. To control how areas at the edges of the image are treated as a result of a distortion correction, do any of the following:

   In the Auto Correction tab, check **Auto Scale Image**, then from the **Edge** menu, choose to have the empty areas fill with an Edge Extension (extension of the image), Transparency, Black Color, or White Color.

   In the Custom tab, increase the **Scale** value.

   Crop the image after exiting the dialog.

10. *Optional:* To save all the current settings as a preset, from the Manage Settings menu ▾≡ in the Custom tab, choose Save Settings, enter a name (keep the .lcs extension and default location), then click Save. The preset can now be chosen from the Settings menu for any image.

    Or if you prefer to save all the settings except the Transform settings as a preset for photos that contain camera EXIF metadata, choose Set Lens Default from the Manage Settings menu. ▾≡

11. Click OK (**D**, next page).

➤ To change the Lens Correction settings at any time, double-click the Smart Filter listing on the Layers panel.

➤ From the Settings menu in the Custom tab, you can choose Previous Correction to apply the last-used settings or Default Correction to restore the default values to all the options.

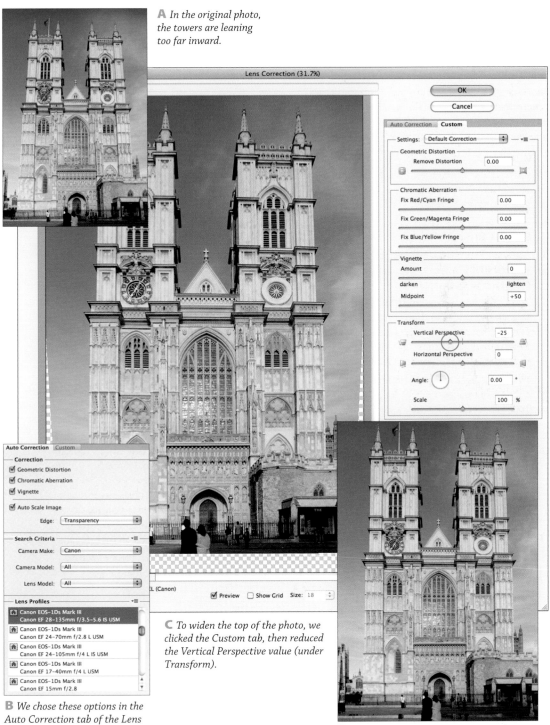

**A** *In the original photo, the towers are leaning too far inward.*

Lens Correction (31.7%)

OK

Cancel

Auto Correction | **Custom**

Settings: Default Correction

Geometric Distortion
Remove Distortion | 0.00

Chromatic Aberration
Fix Red/Cyan Fringe | 0.00
Fix Green/Magenta Fringe | 0.00
Fix Blue/Yellow Fringe | 0.00

Vignette
Amount | 0
darken | lighten
Midpoint | +50

Transform
Vertical Perspective | -25
Horizontal Perspective | 0
Angle: | 0.00 | °
Scale | 100 | %

Auto Correction | Custom

Correction
☑ Geometric Distortion
☑ Chromatic Aberration
☑ Vignette

☑ Auto Scale Image
Edge: Transparency

Search Criteria
Camera Make: Canon
Camera Model: All
Lens Model: All

Lens Profiles
🔒 Canon EOS-1Ds Mark III
Canon EF 28–135mm f/3.5–5.6 IS USM
🏠 Canon EOS-1Ds Mark III
Canon EF 24–70mm f/2.8 L USM
🏠 Canon EOS-1Ds Mark III
Canon EF 24–105mm f/4 L IS USM
🏠 Canon EOS-1Ds Mark III
Canon EF 17–40mm f/4 L USM
🏠 Canon EOS-1Ds Mark III
Canon EF 15mm f/2.8

EL (Canon)
☑ Preview ☐ Show Grid Size: 18

**C** *To widen the top of the photo, we clicked the Custom tab, then reduced the Vertical Perspective value (under Transform).*

**B** *We chose these options in the Auto Correction tab of the Lens Correction dialog, but they produced only a minor correction.*

**D** *As a result of the Lens Correction adjustments, now the towers look more vertical.*

## Applying the Motion Blur filter

One way photographers capture the blur of motion (e.g., in sports or wildlife photography) is by panning the camera as the subject is moving. In Photoshop, you can create a similar illusion of motion by using the Motion Blur filter. In the following instructions, you'll blur the whole image by applying the filter as a Smart Filter, then to bring a key area back into focus, remove the effect from part of the image by painting on the filter mask.

### To apply the Motion Blur filter to part of an image:

1. Click an image layer and duplicate it by pressing Ctrl-J/Cmd-J.**A**

2. Right-click the duplicate layer and choose **Convert to Smart Object**.

3. Choose Filter > Blur > **Motion Blur**. The Motion Blur dialog opens.**B**

4. Lower the zoom level for the preview. Choose a **Distance** value for the amount of blurring, choose an **Angle** value for the direction of the blur, then click OK.**C**

5. On the Layers panel, click the filter mask thumbnail for the Smart Filters listing.

6. Choose the **Brush** tool 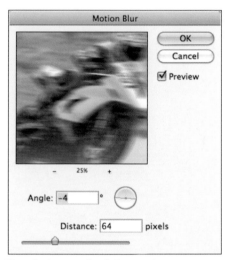 (B or Shift-B). On the Options bar, choose a medium-sized Soft Round brush and an Opacity of 80%. Choose black as the Foreground color.

7. Paint over the area of the image that you want to hide the Motion Blur effect from and restore focus to (**A–B**, next page). Since your brush isn't at full opacity, you can repeat your strokes in any area to hide even more of the motion blur.

8. If you have masked too much of the Motion Blur effect, press X to make the Foreground color white, then apply strokes to restore it.

➤ To readjust the Motion Blur filter settings, double-click the filter listing on the Layers panel.

**A** *This is the original photo.*

**B** *In the Motion Blur dialog, we chose a Distance value of 64 px and set the Angle dial to match the angle of the motorcycle.*

**C** *The Motion Blur filter was applied to the whole image.*

*B The final results convey fast motion. We were careful not to remove the Motion Blur effect from the tires, since they would be moving too fast to stay in focus.*

*A We clicked the filter mask thumbnail on the Layers panel, then applied strokes with black to hide the Motion Blur effect.*

*C This photo has a soft focus.*

## Using the Sharpen tool

When used with the new Protect Detail option checked on the Options bar, the Sharpen tool enhances details without introducing noticeable artifacts. With this tool, you can sharpen areas selectively without having to use a mask. Note: To sharpen an entire image, see the remaining pages in this chapter.

### To use the Sharpen tool: ★

1. Click an image layer, then duplicate it by pressing Ctrl-J/Cmd-J.**C**

2. Choose the **Sharpen** tool.△

3. On the Options bar, choose a **Strength** value, and check **Sample All Layers** and **Protect Detail**.

4. Press [ or ] to adjust the brush diameter, then drag across any area that needs sharpening.**D** For stronger sharpening, drag again in the same area.

*D With the Sharpen tool, we easily sharpened just the eyes.*

# Applying the Smart Sharpen filter

Most digital photos need to be sharpened, and the need becomes greater if you change the file's dimensions or resolution with the Resample Image option checked, convert it to CMYK Color mode, or apply a transformation command to it.

To sharpen an image, you can use either the Smart Sharpen filter or the Unsharp Mask filter (the latter, despite its name, has a sharpening effect). These filters can add noise to an image and therefore should be applied after image-editing, adjustment, and color correction.

High-resolution printing also causes some minor blurring due to dot gain. You can anticipate and compensate for this by sharpening the image once again as you prepare it for output. Experience will teach you how much sharpening is needed.

The Smart Sharpen filter, discussed first, gives you the ability to sharpen (and fade the sharpening) in the shadow and highlight areas separately, whereas Unsharp Mask (see pages 299–300) doesn't provide that control. We usually use the Smart Sharpen filter for targeted sharpening and the Unsharp Mask filter for output sharpening. (See also the sidebar below.)

## To apply the Smart Sharpen filter:

1. Open a photo that needs sharpening. **A** On the Layers panel, click an image layer or the Background, then press Ctrl-J/Cmd-J to duplicate it. Right-click the duplicate layer and choose **Convert to Smart Object**.

2. Choose Filter > Sharpen > **Smart Sharpen**. The Smart Sharpen dialog opens. Move it out of the way so the document is still in view.

   ➤ Keep the zoom level for the preview at 67% or 100%. To bring a different area of the image into view, either drag in the preview or click in the document.

3. Check **More Accurate** to produce high-quality sharpening by allowing multiple passes of the filter. This takes longer but is worth the wait.

4. From the **Remove** menu, choose an algorithm for the correction: Gaussian Blur is a good, all-purpose choice; Lens Blur sharpens details with fewer resulting halos (we like this option); and Motion Blur is useful for correcting blurring due to movement of the camera or subject, but for this option you need to know that angle of movement.

---

**ADVANTAGES TO USING THE SMART SHARPEN FILTER**

We use both the Smart Sharpen and Unsharp Mask filters on a regular basis. Smart Sharpen offers the following advantages, though, in addition to the one mentioned in the paragraph above:

➤ With the More Accurate option checked, Smart Sharpen applies sharpening in multiple passes.

➤ Smart Sharpen has the ability to detect edges, so it produces fewer color halos than Unsharp Mask.

➤ Smart Sharpen lets you choose from three algorithms (to correct Gaussian blur, lens blur, or motion blur), whereas Unsharp Mask corrects only Gaussian blur.

➤ Smart Sharpen lets you save and reuse your settings, for greater speed and consistency in your workflow.

**A** *Because the Smart Sharpen filter will let us control which tonal areas in the image are sharpened, it will be the right choice for correcting this blurry portrait (the resolution of this image is 300 ppi).*

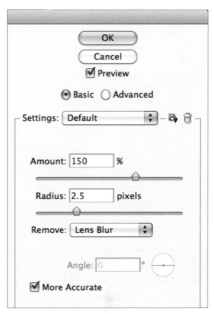

**A** *The settings we chose in the Basic panel of the Smart Sharpen dialog (shown above) successfully sharpened key details in the photo, such as the eyes and lips, but in the process, also oversharpened the skin (now the pores look too pronounced).*

5. Try an **Amount** value of 60–150% for the degree to which contrast will be increased, and a **Radius** value between 1 and 2.5 pixels. You can use the scrubby slider for all the sliders in this dialog. The image should now look slightly oversharpened.**A** You'll fade the effect next.

6. To control the amount of sharpening in the shadow and highlight areas, click **Advanced**, then click the **Shadow** tab.**B** Drag in the preview to display an area of the image that contains both shadows and midtones, then make the following adjustments:

   Choose a **Radius** value (between 5 and 10) to control how many neighboring pixels will be compared to a specific pixel. The higher the Radius, the larger the area to be compared.

   Change the **Tonal Width** value to control the range of midtones to be affected by the Fade Amount. The higher this width, the wider the range of midtones affected and the more gradually the sharpening will fade into the shadows.

   Move the **Fade Amount** slider until you see the desired reduction of oversharpening in the

*Continued on the following page*

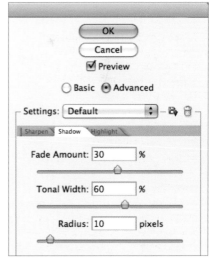

**B** *In the Shadow tab (Advanced panel), we chose a moderate Fade Amount to soften the sharpening in the shadows (such as around the eyes) and a moderate Tonal Width value to fully sharpen the shadows but only partially sharpen the midtones.*

shadows. If the Tonal Width value is too low, the effectiveness of this slider will be limited.

7. Click the **Highlight** tab.**A** Drag the image in the preview to display an area that contains both highlights and midtones. Adjust the **Radius**, **Tonal Width**, and **Fade Amount** values, as in the preceding step.

8. Hopefully, just the key details or features of the image are sharper. If the overall image now looks too sharp, click the **Sharpen** tab and reduce the **Amount** value slightly.

9. Click OK.**B–C**

➤ To save the current settings as a preset, click the Save a Copy button 🖫 in the dialog, enter a name, then click OK. Saved settings can be chosen from the Settings menu for any image.

➤ To compare the unsharpened and sharpened versions of the image, press on the dialog preview, then release.

➤ To modify the Smart Sharpen results, double-click the Smart Sharpen listing on the Smart Object layer; the dialog reopens.

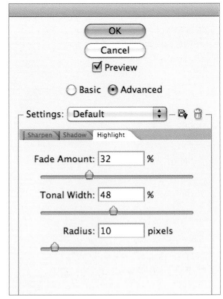

**A** *Finally, in the Highlight tab of the Smart Sharpen dialog, we chose a moderate Fade Amount to soften the sharpening in the broad, flat highlight areas of skin and a moderate Tonal Width value to fully sharpen the highlights and partially sharpen the light midtones.*

**B** *Compare this original image to the final image at right.*

**C** *The Smart Sharpen filter added clarity to the facial features without applying unflattering sharpening to the cheeks and forehead.*

# Applying the Unsharp Mask filter

To do its job of sharpening an image, the Unsharp Mask filter increases the contrast between adjacent pixels. You will need to choose three variables in the dialog: Amount, Radius, and Threshold.

### To apply the Unsharp Mask filter:

1. Choose a zoom level of 50–100% for your image, then duplicate an image layer (Ctrl-J/Cmd-J).**A**

2. Right-click the duplicate layer and choose **Convert to Smart Object**.

3. With the Smart Object layer selected, choose Filter > Sharpen > **Unsharp Mask**. The Unsharp Mask dialog opens. Move it out of the way, if necessary, so the document is still in view.

4. Choose an **Amount** percentage to control how much the contrast is increased. Use a low setting (try 80–100) for figures or natural objects or a higher setting (150–170) for sharp-edged objects. For a high-resolution image (2000 x 3000 pixels or higher), try an Amount of 130–170.**B**

   ➤ Uncheck, then recheck Preview to compare the original and sharpened images. Choose a zoom level for the preview of 50–100%. To bring a different area of the image into view, either drag in the preview or click in the document.

5. The **Radius** affects how many neighboring pixels around high-contrast edges the filter affects. When choosing an appropriate Radius, you need to consider the pixel count of the image and its subject matter.**C** The higher the pixel count, the higher the Radius value needed to achieve the desired result. For a low-contrast image that contains large, simple objects and smooth transitions, try a high Radius of 2 (you'll rarely need to use a higher value), whereas for an intricate, high-contrast image containing many sharp transitions, try a lower Radius of around 1.

   Note: The Amount and Radius settings are interdependent, meaning if you raise the Radius, you'll need to lower the Amount, and vice versa.

6. Choose a **Threshold** value (0–255) to establish how different in value an area of pixels must be from a high-contrast edge to be affected by the filter (**A**, next page). Start with a Threshold value of 0 (to sharpen the entire image), then increase

*Continued on the following page*

**A** *The original 300 ppi image is slightly blurry.*

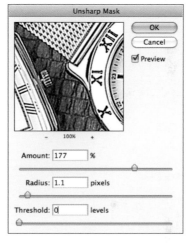

**B** *A high Amount percentage for the Unsharp Mask filter produced halos along the edges of the watches...*

**C** *...and a high Radius value of 3.3 produced halos around the watch hands and numerals.*

it slowly. At a Threshold of 5–10, high-contrast areas will be sharpened and areas of lesser contrast will be sharpened much less. When increasing the Threshold, you can also increase the Amount and Radius to sharpen the edges. Thankfully, the filter won't oversharpen the low-contrast areas.

7. Click OK.**B** To adjust the settings at any time, double-click the Unsharp Mask listing on the Layers panel.

➤ If the sharpening produced color halos along the edges of the objects, choose Luminosity as the blending mode for the Smart Object layer. This will limit the sharpening to luminosity values and remove it from hue and saturation values.

### SUGGESTED SETTINGS FOR UNSHARP MASK

For an image that is 2000 x 3000 pixels or larger, try using these values:

| | |
|---|---|
| Soft-edged subjects, such as landscapes | Amount 100–150, Radius 1–1.5, Threshold 6–10 |
| Portraits | Amount 100–120, Radius 1–2, Threshold 4–6, or to the point where skin areas start to look smoother |
| Buildings, objects, etc. for which contrast is a priority | Amount 150–200 or more, Radius 1.5–3, Threshold 0–3 |

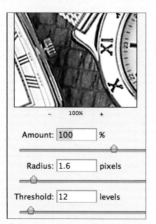

**A** With a high Threshold value of 12 chosen in the Unsharp Mask dialog, the filter sharpened only high-contrast edges but left the watchbands and background still blurry.

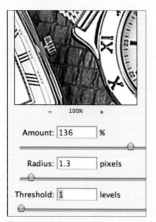

**B** The values shown above (note especially the lower Threshold value) produced this final, and properly sharpened, version of the image.

By this point, hopefully, you've got the hang of using the Layers panel and its basic controls and are ready to explore it more in depth. In this chapter, you'll learn how to blend pixels between layers, create and use clipping masks, link layers, create and edit Smart Object layers, transform layers—and, to entertain yourself, apply the Puppet Warp and Warp commands.

## Changing layer opacity and fill values

The Opacity setting on the Layers panel controls the opacity of a layer, including any layer effects, whereas the Fill setting controls the opacity of a layer, excluding any layer effects (for layer effects, see Chapter 21). Both settings are available for image, type, adjustment, fill, Smart Object, and shape layers. Each layer has its own Opacity and Fill percentages.

### To change the opacity or fill setting of one or more layers:

1. Click a layer (not the Background) or select multiple layers.★

2. On the Layers panel, choose an **Opacity** or **Fill** percentage (you can use the scrubby slider).**A–B** The lower the Opacity or Fill value, the more pixels from the underlying layer will be visible.

18

**A** *The original image contains four layers, including an editable type layer.*

**B** *We lowered the Opacity of the three image layers, and also lowered the Fill percentage of the type layer to keep the drop shadow (a layer effect) at full opacity.*

# Blending layers

The blending mode of a layer controls how its pixels blend with those in the layer directly below it. You can change the blending mode for any kind of layer. Some modes, such as Soft Light, produce subtle effects, whereas others, such as Difference, produce dramatic color shifts. The default mode is Normal. The individual blending modes are described and illustrated on pages 192–196.

## To choose a blending mode (and opacity) for a layer:

1. Click any kind of layer (not the Background),**A** such as a duplicate or silhouetted image layer or a type, adjustment, fill, or Smart Object layer.

2. From the menu in the upper left corner of the Layers panel, choose a **blending mode.B–C**

3. *Optional:* Adjust the opacity of the duplicate layer.

➤ If you don't have a painting or editing tool selected, you can press Shift- + (plus) or Shift- – (minus) to cycle through the blending modes for the current layer. If a painting or editing tool is selected, the same shortcut changes the mode for the tool.

➤ To choose blending options (mode and opacity settings) for a Smart Filter, see page 321.

**A** *We duplicated the Background image in this original document.*

**B** *We chose Color Dodge mode for the duplicate layer, and lowered the layer Opacity to 57%.*

**C** *The final image is a combination of the two layers.*

In these instructions, you'll edit a duplicate image layer and then blend the original and duplicate layers by using the opacity and blending mode controls on the Layers panel. You can use this method to soften the effect of a filter or other image-editing command or simply to try out various blending modes. If you don't like the results, simply discard the duplicate layer (or the Smart Filter) and start over.

## To blend a modified layer with the original one:

1. Click a layer, then press Ctrl-J/Cmd-J to duplicate it.

2. *Optional:* If you want to apply a filter as an editable Smart Filter in the next step, right-click the duplicate image layer and choose Convert to Smart Object (see page 320).

3. Apply some creative edits to the duplicate layer, such as brush strokes or filters.  Learn about the Filter Gallery on pages 318–319.

4. Keep the duplicate layer selected, then on the Layers panel, do either or both of the following:

   Choose a different **blending mode**.

   Adjust the **Opacity** to achieve the desired level of transparency. **B–C**

**A** *We duplicated the Background image in the original document (see* **A***, preceding page), converted the layer to a Smart Object, then applied the Ocean Ripple filter to the duplicate layer.*

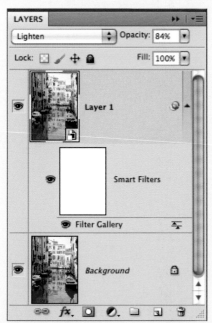

**B** *We chose Lighten mode for the duplicate layer and lowered the layer Opacity to 84%.*

**C** *The final image is a combination of the original image layer and the Smart Object layer.*

The blending options in the Layer Style dialog—in addition to the blending mode, opacity, and fill controls we have already discussed—let you control how a layer and layer effects blend with underlying layers.

## To choose blending options for a layer:

1. Double-click next to a layer name on the Layers panel, or right-click a layer and choose **Blending Options**.

2. The Layer Style dialog opens, with Blending Options selected in the upper left. **A** Check Preview.

3. The first three controls are the same as on the Layers panel:

   Under General Blending, you can change the layer **Blend Mode** or **Opacity**.

   In Advanced Blending, adjust the **Fill Opacity** to control the opacity of the layer without altering the opacity of any layer effects.

4. Via the **Blend If** sliders, you can control which pixels in the current layer stay visible and which pixels from the underlying layer show through the current layer (**A–D**, next page):

   Move the black **This Layer** slider to the right to drop out shadow areas from the current layer.

   Move the white **This Layer** slider to the left to drop out highlight areas from the current layer.

   Move the black **Underlying Layer** slider to the right to reveal shadow areas from the underlying layer.

   Move the white **Underlying Layer** slider to the left to reveal highlight areas from the underlying layer.

   To adjust the midtone colors separately from the lightest and darkest colors, Alt-drag/Option-drag a slider (it will divide in two) (**E**, next page).

5. Click OK.

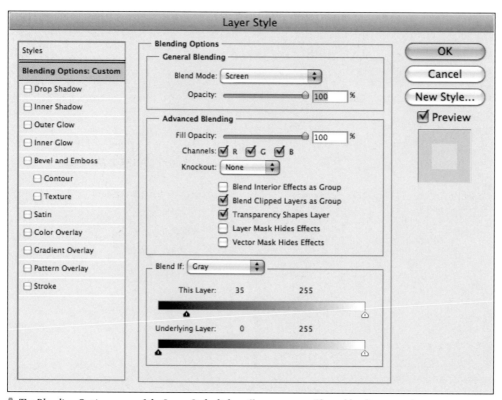

**A** *The Blending Options area of the Layer Style dialog offers an array of layer blending controls.*

> For the sake of simplicity, you can work with all the channels at once by leaving the Blend If menu set to Gray, or if you want to experiment with blending each color channel separately, choose a channel from the menu before moving the sliders.

**A** *This is the original image.*

**B** *We chose black as the Foreground color and a light tan as the Background color, duplicated the Background, then applied the Sketch > Charcoal filter to the duplicate layer (the filter used our chosen colors).*

**C** *To allow some of the dark tones in the photo to show through the filter layer, we moved the black Underlying Layer slider in the Blending Options panel of the Layer Style dialog.*

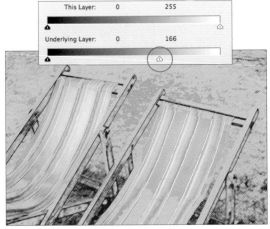

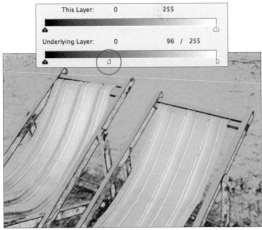

**D** *A second option was to restore some of the light tones from the photo by moving the white Underlying Layer slider.*

**E** *And a third option was to restore only the midtone colors (not the lightest colors) by dividing and then moving the white Underlying Layer slider.*

# Using clipping masks

When layers are formed into a clipping mask, the content of the bottommost layer, called the "base" layer, clips (limits the display of pixels on) the layers above it. The mode and opacity of the base layer — which can be a type, image, Smart Object, or shape layer — is applied to the clipped layers.

### To create a clipping mask:

1. Position the base layer so it is stacked directly below the successive layers to be clipped.

2. Do one of the following:

   Shift-click the layers to be clipped (not the base layer), then press Ctrl-Alt-G/Cmd-Option-G.**A–B**

   Alt-click/Option-click the line between two layers (the pointer becomes two overlapping circles).

   Right-click a layer to be clipped (not the base layer) and choose Create Clipping Mask.

   The base layer name has an underline; the thumbnail for each clipped layer has a downward-pointing arrow ⬐ and is indented.

3. *Optional:* To include more layers in the mask, either repeat the preceding step or restack other layers between existing layers in the mask.**C–D**

➤ All the layers to be put in a clipping mask must be listed consecutively. When creating a clipping mask of layers in a group, all the layers (including the base layer) must be part of the group.

Note: When a layer is released from a clipping mask, any masked layers above it are also released.

### To release a layer from a clipping mask:

Do either of the following:

Alt-click/Option-click the line below the layer to be released.

Click a layer to be released (not the base layer), then press Ctrl-Alt-G/Cmd-Option-G.

### To release an entire clipping mask:

Alt-click/Option-click the line above the base layer.

➤ To merge all the layers in a clipping mask into a base image layer and apply the clipping effect to the result, click the base layer, then press Ctrl-E/Cmd-E.

**A** *The original image contains five layers. (An editable type layer is obscured by the image layers.)*

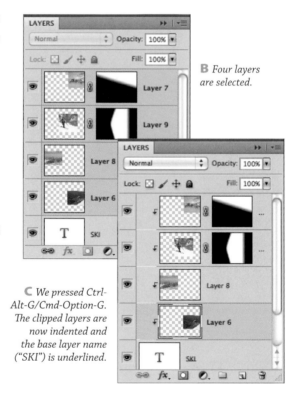

**B** *Four layers are selected.*

**C** *We pressed Ctrl-Alt-G/Cmd-Option-G. The clipped layers are now indented and the base layer name ("SKI") is underlined.*

**D** *The type (base) layer is clipping the four image layers.*

# Linking layers

Layers that are linked together will move as a unit in the document window and drag-and-drop as a unit to other files. If you align, distribute, or transform (e.g., scale or rotate) a linked layer, your edits will also be applied to the layers it's linked to.

## To link layers:

1. On the Layers panel, select two or more layers (Ctrl-click/Cmd-click to select nonconsecutive layers).**A–B**

2. Click the **Link Layers** button ⊕ at the bottom of the Layers panel. A link icon appears to the right of that layer and the layers it's linked to.**C**

➤ To unlink a layer, click the layer, then click the Link Layers button. The link icon disappears.

➤ To deactivate a link temporarily, Shift-click the link icon for a layer. A red X appears over the icon. (To reactivate the link, Shift-click it again.)

## To move layers that are linked:

1. Click a linked layer.

2. Hold down the V key to spring-load the Move tool, drag in the document window, then release the V key.**D**

➤ Don't link any layers to the Background, because you won't be able to move them.

➤ To align or distribute multiple layers, see page 247.

**A** *This image contains multiple layers (and a clipping mask).*

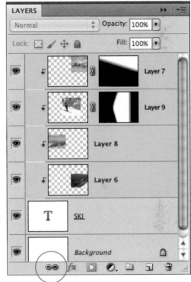

**B** *We selected four layers (they happen to be in a clipping mask). To link them, we will click the Link Layers button.*

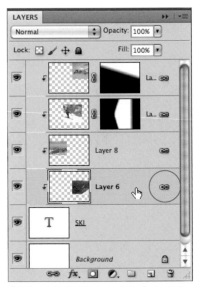

**C** *When a linked layer is clicked, the link icon displays for that layer and the layers it's linked to.*

**D** *We moved the linked image layers to the left, while the base layer (the type layer) stayed put.*

# Creating Smart Object layers

A Smart Object layer is created when you convert one or more layers in a Photoshop document to a Smart Object. It is also an option when you open, paste, or place an AI (Adobe Illustrator), PDF, PSD, or Camera Raw file into a Photoshop document. If you double-click the thumbnail for a Smart Object made from Photoshop layers, a separate document opens in Photoshop, containing the embedded layers, whereas if you double-click the thumbnail for a Smart Object made from imported contents, the embedded file opens in the creator application. In either case, when you edit, save, and close the new window, your changes will appear in the Photoshop document. (To edit a Smart Object layer, see page 310.)

### To create a Smart Object layer by converting existing Photoshop layers:

1. Open a Photoshop document.
2. Select one or more layers on the Layers panel (such as an image or type layer).
3. Right-click a selected layer and choose **Convert to Smart Object** (this command is also available on the Layers panel menu).**A–B**

### To open a PSD, AI, PDF, or TIFF file as a Smart Object layer in a new Photoshop document:

1. In Photoshop, choose File > **Open as Smart Object**. Locate and click a PSD, AI, PDF, or TIFF file, then click Open.
2. For an AI or PDF file, the Open as Smart Object dialog opens.**C** Choose Thumbnail Size: Fit Page and a Crop To option, then click OK. A Smart Object layer appears in a new document.

### To create a Smart Object layer from a Camera Raw file:

1. From Bridge, open a photo into Camera Raw.
2. Apply any needed adjustments, then hold down Shift and click (or just click) **Open Object** (see page 86). The image appears as a Smart Object layer in a new Photoshop document.

### To create a Smart Object layer from an AI or PDF file by using the Paste command:

1. In Illustrator, copy art by pressing Ctrl-C/Cmd-C.
2. Click in a Photoshop document, then press Ctrl-V/Cmd-V. The Paste dialog opens.**D** Click Paste As: **Smart Object**, then click OK. A Vector Smart Object layer appears on the Layers panel.

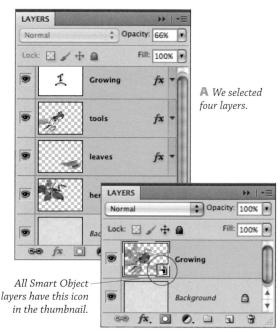

**A** *We selected four layers.*

*All Smart Object layers have this icon in the thumbnail.*

**B** *The Convert to Smart Object command combined the layers into one Smart Object layer.*

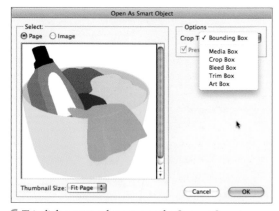

**C** *This dialog opens when you use the Open as Smart Object command to open an AI or PDF file into Photoshop.*

**D** *This dialog opens when you paste an AI or PDF file into Photoshop.*

You can use the Place command to place files of many formats into a Photoshop document, such as an AI or PDF file.

### To place a file into Photoshop as a Smart Object layer:

1. *Optional:* Open a document in Photoshop.

2. Go to Edit/Photoshop > Preferences > General and check **Resize Image During Place** to allow the image to be scaled automatically and **Place or Drag Raster Images as Smart Objects** to have it arrive as a Smart Object layer. Click OK.

3. Do either of the following:

   Choose File > **Place**, locate and click a file, then click Place.

   In Mini Bridge, click the thumbnail for the file to be placed, then from the Tools menu,  choose Place > **In Photoshop**. (Or in Bridge, choose File > Place > In Photoshop.)

4. For an Illustrator or PDF file, the Place PDF dialog opens.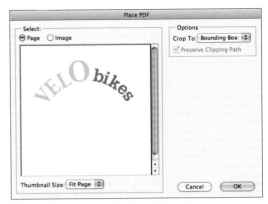 Choose a Thumbnail Size to preview the file. For a multipage PDF file, choose the desired page. Also choose a Crop To option (to exclude any white areas outside the artwork, choose Bounding Box).

5. Click OK. The art appears in a bounding box in the current document or in a new Photoshop document.

6. To transform the placed art, do any of these optional steps:

   To scale it, drag a handle on the bounding box (Shift-drag to maintain the aspect ratio).

   To reposition it, drag inside the bounding box.

   To rotate it, position the pointer outside the bounding box (two-headed arrow), then drag.

   ➤ To undo the last transformation, use Undo.

7. Double-click inside the bounding box, or click the Commit Transform button ✔ on the Options bar, or press Enter/Return. The art becomes a Smart Object layer.

➤ If you change your mind, you can delete the placed art before accepting it by pressing Esc.

➤ For another way to create a Smart Object, drag an object or group from an Illustrator document window into a Photoshop document window, then follow steps 6–7, above.

**A** *The file previews in the Place PDF dialog.*

**B** *Reposition and transform the placed object, if desired, then double-click inside it to accept it.*

**C** *When we accepted the object, it became an embedded Smart Object layer. (We added a drop shadow effect to it in Photoshop; see pages 356–357.)*

# Editing and replacing Smart Objects

To apply some types of edits to a Smart Object layer, such as Smart Filters (see pages 320–324), blending mode and opacity changes, and layer effects, you simply click the layer first. Edits that change pixel data, however, such as those made by the painting, healing, sharpening, and cloning tools, can't be made directly to a Smart Object layer (try it, and you'll get an alert prompt about rasterizing the layer; click Cancel). To make those types of edits, you double-click the Smart Object layer thumbnail first. The embedded object opens in a temporary new document in Photoshop, in the creator application (Illustrator), or in the Camera Raw dialog. When you close the temporary window or dialog, your changes will appear in the Photoshop document. The original file, from which the Smart Object layer was created, remains unchanged.

## To edit a Smart Object layer:

1. Double-click the Smart Object layer thumbnail. If an alert regarding saving changes appears, click OK. If the PDF Modification Detected alert appears next, **A** ★ click "Discard Changes, Preserving Illustrator Editing Capabilities," then click OK (don't worry... the "changes" are internal and inconsequential).

   If the Smart Object layer contains one or more Photoshop layers, a separate document will open in Photoshop, containing those layers; if it contains imported content, that content will open in a document in the creator application; and if it's a Camera Raw image, the photo will open into the Camera Raw dialog.

2. For a Camera Raw file, adjust the settings, then click OK. For any other type of Smart Object, edit the temporary document, save it without changing the file name or location (press Ctrl-S/ Cmd-S), and then close it. Your edits will display in the Smart Object layer in Photoshop.

➤ When you place vector art as a Smart Object into a Photoshop document, it stays as vector art. When you output the Photoshop file, the vector art is rendered at the resolution of the printer.

There are two ways to duplicate a Smart Object layer. If the duplicate is linked to the original Smart Object layer, any pixel edits made to the original embedded file will automatically appear in the copy, and vice versa. This is useful, say, if you want to apply identical pixel edits to both the original and duplicate but apply a different Smart Filter or transformation, or different opacity, mask, or layer style settings. If the duplicate isn't linked to the original, you will be able to rasterize the copy, while keeping the original as a Smart Object layer.

## To duplicate a Smart Object layer:

1. Click a Smart Object layer.

2. Do either of the following:

   To create a duplicate of the layer that is linked to the original Smart Object layer, press Ctrl-J/ Cmd-J. Pixel edits to the original will appear in the copy, and vice versa (**A–B**, next page).

   To create a duplicate of the layer that isn't linked to the original, right-click the layer and choose **New Smart Object via Copy**. Edits made to the original Smart Object layer won't affect the copy, and vice versa (**C**, next page).

   A new Smart Object layer appears in the Layers panel, bearing the same name as the original layer, and by default, the word "copy" is added.

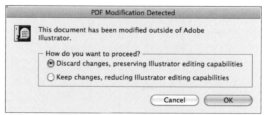

**A** *This alert dialog will appear if you try to edit a Smart Object that was created from an Adobe Illustrator file.*

---

### RASTERIZING A SMART OBJECT LAYER

If you rasterize a Smart Object layer (convert it to a standard image layer), the contents of the embedded file become inaccessible, and some edits, such as Smart Filters, are applied. For this reason, we recommend copying the Smart Object layer first by using the New Smart Object via Copy command (see above). Then to rasterize the duplicate layer, right-click it and choose Rasterize Layer.

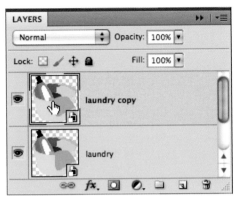

**A** *We duplicated a Smart Object layer via the Ctrl-J/ Cmd-J shortcut, then double-clicked one of the layers.*

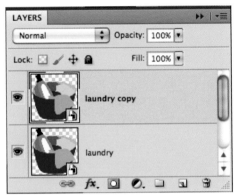

**B** *The Smart Object opened in a temporary window in Illustrator, and we changed the color of the laundry basket to green. In the Photoshop document, the change registered in both Smart Objects.*

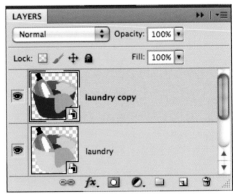

**C** *Here we copied the layer using the New Smart Object Via Copy command, then edited one of them in Illustrator. The change appeared only in that layer.*

Via the Replace Contents command, you can swap existing Smart Object content with a different file. Or if you open the creator application and edit the original file that a Smart Object was created from (not by double-clicking the Smart Object thumbnail), you will need to use the Replace Contents command to update the embedded file. Any transformations, filters, or layer style settings that were applied to the Smart Object layer are applied to the replacement content.

### To replace the contents of a Smart Object with another file:

1. Right-click a Smart Object layer (not the thumb-nail) and choose **Replace Contents**. The Place dialog opens.

2. Locate a replacement file (either the same file that you have edited separately or an altogether new file), then click **Place**. Respond to any dialogs that open (e.g., the Camera Raw dialog or the Place PDF dialog). The new image appears in the Smart Object layer.

Photoshop layers that are converted to a Smart Object become embedded in the layer, and are acces-sible for editing only in the temporary document that opens when you double-click the layer thumbnail. If you need to, however, you can bring a copy of an embedded layer back into your document by follow-ing these steps.

### To reclaim embedded Photoshop layers from a Smart Object:

1. In Photoshop, double-click a Smart Object layer thumbnail, then click OK if an alert appears. The embedded file opens in a separate document tab.

2. Via the Arrange Documents menu, display both documents. With the window for the embedded file active, drag a layer from the Layers panel into the original document window. Or to copy multiple layers, Ctrl-click/Cmd-click the ones you want to copy first.

3. Close the window for the embedded file. (Any Smart Filters or layer styles that you applied to the Smart Object layer won't be applied to the copies.)

4. *Optional:* Delete the Smart Object layer.

# Applying transformations

In Photoshop, you can apply scale, rotate, skew, distort, and perspective transformations to a layer, layer group, or selection, among other things (see the sidebar at right). We'll show you how to apply multiple transformations via the Free Transform command and the Move tool, which are the quickest and most intuitive methods.

Note: To help preserve the image quality, if you need to apply multiple transformations, do it in one pass and then accept the edits at the end, so the image data is resampled only once.

## To apply transformations using the Free Transform command or the Move tool:

1. On the Layers panel, click a layer, a layer group, or the Background, or Shift-select multiple layers.**A** Any layers that are linked to the one(s) you have selected will also be transformed.

   Note: To transform the Background, you *must* create a selection, and you must use the Free Transform command in step 3.

2. *Optional:* If you selected a single image layer, you can create a selection to limit which part of it is transformed.

3. Do either of the following:

   Choose Edit > **Free Transform** (Ctrl-T/Cmd-T).

   Choose the **Move** tool, then check **Show Transform Controls** on the Options bar.

4. A transform box with handles now surrounds either the opaque part of the layer or the whole selection. To transform the layer, do one or more of the following:

   To **scale** it horizontally and vertically, drag a corner handle; to scale it only horizontally or vertically, drag a side handle; to scale it proportionally, Shift-drag a corner handle; or to scale it from the current reference point, Alt-drag/Option-drag a handle (add Shift to scale it proportionally from the reference point).**B**

   To **rotate** it, position the pointer just outside a corner handle (the pointer becomes a curved, two-headed arrow), then drag in a circular direction. Shift-drag to constrain the rotation to a multiple of 15°.

   To **skew** it, Ctrl-drag/Cmd-drag a side handle. (Include Shift to constrain the movement.)

**A** *This is the original image.*

**B** *We selected the car, then copied it to a new layer. Here, we're scaling the new layer.*

To **distort** it, Ctrl-drag/Cmd-drag a corner handle.**A**

To apply **perspective** to it, Ctrl-Alt-Shift-drag/ Cmd-Option-Shift-drag a corner handle along the horizontal or vertical axis to create one-point perspective along that axis (the pointer becomes a gray arrowhead). The adjacent corner will move symmetrically.**B**

5. To accept the transformation, double-click inside the bounding box or click the Commit Transform button ✔ on the Options bar (Enter/Return).

   To cancel the transformation, click the Cancel Transform button ⊘ or press Esc. You must either accept or cancel to resume normal editing.

   Note: If you transform an image layer or a selection on an image layer, pixels outside the transform box will become transparent. If you transform a selection on the Background, areas outside the transform box will be filled with the current Background color.

➤ To undo the last handle edit, choose Edit > Undo.

➤ As you perform a transformation, you can view readouts pertaining to your edits on the Options bar and the Info panel.

➤ You can drag the reference point, from which the layer or selection is transformed, to a different location from its default location in the center. For a rotation transformation, it helps to move the reference point outside the transform box.

➤ To free transform a copy of a layer, hold down Alt/Option and choose Edit > Free Transform. To repeat the last transformation, choose Edit > Transform > Again or press Ctrl-Shift-T/Cmd-Shift-T (the newest transformation is added to the last one). To repeat the last transformation and make a copy of the current layer, press Control-Shift-Alt-T/Cmd-Shift-Option-T.

➤ The current Image Interpolation setting in Preferences > General applies to transformations, among other things (see page 386).

**A** We're applying distortion to the car to widen the lower right corner.

**B** We're applying perspective to make the front of the car wider than the back.

---

### APPLYING TRANSFORMATIONS VIA THE OPTIONS BAR

When you choose the Edit > Free Transform command (Ctrl-T/Cmd-T), features become available on the Options bar for applying transform edits. You can either enter specific values or use the scrubby sliders. If you want to change the reference point for a transformation, click one of the squares on the Reference Point Location icon.

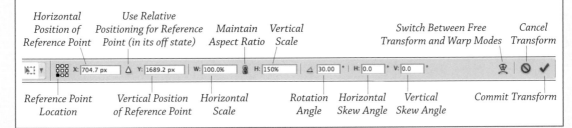

| | | | | | | | |
|---|---|---|---|---|---|---|---|
| Horizontal Position of Reference Point | Use Relative Positioning for Reference Point (in its off state) | Maintain Aspect Ratio | Vertical Scale | | | Switch Between Free Transform and Warp Modes | Cancel Transform |

X: 704.7 px   Y: 1689.2 px   W: 100.0%   H: 150%   30.00°   H: 0.0°   V: 0.0

| Reference Point Location | Vertical Position of Reference Point | Horizontal Scale | Rotation Angle | Horizontal Skew Angle | Vertical Skew Angle | Commit Transform |

# Applying the Puppet Warp command

The new Puppet Warp command lets you distort areas of a layer by dragging pins on a mesh, like you might pull strings on a puppet. The pins that you don't drag serve to anchor image areas in place. The results from this command can range from subtle reshaping or retouching to extreme contortion.

**To apply the Puppet Warp command:** ★

1. Duplicate an image layer or the Background.

   *Optional:* To apply the command as an editable Smart Filter, convert the duplicate layer to a Smart Object layer. To warp a subject but not its background, click a silhouetted image layer.

2. Choose Edit > **Puppet Warp**.

3. On the Options bar, choose these settings:

   A **Mode** option to control the elasticity of the mesh: Rigid for limited 2-dimensional distortion, Normal for 2-dimensional distortion of a larger area, or Distort for 3-dimensional distortion.

   A **Density** option to control the spacing of points in the mesh: Fewer Points for faster but less precise warpage; Normal for an average number of points; or More Points for more precision (and more processing time).

   An **Expansion** value to expand or contract the total area to be warped.

   *Optional:* Uncheck Show Mesh.

4. In the document, click to set pins in both the areas to be warped and the areas to remain anchored in place.**A**

5. To warp the image, drag any individual pin.**B** Or to move multiple pins, Shift-click them first.

6. To apply rotation, do either of the following:

   Choose **Auto** from the **Rotate** menu on the Options bar, then drag a pin. The angle of rotation changes as you drag, and is listed on the Options bar.

   To rotate imagery around a pin, select it, position the cursor near (but not over) it, hold down Alt/Option, and when a circle with handles appears, drag in a circular direction. The Rotate menu for that pin will now be set to **Fixed** and the angle of rotation won't change, even if you drag that pin (or another pin). To unfix the rotation angle of a pin at any time, select it, then choose Auto from the Rotate menu.

   ➤ To remove a pin, Alt-click/Option-click it (scissors pointer). To remove all the pins, click the Remove All Pins button ⟳ on the Options bar, or right-click in the image and choose Remove All Pins from the context menu.

7. To hide the mesh, if displayed, press Ctrl-H/Cmd-H. To hide all the pins temporarily, press and hold down H.

8. Make any further adjustments, then press Enter/Return or click the Commit Puppet Warp button ✔ (Options bar). (To cancel the warp, press Esc.)

   ➤ To reveal a pin that is hidden behind another one, click the pin that is on top, then click one of the Pin Depth buttons on the Options bar.

**A** *To reshape the flat horizon in this photo, we duplicated the image layer, chose the Puppet Warp command, then added two rows of pins.*

**B** *We dragged the central pins upward, one at a time, while the stationary pins anchored the ground in place.*

**APPLYING THE PUPPET WARP COMMAND TO A SILHOUETTED IMAGE**

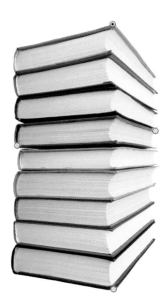

**A** *To add some character to this boring stack of books (not the books, mind you, the photo!), we chose the Puppet Warp command, then clicked to place four pins.*

**B** *To accentuate the perspective, we dragged the top and bottom pins away from each other (one at a time), letting the pin on each side anchor that side in place.*

**C** *We deleted the pin from the middle right side and added a pin to the upper left corner.*

**D** *Finally, to bend and rotate the books, we dragged the two pins (shown in the highlight circles) toward the right simultaneously.*

*We pivoted the stack of books around the two unselected stationary pins on the right side.*

# Applying the Warp command

After choosing the Warp command, you distort a layer by choosing a warp preset, orientation, and other settings on the Options bar, or by manipulating an editable grid that appears over the layer.

## To warp a layer:

1. Click a type, image, or shape layer.

2. Choose Edit > Transform > **Warp**. A grid with handles displays on top of the image layer.

3. Do either of the following:

   On the Options bar, choose a preset style from the **Warp** menu.**B–C** You can also click the **Warp Orientation** button to toggle horizontal and vertical distortion, or reshape the grid by using the scrubby sliders for **Bend**, **H** (horizontal distortion), or **V** (vertical distortion).

   Choose **Warp: Custom** on the Options bar (not available for editable type), then drag any of the squares, diamond-shaped points, grid lines, or direction line handles on the grid. Note: If you don't see the grid, press Ctrl-H/Cmd-H to turn on View > Extras.

4. To accept the warp, press Enter/Return or click the Commit Transform button ✔ on the Options bar (to cancel it, click the Cancel Transform button ⊘ or press Esc).**D**

   ▶ The Warp Text dialog has the same controls as the Warp command, except that it works only on type (see page 347).

---

**RESAMPLE JUST ONCE**

To help preserve the image quality when performing multiple transformations, a transform plus a warp, or transformations to multiple layers, apply them consecutively and accept them in one pass. Resampling will occur once rather than separately for each command.

▶ While the warp or transform controls are showing in your document, you can click the Switch Between Free Transform and Warp Modes button 🏛 on the Options bar to toggle between the two modes.

**REMOVING OR UNDOING A WARP**

▶ To edit the warp settings for a selected layer, choose Edit > Transform > Warp (the warp controls reappear).

▶ To remove a warp, click the prior state on the History panel; or choose the Warp command, then choose None from the Warp menu on the Options bar.

---

*A This image contains a type layer and an image layer.*

Reference Point Location | Warp menu | Warp Orientation | Bend | Horizontal Distortion | Vertical Distortion | Switch Between Free Transform and Warp Modes | Cancel Transform

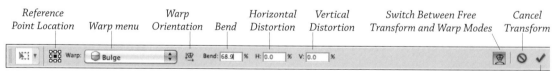

*B When the Edit > Transform > Warp command is chosen, these commands appear on the Options bar.* Commit Transform

*C The type layer is warped using the preset Bulge style.*

*D We chose Overlay mode for the type layer to blend it in with the lime rind.*

You've probably already used a filter or two in an earlier chapter. In this chapter, they are the star players. Depending on which filters you apply and which settings you choose for them, the results can range from a subtle tweak to a total morph. **A–B** You can make an image look hand painted, silkscreened, or sketched; apply distortion or noise; produce patterns or textures; make an image look like a mosaic or like it's being viewed through mottled glass — the creative possibilities are infinite. Once you start using the Filter Gallery, you'll see... time will fly by.

Using this chapter, you will learn techniques for applying filters, learn how to create and use Smart Filters, peruse an illustrated compendium of Photoshop filters, and combine a few filters to make a photo look hand drawn or painted (two quick exercises, just to get you started).

## Applying filters

You can apply filters to a whole layer or just to a selection on a layer. Most of the filters are applied either via the Filter Gallery or via an individual dialog; a small handful of them, such as Clouds and Blur, are applied in one step simply by choosing the filter name from a submenu on the Filter menu. If you apply a filter to a Smart Object layer, it becomes an editable, removable Smart Filter (see pages 320–324).

If you try to select a filter and discover that it's not available, the likely cause is that it's incompatible with the current document color mode or bit depth. All the filters are available for RGB and Grayscale files; most filters are available for Lab Color files; fewer are available for CMYK Color and 16-bits-per-channel files; still fewer are available for 32-bits-per-channel files; and none are available for Bitmap and Indexed Color files.

FILTERS

19

**A** *This is the original image.*

**B** *The Charcoal filter is applied.*

Most of the Photoshop filters are housed conveniently under one roof in the Filter Gallery dialog. The dialog lets you preview dozens of filters and filter settings, show and hide each filter effect that you've previewed, and change the sequence in which they're applied.

### To use the Filter Gallery:

1. Click an image layer (or for more flexibility, a duplicate image layer) or click a Smart Object layer (see "To apply a Smart Filter" on page 320). *Optional:* To limit the filter to a specific area, create a selection.

2. The Foreground and/or Background colors are used by many filters (see the sidebar at right), and you must choose those colors now, before opening the Filter Gallery.

3. Choose Filter > **Filter Gallery**. The resizable gallery opens (**A**, next page).

4. To change the zoom level for the preview, click the Zoom Out button ⊟ or Zoom In button ⊞ in the lower left corner of the dialog or choose a preset zoom level from the menu. (You can drag a magnified preview in the window.)

5. Do either of the following:

   In the middle pane of the dialog, click an arrowhead to expand any of the six filter categories, then click a filter thumbnail.

   Choose a filter name from the menu below the Cancel button (you may need to click a filter thumbnail to make the menu listings appear).

6. On the right side of the dialog, choose settings for the filter. Note that the filter you've chosen is now listed in the right section of the dialog.

7. Do any of the following optional steps:

   To apply another filter effect, click the **New Effect Layer** button, click a filter thumbnail in any category, then choose settings. The filter may take a moment or two to process.

   To **replace** one filter effect with another, click a filter effect name on the scroll list (don't click the New Effect Layer button), then choose a replacement filter and settings.

   To **hide** a filter effect, click the visibility icon 👁 next to the effect name (click again to redisplay).

   To change the **stacking order** of a filter effect to produce a different result in the image, drag the effect name upward or downward on the list.

To remove a filter effect from the list, select it, then click the **Delete Effect Layer** button. 🗑

8. When you're satisfied with the filter(s) and settings that you've chosen, click OK.

➤ To remove a non-Smart Filter, click a prior document state or snapshot on the History panel.

➤ Alt-click/Option-click the visibility icon for a filter effect to hide or show the previews for all the other effects.

➤ If you choose an individual filter from the Filter menu in Photoshop that also happens to be in the Filter Gallery, the Filter Gallery opens automatically.

➤ Plug-in filters for Photoshop are also available for purchase from third-party suppliers.

---

### FILTERS THAT USE THE FOREGROUND AND BACKGROUND COLORS

The filters listed below use the current Foreground and/or Background colors. Some filters, such as Charcoal, Graphic Pen, and Photocopy (in the Sketch category), look good in the default Photoshop colors of black and white, whereas others look better in color. But don't just take our word for it — experiment and see for yourself.

➤ Artistic > Colored Pencil (Background color), Neon Glow (Foreground and Background colors)

➤ Distort > Diffuse Glow (Background color)

➤ Pixelate > Pointillize (Background color)

➤ Render > Clouds, Difference Clouds, Fibers (Foreground and Background colors)

➤ Sketch > Bas Relief, Chalk & Charcoal, Charcoal, Conté Crayon, Graphic Pen, Halftone Pattern, Note Paper, Photocopy, Plaster, Reticulation, Stamp, Torn Edges (Foreground and Background colors)

➤ Stylize > Tiles (Foreground or Background color)

➤ Texture > Stained Glass (Foreground color)

### REAPPLYING THE LAST-USED FILTER

➤ To reapply the last-used filter using the same settings, choose Filter > [last filter name] (Ctrl-F/Cmd-F).

➤ To reopen either the last-used filter dialog or the Filter Gallery with the settings for the last-used filter displayed, press Ctrl-Alt-F/Cmd-Option-F.

Click this button to hide the thumbnails and expand the preview area; click it again to redisplay the thumbnails.

To preview a filter effect, either click a thumbnail or choose a filter name from the menu.

Zoom controls

Hide or show the filter effect preview

New Effect Layer

Drag to resize the dialog

**A** *The Filter Gallery dialog has three sections: a preview area on the left, filter categories with thumbnails in the middle, and on the right the settings for the currently selected filter and a list of the filter effects you've previewed thus far.*

---

### USING THE PREVIEW IN AN INDIVIDUAL FILTER DIALOG

► For individual filter dialogs that have a preview window, you can click the + button to zoom in or the − button to zoom out (we usually do the latter). When the preview is magnified, you can drag it inside the preview window. You can also click and hold in the preview, then release, to compare the image with and without the filter effect. Some filter dialogs also have a Preview check box that you can click on or off.

► When some filter dialogs are open (such as Blur > Gaussian Blur or Motion Blur), if you click in the document window (square pointer), that area of the image will appear in the preview window.

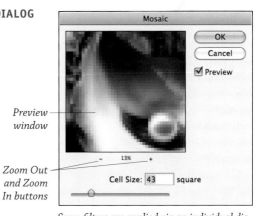

Preview window

Zoom Out and Zoom In buttons

*Some filters are applied via an individual dialog. Of those dialogs, some contain a preview window and some don't.*

# Creating and editing Smart Filters

When you apply a filter to a Smart Object, it becomes a Smart Filter. As with layer effects, you can edit, hide, or remove Smart Filters at any time, apply multiple filters to the same Smart Object layer, hide individual filters while keeping others visible, and move or copy filters from one Smart Object layer to another. You can also edit the filter mask (which is created automatically), change the stacking order of the filters, and of course edit the Smart Object. To learn about Smart Object layers, see pages 308–311.

The file formats that support Photoshop layers — including PSD, PDF, and TIFF — also support Smart Filters. Some third-party (non-Adobe) filters can also be applied as Smart Filters.

## To apply a Smart Filter:

1. Do either of the following:

   Click an existing Smart Object layer.

   Click an image layer, then choose Filter > **Convert for Smart Filters** (or right-click the layer and choose Convert to Smart Object).

2. *Optional:* Create a selection to restrict which part of the image the filter affects. (The selection shape will appear in the filter mask after you apply a filter.)

3. Apply a filter. A Smart Filters listing and mask thumbnail appear on the Layers panel, with the filter name nested below.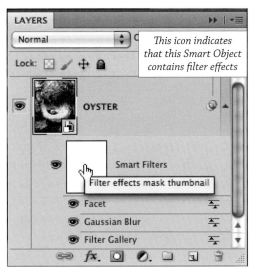 (Note: Filter > Liquify and Vanishing Point can't be applied as Smart Filters.)

The greatest advantage to using Smart Filters is that you can edit the filter settings at any time.

## To edit the settings for a Smart Filter:

1. Do either of the following:

   Double-click on or next to the Smart Filter name on the Layers panel.

   Right-click the Smart Filter name and choose **Edit Smart Filter** from the context menu.

2. If any Smart Filters are listed above the one you're editing, an alert will appear, indicating that those filter effects will be hidden until you exit the Filter Gallery or filter dialog. Check Don't Show Again to prevent the warning from appearing again, if desired, then click OK.

3. Make the desired changes in the filter dialog, then click OK.

*This icon indicates that this Smart Object contains filter effects*

**A** *If you apply a Smart Filter by choosing Filter > Filter Gallery, the filter listing will be a generic "Filter Gallery"; if you apply a Smart Filter by choosing its individual name from the Filter menu, its name will be listed.*

**B** *If you edit a Smart Filter and other filters are listed above it on the same layer, this alert dialog appears.*

## CHANGING THE COLOR MODE OR BIT DEPTH

When changing the document color mode or bit depth, if the document contains Smart Filters that aren't supported by the new mode or depth, an alert appears (shown below). If you click Don't Rasterize and then click Don't Flatten, this symbol ⚠ will display next to the filter names, indicating that the filter effect is inaccessible. If you then convert the file to a mode or depth that does support the filter (and respond to the alerts again the same way), the icon will disappear and the filter effect will become available again.

Not only can you change the blending mode and opacity of any Smart Object layer, but each Smart Filter can also have its own blending mode and opacity setting. Granted, this can be a lot to keep track of. And unfortunately, no indicator appears on the Layers panel to let you know if those settings have been changed from the defaults.

### To edit the blending options for a Smart Filter:

1. Double-click the **Blending Options** icon next to the filter name on the Layers panel, and click OK if an alert dialog appears.**A–B** The Blending Options dialog opens.**C** Check Preview.

2. Lower the zoom level, if desired, change the blending **Mode** and/or **Opacity** (use the latter to fade the filter effect), then click OK.**D**

## Hiding, copying, and deleting Smart Filters

### To hide or show Smart Filter effects:

Do either of the following:

Click the visibility icon 👁 for the Smart Filters listing to hide all the Smart Filters on that layer.

Click the visibility icon 👁 for any individual Smart Filter. This may take longer to process than clicking the visibility icon for all the filters.

Click the icon again to redisplay the hidden filter effects.

### To copy Smart Filters from one Smart Object layer to another:

Expand the list of Smart Filters on a Smart Object layer, then Alt-drag/Option-drag either the Smart Filters listing or an individual filter listing into another Smart Object layer.

➤ You can restack any Smart Filter within a Smart Object layer.

➤ If you drag a filter or the Smart Filters listing from one Smart Object layer to another without holding down Alt/Option, the filters will be removed from the source layer and will be added to any existing Smart Filters on the target layer. Pause to let Photoshop process the change.

**A** *We applied the Fresco and Dry Brush filters to this image.*

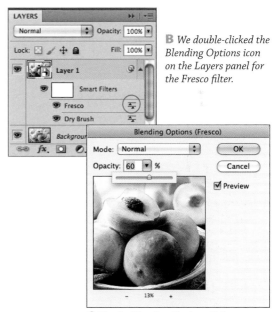

**B** *We double-clicked the Blending Options icon on the Layers panel for the Fresco filter.*

**C** *Via the Blending Options dialog, we lowered the opacity of the Fresco filter.*

**D** *Now more of the Dry Brush filter is showing through.*

If you delete a Smart Filter from a layer that contains other filters, Photoshop may take a moment or two to update the display.

### To delete a Smart Filter:

Do either of the following:

Right-click a Smart Filter and choose **Delete Smart Filter**.

Drag the Smart Filter to the **Delete Layer** button. 🗑

## Working with the Smart Filter mask

All Smart Filters have a filter mask. If you create a selection before applying a filter, the selection shape will appear in the mask. To work with the mask, see the next instructions. To create a filter mask if there is none (someone deleted it), do as follows.

### To create a filter mask:

1. *Optional:* Create a selection.
2. Do either of the following:

Right-click Smart Filters on the Layers panel and choose **Add Filter Mask.**

Click the Smart Object layer on the Layers panel, then on the Masks panel,🔲 click the **Add Filter Mask** button.⊕

A filter mask is edited the same way as a layer mask. For an illustration of how this works, see the next two pages.

### To edit a filter mask:

Do any of the following:

To edit the mask by applying brush strokes, click the mask thumbnail, then with the **Brush** tool, ✏ apply strokes with black to hide the filter effect or with white to reveal areas you've hidden. To hide areas partially, apply strokes with black and a lower tool opacity.

For a gradual transition between the filtered and nonfiltered areas, click the filter mask thumbnail on the Layers panel, then on the Masks panel, 🔲 adjust the **Feather** value (you can also reduce the mask effect via the Density slider). Another option is to apply a gradient to the filter mask with the **Gradient** tool. ▬

➤ To display the filter mask by itself in the document, Alt-click/Option-click the mask; repeat to redisplay the full Smart Object layer.

➤ To load a filter mask as a selection, Ctrl-click/Cmd-click the filter mask thumbnail.

### To deactivate or delete a filter mask:

To **deactivate** a filter mask temporarily, Shift-click the mask thumbnail (a red X appears over the thumbnail); repeat to reactivate it.

To **delete** a filter mask, drag it to the Delete Layer button on the Layers panel; or click it, then on the Masks panel, click the Delete Mask button. 🗑

---

**BECOMING A FILTER WIZARD**

➤ To make your filter results look less uniform or machine made, apply more than one to the same layer. That way, no single effect will stand out.

➤ To intensify the filter results, before applying them, pump up the brightness and contrast of the image via a Levels adjustment layer. Move the black Input Levels slider slightly to the right and the white Input Levels slider slightly to the left.

➤ If a filter has been applied to a duplicate image layer (not to a Smart Object layer), you can lessen its effect by lowering the layer opacity, or selectively limit its effect by applying black strokes in the document with the layer mask thumbnail selected.

➤ If multiple filters are applied to a Smart Object layer, you can selectively reduce the effect of any individual one via the Blending Options dialog (see the preceding page).

➤ If you encounter memory problems when applying filters (Photoshop memory, that is, not your own forgetfulness!), some possible solutions are to use Edit > Purge > All first to free up memory, exit/quit other open applications, or if necessary, allocate more RAM to Photoshop. Also, keep in mind that for the same filter, some settings may require more RAM to process than others. For example, a setting that produces many small shapes may take more processing time than one that produces a few large ones.

## WORKING WITH SMART FILTERS, BY EXAMPLE

**A** *This is the original image.*

**B** *We duplicated the image layer, converted it to a Smart Object layer, pressed D to reset the default Foreground and Background colors, then applied Filter > Sketch > Charcoal.*

**C** *We reduced the Smart Object layer opacity to 62%.*

**D** *We clicked the filter mask, then with the Brush tool at 50% Opacity and black as the Foreground color, applied strokes to partially restore the tiger's face to its virgin state.*

**E** *This is the Layers panel for the figure shown at left.*

*Continued on the following page*

**A** *Next, to wipe the mask clean in order to try a different approach, we erased our brush strokes from the filter mask with the Eraser tool. (Alternatively, we could have pressed Ctrl-A/Cmd-A to select the whole layer, pressed Backspace/Delete, then deselected all.)*

**B** *To fade the filter effect gradually, we clicked the filter mask, then with the Gradient tool at 100% Opacity, applied the "Black, White" gradient (radial type) by dragging from the center of the image outward. The filter effect is full where the mask is white, and fades to nil where the mask is black.*

**C** *The gradient in the filter mask is diminishing the impact of the filter in the center of the image (the tiger's face) — where we want the focal point to be.*

# (Most of) the filters illustrated
## Artistic filters

*Original image*

*Colored Pencil\**

*Cutout*

*Dry Brush*

*Film Grain*

*Fresco*

*Neon Glow (choose Foreground and Background colors first, and choose a glow color in the Filter Gallery)*

*Paint Daubs*

*Palette Knife*

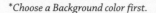

*\*Choose a Background color first.*

## Artistic filters (continued)

*Original image*

*Plastic Wrap*

*Poster Edges*

*Rough Pastels*

*Smudge Stick*

*Sponge*

*Underpainting*

*Watercolor*

# Brush Strokes filters

*Original image*

*Accented Edges*

*Angled Strokes*

*Crosshatch*

*Dark Strokes*

*Ink Outlines*

*Spatter*

*Sprayed Strokes*

*Sumi-e*

## Pixelate filters

*Color Halftone*

*Crystallize*

*Facet*

*Fragment*

*Mezzotint*

*Mosaic*

## Two of the Render filters

*Pointillize (choose a Background color first)*

*Clouds (choose Foreground and Background colors first)*

*Lens Flare*

## Sketch filters

*Bas Relief**

*Chalk & Charcoal**

*Charcoal**

*Chrome*

*Conté Crayon**

*Graphic Pen**

*Halftone Pattern**

*Note Paper**

*Photocopy**

*Choose Foreground and Background colors first.*

## Sketch filters (continued)

*Original image*

*Plaster\**

*Reticulation\**

*Stamp\**

*Torn Edges\**

*Water Paper*

## A few of the Distort filters

*Diffuse Glow (choose a Background color first)*

*Displace*

*\*Choose Foreground and Background colors first.*

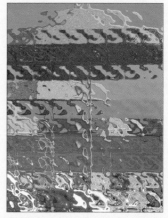

*Glass*

## Stylize filters

*Diffuse*

*Emboss*

*Extrude*

*Find Edges*

*Glowing Edges*

*Solarize*

*Tiles (choose a Foreground or Background color first)*

*Trace Contour*

*Wind*

## Texture filters

*Original image*

*Craquelure*

*Grain (Soft)*

*Grain (Speckle)*

*Grain (Vertical)*

*Mosaic Tiles*

*Patchwork*

*Stained Glass (choose a Foreground color first)*

*Texturizer*

# Turning photos into drawings or paintings

In the instructions on this page, you'll turn a photo into a drawing by reducing it to lines and then painting on the filter mask. On the next page, you'll turn a photo into a watercolor by applying a series of filters. We hope these exercises will inspire you to develop your own formulas.

## To turn a photo into a tinted drawing:

1. Duplicate an image layer in a high-resolution photo.**A**

2. Choose Filter > Stylize > **Find Edges**.**B**

3. Choose the **Brush** tool. Choose a large, Soft Round brush, Normal mode, and an Opacity below 50% on the Options bar. Also make the Foreground color black.

4. Click the **Add Layer Mask** button on the Layers panel, then with the layer mask thumbnail selected, apply strokes to the image to reveal areas of the underlying layer.

5. Do either or both of the following optional steps:

   Lower the opacity of the duplicate layer.

   Change the blending mode of the duplicate layer (try Lighter Color, Hard Light, Pin Light, or Luminosity mode).**C–D**

**A** We duplicated the Background in this original image.

**B** We applied the Find Edges filter to the duplicate layer.

**C** This is the Layers panel for the image shown at right.

**D** We applied brush strokes to the layer mask to reveal some of the underlying image, and changed the blending mode of the duplicate layer to Hard Light.

There are so many ways to combine filters. In these instructions, you'll turn an image into a watercolor by applying the Median and Minimum filters — two filters that you probably wouldn't ordinarily use. A medium- to light-toned image would work best for this exercise.

## To turn a photo into a watercolor:

1. Duplicate an image layer, then right-click the duplicate and choose Convert to Smart Object. Keep the new layer selected. **A**

2. Choose Filter > Noise > **Median**. In the Median dialog, choose a Radius value between 2 and 8, then click OK.

3. Choose Filter > Other > **Minimum**. In the Minimum dialog, choose a value that produces a pleasing simulation of a watercolor; click OK.

4. *Optional:* Choose Filter > Sharpen > Smart Sharpen, click Basic, try an Amount of 80–100% and a Radius of 4–8 px, then click OK. **B–C**

**A** *This is the original photo.*

**B** *This watercolor was created by following the steps above.*

**C** *This is the result of using Photoshop's Artistic > Watercolor filter. We think it's a bit harsh compared to the results of our steps, as shown at left.*

We've never heard the phrase "A word is worth a thousand pictures," but in Photoshop, where you can do such artful things with type, the line between pictures and words is blurred (sometimes literally!). In this chapter, you'll learn how to create and select editable type and apply a wide assortment of character and paragraph attributes. You'll also learn some tricks, such as how to transform, warp, fade, and screen back type, and how to fill it with imagery. Finally, you will learn how to put type in a spot color channel.

When you use the Horizontal Type tool or Vertical Type tool, a new layer appears on the Layers panel and editable type appears in the document. You can easily change the font, style, size, or color of editable type, and such settings as the kerning, tracking, leading, alignment, and baseline shift. Moreover, you can transform, warp, or apply layer effects to editable type, change its blending mode, and change its opacity and fill values. To style type, you'll use the Character panel **A** (shown below in **A**), the Paragraph panel **¶** (on page 345), and the Options bar (**A**, next page).

Note: To apply some kinds of edits to type, such as filters or brush strokes, or to fill type with a gradient or pattern by using the Fill command, the type layer must be rasterized first. However, you can't have your cake and eat it, too: Once type is rasterized, you can't edit its character attributes, such as the font, or its paragraph attributes, such as the alignment.

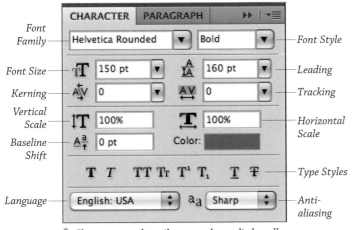

**A** *Character panel attributes can be applied to all the type on a layer or to select characters or words.*

# Creating editable type

Because editable type automatically appears on its own layer, it can be edited, moved, transformed, warped, restacked, etc., without affecting any other layers. You can be very casual about where you position editable type initially and about which typographic attributes you choose for it, because it's so easy to move and edit.

## To create an editable type layer:

1. Choose the **Horizontal Type** tool T or **Vertical Type** tool ↓T (T or Shift-T).

2. On the Options bar, A do all of the following:

   Choose a **font family**, and from the adjacent menu, choose a **font style**. A sample of each font displays on the menu.

   Choose or enter a **font size** (you can use the scrubby slider).

   Choose an **anti-aliasing** method: Sharp (sharpest), Crisp (somewhat sharp), Strong (heavier), or Smooth (smoothest). Photoshop will introduce partially transparent pixels along the edges of the characters to make them look smoother. With anti-aliasing off (None), the edges of the type will be jagged; this is the best option for Web output. B–C

   Click an **alignment** button to align point type relative to your original insertion point or to

align paragraph type to the left edge, right edge, or center of the bounding box (see also page 345).

Click the **Text Color** swatch, then choose a color from the Color Picker or the Swatches panel, or click a color in the document.

3. Do either of the following:

   To create **point** type (suitable for a small amount of text), click in the document to establish an insertion point, then type the desired text. You can press Enter/Return to create line breaks, where necessary, to prevent the type from disappearing off the edge of the canvas. (You can also move the type later with the Move tool.)

   To create **paragraph** type (suitable for a larger block of text*), drag a marquee to define a bounding box for the type to fit into, then type the desired text. Let the words wrap naturally to the edges of the bounding box; press Enter/Return only when you need to start a new paragraph. If you prefer to specify dimensions for the bounding box, Alt/Option click in the document, then enter dimensions in the Paragraph Text Size dialog.

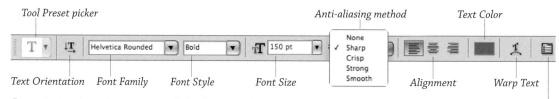

**A** The Options bar offers many controls for the type tools.

**B** With Anti-aliasing off, type edges look jagged.

**C** With Anti-aliasing on, type edges look smoother.

*If your project requires you to typeset a fair amount of text, it may be more efficient to create the imagery in Photoshop and add the type in a layout or Web page creation program.

**4.** To accept the new text, press Enter on the keypad (not on the main keyboard) or click the Commit ✔ button on the right end of the Options bar. (To cancel the type, press Esc or click the Cancel button ⊘ on the Options bar.) Each time you use the Horizontal or Vertical Type tool, Photoshop creates a new layer automatically.**A–B**

Note: Photoshop uses the vector outlines for a typeface when resizing editable type, when saving the file to the PDF and EPS formats, and when outputting it to a PostScript printer. Like vector graphics, editable type outputs at the printer resolution, not at the file resolution.

➤ You can right-click an editable type layer name and choose a different anti-aliasing method from the context menu.

➤ In Edit/Photoshop > Preferences > Type, from the Font Preview Size menu, you can turn font menu previewing on or off and change the preview size for the Font menu. If previewing is on but it's working too slowly on your machine, turn it off.

➤ For documents in Bitmap, Indexed Color, and Multichannel color mode, type appears on the Background, not on a layer, and cannot be edited.

➤ If you prefer not to establish new default Options bar settings for your type tool, click or drag with the tool in the document before choosing settings for it.

➤ If you place individual phrases, words, or characters on separate layers, you'll be able to move them around and apply effects to them individually. If your type layers start to overpopulate, on the other hand, you can periodically delete any layers that you don't need and gather the ones you do want to preserve into layer groups.

**A** *After typing the first word shown at left, we pressed Enter/Return to start the second word on the next line.*

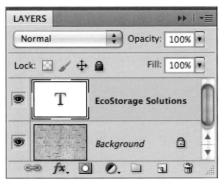

**B** *Editable type layers have a **T** in the thumbnail and are named automatically by the first word or few words of type they contain.*

## Selecting type

Before you can change the character or paragraph attributes of type or make any copy changes, you have to select the characters to be edited. You can edit either all the type on a layer or a series of sequential characters or words.

### To select type for editing or style changes:

1. Do any of the following:

   To highlight characters for editing, click a type layer, choose the **Horizontal Type** tool T or **Vertical Type** tool !T (T or Shift-T), click in the type to create an insertion point, then drag across characters or words to select them.A For other methods, see the sidebar on this page.

   To select all the type on a layer, and to make the type controls available on the Options bar, with any tool selected, double-click the **T** icon on the Layers panel. (The Horizontal Type tool will also become selected, if it was the last type tool you had selected.)

   To change the attributes of all the type on a layer via the Character or Paragraph panel, such as the scale, tracking, leading, style, or alignment, simply click the layer (you don't need to select a type tool).

2. After performing text edits or after changing the type attributes via the Options bar, to commit to the changes, do one of the following:

   Click the Commit button ✔ on the Options bar.

   Press Enter on the keypad (not on the main keyboard).

   Click a different tool.

   Click a different layer.

   (To cancel your editing changes before committing to them, click the Cancel button ⊘ on the Options bar or press Esc.)

➤ To move type to a different location in the document, click the type layer, click the Move tool ▶⊹ or hold down Ctrl/Cmd, then drag the type.

➤ To delete selected type, press Backspace/Delete on the keyboard. Or to delete one character at a time, click with a type tool to create an insertion point, then press Backspace/Delete.

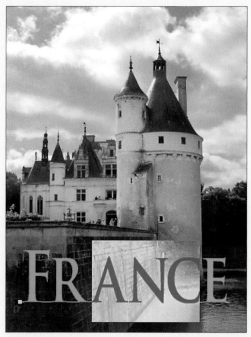

**A** *Drag across the characters to be selected.*

---

### SELECTING TYPE CHARACTERS

To select type for copy editing or restyling, choose the Horizontal Type or Vertical Type tool, then do any of the following:

| | |
|---|---|
| Select consecutive characters or words | Drag across them. Or click at the beginning of a series of words, then Shift-click at the end. |
| Select a word | Double-click a word |
| Select consecutive words | Double-click a word, then drag (without releasing the mouse) |
| Select a line | Triple-click a line |
| Select a paragraph | Quadruple-click in the paragraph |
| Select all the characters in the type object | Double-click the **T** thumbnail on the Layers panel; or click in the text, then press Ctrl-A/Cmd-A |

## Recoloring type

### To recolor all the type on a layer:

1. On the Layers panel, click a type layer.

2. Do either of the following:

   Choose the **Horizontal Type** tool T or **Vertical Type** tool, ↓T then click the **Text Color** swatch on the Options bar.

   Click the **Color** swatch on the Character panel.

3. Choose a color in the Color Picker, then click OK.

➤ You can also apply a color, gradient, or pattern to a type layer via an editable Overlay effect (see pages 362–364).

### To recolor select characters or words:

1. Choose the **Horizontal Type** tool T or **Vertical Type** tool. ↓T

2. Click in the type to create an insertion point, then drag across the characters or words to be recolored. A

3. On the Options bar, click the **Text Color** swatch, choose a color in the color picker B or click a color in the image, then click OK. You can also choose a color via the Color panel or Swatches panel.

## Changing the font family and font style

### Method 1

1. On the Layers panel, 🔲 double-click a **T** icon. If you don't want to change all the selected type, select the characters or words to be restyled.

2. On the Options bar or the Character panel, A choose from the **Font Family** menu, then from the **Font Style** menu (to show the Character panel, see the sidebar on page 342).

### Method 2

To change the font for all the type on a layer, click the layer without selecting anything, then use the Character panel, as described above.

➤ To deal with missing fonts in a file, see page 58.

---

**REMEMBER TO USE SMART QUOTES!**

To specify that curly typographer's quotes be used for quotation marks and apostrophes — a basic rule of proper typesetting that is too often ignored — go to Edit/Photoshop > Preferences > Type and check Use Smart Quotes. Straight quotes should be used only as abbreviations for foot and inch measurements!

---

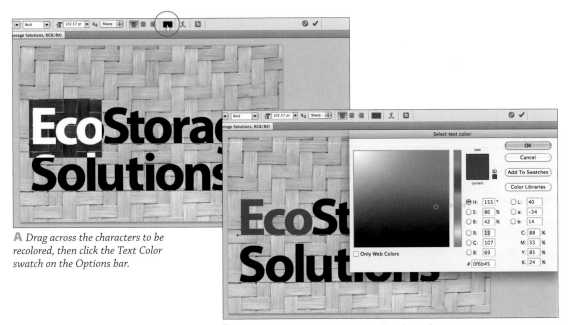

**A** Drag across the characters to be recolored, then click the Text Color swatch on the Options bar.

**B** Choose a replacement color from the color picker.

# Converting type

## To convert paragraph type to point type:

On the Layers panel, right-click a type layer name and choose **Convert to Point Text**. A return will be added to the end of every line of type except the last one. If the type object contains hidden (overflow) text, an alert dialog will warn you that the hidden text will be deleted if you proceed; click OK.

➤ We don't know of a command in Photoshop that reveals hidden characters (paragraph returns and the like). We do wish there was one.

## To convert point type to paragraph type:

On the Layers panel, right-click a type layer name and choose **Convert to Paragraph Text**. To reshape the resulting bounding box, follow the steps on page 346. Be sure to delete any unwanted hyphens that Photoshop may have inserted.

## Importing type from Illustrator into Photoshop as a Smart Object

If you create type in Adobe Illustrator and then import it into Photoshop using the method outlined below, it will arrive as a Smart Object layer in Photoshop. To edit or restyle the type at any time in Illustrator, simply double-click the Smart Object layer. When you return to Photoshop, your edits will appear in the Photoshop document.

## To import type from Adobe Illustrator as a Smart Object:

1. In Adobe Illustrator, make sure the type is on its own layer, then via File > Save As, save the file in the Illustrator Document (.ai) format.

2. Open a document in Photoshop, then do either of the following:

   In Photoshop, use File > **Place** to import the Illustrator file; or in Bridge, click the Illustrator file thumbnail, then choose File > Place > **In Photoshop**.

   In Illustrator, copy the type by pressing Ctrl-C/Cmd-C. Click in the Photoshop document, then press Ctrl-V/Cmd-V. In the Paste dialog, click **Paste As: Smart Object**, then click OK.

3. To scale the type proportionally from its center, Alt-Shift/Option-Shift drag a corner handle. **A**

To accept the type, click the **Commit** button ✔ on the Options bar or press Enter/Return.

4. A new Smart Object layer appears on the Layers panel. **B**

5. To edit the Smart Object, double-click the Smart Object layer thumbnail. If an alert regarding saving changes appears, click OK. If the PDF Modification Detected alert appears next, ★ click "Discard Changes, Preserving Illustrator Editing Capabilities," then click OK.

   The embedded file (not the original one) will open in Illustrator. You can edit the type or any of its attributes or effects. Save and close the file. Your edits will appear in the Photoshop document.

➤ To learn more about Smart Object layers, see pages 308–311.

**A** *We used the Place command to import a type object from Illustrator. Here, we are scaling it proportionally.*

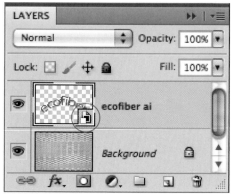

**B** *When we accepted the object from Illustrator, the Smart Object icon appeared in the layer thumbnail.*

## Changing the font size

To assign the same font (point) size to all the characters you select, you can use either the Options bar or the Character panel.

### To change the font size:

**Method 1 (Options bar)**

1. Select the type to be scaled (see step 1 on page 338).

2. Choose the **Horizontal Type** or **Vertical Type** tool; then, on the Options bar, use the **Font Size** icon **T** as a scrubby slider (Alt-drag/Option-drag for smaller increments), 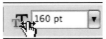 **A** or enter a value, or choose from the menu.**B**

**Method 2 (Character panel)**

On the Layers panel, click a type layer, then change the Font Size on the Character panel.**C**

If the type characters you select are in more than one size and you want to preserve their relative size differences while scaling them, do so interactively with the Move tool.

### To scale type with the Move tool:

1. On the Layers panel, click a type layer.

2. Click the **Move** tool **+** and check **Show Transform Controls** on the Options bar. On the bounding box for the type, click any handle.

3. Do one of the following:

   To scale both the height and the width, drag a corner handle. To preserve the proportions of the characters while scaling them (better!), Shift-drag a corner handle.**D**

   To scale just the height or the width, drag a side handle.

4. To commit to the scale transformation, click the Commit ✔ button on the Options bar or double-click in the text block. (To cancel the edit before committing to it, click the Cancel ⊘ button on the Options bar or press Esc.)

➤ To typeset narrow or wide characters — type purists that we are — we use a condensed or extended font in which the proportions are balanced. If you use the Vertical Scale **IT** or Horizontal Scale **T** control on the Character panel to squeeze or widen type, be aware that this will distort the shape of the characters.

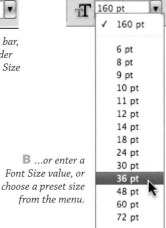

**A** *On the Options bar, use the scrubby slider to change the Font Size of type...*

**B** *...or enter a Font Size value, or choose a preset size from the menu.*

**C** *You can also change the type size via the Font Size scrubby slider, field, or menu on the Character panel.*

**D** *To scale type proportionally with the Move tool, hold down Shift while dragging a corner handle on the transform box.*

# Applying kerning and tracking

Kerning changes the spacing between a pair of text characters, whereas tracking changes the spacing between multiple characters.

## To apply kerning:

### Method 1 (Character panel)

1. On the Layers panel, double-click a **T** icon.

2. Click to create an insertion point between any two characters, and show the Character panel.

3. Do one of the following: From the **Kerning** menu, choose Metrics to apply the kerning value built into the current font or Optical to let Photoshop control the kerning; or use the Kerning icon ᴬⱽ as a scrubby slider; **A** or enter or choose a positive or negative value.**B**

➤ If you need to restore the kerning setting to Optical, select two or more type characters, then choose Optical from the Kerning menu.

### Method 2 (keyboard)

Choose a type tool, insert the cursor between two characters, then press Alt/Option plus the left or right arrow key. Or to kern in a larger increment, press Ctrl-Alt/Cmd-Option and an arrow key.

## To apply tracking:

1. On the Layers panel, do either of the following:

   To apply tracking to a whole layer, click the layer.

   To apply tracking to part of a layer, double-click a **T** icon, then select some characters or words.

2. Do either of the following:

   On the Character panel, use the **Tracking** icon ᴬⱽ as a scrubby slider or enter or choose a positive or negative tracking value.**C**

   If type is selected, you can press Alt/Option and the left or right arrow key (or hold down Ctrl-Alt/Cmd-Option for a larger tracking increment).

➤ To reset the tracking value of selected characters to 0, press Ctrl-Shift-Q/Cmd-Control-Shift-Q.

---

**DISPLAYING THE CHARACTER PANEL**

➤ If the Character panel is open but collapsed to an icon, click the **A** icon.

➤ Select the Horizontal Type tool or Vertical Type tool, then click the Toggle the Character and Paragraph Panels 🗎 button on the Options bar.

➤ Choose Window > Character.

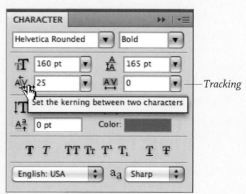

**A** *The Kerning and Tracking controls on the Character panel don't have equivalents on the Options bar. To change either value quickly, use the scrubby slider (or shortcut).*

**B** *Use a negative kerning value to tighten the gap between a pair of characters (we chose a value of –100).*

**TRACKING IT OUT**

Tracking can make type more or less readable, depending on the tracking value used. Try not to overdo it!

**C** *On occasion, we might spread out a few words, as in the header in this figure, but never a whole paragraph (that's a typesetting no-no!).*

## Adjusting the leading

The Leading value controls the spacing between each line of paragraph type and the line above it. Although theoretically each character could have a different leading value (the highest value in a line controls the spacing for the entire line), the spacing will be more uniform and will look better if you apply one value to either a whole line or block of text.

**To adjust leading in horizontal type:**

1. On the Layers panel, do either of the following:

   Double-click the **T** icon for a type layer. *Optional:* Select a line or lines of text that you want to limit the leading change to.

   Click a type layer.

   Note: Leading has no effect on the spacing above the first line in a paragraph.

2. Show the Character panel.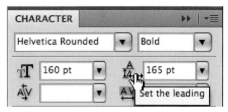 Use the **Leading** icon as a scrubby slider **A–C** (Alt-drag/Option-drag for finer increments), or enter a value in the field (.01 to 5000 pt.), or choose a preset value from the menu. The leading will change from Auto to a numerical value. If you're not sure what value to use, start with a number that's a couple of points larger than the current font size, then readjust it if needed.

   ➤ The Auto setting for leading is calculated as a percentage of the font size, and is set in the Justification dialog. To open that dialog, choose Justification from the Paragraph panel menu. For instance, with Auto Leading set to the default percentage of 120%, the leading for 30-point type would be 36 points. To restore the Auto setting to selected type, press Ctrl-Alt-Shift-A/ Cmd-Option-Shift-A.

   ➤ To reset all of the factory-default settings to the Character panel and to any selected type, choose Reset Character from the Character panel menu.

   ➤ To adjust the vertical spacing between characters in vertical type, highlight the characters to be adjusted, then change the Tracking value (not the leading value) on the Character panel.

   ➤ To choose a unit for the Character and Paragraph panels, and to see a list of abbreviations for the units that can be entered in Photoshop fields, see page 393.

**A** *This is the Leading area on the Character panel.*

**B** *This type has a leading value of 154 pt.*

**C** *A leading value of 120 pt. brings the bottom line of type closer to the top one.*

---

**CREATING PRESETS FOR YOUR TYPE TOOL**

After styling your type, choose the Horizontal or Vertical Type tool, click the type layer, click the Tool Preset picker thumbnail or arrowhead T on the left end of the Options bar, click the New Tool Preset button, rename the new preset, then click OK. You can choose your new preset from the Tool Preset picker or Tool Presets panel any time you create type. It's sort of like having a style sheet, because all your carefully chosen attributes are saved in the preset—except in this case you click the preset before creating the type. You could create presets for print and Web work or for different kinds of projects.

## Changing the type style

### To change the type style:

1. To modify a whole type layer, click the layer; or to style some of the type on the layer, double-click the **T** icon, then select the type to be styled.

2. Click any **style** button on the Character panel. To identify the buttons, use the tool tips onscreen or refer to Figure **A** at right.

➤ The Fractional Widths option on the Character panel menu tells Photoshop to use fractions of pixels to control the spacing of type in order to optimize its appearance (this applies to the entire layer). Keep this option checked unless you're setting small type for Web output.

➤ To choose a "real" italic, bold, or other font style, see "Changing the font family and font style" on page 339.

## Shifting type from the baseline

Use the baseline shift feature to raise or lower type characters from the normal baseline by 1 point at a time.

### To shift characters from the normal baseline:

1. On the Layers panel, double-click a **T** icon, then select the characters or words to be shifted.

2. On the Character panel, use the **Baseline Shift** icon **Aa** as a scrubby slider (Alt-drag/Option-drag for finer increments), or enter a value.**B** A positive value raises characters upward, a negative value moves them downward.**C–D**

   Note: To shift whole lines of paragraph type, use leading—not baseline shift. To shift a whole layer, drag it with the Move tool (so simple, it's easy to forget!).

➤ To change the orientation of type from horizontal to vertical, or vice versa, right-click a type layer name on the Layers panel and choose Horizontal or Vertical. Or double-click a type layer thumbnail and then, on the Options bar, click the Change Text Orientation button.⤶**T** After changing the orientation, you may need to reposition the type or adjust the tracking. For vertical type, another option is to click the type layer, then uncheck Standard Roman Vertical Alignment on the Character panel menu.

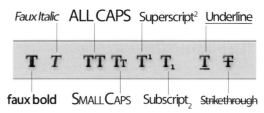

**A** Click a style button on the Character panel.

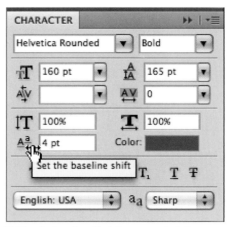

**B** Use the Baseline Shift feature to shift characters or words upward or downward by a few points.

# Upanddown

**C** These characters have a Baseline Shift value of 0.

# Upanddown

**D** These characters have different Baseline Shift values, some positive and some negative.

# Applying paragraph settings

With paragraph type, you forgo the manual control of point type but gain some powerful typesetting tools. The Paragraph panel offers controls for justification, alignment, indents, and paragraph spacing, like those you would use in a page layout program.

## To choose a paragraph alignment or justification option for horizontal type:

1. Do either of the following:

   On the Layers panel, double-click a **T** icon, then click in a paragraph or select a series of paragraphs.

   To apply settings to all the type in a layer, click the layer, but don't select anything.

2. If the Paragraph panel is open but collapsed to an icon, click the ¶ icon. If the panel is closed, choose a type tool, click the Toggle Character and Paragraph Panels 🗐 button on the Options bar, then click the Paragraph tab.

3. Click an alignment and/or justification button at the top of the panel: **A**

   The buttons in the first group—**Left-Align Text**, **Center Text**, and **Right-Align Text**—align type to the center or an edge of the bounding box that surrounds the type. (Note: These options can also be used on point type.)

   The buttons in the second group—**Justify Last Left**, **Justify Last Centered**, and **Justify Last Right**—justify the type, forcing all but the last line to span the full width of the bounding box.

The last button, **Justify All**, forces all lines, including the last one, to span the full width of the bounding box.

4. Check **Hyphenate** at the bottom of the panel to enable automatic hyphenation. If you chose a justified alignment option, turning on hyphenation is especially recommended, because it will help to minimize the gaps between words.

➤ To change the alignment and/or justification values for vertical type, the procedure is the same as described on this page, except the buttons have different labels.

➤ To reset all currently selected paragraphs to the factory-default settings, choose Reset Paragraph from the Paragraph panel menu.

➤ To specify parameters for hyphenation, choose Hyphenation from the Paragraph panel menu.

---

**CHOOSING YOUR FAVORITE COMPOSER**

The Adobe Single-Line Composer and Adobe Every-Line Composer algorithms on the Paragraph panel menu control how lines of type wrap within the bounding box, and affect the overall shape of the paragraph. We prefer the Adobe Every-Line option because it automatically adjusts word breaks at the beginning of a paragraph, when necessary, to improve the line breaks and appearance of the paragraph toward the end. Both composers abide by the current Word Spacing and Letter Spacing values in the Justification dialog, which also opens from the panel menu.

---

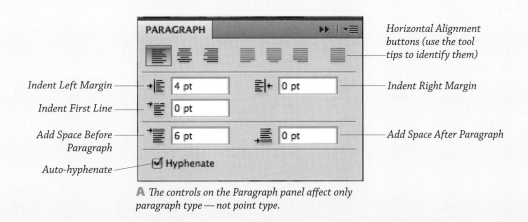

*Horizontal Alignment buttons (use the tool tips to identify them)*

*Indent Left Margin* — 4 pt    *Indent Right Margin* — 0 pt

*Indent First Line* — 0 pt

*Add Space Before Paragraph* — 6 pt    *Add Space After Paragraph* — 0 pt

*Auto-hyphenate* — ☑ Hyphenate

**A** *The controls on the Paragraph panel affect only paragraph type—not point type.*

# Transforming the bounding box for paragraph type

By changing the shape of the bounding box that surrounds paragraph type, you can change the line lengths of the type without distorting the characters. Enlarging the bounding box is a necessity when you want to reveal overflow type (when a bounding box contains overflow type, a plus sign displays in the handle in the lower right corner). You will find less of a need to rotate type, but instructions for doing so are also included.

### To transform paragraph type via its bounding box:

1. On the Layers panel, double-click the **T** icon for a paragraph type layer, then click anywhere in the text. A dashed bounding box surrounds the type.

2. Do one of the following:

   To **reflow** the type by reshaping the bounding box, position the cursor over a control handle, then drag. **A** To preserve the proportions of the bounding box while scaling it, start dragging a corner handle, then hold down Shift and continue to drag. The type will reflow into the new shape. **B**

   To **rotate** the box, position the pointer just outside one of the corners (it will become a curved, double-arrow pointer), then drag in a circular direction.

3. To accept the transformation, press Enter on the keypad or click the Commit button ✔ on the Options bar. (To cancel it, press Esc or click the Cancel button ⊘ on the Options bar.)

➤ To align or distribute multiple type layers, follow the instructions on page 247.

➤ To access the Move tool temporarily when you're working with type (perhaps to move the type), hold down Ctrl/Cmd instead of using the letter shortcut (V). If you do press "V," make sure your type cursor isn't inserted in type, or you will unintentionally either replace selected type with that letter or insert it into your text.

**A** Drag a control handle to transform the bounding box.

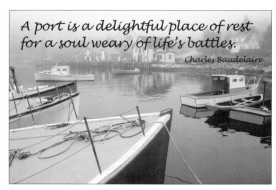

**B** When we made the bounding box wider, the type reflowed into the new shape.

---

**TRANSFORMING TYPE**

➤ When applied to paragraph or point type, the transform commands, such as Free Transform, affect both the bounding box and the characters within it (see pages 312–313).

➤ You can move, scale, rotate, and skew both editable and rasterized type, plus you can apply a distortion or perspective transformation to rasterized type.

➤ If you want to transform individual characters, create them on separate layers.

## Using the Warp Text command

The Warp Text dialog transforms the type bounding box, and the characters within it are warped accordingly. The command offers many customizable style choices, such as arc, arch, shell, wave, and fish. Best of all, warped type remains fully editable.

### To warp editable type:

1. Do either of the following:

   On the Layers panel, double-click a **T** icon, then click the **Warp Text** button ↓ on the Options bar.

   Right-click an editable type layer name and choose **Warp Text**.

2. The Warp Text dialog opens.**A** Move it aside if it's in the way.

3. From the **Style** menu, choose a preset style.

4. Click **Horizontal** or **Vertical** as the overall orientation for the distortion.

5. *Optional:* Move the Bend, Horizontal Distortion, or Vertical Distortion sliders.

6. Click OK.**B–E** A Warp Text icon ↓ appears in the layer thumbnail.

   Note: Characters that are added to warped type adopt the same warp characteristics.

➤ To reopen the Warp Text dialog at any time, repeat step 1 on this page. For example, you could choose a different style or adjust the sliders (or to undo the warp, choose Style: None).

➤ Once you move the sliders in the Warp Text dialog, those settings are applied to all the other Styles in the dialog. To restore the default settings to all the sliders, choose a Style of None.

➤ To warp type using manual controls, see page 316.

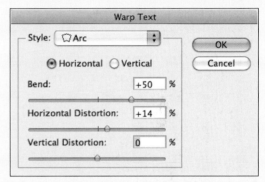

**A** *The Warp Text dialog offers many Style presets, as well as three sliders that enable you to customize the effect.*

**B** *Styles: Shell Lower for "Greg's," Bulge for "Boat Yard"*

**C** *Style: Arc (layer effects are also applied)*

**D** *Style: Flag (layer effects are also applied)*

**E** *Style: Rise*

## Rasterizing type

To edit type by applying a filter or the Transform > Distort or Perspective command, or to draw strokes on it with a tool such as the Brush, you have to convert it to pixels first via the Rasterize Type command. Unfortunately, you can't change the typographic attributes of rasterized type.

### To rasterize type into pixels:

1. *Optional:* To preserve the editable type layer, duplicate it (Ctrl-J/Cmd-J), then hide it. Keep the duplicate layer selected.

2. Right-click an editable type layer name and choose **Rasterize Type**. The layer thumbnail now has a checkerboard pattern, which represents areas of transparency.

3. Be creative!

## Filling type with imagery

To spark your imagination, these are some of the ways you can make editable type look as if it's filled with imagery (and good news: you don't need to rasterize the type layer first):

➤ Use an editable type layer as the base layer in a **clipping mask** to clip the image layers above it.**A–B** You can edit the image layers (e.g., apply filters or brush strokes to them) or reposition them without disturbing the type. To learn more about clipping masks, see page 306.

➤ Apply the **Pattern Overlay** effect to an editable type layer (see pages 363–364). While the Layer Style dialog is open, you can scale the pattern by using the Scale slider or move the pattern within the type by dragging in the document. To create a custom pattern, with the Rectangular Marquee tool, select all or part of an image to use as a pattern tile, choose Edit > Define Pattern, then click OK. Choose your new pattern from the Pattern Preset picker in the Pattern Overlay panel of the Layer Style dialog.**C**

➤ Use a type selection in a **layer mask** (follow the instructions on the next page).**D** For an extra bit of fun, try warping some type, then use the resulting shapes as a layer mask.

**A** *In this image, the type is the base layer in a clipping mask.*

**B** *This image was created the same way as the one above, except here we also rasterized the type layer (which is the clipping mask), then softened the edges via the Gaussian Blur filter to make it look more "snowy."*

**C** *We applied the Pattern Overlay layer effect to the type layer using a custom pattern that we made from an image (we also applied the Drop Shadow, Inner Shadow, Outer Glow, and Emboss effects).*

**D** *In this image, a type selection that we converted to a layer mask is masking a group of image layers. We also applied a gradient to the mask on each image layer to hide part of the imagery (see also pages 244–245).*

## To use type shapes as a layer mask:

1. Create an editable type layer.

2. Ctrl-click/Cmd-click the type layer thumbnail to load the type shapes as a selection. **A**

3. Hide the type layer by clicking its visibility icon. **B** The selection marquee will remain visible. Don't deselect it.

4. Click the image layer to which you want to add a mask.

5. On the Layers panel, do either of the following:

   To **reveal** layer pixels within the selection area, click the Add Layer Mask button. 🔲 **C–E**

   To **hide** layer pixels within the selection area, Alt-click/Option-click the Add Layer Mask button.

The type shapes are now represented by white or black areas in the layer mask thumbnail.

➤ To reposition the layer mask, unlink it from the layer by clicking the link icon 🔗 (the icon disappears), click the layer mask thumbnail, then with the Move tool, drag in the document. Or to move the layer imagery within the mask, click the layer mask thumbnail, then drag. When you're done, click to restore the link.

➤ You can also add a layer mask by clicking the Add Pixel Mask button 🔲 on the Masks panel. To toggle the function of the mask between hiding and revealing pixels, click Invert on the panel.

**A** *Ctrl-click/Cmd-click a type layer thumbnail to create a selection from type.*

**B** *Hide the type layer — but don't deselect!*

**C** *To reveal layer imagery within the selection, click the Add Layer Mask button (it's a "ski mask," ha-ha).*

**D** *To create a solid backdrop for the type shapes, we added a layer below the image layer, which we filled with white.*

**E** *This is the Layers panel for the final image, which is shown in Figure* **D***.*

# Making type fade

To make it seem as though type is fading into thin air, apply a gradient to a layer mask.

## To make type fade:

1. Click an editable or rasterized type layer (for this exercise, make the type relatively large).

2. On the Masks panel, click the **Add Pixel Mask** button. A layer mask thumbnail appears on the type layer.

3. Choose the **Gradient** tool (G or Shift-G).

4. On the Options bar:

    Click the Gradient picker arrowhead, then click the "Black, White" preset in the picker (it's the third swatch in the default gradient library).

    Click the Linear gradient button.

    Choose Mode: Normal and 100% Opacity.

5. Make sure the layer mask thumbnail is still selected, then in the document, Shift-drag vertically or horizontally from the middle of the type to one of its edges (we dragged from the middle to the left). The type layer mask will fill with a white-to-black gradient **A** and the type will be hidden where black is present in the layer mask.**B**

6. On the Masks panel, lower the **Density** value to reveal more of the type and soften the transition between the visible and hidden areas.**C–D**

➤ To modify the type or the layer, click the type layer thumbnail; to modify the layer mask, click the layer mask thumbnail; or to toggle the two thumbnails, click the layer, then click the Select Pixel Mask button on the Masks panel on or off. To learn more about layer masks, see pages 168–173.

> **DON'T FORGET ABOUT LAYER EFFECTS!**
>
> Layer effects can be applied to both editable and rasterized type layers. To open the Layer Style dialog, double-click next to a layer name. Browse through the next chapter and you'll see many examples of effects that we've applied to type.

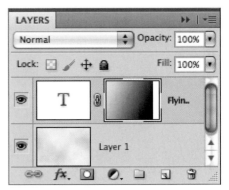

**A** We clicked the layer mask thumbnail, then dragged with the Gradient tool in the image from the middle of the type to the left edge of the layer.

**B** The type is now fading, but a bit too abruptly.

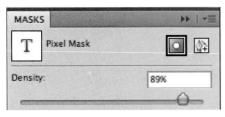

**C** To fade the type more gradually, we lowered the Density of the layer mask to 89%.

**D** In the final image, the type fades gradually.

## Screening back type

In these instructions, you'll use a Levels adjustment layer to screen back type. A lightened version of the image will be visible only within the type shapes.

### To screen back type:

1. Create a document that contains a medium to dark image layer and an editable type layer (the type color won't matter). We recommend using a large font size and a bold or black font style. **A**

2. On the Layers panel, Ctrl-click/Cmd-click the **T** icon, hide the type layer, then click the underlying image layer or Background.

3. On the Adjustments panel, click the **Levels** button. The Levels controls display and the type disappears from view temporarily.

4. Move the gray Input Levels slider to the left to lighten the midtones in the type. You also can move the Input Levels highlights slider. Move the Output Levels shadows slider to the right to reduce the contrast in the type. **B–C**

➤ To screen back the imagery instead of the type, after the last step above, click the Levels adjustment layer, then on the Masks panel, click Invert.

➤ To reposition the type over the imagery, click the adjustment layer, then drag the type shape in the document with the Move tool.

➤ You can apply layer effects to the adjustment layer, for some great results (try Drop Shadow, Inner Shadow, or Bevel and Emboss).

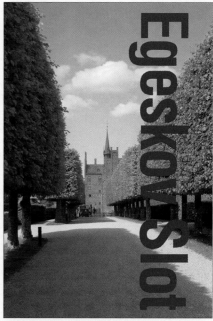

**A** *The original document contains an image layer and an editable type layer.*

**B** *The mask on the Levels adjustment layer is restricting the adjustment to the type shapes.*

**C** *The type is now screened back. Only pixels within the character shapes are affected by the Levels adjustment layer.*

## Putting type in a spot color channel

### To create type in a spot color channel:

1. Display the Channels panel, 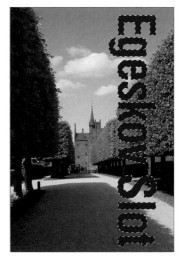 then from the panel menu, choose **New Spot Channel**.

2. In the New Spot Channel dialog, click the **Color** swatch, and if necessary, click **Color Libraries** to display the Color Libraries dialog.

3. From the **Book** menu, choose a spot color matching system, such as a PANTONE system (non-process), click the desired color or type a number from a swatch book, then click OK twice.

4. Display the Layers panel, and create some editable type.

5. Ctrl-click/Cmd-click the **T** icon on the Layers panel to select the type shapes, then hide the type layer.**A**

6. On the Channels panel, click the new spot color channel.

7. Choose Edit > **Fill** (Shift-Backspace/Shift-Delete). In the dialog, choose Use: Black; Mode: Normal; and an Opacity value that matches the tint, or density, value of the spot color ink to be used on press. If you don't know what value that should be, ask the production manager on the project. Click OK. The selection will fill with the color that you chose for the spot color channel.

8. Deselect (Ctrl-D/Cmd-D). The type shapes should appear in the new spot channel on the Channels panel (but a layer isn't created on the Layers panel).**B**

➤ To reposition the type shapes in the spot color channel, click the spot color channel, then with the Move tool, drag in the document.

➤ You can't edit the type characters in a spot color channel. Instead, you have to redo it from scratch. Fill the channel with White, 100% Opacity, edit the original type layer, then repeat steps 5–8 above.

*A The type is converted to a selection.*

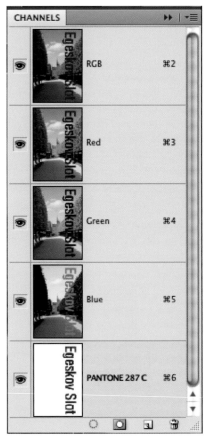

*B Because our type shapes are now in a spot color channel, our commercial printer will be able to create a special printing plate for them.*

As a Photoshop user, you're in the business of creating illusions. With layer effects, you can accomplish this in short, easy steps. The Photoshop effects that you can apply alone or in combination include Drop Shadow, Inner Shadow, Outer Glow, Inner Glow, Bevel and Emboss, Satin, Color Overlay, Gradient Overlay,  Pattern Overlay, and Stroke. Once applied, layer effects can be edited, hidden, or removed at any time. And best of all, when you modify layer pixels, the effects update accordingly (they should be called "Smart Effects"!).

In this chapter, we include generic instructions for applying, copying, moving, and removing layer effects; individual instructions for each effect; and finally, the steps to save and apply effects, combined with other Layers panel settings, as styles via the Styles panel.

## Applying layer effects (general info)

Layer effects can be applied to any layer (even to editable type), but not to the Background. They affect all the visible pixels on a layer and update instantly if you add, modify, or delete pixels from the layer that contains them. Each individual effect can be turned on or off at any time via its own visibility icon.

Layer effects are applied and edited via the Layer Style dialog and are listed on the Layers panel below the layer they belong to. Before exploring the individual effects, familiarize yourself with these generic instructions.

### To apply layer effects (generic instructions):

1. Do any of the following:

   Double-click to the right of a layer name; or for an image layer (not a type or Smart Object layer), you can double-click the layer thumbnail instead.

   Click a layer, then choose an effect from the **Add Layer Style** menu _fx_ at the bottom of the Layers panel.

_Continued on the following page_

**LAYER STYLES**

# 21

## IN THIS CHAPTER

**A** _Three effects are applied to this editable type: Drop Shadow, Bevel and Emboss, and Gradient Overlay._

The Layer Style dialog opens. **A**

2. Click an effect name on the left side, check Preview to preview the effect in the image, then choose settings.

3. *Optional:* Click other effect names to apply additional effects to the same layer.

4. Click OK.

5. Edit the layer (e.g., for a type layer, edit the type; for an image layer, add or erase some pixels). Watch as the "smart" effect(s) update instantly!

   On the Layers panel, layers that contain effects have this icon: *fx*. Click the arrowhead next to the icon to expand or collapse the list of effects for that layer (**B**, next page).

6. To change the settings for an effect or to add more effects to a layer, double-click the layer or the Effects listing, or double-click the effect name, which is nested below the layer name.

7. To hide or show one layer effect, expand the effects list for the layer, then click the visibility icon 👁 for the effect.

   To hide all the effects on a layer, click the visibility icon for the "Effects" listing.

➤ If you readjust the Angle for an individual effect while Use Global Light is checked, that angle will be applied to any other effects that are using the Global Light option. This option unifies the lighting across multiple layer effects.

➤ If you move layer pixels, any effects on the layer will also move.

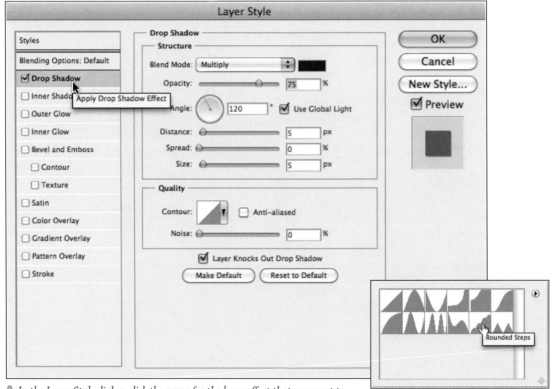

**A** *In the Layer Style dialog, click the name for the layer effect that you want to display and choose settings for (the box becomes checked automatically).*

*The Contour presets define the effect profile. Gray areas in the thumbnail represent opaque pixels, and white areas represent transparency. To close the preset picker, either double-click a contour or click in the dialog.*

## What kind of imagery can layer effects be applied to?

➤ We recommend applying the layer effects that work inward or outward from edges — Drop Shadow, Inner Shadow, Outer Glow, Inner Glow, Bevel and Emboss, and Stroke — to a type layer, shape layer, or any layer imagery that's surrounded by transparent pixels.**A** To isolate a subject from its background before applying layer effects, select an area of a layer, then press Ctrl-J/Cmd-J (the Layer via Copy command).

➤ You can apply the Satin, Color Overlay, Gradient Overlay, and Pattern Overlay effects either to fully opaque layers or to layers that contain transparency.

Note: Don't bother creating a selection before applying a layer effect. Your selection will be ignored by the Layer Style command.

---

**CHOOSING DEFAULT LAYER STYLE SETTINGS** ★

➤ To establish new default settings for a particular layer effect, choose the desired settings in the Layer Style dialog, then click Make Default.

➤ To restore the default settings to a layer effect that you established by clicking Make Default (or to restore the factory default settings, if you didn't establish user default settings), click Reset to Default.

➤ To restore the settings that were in place in all the panels when you opened the Layer Style dialog, Alt-click/Option-click Reset (Cancel becomes Reset).

➤ Unfortunately, the only way to restore the factory default settings to all layer effects is by resetting all the Photoshop preferences. Hold down Ctrl-Alt-Shift/Cmd-Option-Shift while relaunching the program, and click Yes in the alert dialog.

---

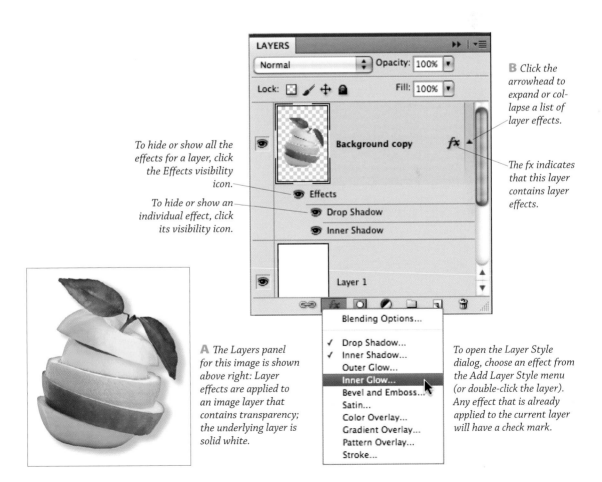

**B** Click the arrowhead to expand or collapse a list of layer effects.

The fx indicates that this layer contains layer effects.

To hide or show all the effects for a layer, click the Effects visibility icon.

To hide or show an individual effect, click its visibility icon.

**A** The Layers panel for this image is shown above right: Layer effects are applied to an image layer that contains transparency; the underlying layer is solid white.

To open the Layer Style dialog, choose an effect from the Add Layer Style menu (or double-click the layer). Any effect that is already applied to the current layer will have a check mark.

# Applying a shadow effect

You can create a drop shadow or inner shadow with just a few clicks of the mouse.

## To apply the Drop Shadow or Inner Shadow effect:

1. On the Layers panel, double-click next to a layer name to open the Layer Style dialog.**A**

2. Click **Drop Shadow** or **Inner Shadow**.

3. Choose a **Distance** value (in pixels) by which you want to offset a drop shadow from the original layer shapes,**B** or for the width of an inner shadow.**C–D**

   ➤ You can also change the position of a shadow by dragging in the document while the dialog is open, but be aware that this will also reposition any other effects that are using the Global Light option.

   Choose a **Spread** percentage for a Drop Shadow or a **Choke** percentage for an Inner Shadow to control where the shadow begins to fade.

   Choose an overall **Size** for the shadow (in pixels).

4. You can also change any of these settings:

   Choose a **Blend Mode** from the menu. (For a drop shadow, we usually keep the default setting of Multiply.)

   To choose a different shadow **color**, click the color swatch, then choose a color from the Color Picker or click a color in the document with the eyedropper (the new color previews immediately). Click OK. Note: If you change the color for an inner shadow, you may also want to change the Blend Mode to Normal.

   Choose an **Opacity** percentage for the transparency level of the shadow (the default value is 75%, but we usually lower it).

   Choose an **Angle** for the angle of the shadow relative to the original layer shapes.

   In the Quality area, you can click the **Contour** arrowhead and choose a preset from the picker for the edge profile of the shadow (we're usually satisfied with the shape of the default Contour).

   Check **Anti-aliased** to soften any jagged edges between the shadow and the layer imagery.

   Adjust the **Noise** level. The addition of noise (speckling) can help prevent banding on print output, but a low value is best.

**A** *The original image consists of some garden tools on one layer and a background pattern on another layer (we created the pattern via Filter > Render > Clouds).*

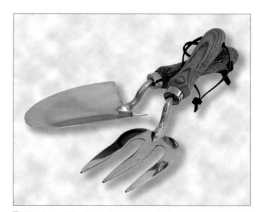

**B** *The Drop Shadow effect is applied.*

**C** *The original image consists of editable type on one layer and a blue-gray background pattern on another.*

**D** *The Inner Shadow effect is applied.*

For the Drop Shadow effect, if the layer Fill opacity is below 100% or the layer blending mode isn't set to Normal, check **Layer Knocks Out Drop Shadow** to prevent the shadow from showing through transparent areas on the layer.

5. Click OK. If you're not satisfied with the shape of the resulting shadow, follow the steps below.

➤ To scale the effects on a layer without scaling the other layer content, right-click the Effects listing and choose Scale Effects, then specify the desired Scale percentage in the dialog.

Depending on the time of day and the angle of the sun or another light source, cast shadows are either short or elongated. You can reshape a drop shadow via the Distort command.

## To transform a Drop Shadow effect:

1. Apply the Drop Shadow effect (see the preceding instructions), and keep that layer selected.

2. To transfer the shadow effect to its own layer, right-click the Effects listing on the Layers panel, choose **Create Layer(s)** from the context menu, then click OK in the alert dialog, if one appears.

3. Click the new Drop Shadow layer.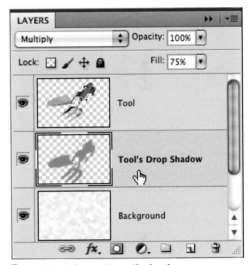

4. Choose Edit > Transform > **Distort**, drag the handles of the transform box to slant the shape, then press Enter/Return. For a symmetrical perspective distortion, hold down Ctrl-Alt-Shift/Cmd-Option-Shift as you drag a corner handle. Note: If you don't see all the handles, press Ctrl-0/Cmd-0 (zero) to enlarge the document window.

➤ To limit any painting or fill changes to just the shadow shape, on the Layers panel, activate the Lock Transparent Pixels button.

➤ To ensure that the image and shadow layers will move and transform as a unit, Shift-click them, then click the Link Layers button 🔗 at the bottom of the panel.

---

**LAYER OPACITY AND FILL SETTINGS**

A quick reminder from the preceding chapter: The Opacity setting on the Layers panel controls the opacity of layer imagery — including any layer effects — whereas the Fill setting controls only the opacity of layer imagery — not of layer effects.

---

**A** *The original layer has a Drop Shadow effect.*

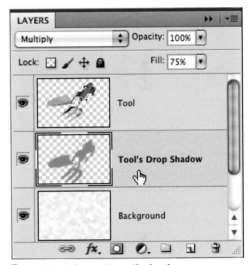

**B** *We clicked the new Drop Shadow layer...*

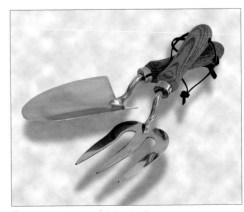

**C** *...then we elongated the shadow.*

# Applying a glow effect

The Outer Glow and Inner Glow effects add a soft, airbrushed rim of color to the edges of layer imagery or to type.

### To apply the Outer or Inner Glow effect:

1. Display the Swatches panel.▦

2. On the Layers panel, double-click a layer to open the Layer Style dialog. Note: For the Outer Glow effect, we recommend using a silhouetted image layer above a solid-color layer or the Background.**A**

3. Click **Outer Glow** or **Inner Glow**. In the Elements area, increase the **Size** value.

4. Under **Structure,** **B–C** do any of the following optional steps:

   To change the glow color, click the color square, choose a color from the Color Picker (or, while the picker is open, choose from the Swatches panel or click a color in the document), then click OK to exit the picker. (For the gradient option, see the next chapter.)

   Change the **Blend Mode**.

   Change the **Opacity** level for the glow.

   To prevent banding on print output, increase the **Noise** level slightly to add speckles.

5. Choose other **Elements** settings:

   From the **Technique** menu, we recommend choosing **Softer** for smooth color transitions.

   For an Inner Glow, click **Source: Center** to create a glow that spreads outward from the center of the layer pixels (this looks good on type), or click **Edge** to create a glow that spreads inward from the inside edges of the layer imagery.

   Choose a **Spread** percentage for an Outer Glow or a **Choke** percentage for an Inner Glow to control the point at which the glow starts to fade. We keep these values relatively low.

6. Choose **Quality** settings:

   *Optional:* Click the Contour arrowhead and choose a preset from the picker to add rings of transparency to the edges of the glow.

   Choose a **Range** value to control where the glow is applied relative to the contour.

7. Click OK (**A**, next page).

**A** *The original image contains a silhouetted image of a watch above a solid-color Background.*

**B** *We chose these Structure and Elements settings for the Inner Glow effect in the Layer Style dialog...*

**C** *...and we chose these Structure and Elements settings for the Outer Glow effect.*

**A** *The Layer Style settings shown in Figures* **B** *and* **C** *on the preceding page produced these inner and outer glow effects.*

## BECOMING A LAYER EFFECTS PRO

➤ When deciding which effect or effects to use, consider what kind of surface texture you want to create. Stone? Metal? Paper? Type that looks as if it's embedded, or embossed, into porous paper, or satin text that looks as if it's cast in metal?

➤ With the exception of Drop Shadow and Overlay, layer effects usually look better, or more convincing as an illusion, when applied in combination (see the figures below).

➤ If you achieve a layer effect or combination of effects and Layers panel settings that you like, save that collection of settings as a style on the Styles panel (see pages 365–366). This can be a great timesaver.

➤ While the Layer Style dialog is open, you can click Blending Options on the upper left side, then use the options to control how the current layer blends with underlying layers. (Note that the same blending mode, Opacity, and Fill controls are also available on the Layers panel.) See pages 304–305.

*This is plain editable type (in the Bodoni Highlight font) on top of a pattern layer.*

*The Drop Shadow effect is applied.*

*We also added the Bevel and Emboss effect — two effects look better than one.*

*A total of the three layer effects — Drop Shadow, Bevel and Emboss, and Gradient Overlay — look better still.*

# Applying a bevel or emboss effect

The Bevel and Emboss effect creates an illusion of volume by adding a highlight and some shading. The results can range from a chiseled bevel that looks factory-made to a pillowy emboss that looks as if it's been stamped onto porous paper. For variety, experiment with the Contour options.

## To apply the Bevel or Emboss effect:

1. Display the Swatches panel.⊞

2. On the Layers panel, double-click a layer **A** to open the Layer Style dialog.

3. Click **Bevel and Emboss**.

4. Under Structure, choose a **Size** for the depth of the bevel or emboss effect.

5. Choose other **Structure** settings: **B**

   Choose a **Style**: Outer Bevel, Inner Bevel, Emboss, Pillow Emboss, or Stroke Emboss **C–D** (and **A–C**, next page).

   From the **Technique** menu, choose **Smooth**, **Chisel Hard** (best for type), or **Chisel Soft**.

   Choose a **Depth** for the intensity of the highlight and shading.

   Click the **Up** or **Down** button to swap the positions of the highlight and shading.

   Raise the **Soften** value to blur the effect.

6. Choose **Shading** settings:

   Choose an **Angle** and an **Altitude** (height) to change the location of the light source. These settings in turn will affect the position of the highlight and shading. Check **Use Global Light** to use the same Angle and Altitude settings for all effects that are using the Global Light option, to produce uniform lighting; or uncheck it to use a unique setting for just this effect. Note: If you change the Angle or Altitude for an individual effect while Use Global Light is checked, any other effects that are using the Global Light option will adopt those values.

   Click the **Gloss Contour** arrowhead, then choose a profile from the Contour Preset picker.

   Choose a **Highlight Mode** and **Opacity** for the highlight and a **Shadow Mode** and **Opacity** for the shading.

   To change the highlight or shading **color**, click the corresponding color swatch, then choose a color from the Color Picker (or, while the picker

**A** *The original image contains two layers.*

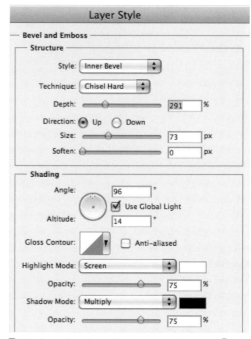

**B** *We chose these Layer Style options for Figure **C**.*

**C** *The Inner Bevel effect is applied (and also the Drop Shadow effect).*

**D** *Here the Outer Bevel effect is applied (plus a Drop Shadow).*

is open, choose from the Swatches panel or click a color in the document); click OK.

7. To add a **Contour** to the edges of the bevel or emboss, click Contour on the left side of the dialog, below Bevel and Emboss. Click the Contour arrowhead, then click a preset contour in the picker. This option can dramatically alter the appearance of the effect.

Check **Anti-aliased** to soften the transition between the dark and light areas in the contour.

For the Outer Bevel or Inner Bevel style option, adjust the **Range** (the position of the bevel on the chosen contour) to minimize or maximize the prominence of the bevel.

8. To add a texture to the effect, click **Texture** on the left side of the dialog, click the Texture arrowhead, choose a pattern from the picker, then do any of the following:

Adjust the **Scale** of the pattern.

Change the **Depth** to increase or reduce the contrast between the shadows and highlights in the pattern.

Check **Invert** to swap the highlight and shading. This has the same effect as changing the Depth percentage from negative to positive, and vice versa.

Check **Link with Layer** to ensure that the texture and the layer move as a unit.

Drag in the document to reposition the texture within the effect; click **Snap to Origin** to realign the pattern with the upper left corner of the image.

9. Click OK.

**A** *This is the original editable type.*

**B** *Emboss (Chisel Soft) is applied.*

**C** *Pillow Emboss (Technique: Smooth) plus a Drop Shadow are applied.*

**D** *Pillow Emboss with a Texture, plus a Drop Shadow, are applied.*

## Applying the Satin effect

Use the Satin layer effect to apply light and dark shades to the surfaces of objects or type to make them look reflective or metallic.

Notes: The default Blend Mode for the Satin layer effect, Multiply, deepens some tonal values and heightens contrast, so we recommend applying this effect to an image layer that has a good range of tonal values. For this effect to show up well on type, make the type a medium to light color, and apply a strong Inner Glow or Bevel and Emboss effect first.

### To apply the Satin effect :

1. Double-click a layer **A** on the Layers panel to open the Layer Style dialog.

2. Click **Satin**.

3. Do any of the following. **B**

   Change the **Blend Mode**.

   To change the overlay **color**, click the color swatch, then choose a color from the Color Picker or click a color in the document; click OK.

   Adjust the **Opacity** of the effect.

   Change the **Angle** of the effect. This angle is independent of the Global Light settings.

   Set the **Distance** and the **Size** of the effect.

   Change the edge profile of the effect by choosing a profile from the Contour Preset picker.

   Check **Anti-aliased** to soften the transition between the dark and light areas in the contour.

   Check **Invert** to swap the shadows and highlights in the effect.

4. Click OK. **C**

## Applying the Overlay effects

The Gradient Overlay and Pattern Overlay effects can be applied to image, shape, and type layers. The same holds true for the Color Overlay effect, which isn't discussed here.

### To apply the Gradient Overlay effect:

1. Double-click a layer on the Layers panel to open the Layer Style dialog. **D**

2. Click **Gradient Overlay**.

3. Click the **Gradient** arrowhead, then click a gradient on the Gradient picker. Also choose a **Style** of **Linear**, **Radial**, **Angle**, **Reflected**, or **Diamond**.

**A** *The Bevel and Emboss effect is applied to this editable type.*

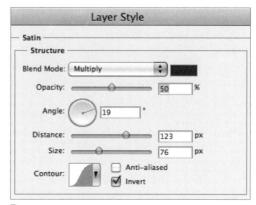

**B** *We chose these options for the Satin layer effect.*

**C** *The addition of the Satin effect makes the surface of the letters look even more reflective.*

**D** *The Bevel and Emboss effect is applied to this type.*

➤ To load gradients from another library, choose a library name from the lower part of the picker menu (see page 401).

4. Do any of the following:

Choose a **Blend Mode**.

Adjust the **Opacity** of the overlay.

Check **Reverse** to switch the direction of the gradient.

Check **Align with Layer** to confine the gradient to visible pixels in the layer, or uncheck it to have the gradient fill the whole canvas.

Set the **Angle** of the gradient.

Choose a **Scale** percentage to control how gradually the gradient transitions across the layer.

Drag in the document to **reposition** the gradient within the layer shapes.

5. Click OK. **A–B** To learn more about creating and editing gradients, see the next chapter.

➤ If you apply two overlay effects, such as Gradient Overlay and Pattern Overlay, lower the opacity of the one that's listed first in the dialog; otherwise the bottom one won't be visible.

Patterns applied via the Pattern Overlay effect can range from those with an obvious repeat, such as polka dots or stripes, to overall textures resembling such surfaces as gritty sandpaper, handmade paper, woven fabric, or variegated stone.

## To apply the Pattern Overlay effect:

1. Double-click a layer on the Layers panel to open the Layer Style dialog. **C**

2. Click **Pattern Overlay**.

3. Click the **Pattern** arrowhead, then choose a pattern preset in the picker. Also adjust the **Opacity** of the overlay. **D**

   ➤ To load patterns from another library, choose a library name from the lower part of the picker menu (see page 401).

4. Do any of the following:

Change the **Blend Mode**.

Drag in the document to reposition the pattern; click **Snap to Origin** to realign the pattern with the upper left corner of the document.

Choose a **Scale** percentage for the size of the pattern.

*Continued on the following page*

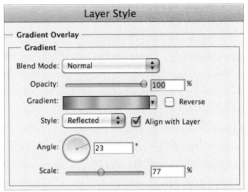

**A** *We chose these options for the Gradient Overlay layer effect.*

**B** *The Gradient Overlay effect is applied to the original image (shown in Figure* **D** *on the previous page).*

**C** *The original type contains the Bevel and Emboss and Satin layer effects.*

**D** *For our Pattern Overlay layer effect, we chose the Mountains pattern, which is in the Texture Fill library. With the pattern overlay added to the mix, now the type looks like polished granite.*

Check **Link with Layer** to link the pattern to the layer so they'll move as a unit if you drag the layer.

5. Click OK.

## Applying the Stroke effect

If you're partial to neon, you can achieve that illusion in Photoshop by using the Stroke effect. This works especially well on type, and also on geometric shapes.

### To apply the Stroke effect:

1. Double-click a layer on the Layers panel to open the Layer Style dialog.

2. Click **Stroke**.

3. Do any of the following:

   Choose a **Size** (width) for the stroke.

   From the **Position** menu, choose whether you want the stroke to be applied to the **Outside**, **Inside**, or **Center** of the edges of the layer content.

   Choose a **Blend Mode**.

   Choose an **Opacity** percentage.

   For the **Fill Type**, choose **Color**, **Gradient**, or **Pattern**, and choose settings for the options that become available (see the preceding page).

4. Click OK. A

A *The Bevel and Emboss, Gradient Overlay, and Stroke effects are applied. We did this in one easy step by applying the Liquid Rainbow layer style, which is in the Text Effects style library (see the next page).*

## Copying, moving, and removing layer effects

If you like how an effect looks on one layer, you can copy it to another one. The more, the merrier.

### To copy individual effects between layers:

Alt-drag/Option-drag any individual effect name from one layer to another.

You can move an individual effect from one layer to another without deleting any effects on the target layer.

### To move an effect from one layer to another without replacing existing effects:

Drag any individual effect name from one layer to another. The effect will be removed from the source layer and copied to the target layer.

And finally, you can also move all the effects from one layer to another (that is, replace any existing effects on the target layer and remove them from the source layer).

### To move all the effects from one layer to another, replacing existing effects:

Drag the Effects listing from one layer to another.

Clicking to remove the visibility icon for a layer effect or unchecking the box for an effect in the Layer Style dialog doesn't remove the effect — it merely hides it from view. If you want to permanently delete effects from a layer, do as follows.

### To remove layer effects:

Do either of the following:

Drag a single effect name to the Delete Layer button 🗑 at the bottom of the Layers panel.

To remove all the effects from a layer, drag the Effects listing over the Delete Layer button.

➤ If you turn off an effect via the check box in the Layer Style dialog and then turn it back on again the same way, the last-used options for that effect will redisplay.

➤ To flatten all the layer effects in a document, choose File > Scripts > Flatten All Layer Effects. ★ If any type layers contain effects, the script will also rasterize those layers.

## Applying layer styles

You can conveniently store multiple layer settings collectively as a style on the Styles panel. The style will include layer effects and/or blending options, such as the layer opacity, blending mode, and fill opacity settings. Once stored, styles can be quickly applied to any layer. To get acquainted with this panel, start by applying one of the predefined styles to a type layer or to a layer that contains some transparency. You can edit the effects from any predefined style, or create and save your own styles, as we show you on the next page.

### To apply a style to a layer:

1. Show the Styles panel. ![icon] Via the panel menu, you can change the panel display mode to Text Only or to a Thumbnail or List mode, and you can load more style libraries onto the panel by choosing a library name (see page 401).

2. Do one of the following:

   Click a layer (not the Background) on the Layers panel, then click a style on the Styles panel. **A–F**

   Drag a style name or thumbnail from the Styles panel over any selected or unselected layer on the Layers panel.

   Double-click a layer to open the Layer Style dialog, click Styles at the top, click a style thumbnail, then click OK (**A**, next page).

➤ Normally, when a style is applied, it replaces any and all existing effects on the current layer. If you prefer to combine the effects from a style with the existing effects on a layer, Shift-click or Shift-drag the style. Note that whether Shift is held down or not, if two effects have the same name, effects in the new style will replace the old.

**A** *Click a layer, then click a style thumbnail (or name) on the Styles panel.*

**B** *Web Styles library > Blue Paper Clip*

**C** *Text Effects library > Sprayed Stencil*

**D** *Text Effects library > Shaded Red Bevel*

**E** *KS Styles library ★ > Lightning*

**F** *Image Effects library > Water Reflection*

### CLEARING A STYLE FROM A LAYER

To remove a style from a layer (and also restore the default opacity of 100% and the layer blending mode of Normal), right-click the layer and choose Clear Layer Style.

**A** *Styles can also be applied to a layer via your old pal, the Layer Style dialog. Click Styles at the top left side of the dialog, then click a thumbnail.*

## Creating layer styles

When creating a layer style, you can control whether the style will include the layer effects that are currently applied to the selected layer and/or the current blending option settings (such as the layer opacity, blending mode, and fill opacity).

### To save a style to the Styles panel:

1. To a layer, apply the effects settings and/or blending option settings that you want to save collectively as a style.

2. Do either of the following:

   On the Layers panel, click the layer that contains the desired settings, **B** then on the Styles panel, *fx* click either the blank area or the **New Style** button. **C–D**

   On the Layers panel, double-click the layer that contains the desired settings, then on the right side of the Layer Style dialog, click **New Style**.

3. The New Style dialog opens. Enter a **Name** for the new style, check whether you want to **Include Layer Effects** and/or **Include Layer Blending Options** in the style, then click OK. If the Layer Style dialog is open, click OK again. The new style appears as the last listing or thumbnail on the Styles panel.

➤ To create a library of styles, see page 401.

➤ To copy a style from one layer to another, right-click the layer that contains the desired settings and choose Copy Layer Style. Click another layer, then right-click that layer and choose Paste Layer Style. If the target layer already has a style, the new one will replace it.

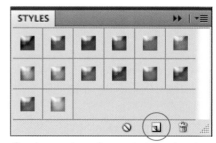

**B** *On the Layers panel, click a layer that contains the effects and/or other settings to be saved as a style...*

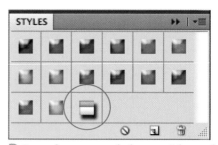

**C** *...then on the Styles panel, click either the blank area or the New Style button.*

**D** *Our style appears at the bottom of the panel.*

A gradient is a soft blend between two or more opaque or semitransparent colors. Gradients can be used to enhance the background behind imagery or type or to add color to objects. In this short but fun chapter, you will learn how to apply gradients via a Gradient fill layer and the Gradient tool, and how to create and modify gradients via the Gradient Editor.

## Creating a Gradient fill layer

A gradient that you apply via a Gradient fill layer appears in its own layer, complete with a layer mask that can be used to control how much of the gradient is visible. Like an adjustment layer, this type of gradient is editable, restackable, and removable — unlike a gradient that you apply directly to a layer. A good use for a Gradient fill layer is to add color behind silhouetted imagery or type.

### To apply a gradient via a fill layer:

1. If you want the gradient fill to display behind silhouetted imagery or type, click the layer directly below the image layer or type layer. **A**

2. *Optional:* To confine the gradient to an area of the layer, create a selection.

3. From the **New Fill/Adjustment Layer** menu ⬤. on the Layers panel, choose **Gradient**. The Gradient Fill dialog opens.

*Continued on the following page*

GRADIENTS

# 22

**A** *The original image contains a silhouetted image layer and a separate white Background. We clicked the Background.*

4. Click the Gradient picker arrowhead at the top of the dialog, click a gradient preset on the picker, A then click back in the dialog and keep it open.

   ➤ To load in more gradients, open the preset picker menu, ▶ choose a library name from the assortment at the bottom, then click Append in the alert dialog (see also page 401).

5. Choose a gradient **Style** of Linear, Radial, Angular, Reflected, or Diamond. B

6. Do any of the following optional steps:

   Change the **Angle** for the gradient by moving the dial or by entering a value.

   Use the **Scale** slider to scale the gradient relative to the layer. The greater the scale percentage, the more gradual the transition between colors in the gradient.

   Drag in the document window (with the dialog still open) to **reposition** the gradient.

   Check/uncheck **Reverse** to swap the order of colors in the gradient.

Check **Dither** to minimize banding (stripes) in the gradient on print output.

If you created a selection in step 2, check **Align with Layer** to fit the complete gradient within the selection, or uncheck this option to have the gradient stretch across the whole layer. With this option unchecked, only part of the gradient will display within the selection area.

7. Click OK. C Note: If the Gradient fill layer is now obscuring all the layers below it, do any of the following: lower the opacity of the the the fill layer, restack it below the layers you want to keep visible, or lower the opacity of some of its color stops (see page 370).

   ➤ To edit the settings for the Gradient fill layer, double-click the Gradient fill layer thumbnail. The Gradient Fill dialog reopens.

   ➤ To apply a gradient as an editable Gradient Overlay layer effect, see pages 362–363.

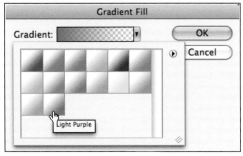

**A** In the Gradient Fill dialog, click the Gradient picker, then click a preset in the picker.

**C** We reduced the opacity of the Gradient fill layer to 80%.

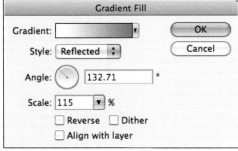

**B** After clicking the Background and opening the Gradient Fill dialog, we chose the "Light Purple" preset (in the Simple library) and the settings shown above.

---

**EDITING THE GRADIENT FILL LAYER MASK**

If you create a selection before creating a Gradient fill layer, the selection will be represented as a white area within the layer mask thumbnail for the Gradient fill layer on the Layers panel. To reshape the mask, click the layer mask thumbnail, then with the Brush tool, paint with white to enlarge the white area or with black to enlarge the black area. Via the Masks panel, you can adjust the density of the black area in the mask or feather its edge.

## Using the Gradient tool

With the Gradient tool, you create a gradient by dragging in the document window. Each time you drag, an additional gradient is applied. Although you can't edit the results in the same way that you would edit a Gradient fill layer, if you use the tool on a separate layer, at least you will be able to change the layer blending mode or opacity.

### To apply a gradient with the Gradient tool:

1. Create a new, blank layer for the gradient.
   *Optional:* To confine the gradient to an area of the layer, create a selection.

2. Choose the **Gradient** tool ■ (G or Shift-G).

3. On the Options bar, do all of the following:
   Click the Gradient picker arrowhead, then click a preset on the picker.
   Click a Style button: Linear, Radial, Angle, Reflected, or Diamond.
   Choose Mode: Normal and Opacity 100%.

4. Do any of the following on the Options bar (optional):
   Check Reverse to swap the order of colors in the gradient.
   Check Dither to minimize banding (stripes) in the gradient on print output.
   Check Transparency to enable any transparency that was edited into the gradient, or turn this option off to apply a fully opaque gradient.

5. For a Linear gradient, drag from one side or corner of the image or selection to the other. For any other gradient style, drag from a center point outward (Shift-drag to constrain the angle to a multiple of 45°).**A–C** Drag a long distance to produce subtle transitions between colors or a short distance to produce abrupt transitions; this has the same effect as changing the Scale value in the Gradient Fill dialog.

6. Change the gradient layer mode or opacity.

➤ To delete the last results of the Gradient tool, click the prior state on the History panel.

➤ For a gradual transition between the masked and unmasked areas, click the mask thumbnail for an image, editable type, adjustment, or fill layer, or for a Smart Filter, then drag in the document with the Gradient tool. See pages 244–245 and 350.

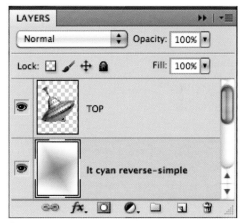

**A** *With the Gradient tool (Diamond style chosen), we dragged diagonally from the middle to the lower right on a new, blank layer.*

**B** *This is the Layers panel for the image shown below.*

**C** *This is the final image.*

# Creating and editing gradient presets

You can create a variation of any gradient preset in the picker or create new, custom presets. When you edit a preset, Photoshop forces you to work on a copy automatically so the one in the library is preserved. We'll show you how to add and change the colors in a gradient, adjust the color transitions, and make individual colors semi- or fully transparent.

## To create or edit a gradient preset:

1. Open the Swatches and/or Color panels (they can be collapsed to icons).

2. To open the Gradient Editor, do either of the following:

   Choose the **Gradient** tool ▉ (G or Shift-G), then click the Gradient thumbnail on the Options bar.**A**

   Double-click the thumbnail for an existing **Gradient Fill** layer, then click the gradient thumbnail at the top of the Gradient Fill dialog.

3. Click the preset swatch that you want to create a variation of. (When you begin editing the gradient, the Name will change to Custom.) Keep the Gradient Type as **Solid** and the Smoothness setting at 100%.

   If you want to create a gradient that uses whichever Foreground and Background colors are in effect when the gradient is applied, click the Foreground to Background preset.*

4. For any gradient except Foreground to Background, click the starting (left) or ending (right) color stop under the gradient bar, then do either of the following:

   Click a color on the Swatches panel, or on the color ramp at the bottom of the Color panel, or in any open document window (the pointer becomes a temporary Eyedropper tool).

   Click the Color swatch at the bottom of the Gradient Editor, choose a color from the color

picker, then click OK (you can also open the picker by double-clicking a color stop).

5. Do any of these optional steps:

   To add an **intermediate** color to the gradient, click below the gradient bar to produce a stop, then choose a color for that stop, as described in the preceding step.

   To control the abruptness of a transition between colors, click a color or opacity stop, then drag the **midpoint diamond** (located on either side of the stop) to the left or right (**A**, next page). The diamond marks the point at which two adjacent colors are evenly mixed.

   To add an **opacity** stop, click above the gradient bar, then use the scrubby slider to change the Opacity percentage. You can also click any existing opacity stop and change its Opacity percentage (**B–C**, next page). Transparency is represented by a checkerboard pattern.

   To change the **location** of a color or opacity stop in the gradient, drag it to the left or right.

   To **delete** an unwanted opacity or color stop, drag it upward or downward off the bar.

   ➤ Use Ctrl-Z/Cmd-Z if you need to undo the last edit (some edits can't be undone).

6. Don't click OK yet! To create a preset of your custom gradient, type a name in the **Name** field, then click **New** (**D**, next page).

   Note: Your new presets will be deleted from the picker if you allow them to be replaced by another gradient library or if the Photoshop Preferences file is deleted or damaged. To save all the presets currently on the picker as a permanent library, click Save, enter a name, keep the default location, then click Save again. See also page 401.

7. Click OK to exit the Gradient Editor (**E**, next page), and then the Gradient Fill dialog. The gradient displays on the Gradient picker.

   ➤ To delete a gradient preset from the picker, Alt-click/Option-click the preset thumbnail.

   ➤ To rename a gradient preset, double-click the swatch in the Gradient Editor; the Gradient Name dialog opens.

*A* *We are opening the Gradient Editor by clicking the Gradient thumbnail on the Options bar.*

*Foreground to Background is the first preset in the default gradient library. To reload that library, choose Reset Gradients from the Gradient picker menu, then click Append or OK.*

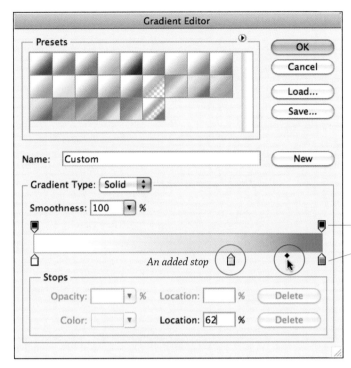

**A** *In the Gradient Editor dialog, we clicked below the gradient bar to add an intermediate (third) color to our two-color gradient, chose a color for that stop, then moved the midpoint diamond to make the transition between the middle and end colors more abrupt.*

—*An opacity stop*

—*A color stop*

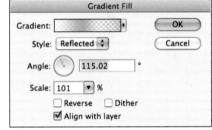

**B** *We clicked above the bar to add a couple of intermediate opacity stops (note the checkerboard pattern in the bar). We also lowered the opacity of the second stop.*

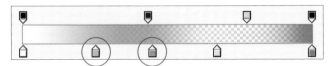

**C** *We added two more color stops.*

**D** *We lowered the opacity of the first and last opacity stops. Finally, we named our custom gradient, clicked New, then exited both dialogs.*

**E** *We applied our custom gradient via a Gradient fill layer (above an image layer). The dialog settings we chose are shown above. Note that we chose the Reflected style.*

## USING BLENDING MODES TO ENHANCE A GRADIENT

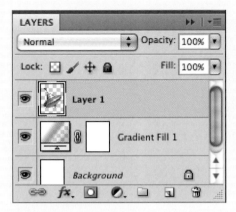

A *In all the images on this page, the gradient is supplied by a Gradient fill layer below a silhouetted image layer. A different blending mode is chosen for the image layer in Figures* **B** *through* **G**.

**B** *Color Burn blending mode*

**C** *Luminosity blending mode*

**D** *Linear Light blending mode*

**E** *Difference blending mode*

**F** *Pin Light blending mode*

**G** *Multiply blending mode*

In this chapter, you'll learn various ways to finish and present your photos to clients in print and onscreen. You'll learn how to frame your subject matter as a vignette, add an artistic border, embed a watermark, create a contact sheet or PDF presentation, and create and present layer comps (multiple variations within the same document) manually and via a PDF slide show.

## Creating a vignette

Aside from the fact that vignettes look beautiful, they also can be used as a cropping device to feature (or hide) part of a composition.

**To create a vignette:**

1. Open an image, and press Ctrl-J/Cmd-J to duplicate the Background.

2. Click the Background, then press Shift-Backspace/Shift-Delete. In the Fill dialog, choose Use: White, Mode: Normal, and Opacity: 100%, then click OK.

3. Click the duplicate image layer. Choose the **Elliptical Marquee** tool ⬭ (M or Shift-M), then select the area of the image you want to keep visible. Hold down Alt/Option while dragging to draw the marquee from the center.

4. Display the Masks panel. ▣ Click the **Add Pixel Mask** button, ▣ then adjust the **Feather** value to fade the edge of the mask. **A**

➤ To reposition the mask to reveal a different area of the image, on the Layers panel, click between the layer and mask thumbnails to unlink them, then hold down V (for a temporary Move tool) and drag in the document window.

**23**

**A** *An oval, feathered mask lends this garden photo an old-fashioned appeal.*

# Adding an artistic border

Using options in the Refine Edge dialog, it's incredibly easy to add artistic borders to an image.

## To add an artistic border to an image: ★

1. Open a one-layer document, then click the Background on the Layers panel.

2. Choose the **Rectangular Marquee** tool ⬚ (M or Shift-M), then draw a selection marquee. Position the marquee where you want the border to be.**A**

3. On the Options bar, click **Refine Edge**.

4. In the Refine Edge dialog, choose **On White** view (W), then adjust the **Radius**, **Smooth**, **Contrast**, and **Shift Edge** values to roughen the edges.**B**

5. From the Output To menu, choose **New Layer with Layer Mask**, then click OK.**C**

6. Click the Background, then press Shift-Backspace/ Shift-Delete. In the Fill dialog, choose Use: White, Mode: Normal, and Opacity: 100%, then click OK.

**A** *We created a rectangular selection.*

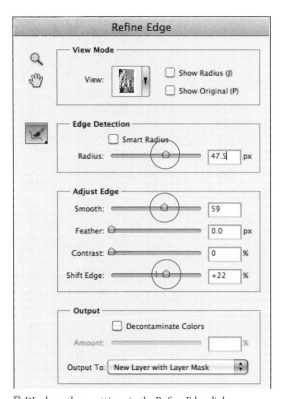

**B** *We chose these settings in the Refine Edge dialog.*

**C** *So easy!*

## USING HAND-PAINTED FRAMES IN A MONTAGE

**A** *To create this Paris montage, we applied a hand-painted border to each image separately in its own file, using the technique described on the preceding page. We dragged each image layer into a larger document, which contains a photo of burlap as the Background image. To complete the composition, we scaled and moved — and rotated two of — the layers.*

# Adding a watermark

If you're planning to display any of your images online, you can help protect them from unauthorized use by embedding a copyright or other watermark into them, analogous to traditional watermarking on paper. In these instructions, you'll create a copyright shape with the Custom Shape tool, then save the shape as a tool preset for use in any document.

## To embed a watermark into a file:

1. Choose the **Custom Shape** tool 🔯 (U or Shift-U).

2. On the Options bar, do the following:

   Click the **Shape Layers** button. 🔲

   Click the **Shape** picker thumbnail, then click the copyright symbol © (it's in the default custom shape preset library) **A** or click a custom shape that you've created for this purpose (see the instructions on the following page).

   Click the **Style** picker thumbnail, then click the **Default Style (None)**. 🔲

   Click the **Color** swatch. In the Color Picker, choose white as the Foreground color, then click OK.

3. Shift-drag with the tool in the document window until the symbol is the desired size. A shape layer will appear on the Layers panel.

4. On the Layers panel, change the **Fill** value for the shape layer to 0%.

5. Double-click next to the shape layer name to open the Layer Style dialog, then click **Bevel and Emboss** (don't check Contour). Choose Style: Inner Bevel, Technique: Smooth, Depth around 60–90%, Size 16–30, and Soften 8–12, then click OK. **B**

6. You can use the Move tool to reposition the shape on the image. For a better view of the copyright symbol, **C** click another layer.

7. To save the layer settings and layer effects to the Styles panel for future use, click the shape layer for the copyright mark on the Layers panel. On the Styles panel, 🔳 click the **New Style** button. 🔳 Type a name in the dialog, then click OK.

   To save the shape style as a tool preset, see the second task on the next page.

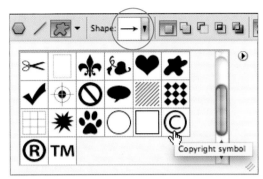

**A** *Click the copyright symbol (or a custom shape) on the Custom Shape picker.*

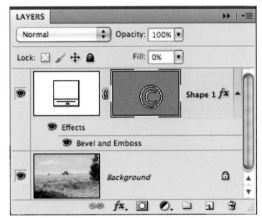

**B** *The © symbol appears in the mask for the shape layer on the Layers panel.*

**C** *This is the final watermark in the image.*

You can also create a custom watermark by using the Type tool.

## To create a custom watermark from text:

1. Choose the **Horizontal Type** tool, T create the desired text for the watermark, then scale and style it as desired. (To create the copyright symbol, we typed Alt + 0169/Option-G.)

2. Choose Layer > Type > **Convert to Shape.**

3. Choose Edit > **Define Custom Shape**, enter a name (we entered the same name as in our watermark), then click OK.

4. Delete the shape layer.

5. Follow the steps on the preceding page, except in step 2, choose your new custom shape from the Custom Shape picker. **A** Note: If you already saved a watermark style to the Styles panel, follow only steps 1–3. In step 2, click your custom shape on the Custom Shape picker and click your watermark style on the Style picker.

By saving your custom watermark as a preset for the Custom Shape tool, you'll be able to use it to quickly add your watermark to any image.

## To save a watermark shape and style as a tool preset:

1. Follow steps 1–7 on the preceding page.

2. Choose the **Custom Shape** tool ☁ (U or Shift-U).

3. On the Options bar, **B** make sure either the copyright symbol or your custom shape is chosen on the **Shape** preset picker.

4. Click the **Style** thumbnail on the Options bar to open the Style picker, then click your custom style.

5. Click the Tool Preset picker thumbnail at the left end of the Options bar, or display the Tool Presets panel. ✖

6. On the picker or panel, click the **New Tool Preset** button, ⬛ enter a name (we entered the text we used for our watermark), keep Include Color unchecked, and click OK. **C**

7. To place the watermark in any image, with the Custom Shape tool selected, click your tool preset on the Tool Preset picker or the Tool Presets panel, then Shift-drag in the document.

   Note: If Current Tool Only is checked on the picker or panel, you'll have to choose the Custom Shape tool to make the preset appear as a listing.

**A** *To create a custom watermark, we converted this text into a shape.*

**B** *On the Options bar for the Custom Shape tool, we chose Shape, Style, and Color settings, clicked our custom watermark on the Shape picker, and clicked our custom style on the Style picker.*

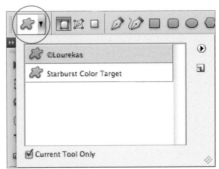

**C** *Our new custom tool preset appears on the Tool Preset picker.*

Next, we'll show you two ways to organize images and display them to clients: contact sheets and PDF presentations. You'll produce both by using the Output panel in Bridge.

## Creating a contact sheet

A contact sheet is an arrangement of image thumbnails in one document, an electronic version of the contact sheets that are traditionally created from film. Use them to catalog images, such as the photos that you back up onto DVDs, for easy reference and identification.

### To create a contact sheet:

1. In Bridge, put all the files to be displayed on the contact sheet in the same folder, in the order in which you want them to appear on the sheet (they can be grouped in a stack), and display the contents of that folder.

2. Click the **Output** workspace (or from the Output menu ◼ on the toolbar, choose Output to Web or PDF).* **A** A Preview panel displays above the Content panel, and an Output panel displays on the right side.

3. At the top of the Output panel, **B** click **PDF**, then from the **Template** menu, choose **4*5 Contact Sheet** or **5*8 Contact Sheet**, for the number of columns and rows.

   If you're content with the default settings for the chosen template, skip ahead to step 10 or 11; or if you prefer to customize the template, follow all the remaining steps.

4. In the **Document** category, do as follows:

   Choose a **Page Preset**, such as U.S. Paper, and a preset **Size**, or to produce a custom-size sheet, enter Width and Height values.

   Choose image **Quality** settings. For onscreen output, for example, choose 150 or 72 ppi and move the Quality slider to 60–70. ★ These settings will affect the file size.

   From the **Background** menu, choose a background color for the contact sheet. For print output, we recommend choosing White.

   For the Password options, see step 4, page 380.

5. Select around 10–15 thumbnails (to minimize the preview time), then click **Refresh Preview** to preview the current settings in a layout.

*If this workspace isn't listed, go to Edit/Adobe Bridge CS5 > Preferences > Startup Scripts, check Adobe Output Module, then relaunch Bridge.

**A** Display a folder of image thumbnails, then click the Output workspace on the Bridge toolbar.

**B** We chose these Document and Layout settings for our PDF contact sheet in the Output panel in Bridge before clicking Refresh Preview.

**6.** In the **Layout** category, change any of the following settings:

Choose an **Image Placement** option for the order in which the images are to be arranged, based on the current order of the thumbnails.

Enter the desired number of **Columns** and **Rows** for the contact sheet, depending on how many images it will contain.

Check **Use Auto-Spacing** to let Bridge calculate the spacing between thumbnails (the easy way); or uncheck this option, enter the desired spacing between thumbnails in the Vertical and Horizontal fields, and enter Top, Bottom, Left, and Right margin values.

*Optional:* Check Rotate for Best Fit to allow thumbnails to be rotated for a better fit (we keep this off, for a uniform orientation).

Keep **Repeat One Photo per Page** unchecked.

**7.** *Optional:* In the Overlays category (scroll downward if you don't see it), check Filename and Extension to have that data appear below each image, and choose a Font, Size, and Color for the text.

**8.** *Optional:* To display a header above all the images, in the Header category, check Add Header, choose an alignment option, enter text, and choose text attributes. Ditto for a Footer.

**9.** In the Playback category, uncheck all options (since the sheet is going to be viewed manually).

**10.** *Optional:* In the Watermark category, check Add Watermark, enter copyright text to appear in the center of each image, choose Font, Size, Color, and Offset options, and choose a low Opacity. ★

**11.** Select all the thumbnails to appear on the contact sheet, then click **Refresh Preview** to preview it. Adjust any settings or rearrange any thumbnails, if needed, then click Refresh Preview once more. **A**

**12.** At the bottom of the panel, check **View PDF After Save**, then click Save. In the Save As dialog, enter a file name, choose a location, then click Save. A PDF file will be created; Adobe Acrobat, Adobe Acrobat Pro, or Adobe Reader will launch; and the PDF file will open onscreen. **B** If it contains multiple pages, you can use the arrow buttons to cycle through them.

**B** *Our contact sheet opened in Adobe Acrobat Pro.*

**A** *When Refresh Preview is clicked again, the contact sheet previews in the Output Preview panel.*

# Creating a PDF presentation

Another way to package and send files to a client or friend is via a PDF presentation, in which images play sequentially onscreen. To view a slideshow, all the viewer has to do is double-click the PDF file.

## To create a PDF presentation:

1. In Bridge, put all the files you want to display in the presentation in the same folder, in the order in which you want them to appear (they can be grouped in a stack). Display the contents of the folder, and click one of the image thumbnails.

2. Click the **Output** workspace (or from the Output menu 🖼 on the toolbar, choose Output to Web or PDF).* **A** A Preview panel displays above the Content panel, and an Output panel displays on the right side (**A**, next page).

3. At the top of the Output panel, click **PDF**, then from the **Template** menu, choose Maximize Size.

4. In the **Document** category, do the following:

   From the **Page Preset** menu, choose Web, and from the **Size** menu, choose 800 x 600 or 1024 x 728.

   Choose **Quality** settings. For Web or other onscreen output, choose 150 ppi or 72 ppi and set the Quality to 60–70.★ These settings affect the file size and the speed of transmission.

   From the **Background** menu, choose a color to be displayed behind the images.

   *Optional:* Check **Open Password** and enter a password. Your viewers will need to enter this password in order to open the PDF file.

   *Optional:* Check **Permission Password** and enter a password to restrict how the PDF file can be used (such as a restriction to print access). Your viewers will need to enter this password in order to print or edit the PDF file.

5. In the **Layout** category, uncheck all the options, including Rotate for Best Fit, to prevent any images from being rotated.

6. In the **Overlays** category, check **Filename** and **Extension** to have that data appear below each image, choose a Font and Size, and set the Color to White (or if you prefer to choose a custom color, click the swatch and use the color picker).

7. *Optional:* To display a header above all the images, in the Header category, check Add

Header, choose an alignment option, enter text, and choose text attributes. Ditto for a Footer.

8. Under **Playback**, choose options for Acrobat:

   To display the presentation images at full-screen size, check **Open in Full Screen Mode**.

   To have the frames advance automatically, check **Automatic Advance to the Next Page**, then enter the **Duration (Seconds)** you want each frame to display.★

   To have the slide show loop continuously (after the last frame displays, the show replays from the first frame), check **Loop After Last Page**.

   To display a transition effect between frames, such as a Dissolve or a Fade, choose from the **Transition** menu. Also choose a **Direction** option (not available for all the Transition options) and a **Speed** option.

9. *Optional:* In the Watermark category, check Add Watermark,★ enter text to be displayed in the center of each image, choose Font, Size (try 60–70 pt), Color, and Offset options, and a low Opacity.★

10. Select all the thumbnails to be included in the presentation, then click **Refresh Preview** to generate a preview of the first frame, based on the settings you have chosen.

11. Check **View PDF After Save** at the bottom of the dialog to have the presentation play automatically when you click Save.

12. Click Save. In the Save As dialog, enter a file name, choose a location, then click Save. A PDF file will be created, and Adobe Acrobat, Adobe Acrobat Pro, or Adobe Reader will launch. If an alert pertaining to Acrobat appears, click Yes. The PDF file will open onscreen, and then finally the slide show will start (**B–C**, next page). To stop the show at any time, press Esc.

**A** *Display a folder of image thumbnails, then click the Output workspace on the Bridge toolbar.*

*If this workspace isn't listed, go to Preferences > Start Scripts (in Bridge), check Adobe Output Module, then relaunch Bridge.

**A** *The first frame of our PDF presentation displays in the Output Preview panel, along with the header. (We dragged the vertical bar of the Folders panel to the left to hide the left pane, to make more room for the other panes.)*

 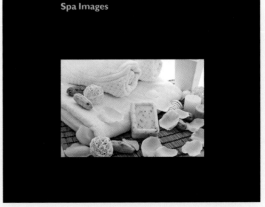

**B** *Adobe Acrobat launched, and the presentation played on the full screen. The image on the left shows a Glitter transition.*

# Creating and using layer comps

A layer comp (short for "composition") is a set of layer characteristics, which can include visibility, position, and layer effect settings. Via the Layer Comps panel, you can store multiple comps in one document. By displaying different comps, you can quickly present multiple design variations to coworkers and clients.

## To create a layer comp:

1. Create multiple image, type, fill, or adjustment layers to be used to create variations in your design. They can have different colors, typefaces, masks, Smart Filter settings, adjustment settings, imagery, etc.

2. To create a first comp, for each layer in the document, do any of the following: Choose a visibility setting, a position (location), and layer style settings (blending mode, opacity setting, etc.).

3. Show the Layer Comps panel,▤ A then click the **New Layer Comp** button 🔲 at the bottom of the panel. The New Layer Comp dialog opens.**B**

4. Enter a **Name** for the comp, then check which layer settings you want it to contain: **Visibility**, **Position**, and/or **Appearance (Layer Style)**.

5. *Optional:* Enter information in the Comment field, to appear on the panel when the list for that layer comp is expanded (such as explanatory notes for a client or coworker).**C**

6. Click OK. To create more comps from different design variations, repeat steps 2–6 (e.g., hide or show different layers, reposition a layer, change the layer style or adjustment settings).

➤ To change which layer settings a comp can store (and therefore display) or to add or edit the Comment, double-click to the right of the comp name; the Layer Comp Options dialog opens.

➤ To bypass the Layer Comp Options dialog as you create a comp, Alt-click/Option-click the New Layer Comp button. The options chosen for the last comp will apply to the new one.

➤ To rename a comp quickly, double-click the comp name on the panel.

## To display a layer comp:

Do either of the following:

On the Layer Comps panel, click in the left column to make the Layer Comp icon ▤ appear.

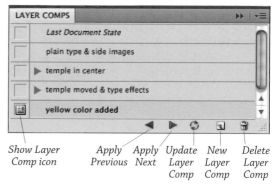

Show Layer Comp icon    Apply Previous    Apply Next    Update Layer Comp    New Layer Comp    Delete Layer Comp

**A** *Use the Layer Comps panel to create, store, apply, edit, update, and delete your layer comps.*

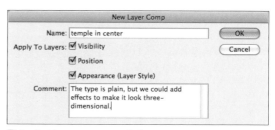

**B** *In the New Layer Comp dialog, type a Name, decide which characteristics are to be saved in the comp, and enter optional comments.*

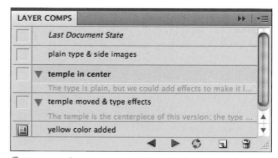

**C** *Two comp lists are expanded to reveal comments.*

### CREATING A LAYER COMP FROM A DUPLICATE

If you don't want to create a new layer comp from scratch, start from a duplicate instead: right-click a layer comp name and choose Duplicate Layer Comp, then to edit and update the duplicate, see "To update a layer comp" on the next page.

To cycle through the layer comps, click the **Apply Next Selected Layer Comp** button ▶ or **Apply Previous Selected Layer Comp** ◀ button.**A**

Let's say you edit your document, then display a layer comp. If you want to restore the document to its state before the comp was displayed, do as follows.

## To restore the last document state:

On the Layer Comps panel, ▦ do either of the following:

Click in the left column next to the **Last Document State** listing.

Right-click a layer comp and choose **Restore Last Document State**.

You can update any existing layer comp to incorporate new edits that you have made to your document.

## To update a layer comp:

1. On the Layer Comps panel, click the name of the layer comp to be updated. Note: If you need to remind yourself which Apply to Layers settings are turned on for the comp (or to change them), double-click it.

2. Add, edit, or delete layers; change their visibility or position; or change the layer style settings.

3. Click the **Update Layer Comp** button ◷ at the bottom of the panel.

If you change the number of layers in a document that are recorded in a layer comp (e.g., delete or merge layers), an alert icon, ⚠ indicating that the "Layer Comp Cannot Be Fully Restored," appears next to the names of any comps that are affected. You can either update or clear the alert, as follows. (If you ignore the alert, layers will remain merged or will be deleted.)

## To clear an alert icon:

Do one of the following:

Click the comp, then click the **Update Layer Comp** button. ◷ Data from the deleted layers will be removed from that comp, but any current edits will be saved to it.

Click the comp, click the alert icon, then click **Clear** in the alert dialog. Data from the deleted layers will be removed from that comp.

Right-click the alert icon and choose **Clear Layer Comp Warning** (or to clear all alert icons, choose Clear All Layer Comp Warnings).

**A** *The three layer comps shown above are variations within the same image.*

---

### CREATING A PERMANENT "SNAPSHOT"

To preserve the original state of a document, create a layer comp when you first open your image (before making any edits). Yes, snapshots on the History panel serve a similar purpose, but they disappear when you close your document, whereas layer comps save with the file and remain accessible.

When you delete a layer comp, no layers are deleted and the appearance of the document is unchanged.

### To delete a layer comp:

1. On the Layer Comps panel, click the layer comp to be deleted.

2. Click the **Delete Layer Comp** button 🗑 at the bottom of the panel.

# Creating a PDF presentation of layer comps

An automated command called Layer Comps to Files produces a flattened PDF file from each layer comp in a document, and from the resulting file, you can produce a PDF presentation. A PDF presentation is a great vehicle for showing document variations to a client, and it can be viewed without Photoshop.

### To create a PDF presentation of layer comps:

1. Open a Photoshop file that contains layer comps. *Optional:* To create the presentation from select layer comps rather than all the comps on the panel, select them now (Ctrl-click/Cmd-click to select nonconsecutive comps).

2. Choose File > Scripts > **Layer Comps to Files**. The Layer Comps to Files dialog opens.**A**

3. Click Browse, choose a location for the PDF files to be saved, then click OK/Open.

4. Enter a **File Name Prefix** to be included in the names of all the comp files.

5. If you selected some layer comps in step 1, check **Selected Layer Comps Only**.

6. In the File Type area, do the following:

   From the **File Type** menu, choose **PDF**.

   Check **Include ICC Profile** to include an assigned or embedded color profile.

   For the **PDF Options**, click **Encoding**: **JPEG** as the compression method, then enter a **Quality** value (1–4 for low quality, 5–8 for medium quality, or 9–12 for high quality).

7. Click Run. The script will save each comp as a flattened PDF file in the designated folder. Click OK in the alert dialog, which will indicate that the script was successful. The PDF file names will include the prefix, plus the title of the layer comp (as listed on the Layer Comps panel).

8. To create a PDF presentation using the new folder of images that the script created, follow the steps on page 380.

**A** *In the Layer Comps to Files dialog, choose a destination folder and options for the files that Photoshop will generate from your layer comps.*

Preferences are settings that you specify for application features, such as the default units for type or the rulers. Most preference changes take effect immediately (but are saved to the Preferences file when you exit/quit Photoshop); a handful of preference changes don't take effect until you relaunch Photoshop or Bridge (such exceptions are noted). In this chapter, in addition to learning about all the panels in the Preferences dialog, you'll learn how to save and load brush, tool, and other presets.

## Opening the Preferences dialogs

To open the Preferences dialog for **Photoshop**, press Ctrl-K/Cmd-K, or choose Edit/Photoshop > Preferences > General or another choice on that submenu. In the dialog, click one of the 10 panel names on the left side,**A** or click Prev or Next, or press Ctrl-1/Cmd-1 through Ctrl-0/Cmd-0 (zero).

To open the Preferences dialog for **Bridge**, in Bridge, press Ctrl-K/Cmd-K or choose Edit/Adobe Bridge CS5 > Preferences.

**A** *The Preferences dialog in Photoshop contains 10 panels.*

---

### RESETTING ALL THE PREFERENCES

▶ To reset all the Photoshop preferences to their default settings, hold down Ctrl-Alt-Shift/Cmd-Option-Shift as you launch the program. When the alert dialog appears, click Yes to delete (and reset) the Adobe Photoshop Settings file.

▶ To reset the Bridge preferences, hold down Ctrl/Option as you launch Bridge. When the Reset Settings dialog appears, check Reset Preferences, then click OK.

# 24

## PREFERENCES & PRESETS

### IN THIS CHAPTER

# General Preferences (A, next page)

As the default **Color Picker**, choose Adobe (the default setting) or the color picker for your system.

For the onscreen **HUD** (Heads-Up Display) **Color Picker**, choose a strip or wheel style and a display size. ★ See page 186.

Choose a default **Image Interpolation** option for Photoshop features, such as the Image Size dialog and the Crop tool, that involve resampling or transforming: Nearest Neighbor (Preserve Hard Edges), the fastest and the best for hard-edged graphics but the least precise; Bilinear, medium quality; Bicubic (Best for Smooth Gradients), higher quality but slower; Bicubic Smoother (Best for Enlargement); or Bicubic Sharper (Best for Reduction). The latter two options also produce high-quality results.

## Options

Check **Auto-Update Open Documents** to have open Photoshop documents that you edit in other applications update automatically when you return to Photoshop, such as when you enter metadata for a file in Bridge.

Check **Beep When Done** to have a beep sound when a command is done processing. This can be handy for commands that take a while to process (so you can grab a snack!).

Check **Dynamic Color Sliders** to have the colors above the sliders on the Color panel update as the sliders are moved.

Check **Export Clipboard** to retain the current Clipboard contents on the system's Clipboard when you switch between Photoshop and other applications.

With **Use Shift Key for Tool Switch** checked, in order to access a tool on a pop-out menu, you must press Shift plus the assigned letter (e.g., press Shift-B to cycle through the Brush, Pencil, Color Replacement, and Mixer Brush tools). If you uncheck this option (as we do), you can cycle through related tools simply by pressing their assigned letter (without pressing Shift). To learn the tool shortcuts, see pages 104–106.

Check **Resize Image During Place** to have pixel images from other Photoshop files or other applications scale to fit the current canvas area automatically when imported via the File > Place command.

Check **Animated Zoom** for smooth, continuous zooming when you change the zoom level by dragging (OpenGL is required and must be enabled in the Performance panel of this dialog).

With **Zoom Resizes Windows** checked, a floating document window will resize when you change the zoom level via the Ctrl/Cmd- + (plus) or Ctrl/Cmd- – (minus) shortcut or the Zoom tool. This preference can be set either here or via the Resize Windows to Fit check box on the Options bar.

If your mouse has a scroll wheel and you check **Zoom with Scroll Wheel**, you can change the zoom level by scrolling the wheel.

Check **Zoom Clicked Point to Center** to center the image, when zooming, at the location you click.

Check **Enable Flick Panning** to enable a magnified image to quickly float across the screen when you drag it with the Hand tool a short distance, then release the mouse (OpenGL is required and must be enabled in the Performance panel of this dialog).

Check **Place or Drag Raster Images as Smart Objects** to have raster images that are imported into Photoshop via the Place command arrive as Smart Object layers. ★

## History Log

Check **History Log** to generate a log of your Photoshop activity from each work session. For **Save Log Items To**, choose where the log is to be saved: to the Metadata of a file, to a separate Text File, or to Both (of the above). For either of the latter two options, choose a location for the text file in the dialog that opens automatically, then click Save (or open the dialog by clicking Choose).

From the **Edit Log Items** menu, choose what data is to be saved in the log: Sessions Only to log only when you launch or exit/quit Photoshop and which files were opened; Concise to log Sessions information plus a list of edits (states on the History panel); or Detailed, to include all of the above data plus any actions used and the options and parameters used in each editing step. These log options can be handy if you need to keep a tally of billable hours for clients or a record of your exact editing steps.

Click **Reset All Warning Dialogs** to reenable any alert dialogs that you may have asked to be hidden by checking Don't Show Again.

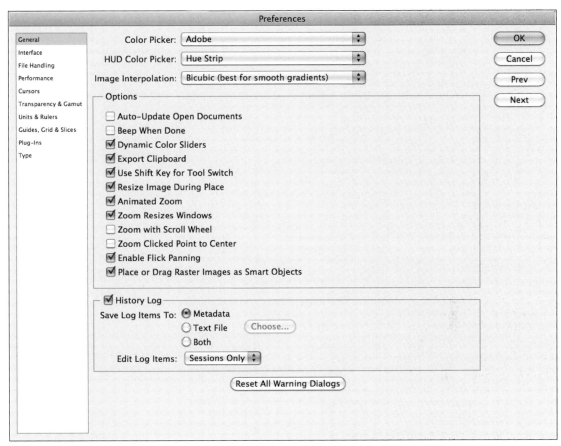

**A** *General Preferences*

# Interface Preferences (A, next page)

### General

To customize the colors for any of the three Photoshop screen modes — **Standard Screen Mode**, **Full Screen with Menus**, or **Full Screen** — choose a background color from the first menu and a border style (or None) from the second. See page 94.

Check **Show Channels in Color** to display RGB or CMYK channels in color when displayed individually on the Channels panel (in the thumbnails), and in the document window. With this option off, individual channels display in grayscale; this can be useful for judging the luminosity values of individual channels.

Check **Show Menu Colors** to enable the display of background colors that are assigned to menu commands via Edit > Menus or by choosing a workspace that contains them, such as the "New in CS5" workspace.

Check **Show Tool Tips** to allow the name or function of whichever bar, dialog, or panel feature the pointer is currently hovering over (with the mouse button up) to appear briefly onscreen so you can identify it. This is a good way to learn the names and shortcuts for tools.

Mac OS users: Check **Enable Gestures** if you have a Windows 7 or MacBook computer with a multi-touch trackpad (or are using a Magic Mouse with an Apple computer) and you want to enable the capability of the trackpad to zoom, rotate, or flick images. ★ Unlock this option if you find that the gestures are causing unwanted changes.

### Panels & Documents

If **Auto-Collapse Iconic Panels** is checked and you open a collapsed panel, it will collapse back to an icon when you click outside it. With this option unchecked, the panel will remain expanded. See pages 96–97.

Check **Auto-Show Hidden Panels** to allow panel docks that you have hidden via the Tab or Shift-Tab shortcut to redisplay temporarily when you let the pointer pause on the dark gray vertical bar at the left or right edge of the Application frame if the document is in Standard Screen mode, or at the edge of your monitor if your document is in either of the Full Screen modes. When the pointer is moved away from the panels, they will disappear again.

Check **Open Documents as Tabs** to have documents dock automatically as tabs when opened instead of in a floating window. (With this option checked in the Mac OS, images dock as tabs in one document window even when the Application frame is hidden.)

**Enable Floating Document Window Docking** to allow a floating document window to be docked as a tabbed window when you drag its title bar below the bar at the top of the Application frame or below the title bar of another window.

Click **Restore Default Workspaces** to restore any predefined Adobe workspaces to the Workspace menu that were deleted. ★

### UI Text Options

To implement choices made from the following two menus, you must relaunch Photoshop.

If you are using a multilingual version of Photoshop, from the **UI Language** menu, choose a language for the interface.

From the **UI Font Size** menu, choose Small (the default choice that we prefer), Medium, or Large as the font size for the Photoshop user interface (menus, panels, tool tips, the Options bar, and the like).

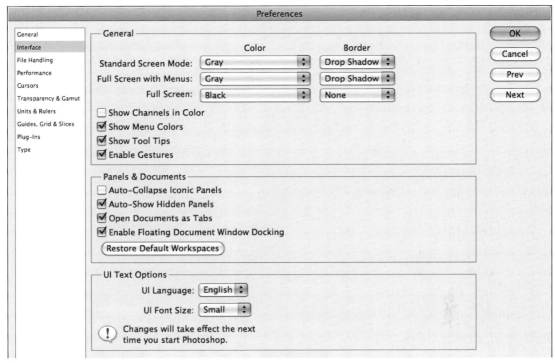

**A** *Interface Preferences*

## File Handling Preferences (A, next page)

### File Saving Options

Choose **Image Previews**: Never Save to save files without a thumbnail preview for the Desktop, or Always Save (our preference) to have an updated preview save with your files each time they're saved, or Ask When Saving to decide which previews to include in each case via Image Previews check boxes in the Save or Save As dialog. See pages 24 and 26.

In the Mac OS, check **Icon** to have a thumbnail of an image display as its file icon on the Desktop and in the File > Open dialog. Check **Windows Thumbnail** to have a file's thumbnail display when the file is selected in File > Open.

In the Mac OS, choose **Append File Extension**: Always (our preference) to automatically include a three-letter abbreviation of the file format (e.g., .tif, .psd) when a file is saved; or Ask When Saving to have the option to decide in each case whether

*Continued on the following page*

to include the extension via File Extension check boxes in the Save As dialog. Extensions are helpful when converting files for Windows, and are necessary when saving files for the Web. Keep Use Lower Case checked to have file extensions appear in lowercase characters instead of uppercase.

In Windows, choose **File Extension**: Use Lower Case or Use Upper Case.

Check **Save As to Original Folder** to have the location in the Save As dialog default to the existing location of the current file. Great new feature! ★

### File Compatibility

Click **Camera Raw Preferences** to open that dialog.

Check **Prefer Adobe Camera Raw for Supported Raw Files** to have raw files that you open via File > Open open into Camera Raw, as opposed to other conversion software (we keep this option checked).

Keep **Ignore EXIF Profile Tag** unchecked to allow Photoshop to read a camera's EXIF metadata color space information when opening files. This option was necessary only for some early digital cameras.

Check **Ask Before Saving Layered TIFF Files** to have an "Including layers will increase file size" alert appear when layered files are saved in the TIFF format. You can use this as a reminder to uncheck the Layers option in the Save As dialog.

The **Maximize PSD and PSB File Compatibility** option includes a flattened version of files in those formats to make them compatible with programs that don't read Photoshop layers (including Adobe Lightroom). This option increases the file size but is often a necessity. Choose Ask to have the compatibility option be offered via an alert when files are saved, or choose Always to produce compatible files upon saving without an alert appearing. See pages 24 and 26.

Note: Upon saving a layered file, if Ask is the current Maximize PSD and PSB File Compatibility preference and you check Maximize Compatibility and Don't Show Again in the Photoshop Format Options dialog, Photoshop will switch the preference setting to Always. If you uncheck Maximize Compatibility but do check Don't Show Again in the alert, the preference setting will be switched to Never. ★

### File list

In the **Recent File List Contains [ ] files** field, enter the maximum number of files (up to 30) that can be listed at a time on the File > Open Recent submenu in Photoshop.

Note: Adobe Drive is not available in, or supported by, Adobe Creative Suite 5.

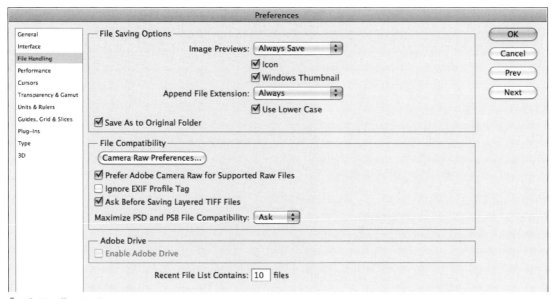

**A** *File Handling Preferences*

# Performance Preferences A

Note: For changes made in this panel to take effect, you must relaunch Photoshop.

In the **Description** window at the bottom of the dialog, read about the feature your pointer is currently hovering over.

### Memory Usage

The **Let Photoshop Use** field and slider control the maximum percentage of your machine's RAM that can be used by Photoshop. We recommend leaving these controls at the default setting.

### History & Cache

Low-resolution versions of the current file are saved in cache buffers to help the image and histograms redraw more quickly onscreen. To optimize the cache levels and tile size for Photoshop, click a generic document type (not your body type!): **Tall and Thin** (for smaller documents with many layers), **Default** (best for general use), or **Big and Flat** (best for larger documents with few layers). ★

Enter the maximum number of **History States** the History panel can list at a time. When this number is reached, older states are deleted.

Choose a higher **Cache Levels** value for large files that contain few layers and a lower Cache Levels value for smaller files that contain more layers.

The **Cache Tile Size** value controls how much data Photoshop processes at a given time. Choose a higher value for large images. ★

### Scratch Disks

Check which hard drives you want made available as **Scratch Disks** for Photoshop when available RAM is insufficient for processing or storing image data. To switch the order of the currently selected drive, click the up or down arrow.

➤ Hold down Ctrl-Alt/Cmd-Option while launching Photoshop to open the Scratch Disk Preferences dialog.

➤ Choose Panel Options from the Info panel 🛈 menu, and check Efficiency under Status Information. When the scratch disk is being used, the Efficiency value at the bottom of the panel registers below 100%.

### GPU Settings

The **Detected Video Card** area lists the video cards in your system.

Check **Enable OpenGL Drawing** if your system has OpenGL graphics capability and you want to take advantage of the OpenGL features of Photoshop, such as Animated Zoom, Scrubby Zoom, flick panning, and the Rotate View tool. For the Advanced Settings options, see Photoshop Help.

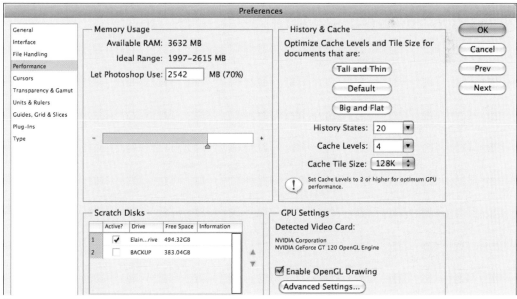

**A** *Performance Preferences*

## Cursors Preferences A

### Painting Cursors

For **Painting Cursors** (the Art History Brush, Background Eraser, Blur, Brush, Burn, Clone Stamp, Color Replacement, Dodge, Eraser, Healing Brush, History Brush, Mixer Brush, Pattern Stamp, Pencil, Quick Selection, Sharpen, Smudge, Sponge, and Spot Healing Brush tools), click the type of cursor to be displayed onscreen as you use the tool: **Standard** for the tool icon; **Precise** for crosshairs; **Normal Brush Tip** for a half-size circle; or **Full Size Brush Tip** for a circle the full size of the current brush. For either of the latter two options, you can also check **Show Crosshair in Brush Tip** to have crosshairs appear in the center of the circle and/or **Show Only Crosshair While Painting** to have only crosshairs display when the mouse is dragged, for faster performance when using large brushes. ★

### Other Cursors

For the **Other Cursors** (all those not listed in the preceding paragraph, such as the Eyedropper and Crop tools), click **Standard** to have the tool icon display onscreen as you use the tool or **Precise** to display crosshairs instead.

➤ Press Caps Lock to turn Standard cursors into Precise cursors (crosshairs) or, if Precise is the current Painting Cursors setting, to turn any Painting cursor into a Full Size Brush Tip.

### Brush Preview

Click the **Color** swatch and choose a color from the Color Picker to represent the brush hardness setting within the brush cursor as you Alt-right-click-drag/Control-Option-drag upward or downward to change that setting (OpenGL must be enabled).

## Transparency & Gamut Preferences B

### Transparency Settings

Choose a **Grid Size** for the checkerboard that Photoshop uses to represent layer transparency.

For the transparency checkerboard, choose one of the **Grid Colors** from the menu, or click each Color swatch and choose a color from the color picker.

### Gamut Warning

To change the color that is used to mark out-of-gamut colors when the View > **Gamut Warning** feature is on, click the Color swatch and use the color picker. You can also lower the Opacity of the Gamut Warning color to see the underlying image more easily.

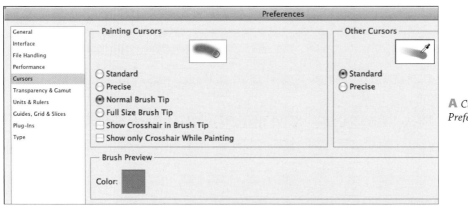

**A** Cursors Preferences

**B** Transparency & Gamut Preferences

# Units & Rulers Preferences A

## Units

From the **Rulers** menu, choose a unit of measure for the horizontal and vertical rulers; for dialogs, such as Image > Canvas Size; and for panels, such as the Info panel.

➤ To show or hide the rulers, press Ctrl-R/Cmd-R or choose Show Rulers from the View Extras menu ▦ ▾ on the Application bar. See page 253.

➤ To change the ruler units without opening the Preferences dialog, right-click either ruler in the document window and choose a unit from the context menu. When changed this way or via the Info Panel Options dialog (Info panel), the ruler units also change here in the Preferences dialog, and vice versa.

Choose a unit for **Type** of Pixels, Points, or Mm to display on the Character and Paragraph panels and on the Options bar when a type tool is selected.

➤ To get directly to the Units & Rulers panel of the Preferences dialog, double-click either ruler.

## Column Size

If you need to fit your Photoshop images into a specific column width in a page layout program, enter values in the **Width** and **Gutter** fields here. When you open the New, Image Size, or Canvas Size dialog, and choose Columns from the units menu next to the Width field, the Width and Gutter preference values will be used to calculate the Width value.

## New Document Preset Resolutions

Enter **Print Resolution** and **Screen Resolution** values in either of the available units to display by default in the New dialog when you choose a preset print or screen size, respectively. The default settings are 300 ppi for print output and 72 ppi for onscreen display. See pages 21–22.

## Point/Pica Size

Click **PostScript** (the default, and preferred setting) to have Photoshop use the standard PostScript value as the points-to-inch ratio.

---

**ENTERING NONDEFAULT UNITS IN ENTRY FIELDS**

When you enter a value in a nondefault unit, it is converted to the equivalent default unit:

| | |
|---|---|
| Pixels | px |
| Inches | in or ″ |
| Centimeters | cm |
| Millimeters | mm |
| Points | pt |
| Picas | p |
| Percent | % |

---

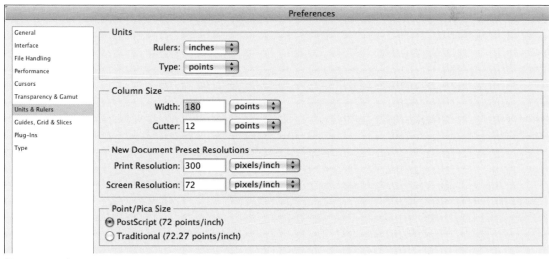

**A** *Units & Rulers Preferences*

# Guides, Grid & Slices Preferences A

Note: Changes in this dialog preview immediately in the document.

## Guides

Choose a **Color** and **Style** for ruler guides (see pages 253–254).

## Smart Guides

Choose a **Color** for Smart Guides, the temporary lines that display onscreen as you move a layer or selection (see page 252).

## Grid

Choose a **Color** and **Style** for the nonprinting grid (choose View > Show > Grid or press Ctrl-'/Cmd-').

To display grid lines onscreen at specific intervals, choose a unit from the menu, then enter a **Gridline Every** value. If you choose Percent from the menu, grid lines will appear at those percentage intervals of the overall document, starting from the left edge. For spacing of the thinner grid lines between the main grid lines, enter a **Subdivisions** value.

➤ To change the color of guides, Smart Guides, or the grid, you can also click the color swatch, then choose a color from the color picker.

## Slices

Choose a **Line Color** for the slice boundaries. Check **Show Slice Numbers** to allow a slice number to display in the upper left corner of each slice. (To learn about the slice tools, see Photoshop Help.)

# Plug-ins Preferences (A, next page)

Note: For changes made in this dialog to take effect, you must relaunch Photoshop.

## Plug-ins

In order to use third-party plug-ins that aren't located in the Plug-ins folder (in the Adobe Photoshop CS5 application folder), you must check **Additional Plug-ins Folder**, locate the folder in which they are installed, then click Open in the dialog.

## Extension Panels

Check **Allow Extensions to Connect to the Internet** to enable Photoshop extension panels to connect to the Internet in order to access updated content. These panels include Window > Extensions > Access CS Live, CS News and Resources, CS Review (an online subscription service), Kuler (see page 115), and Mini Bridge (see pages 46–47). Panels from third-party suppliers are also accessed from this submenu. To learn about the CS online services, use the CS Live menu on the Application bar in Photoshop.

Check **Load Extension Panels** to have the extension panels that are installed in the Plug-ins folder (in the Adobe Photoshop CS5 application folder) load when you launch Photoshop.

Check **Show CS Live in Application Bar** to display the CS Live menu on the Application bar in Photoshop. ★ For CS Live features, see the CS Live menu on the Application bar in Photoshop.

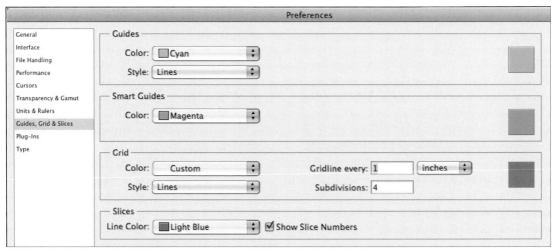

**A** *Guides, Grid & Slices Preferences*

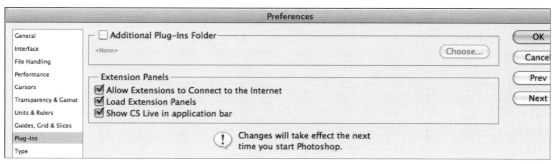

**A** *Plug-ins Preferences*

## Type Preferences B

### Type Options

Be sure to check **Use Smart Quotes** to have Photoshop insert typographically correct (curly) apostrophes and quotation marks automatically when you create type, instead of the incorrect foot and inch marks.

Check **Show Asian Text Options** to display options for Chinese, Japanese, and Korean type on the Character and Paragraph panels and panel menus.

Check **Enable Missing Glyph Protection** to permit Photoshop to substitute Roman characters for missing glyphs, such as Japanese or Chinese characters.

Check **Show Font Names in English** to have non-Roman font names on the Font menus display in English (e.g., "Adobe Ming Std" instead of the equivalent Chinese characters).

Check **Font Preview Size** to show fonts on the Font menu on the Options bar and the Character panel as a preview of the typeface rather than in a generic typeface, and choose a preview size of Small, Medium, Large, Extra Large, or Huge.

**B** *Type Preferences*

# Preferences for Adobe Bridge

## General Preferences A

### Appearance

Choose a value between Black and White for the overall **User Interface Brightness** (for the side panels) and for the **Image Backdrop** (the area behind the Content and Preview panels).

Choose an **Accent Color** for highlighted items.

### Behavior

Check **When a Camera is Connected**, **Launch Adobe Photo Downloader** to make the Downloader the default system utility for acquiring photos (for Mac OS users only).

Check **Double-Click Edits Camera Raw Settings in Bridge** to have raw files open into Camera Raw, hosted by Bridge, when double-clicked. See page 62.

If **Ctrl-Click/Cmd-Click Opens the Loupe When Previewing or Reviewing** is checked, you have to hold down Ctrl/Cmd while clicking an image preview to make the loupe display. With this option unchecked, you can make the loupe appear simply by clicking the preview (see page 38).

For **Number of Recent Items to Display**, enter the maximum number of files (0–30) that can be listed at a time on the Open Recent File menu ▨ and

the Reveal Recent File or Go to Recent Folder menu ▨ on the Path bar, and on the Go to Parent, Recent Items, or Favorites menu in Mini Bridge. ▨

### Favorite Items

Check which items and system-generated folders you want listed in the **Favorites** panel, by default.

## Thumbnails Preferences B

### Performance and File Handling

Note: To implement Performance and File Handling changes, you must purge the folder cache (Tools > Cache submenu).

For **Do Not Process Files Larger Than**, enter the maximum file size that you will permit Bridge to display a thumbnail for (the default value is 1000 MB). Large files preview slowly.

### Details

From the **Additional Lines of Thumbnail Metadata** menus, choose which categories of file information are to be listed below or next to the image thumbnails in the Content panel (see page 42).

Check **Show Tooltips** to allow tool tips to display when you rest the pointer on Bridge features, such as image thumbnails.

**A** *General Preferences, in Bridge*

**B** *Thumbnails Preferences, in Bridge*

## Playback Preferences

Choose options to control whether audio and video files will play and/or loop when viewed in the Preview panel. The **Stack Playback Frame Rate** controls the speed at which a stack of 10 or more video thumbnails play back via the Play button.

## Metadata Preferences

Check which categories of metadata are to be displayed in the **Metadata** panel.

Check **Hide Empty Fields** to hide fields on the Metadata panel that are empty.

Check **Show Metadata Placard** to display camera data at the top of the Metadata panel (see page 36).

## Keywords Preferences

Check **Automatically Apply Parent Keywords** to have the parent keyword apply automatically when a subkeyword check box is clicked in the Keywords panel (we keep this option off). If this option is on and you want to override it (to apply just a sub-keyword), Shift-click the check box. See page 55.

For **Write Hierarchical Keywords**, click an Output Delimiter character to separate keywords in exported files. The **Read Hierarchical Keywords** setting applies to keyword delimiters in imported files.

## Labels Preferences

Check whether to **Require the Control/Command Key** [to be pressed] **to Apply Labels and Ratings** to selected file thumbnails (see page 44). You can also change the label names here, but not the colors.

## File Type Associations Preferences

These settings tell Bridge which application it may open files of different types into. Don't change these settings unless you know what you're doing!

## Cache Preferences

### Options

Check **Keep 100% Previews in Cache** to save a large JPEG preview of image thumbnails to disk for faster previewing when using the loupe and when previewing images in Slideshow mode at 100% or in Full Screen Preview view. We keep this option unchecked, because it uses a lot of disk space.

Check **Automatically Export Caches to Folders When Possible** to have Bridge export the cache (in which thumbnail data is stored) to the same folders as the images. See page 54.

### Location

Click **Choose** to specify a different location for the Bridge cache (then relaunch Bridge).

### Manage

If you have a very large hard drive, you can increase the maximum number of items that can be stored in the cache via the **Cache Size** slider.

Click **Compact Cache** to allow previously cached items that are no longer available to be removed from the cache, for improved performance.

Click **Purge Cache** to purge all cached thumbnails and previews from the central database to free up space on your hard disk, or if Bridge is having trouble displaying your image thumbnails.

## Startup Scripts Preferences

**Startup Scripts** that are checked will be available at startup. We recommend keeping them all checked, unless you have a specific reason to uncheck any particular ones. Changes to these settings take effect when you relaunch Bridge.

## Advanced Preferences

Note: Most changes to the Advanced Preferences settings take effect when you relaunch Bridge.

### Miscellaneous

If (and only if) you encounter display problems in Bridge, check **Use Software Rendering**. This option turns off hardware acceleration for the Preview panel and Slideshow mode.

Check **Generate Monitor-Size Previews** to have Bridge generate previews in a dual-monitor setup based on the resolution of the larger monitor.

Check **Start Bridge at Login** to have Bridge launch automatically at startup.

## Output Preferences

Check **Use Solo Mode for Output Panel Behavior** to display only one expanded category on the Output panel at a time.

Check **Convert Multi-Byte Filenames to Full ASCII** to define Chinese and Japanese file names using the ASCII character system, to prevent problems when transferring files.

Check **Preserve Embedded Color Profile** to preserve any embedded profiles in files being output as PDF files or as a Web gallery.

Click **Reset Panel to Defaults** to restore all the default settings to this panel.

## Using the Preset Manager

If you have practiced the image-editing techniques in other chapters, you have already accessed presets on many of the pickers in Photoshop, such as the Brush Presets, Styles, and Swatches panels. Other presets are found in less obvious locations, such as contours in some panels of the Layer Style dialog and gradients in the Gradient Fill dialog. The preset categories include brushes, swatches, gradients, styles, patterns, contours, custom shapes, and tools. A collection of saved presets that can be loaded onto a picker is called a library. (To learn how presets are created, see the sidebar on page 400.)

Beware! If there are presets on a picker that haven't been saved and you want to be able to access them in the future, you must save them as a library; otherwise, they could be easily replaced by other presets. You can save presets via the Preset Manager dialog (see the instructions at right) or via an individual picker (see "To save the presets on a picker as a library" on page 401). You can load a saved library of presets onto a picker at any time, and you can share them with other Photoshop users.

### To save select presets as a library via the Preset Manager:

1. To open the Preset Manager, do one of the following:

   Choose Edit > **Preset Manager**.

   Choose **Preset Manager** from the menu of any picker or panel (such as the Swatches or Styles panel).

   On the Brush or Brush Presets panel, click the **Open Preset Manager** button. ▦ ★

2. From the **Preset Type** menu, choose the category of presets that you want to create a library for, or press the shortcut that is listed on the menu. **A**

3. From the menu on the right side of the dialog, ▶ choose a view option for the Preset Manager (such as Small Thumbnail or Small List). For Brushes, you can choose Stroke Thumbnail view to display a sample of the brush stroke alongside each thumbnail.

4. Shift-click or Ctrl-click/Cmd-click the presets to be saved in a library, then click **Save Set**.

5. In the Save dialog, enter a name for the new library, keep the default extension and location, then click Save.

6. Click Done to exit the Preset Manager.

7. Relaunch Photoshop.

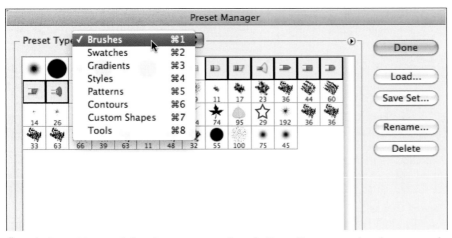

**A** In the Preset Manager dialog, choose a category from the Preset Type menu, select the presets to be saved in a library, then click Save Set.

To load a library of presets onto a picker, you can use either the Preset Manager (instructions here) or an individual preset picker (see pages 400–401). You can reset any category of presets to the factory defaults, append (add) more presets to the current ones on the picker, or replace the current presets with those in a library. Presets on the pickers and panels remain there when you relaunch Photoshop.

Note: Changes made in the Preset Manager also appear in the corresponding picker, and vice versa.

## To load presets onto a picker via the Preset Manager:

1. Choose Edit > **Preset Manager** or choose **Preset Manager** from the menu on any picker or panel.

2. Choose a category of presets from the **Preset Type** menu.

3. Any unsaved presets on the current picker will be deleted in the next step, unless you choose the Append option. To save the current presets as a library before proceeding, follow the steps on the preceding page.

4. From the menu on the right side of the dialog, choose a specific library name; **A** or to reload the default library, choose **Reset** [preset type]. In the

alert dialog, click Append to add the new library to the current ones on the picker, or click OK to replace the current presets with the new ones.

If the picker contains any unsaved presets (you didn't follow step 3), another alert will appear. Click Don't Save or Save.

5. *Optional:* To delete presets from the picker (but not from the library), click a preset to be deleted or Shift-click or Ctrl-click/Cmd-click multiple presets, then click Delete. This can't be undone (but any library can be reloaded).

6. Click Done to exit the Preset Manager.

➤ To load a library that isn't in the default location, click Load in the Preset Manager, locate the library in the Load dialog, then click Open. Or to replace the current presets, choose Replace [preset type] from the menu, locate the desired library in the Open dialog, then click Open.

➤ To rename a preset when the Preset Manager is in a Thumbnail view, double-click the thumbnail, then change the name in the dialog. If the Preset Manager is in Text Only or a List view, double-click the preset name. You can also select multiple presets and then click Rename, in which case naming dialogs will open in succession.

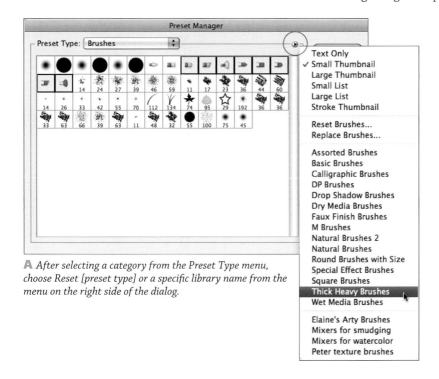

**A** *After selecting a category from the Preset Type menu, choose Reset [preset type] or a specific library name from the menu on the right side of the dialog.*

## Managing presets via the pickers and panels

Presets are created in various ways, such as when you define a new pattern via the Define Pattern command, add a new swatch to the Swatches panel, add a new style to the Styles panel, create a new gradient in the Gradient Editor dialog, or create a new brush or tool preset (see the sidebar at right).

New presets are saved in the Adobe Photoshop Preferences file temporarily. They stay on the picker when you relaunch Photoshop, but are discarded if you replace them with another library or reset the default library to the picker. Thankfully, there's a way to preserve your custom presets and hard work.

When you use the Preset Manager to create a library, you are able to pick and choose which presets are saved. When you create a library via a specific preset picker (accessed from the Options bar or from a dialog, such as the Gradient Editor), all the presets on the picker are included — you can't pick and choose. To outsmart this limitation, before creating the library, delete the presets you don't want saved in the library.

Note: When you delete a preset from a picker or panel, no documents are altered and no saved presets are deleted from the "actual" library they reside in.

### To delete presets from a panel or picker:

1. Display the picker or panel that you want to delete presets from, such as the Brush Presets, Styles, Swatches, or Tool Presets panel.

2. Do either of the following:

   Alt-click/Option-click the preset to be deleted (you'll see a scissors pointer).

   Right-click a preset and choose **Delete** [preset name]. If an alert dialog appears, click OK.

---

**HOW ARE PRESETS CREATED?**

A new preset is created each time you do any of the following:

► Customize a brush using the Brush panel, then click the New Preset button ⬒ on the Brush or Brush Presets panel, or on the Brush Preset picker, which is accessed from the Options bar.

► Add a swatch of the current Foreground color to the Swatches panel by clicking the New Swatch button. ⬒

► Create a tool preset by clicking the New Tool Preset button ⬒ in the Tool Presets panel or on the Tool Preset picker (see page 402).

► Create a gradient by clicking New in the Gradient Editor dialog.

► Create a style by clicking the New Style button ⬒ on the Styles panel or by clicking New Style in the Layer Style dialog.

► Create a pattern via Edit > Define Pattern.

► Create a custom shape via Edit > Define Custom Shape.

## To save the presets on a picker as a library:

1. Make sure the preset picker or panel contains only the presets to be saved in a library (see the instructions on the preceding page).

2. Do one of the following:

   From the Brush Presets, Swatches, Styles, or Tool Presets panel menu, or from the Brush Preset picker menu, choose **Save** [preset type].

   For a gradient, click **Save** in the Gradient Editor dialog; or from the menu in the Gradient Fill dialog (for a fill layer) or in the Gradient picker (on the Options bar), choose **Save Gradients**.

   For a pattern, from the picker menu in the Pattern Overlay panel of the Layer Style dialog, the Edit > Fill dialog, or the Pattern Fill dialog (for a fill layer), choose **Save Patterns**.

3. In the Save dialog, enter a name, keep the default extension and location, then click Save.

4. Relaunch Photoshop to make your new library appear on the panel and/or preset picker menu and on the menu in the Preset Manager.**A**

**A** *The new library appears at the bottom of the Brush Preset picker menu.*

Photoshop supplies an assortment of predefined preset libraries that you can load as needed onto the relevant picker. The libraries are available on the lower portion of the panel or picker menu when you select a tool that uses that panel or picker (for example, from the Brush Preset picker when the Brush or Mixer Brush tool is selected). User-created libraries are also listed on the menu.

## To load a library of presets:

1. From the lower portion of a panel menu ▤ or picker menu, ⊙ choose a preset library name. Libraries are listed on the Brush Presets, Styles, Swatches, and Tool Presets panel menus, and on the Shape and Tool Preset picker menus (on the Options bar). You can also choose a library from the picker menu in the Gradient Editor dialog, the Gradient Fill dialog (for a Gradient Fill layer), the Edit > Fill dialog (for patterns), the Pattern Fill dialog (for a Pattern Fill layer), and the Layer Style dialog (for contours, gradients, patterns, and styles).

2. When the alert appears, click Append to add the additional presets to the panel or picker, or click OK to replace the current presets on the panel or picker with those in the library.

   Note: If the panel or picker contains unsaved presets, another alert dialog appears. Click Don't Save or Save.

➤ To access a library that isn't listed on the menu (because it isn't being stored in the default folder), choose Load [preset name] from the panel or picker menu, locate the desired library, then click Open.

➤ To create document presets for use in the New dialog, see page 23.

You can restore the factory-default library to any panel or picker.

## To restore the default presets to a panel or picker:

1. Choose **Reset** [preset name] from a panel or picker menu.

2. When the alert dialog appears, click OK to replace the existing presets on the panel or picker with the default ones.

   Note: If you made changes to the current presets, another alert dialog will appear. Click Don't Save or Save.

# Creating tool presets

If you're looking for an effective way to streamline your workflow, consider creating some tool presets. For any tool, you can choose a preset (such as a brush or gradient), Options bar settings, and a Foreground color (if applicable), then save that collection of settings as a tool preset. Thereafter, upon selecting that tool, you simply choose your preset from the Tool Preset picker on the Options bar or from the Tool Presets panel; it contains all the settings that you saved with it. Tool presets are a great timesaver and are worth the effort to set up, even for minor variations.

To acquaint yourself with the Tool Presets panel, ✄ uncheck Current Tool Only. The tool presets for all tools display. Click a tool preset, and the tool that uses that preset becomes selected automatically. Now check Current Tool Only. Only presets for the current tool display. Via the panel or picker menu, you can load more presets (see the preceding page). The DP,  M Tool, Mixer Brush Tool, and Splatter Brush Tool preset libraries are new. ★

## To create a tool preset:

1. Choose and customize any tool. Or to create a variation of an existing tool preset, click the preset, then choose custom settings for it.

2. Do either of the following:

   At the far left end of the Options bar, click the Tool Preset picker thumbnail or arrowhead. A

   Display the Tool Presets panel. ✄ B

3. Click the **New Tool Preset** button 🗔 on the picker or panel. The New Tool Preset dialog opens.

4. *Optional:* Change the name of the tool preset, if desired. Also check Include Color, if that option is available and you want to save the current Foreground color with the preset.

5. Click OK. The new tool preset will appear on, and can be chosen from, the Tool Preset picker and the Tool Presets panel.

6. To preserve your user-created tool presets for future use in any document, save them as a library by choosing **Save Tool Presets** from the picker or panel menu.

▶ To restore the default presets for all tools, save any custom tool presets as a library first (if desired), choose Reset Tool Presets from the picker or panel menu, then click OK in the alert dialog.

---

**SOME SUGGESTIONS FOR TOOL PRESETS**

Take note of which tools you use most frequently, and which settings you choose most frequently for them. Here are a few suggestions for presets you can create:

▶ Brush panel settings, Options bar settings, and a Foreground color for the Brush or Mixer Brush tool

▶ Standard photo sizes for the Crop tool

▶ Character panel or Options bar settings for the Horizontal Type or Vertical Type tool, including a color

▶ Frequently used settings for the healing tools, such as the Healing Brush or Spot Healing Brush tool, or for the Clone Stamp or Sharpen tool

▶ Frequently used settings for the selection tools, such as some Fixed Ratio settings for the Rectangular Marquee tool

▶ A basic preset for the Gradient tool, with the "Black, White" gradient chosen

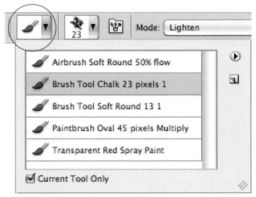

A *Click this thumbnail or arrowhead on the Options bar to open the Tool Preset picker.*

B *Tool presets can also be accessed from the Tool Presets panel.*

When you've finished editing your Photoshop image, it can be output to a color printer (such as an inkjet device) or an imagesetter. In the first task in this chapter, you will create a custom proof setting for your specific inkjet printer and paper and use it to view a soft (onscreen) proof of your print output. Following that, we provide instructions for outputting a document to an inkjet printer. You will also learn how to choose settings for a file to be printed as a monotone, and how to convert your file to CMYK Color mode for commercial printing. (To export your file to another application or to optimize it for the Web, see the next chapter.)

When preparing files for an output service provider, be sure to consult with those experts about which specific settings and formats they need you to select in Photoshop. For additional information beyond the scope of this chapter, refer to Photoshop Help, which contains a wealth of specialized technical information, and to the documentation for your specific printer model. And keep in mind that for both desktop and commercial printing, you can gain a lot of valuable feedback from trial and error. The experts become expert by learning from experience.

# PRINT

# 25

## IN THIS CHAPTER

---

**FOR INKJET PRINTING, KEEP YOUR DOCUMENT IN RGB COLOR MODE**

When printing to a desktop inkjet printer, keep your image in RGB Color mode. Although these printers print using six or more process ink colors, their drivers are designed to receive RGB data and perform the conversion to printer ink colors internally. Be sure to use the installed profile that conforms to your printer model and paper (we'll show you how).

# Proofing colors onscreen

In this next step in color management, you'll create a custom proof setting for your specific inkjet printer and paper, and use it to view a soft proof, or onscreen simulation, of your print output. Although the soft proof won't be perfectly accurate, it will give you a rough idea of how your colors will look (without costing you a penny).

## To proof a document as an inkjet print onscreen:

1. From the View > **Proof Setup** submenu, choose **Custom.** The Customize Proof Condition dialog opens. In the next steps, you will choose custom proofing settings for your output device.**A**

2. Check Preview, then from the **Device to Simulate** menu, choose the correct color profile for your inkjet printer and paper (the profile you either downloaded from a manufacturer's website or installed with your printer driver file).

3. Uncheck **Preserve RGB Numbers**, if available. Photoshop will simulate how the colors will look when converted to the output profile. This option is available only if the color mode of the output profile that you chose from the Device to Simulate menu matches that of the current file (e.g., if your image is in RGB Color mode and you chose an RGB device as the Device to Simulate).

4. Choose a **Rendering Intent** to control how colors will change as the image is shifted from one profile to another (see the sidebar on the next page). We recommend choosing either Perceptual or Relative Colorimetric. You can evaluate a couple of options via the preview and by making some test prints.

Check **Black Point Compensation** to allow adjustments to be made for differences in black points among different color spaces. With this option chosen, the full dynamic range of the image color space is mapped to the full dynamic range of the color space for the output device (the printer). With this option off, black areas in the image may display or print as grays. We recommend checking this option for inkjet printing.

5. *Optional:* For Display Options (On-Screen), check Simulate Paper Color to preview the white of the printing paper as defined in the printer profile; or if you're going to print the file on uncoated paper, check Simulate Black Ink to preview the full range of black values that the printer can produce.

6. To save your custom proof setup, click Save, enter a name, keep the .psf extension, keep the location as the default Proofing folder, then click Save.

7. Click OK. Saved proof setups are available on the Custom Proof Condition menu in this dialog and at the bottom of the View > Proof Setup submenu. View > **Proof Colors** will be checked automatically, so you can see the soft proof. And for the moment, the Device to Simulate profile is listed in the tab of the current document.

Remember, the Proof Setup options control only how Photoshop simulates colors onscreen. Colors in the actual file won't be converted to the chosen profile until you convert the document to a different color mode (such as from RGB to CMYK) or send it to an inkjet printer.

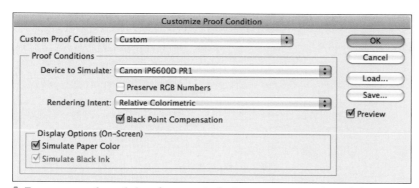

**A** *To generate a soft proof of our document, in the Customize Proof Condition dialog, we've chosen the profile for our Canon Pixma inkjet printer as the Device to Simulate.*

**CHOOSING A RENDERING INTENT**

► **Perceptual** changes colors in a way that seems natural to the human eye, while attempting to preserve the appearance of the overall image. It's a good choice for continuous-tone images.

► **Saturation** changes colors with the intent of preserving vivid colors, but in so doing compromises color fidelity. Nevertheless, it is a good choice for charts and graphics, which normally contain fewer colors than continuous-tone images.

► **Absolute Colorimetric** maintains the color accuracy only of colors that fall within the destination color gamut (i.e., the color range of your printer) but in so doing sacrifices the accuracy of colors that aren't within that gamut.

► **Relative Colorimetric**, the default intent for all the Adobe predefined settings in the Color Settings dialog, compares the white, or highlight, of your document's color space to the white of the destination color space (the white of the paper, in the case of print output), shifting colors where needed. This is the best rendering intent choice for documents in which most of the colors fall within the color range of the destination gamut, because it preserves most of the original colors.

Note: Consult your printer manual when choosing a rendering intent. For example, some inkjet printers favor Perceptual over Relative Colorimetric.

Choosing a Proof Setup preset will cause Photoshop to soft-proof (simulate) the colors in your RGB file onscreen as if it were printed using CMYK inks or displayed online on a Windows or older Macintosh display.

## To proof colors onscreen for commercial printing or online output:

1. From the View > **Proof Setup** submenu, choose the preset for the output display type that you want Photoshop to simulate:

   **Working CMYK** to simulate colors for the commercial press that is currently chosen on the CMYK menu under Working Spaces in the Edit > Color Settings dialog in Photoshop.

   **Legacy Macintosh RGB (Gamma 1.8)** or **Internet Standard RGB (sRGB)** ★ to simulate colors for online output using the legacy Mac gamma (1.8) or Windows gamma (2.2) as the proofing space.

   **Monitor RGB** to simulate colors using the custom display profile for your monitor.

2. View > **Proof Colors** will be checked automatically. To turn off soft proofing at any time, simply uncheck it (Ctrl-Y/Cmd-Y).

# Printing a file on an inkjet printer

In this section, we will show you how to output your file to an inkjet printer and obtain a quality color print that closely matches the document you have been viewing onscreen. You will complete the color management setup that you started in Chapter 1 by choosing settings in the Print dialog. We have divided the steps for using this dialog into three parts: choosing settings for the printer driver, choosing settings in the Print dialog for Photoshop, and finally, turning off color management for the printer and printing the file in Windows or the Mac OS.

*Continued on the following page*

In Photoshop CS5, all the necessary printing options are in the Print dialog. And unlike in previous versions of Photoshop, clicking the Print button sends your file directly to the printer. Upon opening the Print dialog, the first step is to tell Photoshop what type of printer you will be using. You will also click the Print Settings button to gain access to the print dialog for your operating system, in order to specify the paper size, paper type, and other printer-specific options.

## To choose settings in the Print dialog for inkjet printing: ★

### Part 1: Choose settings for your printer driver

1. Open the file to be printed, then choose File > **Print** (Ctrl-P/Cmd-P). The Print dialog opens, complete with a preview.**A**

2. From the **Printer** menu, choose the inkjet printer you're planning to use.

3. Click **Print Settings** to open the [**Printer Name**] **Properties/Print** dialog for your operating system. The driver for your chosen printer and your operating system control which options are available in this dialog.

4. The menu names vary with the chosen printer model, so we will refer to them generically:

   In Windows, in the Main (or other) tab, choose the best-quality option for photo printing. For the paper options, choose the source for your paper, the specific type of paper to be used, and the paper size (**A**, next page).

   In the Mac OS, the inkjet printer you chose in step 2 will be listed on the Printer menu. Choose the desired paper size for the print (for a borderless print, pick a size that includes the word "borderless"). From the fourth menu down, choose the print quality and paper options category (e.g., Quality & Media or Print Settings). From the media or paper type menu, choose the type of paper you will be using (**B**, next page), and from another menu, choose a print quality option (**C**, next page).

5. Click Save to close the [Printer Name] Properties/OS-level Print dialog and return to the Print dialog for Photoshop. Now you're ready to choose print settings for Photoshop (see page 408).

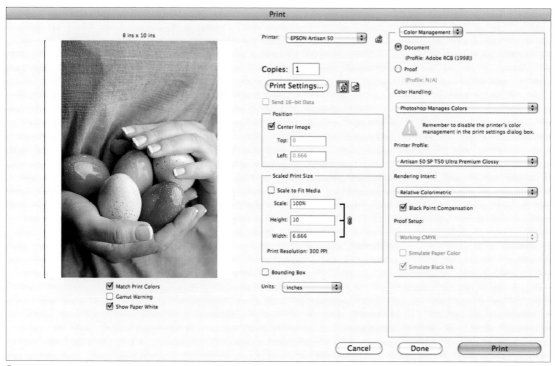

**A** *In the Print dialog for Photoshop, choose your inkjet device from the Printer menu, then click the Print Settings button.*

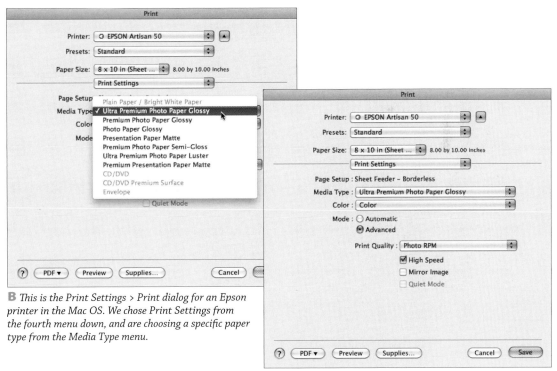

A *This is the Print Settings > [Print Name] Properties dialog for an Epson printer, in Windows 7. We chose a Quality Option and Paper Options.*

B *This is the Print Settings > Print dialog for an Epson printer in the Mac OS. We chose Print Settings from the fourth menu down, and are choosing a specific paper type from the Media Type menu.*

C *Next, in the same dialog, we clicked Mode: Advanced and chose a Print Quality option.*

After choosing print settings by following the steps on page 406, the next step is to choose position, scale, color management, and output options in the Print dialog for Photoshop.

### Part 2: Choose settings in the Print dialog ★

1. In the Print dialog for Photoshop (**A**, next page), click the portrait or landscape orientation button. Check **Center Image** to position the image in the center of the paper. Or to reposition the image on the paper, uncheck Center Image and enter new Top and Left values (note the preview); you can also check **Bounding Box**, if desired, then drag the bounding box in the preview.

2. *Optional:* To scale the print output slightly (not the actual image), do one of the following:

   Check **Scale to Fit Media** to fit the image automatically on the paper size you chose in step 4 on page 406.

   Uncheck Scale to Fit Media, then change the **Scale** percentage or enter specific **Height** and **Width** values (choose a unit from the Units menu). The three values are interdependent; changing one causes the other two to change.

   Note: Use these features to scale the print by only a small amount (i.e., fractions of an inch or a few percentage points). If a larger scale change is needed, cancel out of the dialog, use Image > Image Size to scale the image (see pages 122–124), then resharpen it.

3. From the menu in the upper right, choose **Color Management**, then click **Document** to use the color profile that's embedded in the image, which will be Adobe RGB (1998) if you're continuing with the color management workflow that you began in Chapter 1.

4. From the **Color Handling** menu, choose **Photoshop Manages Colors** to let Photoshop handle the color conversion. This option will ensure optimal color management. (See the sidebar on the next page.)

5. From the **Printer Profile** menu, choose the printer, ink, and paper profile that you have

installed (as per our instructions on pages 14–15), or choose a profile that matches the paper type you chose when you clicked Print Settings (see page 406). The profiles for the currently chosen printer should display at the top of the menu. If you don't see your custom installed profile there, scroll downward on the list.

6. From the **Rendering Intent** menu, choose the same intent that you used when you created the soft-proof setting for your inkjet printer, which most likely was either Perceptual or Relative Colorimetric (see the sidebar on page 405).

   ➤ You could run one test print for the Perceptual intent and one for the Relative Colorimetric intent, and see which one produces better results.

7. Check **Black Point Compensation**. This option preserves the darkest blacks and shadow details by mapping the full color range of the document profile to the full range of the printer profile, and is recommended when printing an RGB image.

8. Below the preview, do the following:

   Check **Match Print Colors** to display a color-managed soft proof of the image in the preview, based on the chosen printer and printer profile settings.

   Uncheck **Gamut Warning**. This option previews out-of-gamut colors as gray. It is necessary only when printing to a commercial CMYK printer.

   Check **Show Paper White** to have the paper color be simulated in any white areas in the preview, based on the current printer profile.

9. Before printing the image, you need to turn off color management for your printer. To do this, carefully follow the steps on page 411 for Windows or on page 412 for the Mac OS.

➤ Click Done in the Print dialog if you want to save all of your settings for the current document and close the dialog.

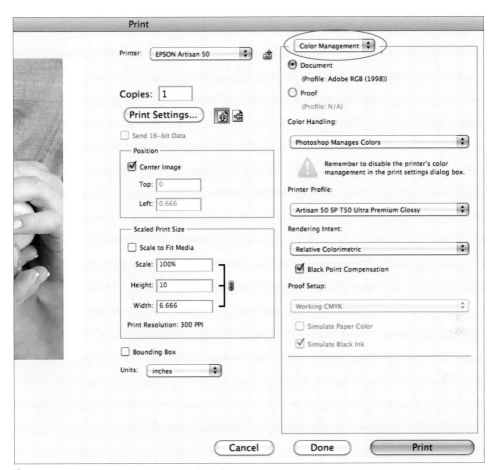

A *Choose settings in the Print dialog in Photoshop.*

## WHY WE LET PHOTOSHOP MANAGE COLORS

From the Color Handling menu of the Print dialog, you can choose to let Photoshop or your printing device manage the colors. What's the difference?

► If you choose Photoshop Manages Colors (the option we recommend), you will be able to select a profile that matches the paper choice you made in the Print Settings dialog. Choose either the printer and paper profile that you downloaded from a paper or print manufacturer's website or a profile that was installed with your printing device. Photoshop will adjust colors to fit that profile, then send the data to the printer. By using the profile, your color-managed workflow is preserved, and you enable Photoshop to use its expertise to produce good color.

► If you choose Printer Manages Colors, the printer driver will handle the color conversion instead of Photoshop. This may limit the print quality, for two reasons. First, the printer won't be aware of your custom paper choice and custom printer profile. And second, color conversion will be subject to the printer's ability to convert colors rather than the color management settings you have been using up to this point. Note that with this option chosen you can adjust the amount of each ink color the printer uses (and thereby override the default printer settings), but we don't recommend doing so.

## CHOOSING OUTPUT OPTIONS

To access options for commercial printing, from the menu in the upper right corner of the File > Print dialog for Photoshop, choose Output. Some key Printing Marks options that we think you should be aware of are listed below. For other options, refer to Photoshop Help.

Under Printing Marks, check any of the following options:

► Calibration Bars prints a grayscale and/or color calibration strip outside the image area.

► Registration Marks prints marks that a print shop uses to align color separations.

► Corner Crop Marks and Center Crop Marks print short little lines that a print shop uses as guide lines when trimming the final print.

► Description prints, outside the image area, whatever information is listed in the File > File Info dialog (in the Description field in the Description tab).

► Labels prints the file name, document color mode, and current channel name on each page (outside the image area).

A few of the options available in the Functions area are as follows:

► Include Vector Data causes the edges of any vector objects (such as type or shapes) to print at the printer resolution, not at the document resolution. This option is checked automatically if the file contains type or a shape layer.

► Click Bleed to specify a Width for the placement of crop marks (a distance between 0 and 3 inches, measured inward from the edge of the canvas area).

► In the Mac OS, if the chosen output device is capable of handling 16-bit files, a Send 16-Bit Data option displays, which, if checked, permits color data from a 16-bits-per-channel file to be sent to the printer. Prints from such files will have finer details and smoother color gradations.

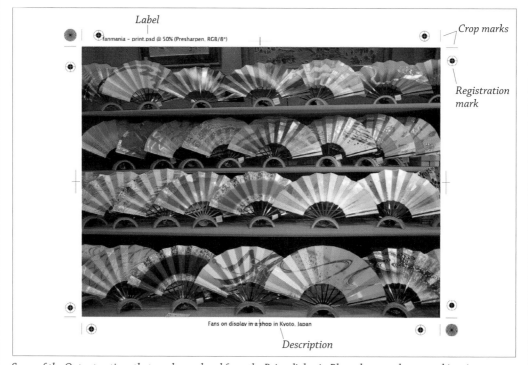

*Some of the Output options that can be produced from the Print dialog in Photoshop are shown on this printout.*

The final step before outputting a file to an inkjet printer is to enable Photoshop to manage the color conversion from RGB color to printing inks. To do this, you will click Print Settings once more and turn off color management for your printer. Note that the color management controls in this dialog will vary depending on the manufacturer of the device, because these options are controlled by the operating system and the printer driver.

In the instructions below, color management will be turned off for an Epson printer driver. If your printing device is a different model, research how to access print quality and color management settings for it, and use our steps as general guidelines.

### Part 3: Turn off color management for your printer in Windows, then print the file: ★

1. In the Print dialog for Photoshop, click **Print Settings** to get to the [Printer Name] Properties dialog for your Windows system.

2. Click the **Advanced** tab. 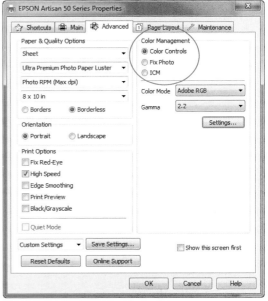 A different set of options appears, including controls for color management.

3. In the Color Management area, click **ICM** to switch control of color management from the Epson driver to the color management system that's built into Windows.

4. Below the ICM button, check **Off** (**No Color Adjustment**) to disable color management for the printer. **B**

5. Click OK to close the Properties dialog and return to the Print dialog for Photoshop.

6. Click **Print**. Phew! You made it.

**A** *In the Print Settings > Properties dialog for an Epson printer in Windows, we clicked the Advanced tab to display these Color Management options.*

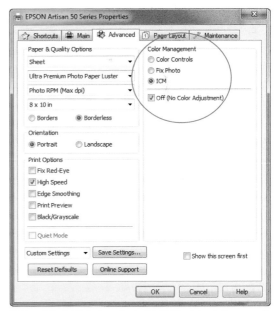

**B** *We clicked ICM, then checked Off (No Color Adjustment).*

The final step before outputting a file to an inkjet printer is to enable Photoshop to manage the color conversion from RGB color to printing inks. To do this, you will click Print Settings once more and turn off color management for your printer. Note that the color management controls in this dialog will vary depending on the manufacturer of the device, because in the Mac OS, these options are controlled by the operating system and the printer driver.

In the instructions below, we'll show you how to turn off color management for an Epson printer driver. If your printing device is a different model, research how to access print quality and color management settings for it, and use our steps as general guidelines.

**Part 4: Turn off color management for your printer in the Mac OS, then print the file:** ★

1. In the Photoshop Print dialog, click **Print Settings** to open the Print dialog for the Mac OS.

2. From the fourth menu, choose **Color Management.**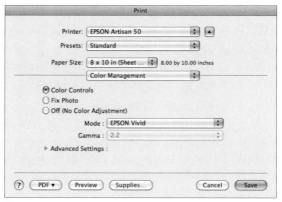

3. Click **Off** (**No Color Adjustment**).  Note that with color management turned off for the printer, depending on the print model, the color controls and the Advanced Settings sliders either won't display at all or will display but be dimmed.

4. Click **Save** to return to the Print dialog for Photoshop.

5. Click **Print**. Congratulations!

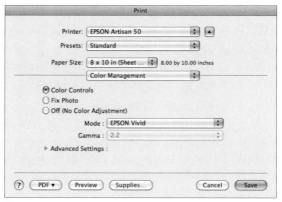

**A** *In the Print Settings > Print dialog for an Epson printer in the Mac OS, we chose Color Management from the fourth menu.*

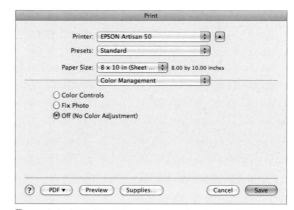

**B** *We clicked Off (No Color Adjustment) to turn color management off for our printer.*

# Creating a monotone print

A low-budget — but effective — way to print a grayscale image in a color tint is to output it as a monotone (from a single plate).

## To print a grayscale image using a spot color tint:

1. Either open a file that's already in Grayscale mode or convert a copy of a file to Grayscale mode.

   ➤ Before performing the actual conversion, you can fine-tune how a layer is switched to grayscale via a Black & White adjustment layer. 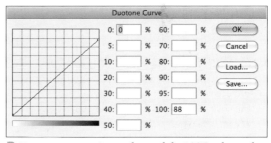A

2. Choose Image > Mode > **Duotone**.

3. In the Duotone Options dialog, choose Type: **Monotone**.

4. Click the **Ink 1** (black) color square, click Color Libraries, if necessary, then choose a spot (non-process) color, such as a PANTONE color. Click OK.

5. In the Duotone Options dialog, click the **Ink 1** curve (the square that contains a diagonal line).

6. The Duotone Curve options dialog opens. In the **100%** field (which controls the darkest shadow value), enter the desired tint percentage.B Keep 0 as the 0% value and keep all the other fields blank, then click OK twice to close the dialogs.C

7. Use File > Save As to save the file in the Photoshop or Photoshop PDF format. It can be imported into Adobe InDesign CS4 or later.

# Preparing a file for commercial printing

Computer monitors display additive colors by projecting red, green, and blue (RGB) light, whereas commercial presses print subtractive colors using CMYK (cyan, magenta, yellow, and black) and/or spot color inks. As you may already know, obtaining high-quality CMYK color reproduction from a commercial press is an art that takes experience and know-how.

Nowadays, with print shops creating their own profiles for their commercial presses, you don't need to concern yourself with creating a custom profile — you can leave that step to the pros. Do concern yourself with saving the custom profile that your print shop has given you to the correct folder (see page 14) so it's available in the Color Settings dialog. The profile will control the CMYK conversion and can also be used to create a soft (onscreen) proof, which we showed you how to do on pages 404–405.

*Continued on the following page*

**A** *We used a Black & White adjustment layer to tweak the conversion of this image layer to grayscale, then converted the document to Grayscale mode.*

**B** *For a monotone print, we lowered the 100% value to the desired percentage for our chosen PANTONE tint.*

**C** *This is a CMYK simulation of the image as if it were printed using a PANTONE Solid Color.*

When preparing a copy of your file to be sent to a print shop for output on a commercial press, you need to establish the CMYK working space, which can either be a custom profile your print shop has supplied you with or a predefined prepress profile. Once the working space is established, the file can be converted to CMYK Color.

## To convert your file to CMYK Color mode:

1. Use the File > Save As dialog to produce a copy of your file.

2. Choose Edit > **Color Settings** (Ctrl-Shift-K/ Cmd-Shift-K).

3. To specify which profile will be used to control the conversion of your image from RGB to CMYK color mode, do either of the following:

   From the **Settings** menu, choose the .csf profile your commercial printer has given you and that you have installed.

   From the **CMYK** menu in the Working Spaces area, choose either the .icc predefined prepress profile that your print shop has given you or the profile your print shop says is the best match for their specific press and the chosen paper type.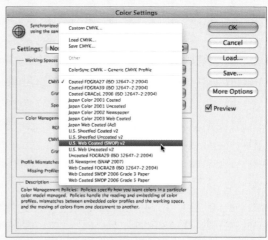

4. Click OK. To convert the file to CMYK color mode, choose Image > Mode > **CMYK Color**.

5. Save the file.

**A** *In the Color Settings dialog, from the CMYK menu in the Workspace Spaces area, choose the correct CMYK profile.*

---

### A WORKFLOW FOR COMMERCIAL PRINTING

The steps needed to prepare a file for commercial printing are too complex to cover in this QuickStart Guide. The basic steps, however, are summarized below.

1. Calibrate your display on a regular basis (see pages 7–9).

2. Ask your commercial printer what type of press your document will be printed on and if they have any special requirements for it. Ask what lines-per-inch setting will be used on the press for your document so you can choose the proper resolution for your Photoshop files.

3. Ask your commercial printer to supply you with a printer profile for their press, ink, and paper, then load it into the Color Settings dialog (see page 14).

4. Use the printer profile to create a custom proof condition, and view a soft proof onscreen of the image for that specific press (see pages 404–405).

5. Make any necessary tonal adjustments, such as improving the contrast, and perform color adjustments, such as removing a color cast.

6. Images that are to be color-separated for commercial printing should be edited in RGB Color mode and then converted to CMYK Color mode for printing. To control the conversion, use the printer profile that your print shop has supplied you with.

7. Sharpen the image (see pages 296–300).

8. Ask in which file format the document should be saved, then save a copy of it in that format.

9. Print a CMYK color proof and analyze it. Tweak the Photoshop document, if necessary, then print and analyze another proof.

When you're ready to export your Photoshop image, you need to save it in the proper format for the specific drawing, layout, multimedia, Web page creation, or other program you're going to import it into. In this chapter, you'll learn how to save and prepare files for export to other programs for print output, and for viewing online.

## Preparing Photoshop files for other applications

### Photoshop to Adobe InDesign

Photoshop PSD files can be imported directly into Adobe InDesign. Photoshop layers (and layer comps) are preserved, and you can turn their visibility on or off in InDesign. InDesign can separate Photoshop PSD and PDF files (RGB or CMYK), and can read ICC color profiles that are embedded in Photoshop files. And because it's part of the Adobe Creative Suite, InDesign lets you use Bridge for file and color management. Alpha channels, layer masks, and transparency are also preserved, eliminating any need to use clipping masks.

If you want to import only part of a Photoshop layer into InDesign CS5, you can use either a layer mask or an alpha channel. In Photoshop, select an area of a layer, then create a layer mask or an alpha channel (if you haven't already done so). In InDesign, choose File > Place, and in that dialog, check Show Import Options. The Image Import Options dialog opens. For a mask, under Show Layers, show the layer that contains the layer mask and hide any other layers; for a channel, click the Image tab, then from the Alpha Channel menu, choose the alpha channel (the alpha channel will clip all layers). Click OK.

### Photoshop to QuarkXPress

To color-separate a Photoshop image from Quark-XPress, you can convert it to CMYK Color mode before importing it into QuarkXPress, or you can let QuarkXPress read the embedded profiles and convert your RGB TIFF into a CMYK TIFF. Ask your output service provider which program to use for the conversion. With the PSD Import XTension installed, layered PSD files can be imported into QuarkXPress 6.5 and later. In QuarkXPress, you can adjust the layer blending mode and opacity. If the PSD file contains layer effects or has a higher color depth than 8 bits per channel, all layers will be flattened upon import.

*Continued on the following page*

EXPORT

# 26

## IN THIS CHAPTER

If you need to place only a portion of a Photoshop image into QuarkXpress 7 or 8, select an area of a layer, then create an alpha channel. In QuarkXPress, import the file using File > Import Picture. Controls for choosing and modifying the alpha channel can be found on the Measurements palette.

## Photoshop to Adobe Illustrator

Not surprisingly, files from Photoshop CS5 and Adobe Illustrator CS5 are compatible in many (although not all) respects.

➤ If you **drag and drop** a Photoshop selection or layer into Illustrator, the imagery will appear on the Layers panel in Illustrator as an image layer in Windows, or as a group with an image layer in the Mac OS. Opacity settings are reset to 100% but are preserved visually, the blending mode is reset to Normal, and layer and vector masks are applied to their respective layers. All transparent areas are filled with white.

➤ If you copy and **paste** a layer from Photoshop into Illustrator, layer masks are discarded without being applied.

➤ Via File > **Place**, you can place either a whole Photoshop image or just a single layer comp into Illustrator. If you place a Photoshop image with the Link option checked, the image will appear on the Layers panel on a single image layer, and any masks will be applied. If you embed the Photoshop image as you place it (uncheck the Link option), you'll have the option via the Photoshop Import Options dialog to convert layers into objects or flatten them into one layer. This choice is also available if you open a Photoshop image via File > **Open** in Illustrator.

Using the Place or Open command, if you decide to convert layers into objects, each layer will appear as an object on its own editable nested layer within a group. The Background (if any) will become a separate, opaque layer. All transparency values are preserved, and blending modes that are also available in Illustrator are preserved; both are listed as editable appearances in Illustrator. (To verify which blending modes are available in Illustrator, click the blending mode menu on the Transparency panel.) Layer masks become opacity masks. Layer effects are applied to the layer; their visual effects are preserved. We prefer the Convert Layers to Objects option because it preserves layer transparency. In the Photoshop Import Options dialog, you can check Import Hidden Layers if you want to allow hidden layers to be imported.

➤ The presence of adjustment layers in a Photoshop document will prevent underlying Photoshop layers from becoming individual layers in Illustrator. To work around this limitation, hide the adjustment layers, or merge the adjustment layers downward. Save the Photoshop file, then open or place it into Illustrator.

➤ If you decide to flatten Photoshop layers into one layer, the effect of all transparency, blending modes, and layer masks will be preserved visually, but won't be editable in Illustrator.

➤ When you open or place a TIFF, EPS, or PSD file into Illustrator, the file resolution stays the same, but the Photoshop image adopts the color mode of the Illustrator file. Via the Effect menu in Illustrator, some Photoshop (raster) effects and some Illustrator (vector) effects can be applied to the imported images.

---

**MAKING FILES COMPATIBLE**

When you open a Photoshop (PSD) file in another application, ideally that target application should be able to read layers. To allow your PSD files to be readable by those that don't, go to Edit/Photoshop > Preferences > File Handling and from the Maximize PSD and PSB File Compatibility menu, choose Always. To apply the preference change, reopen and resave the layered PSD files. A composite preview will be saved with the layered version for applications that don't support layers, and a rasterized copy of any vector art will be saved for applications that don't support vector data. Although this option produces larger files that take longer to save, it's an acceptable trade-off for the needed compatibility.

# Saving a file in the TIFF format

TIFF files are versatile in that they can be imported into most applications and are usable in many color management scenarios. Both InDesign and QuarkXPress can color-separate a CMYK color TIFF. Note that although Photoshop files up to 4 GB can be saved in this format, 2 GB is the largest file size that other applications can read.

### To save a file in the TIFF format:

1. *Optional:* If your commercial printer requests that you convert the color mode of your document to CMYK, choose Image > Mode > CMYK Color.

2. Choose File > Save As, enter a name or keep the current name, choose Format: **TIFF**, and choose a location for the file.

3. In the Save area:

   Check **Save a Copy** to keep the existing file open onscreen and save a copy of it to disk.

   Check **Layers** to preserve any layers in your file. Note, however, that few image or layout programs can work with layered TIFFs, and those that don't will either flatten the layers or ignore the layer data. We recommend unchecking this option to allow the file to be flattened.

   You can also choose to save **Alpha Channels**, **Notes**, or **Spot Colors**, if the file contains them.

4. *Optional:* Check ICC Profile/Embed Color Profile to include the currently embedded color profile with the file. For more about color management, see Chapter 1.

5. Click Save. The TIFF Options dialog opens.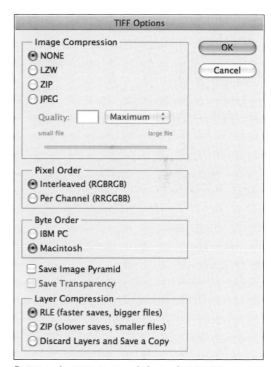

6. If you need to reduce the storage size of the file, choose an **Image Compression** method. The LZW and ZIP methods are nonlossy. Some programs can't open TIFF files that are saved with ZIP compression, so find out which file format your target application supports. We don't recommend choosing the JPEG compression option because it discards some image data. Note that for color separation, output service providers prefer uncompressed files, in which case you should click None.

   Leave the **Pixel Order** on the default setting of **Interleaved** (**RGBRGB**).

Click **Byte Order**: **IBM PC** or **Macintosh**, for the platform the file will be used on.

*Optional:* Check Save Image Pyramid to save multiple resolutions of the image in one file. Photoshop doesn't offer options for opening image pyramids, but Adobe InDesign does.

If your file contains transparency and you want it to be preserved, check **Save Transparency**. To access this option, the bottommost layer in the file must be a layer — not the Background.

If the file contains layers, click a **Layer Compression** method.

7. Click OK.

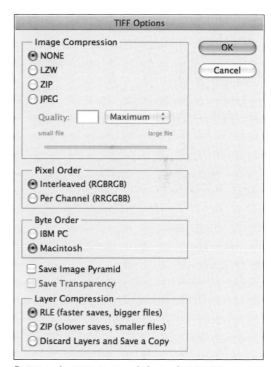

**A** *This is the TIFF Options dialog in the Mac OS.*

# Saving a file in the EPS format

If the drawing or page layout program you're planning to export your files to can't read Photoshop PSD or PDF files, the Photoshop EPS format is the next best option. Note that this format flattens layers and discards alpha channels and spot channels. To access it, your file can be in any color mode except Multichannel, but its color depth must be 8 bits per channel. Printing an EPS file requires using a PostScript or PostScript-emulation printer.

### To save a file in the EPS format:

1. *Optional:* If the file is to be color-separated by another application and you want to see a simulation of how it will look when converted to CMYK mode, choose View > Proof Setup > Working CMYK.

2. Choose File > Save As (Ctrl-Shift-S/Cmd-Shift-S) to open the Save As dialog.

3. Enter a file name or keep the current name, choose Format: **Photoshop EPS**, and choose a location in which to save the file.

   *Optional:* Check ICC Profile/Embed Color Profile to have Photoshop embed the document color profile or current working color space into the file (see pages 10 and 16).

   Click Save. Note that all layers will be flattened. The EPS Options dialog opens.**A–B**

4. From the **Preview** menu, choose **TIFF (1 bit/pixel)** to save the file with a black-and-white preview or **TIFF (8 bits/pixel)** to save it with a grayscale or color preview. Mac OS users, choose a Macintosh preview only if you're certain you won't need to open the file on another platform.

5. If the file is to be used in the Mac OS, choose **Encoding: Binary**, the default method used by PostScript printers. Binary-encoded files are smaller and process more quickly than ASCII files. If the file is to be used in Windows, or for applications, PostScript printers, or printing utilities that can't handle binary files, you must choose **ASCII85** or **ASCII**. **JPEG** is the fastest encoding method, but it causes some data loss. A JPEG file can be printed only on a PostScript printer that is Level 2 or higher.

   Note: The PostScript Color Management Option converts the file's color data to the printer's color space. Don't choose this option if you're going to import the file into another color-managed

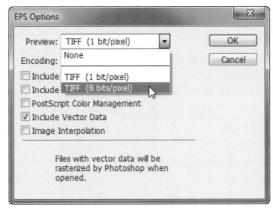

**A** *In the EPS Options dialog in Windows, choose Preview and Encoding options.*

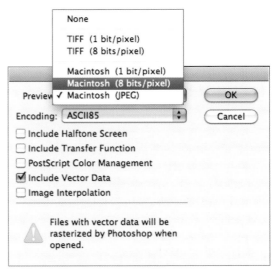

**B** *In the EPS Options dialog in the Mac OS, choose Preview and Encoding options.*

application (such as InDesign), as unpredictable color shifts may result.

6. If your document contains vector elements, such as shapes or type, check **Include Vector Data**. Although saved vector data in EPS files is available to other applications, as an alert will tell you if you reopen the file in Photoshop, that data will be rasterized.

7. For low-resolution output only, check **Image Interpolation** to allow other applications to resample the image pixels, to help reduce jagged edges.

8. Click OK.

## To quickly save multiple files in the JPEG, PSD, or TIFF format:

1. In Bridge or Mini Bridge, click a folder, then select the thumbnails for multiple PSD or JPEG files or raw photos.

2. Choose Tools > Photoshop > **Image Processor**. The Image Processor dialog opens.**A**

3. *Optional:* If you selected raw photos, check Open First Image to Apply Settings to have the Camera Raw dialog open for the first selected photo, enabling you to choose settings. Check this option only if you're certain the other raw photos you have selected need the same adjustments.

4. To choose a location for the new files, do either of the following:

   Click **Save in Same Location**.

   Click **Select Folder**, navigate to the desired location, then click Open.

5. Click the desired **File Type** (or types) and applicable settings.

6. *Optional:* Enter Copyright Info (such as your name) to be added to the files' metadata.

7. Check **Include ICC Profile** to include the file's color profile so its display and output can be color-managed.

8. Click Run. If a file opens into Camera Raw, choose settings, then click **Open Image**. After the files are done processing, a folder containing the new files and bearing the name of the file format appears in the designated location.

▶ Via the Save button, you can save the current settings as a preset. Then, to apply it to other images, use the Load button.

---

**CREATING A COMPRESSED ZIP FILE**

To reduce the storage size of a file without discarding any of its data, you can create a compressed version of it, using the ZIP compression command that's built into your system:

▶ To create a ZIP file in Windows, right-click a file and choose Send To > Compressed (Zipped) Folder from the context menu. A compressed version of the file will appear in a new folder within the current folder.

▶ To create a ZIP file in the Mac OS, right-click a file name in the Finder and choose Compress [file name] from the context menu.

---

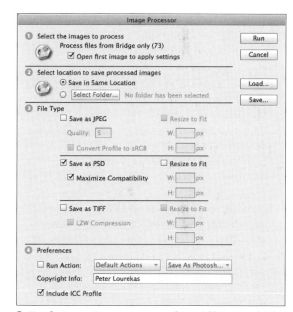

**A** *Use the Image Processor command to quickly save multiple files in the JPEG, PSD, or TIFF format.*

# Saving a file in the PDF format

PDF (Portable Document Format) files can be opened in many Windows and Macintosh applications, as well as in Adobe Reader, Acrobat Standard, and Acrobat Professional. 8-bit and 16-bit files (not 32-bit files) in any color mode except Multichannel can be saved in this format. Photoshop will create one of two kinds of PDF files, depending on which preset you choose in the Save Adobe PDF dialog.

The default PDF format, Photoshop PDF, preserves image, font, layer, and vector data, but it can save only one image per file. To create a Photoshop PDF file, you need to check Preserve Photoshop Editing Capabilities in the Save Adobe PDF dialog. This type of PDF can be opened only in Photoshop CS2 and later. (To save multiple images in one PDF file, see "Creating a PDF Presentation" on pages 380–381.)

Photoshop can also create generic PDF files, which are similar in format to PDFs from a graphics or page layout application. To save a Photoshop image as a generic PDF file, uncheck the above-mentioned Preserve Photoshop Editing Capabilities option. The image will be flattened and rasterized, so your ability to re-edit it in Photoshop will be very limited.

### To save a file in the PDF format:

1. Choose File > Save As, enter a file name or keep the current name in the File Name/Save As field, choose a location in which to save the file, choose Format: **Photoshop PDF**, then click Save. If an alert dialog appears, click OK. The Save Adobe PDF dialog opens.**A**

2. From the **Adobe PDF Preset** menu, choose one of the predefined settings, depending on the

output medium (press, Internet, etc.). The High Quality Print and Press Quality presets create a large Photoshop PDF file that is compatible with Adobe Acrobat 5 and later, compress the file using JPEG at Maximum quality, embed all fonts automatically, and preserve transparency. Note: For commercial printing, ask your shop what settings to use. The Preserve Photoshop Editing Capabilities option is selected for both presets, by default:

**High Quality Print** (the default preset) creates PDF files for desktop printers and color proofing devices. The file won't be PDF/X-compliant. The color conversion is handled by the printer driver.

**Press Quality** is designed for high-quality prepress output. Colors are converted to CMYK.

Preserve Photoshop Editing Capabilities is unchecked for the PDF/X and Smallest File Size presets, so they produce generic PDF files:

**PDF/X-1a:2001**, **PDF/X-3:2002**, and **PDF/X-4: 2008** create PDF files that will be checked for compliance with specific printing standards, to help prevent printing errors. The resulting files are compatible with Acrobat 4 and later; PDF/X-4 files are also compatible with Acrobat 5 and later.

**Smallest File Size** uses high levels of JPEG compression to produce very compact PDF files for output to the Web, transmission via e-mail, etc. All colors are converted to sRGB.

3. Click Save PDF, then click Yes in the alert dialog.

➤ To learn more about the PDF format, see "Saving PDF Files" in Photoshop Help.

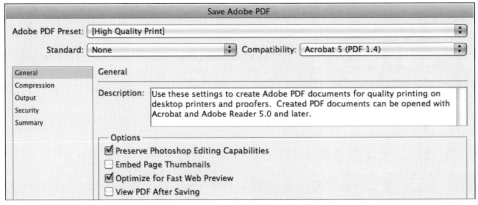

**A** In the Save Adobe PDF dialog, choose a preset from the Adobe PDF Preset menu.

# Saving files for the Web

Optimization is the process by which files are prepared for online viewing, within specific format, storage size, and color parameters. When choosing settings for Web output as opposed to print output, issues of file size and the transmission of data come into play. The goal is to compress your files enough that they download quickly on the Web while keeping their quality as high as possible. Two main parameters that you'll need to focus on as you do this are the file size and the file format (GIF or JPEG).

## File size

The length of time it takes for an image to load into a Web page is related directly to its file size. The size of the optimized file, in turn, is determined by the dimensions of the image (in pixels) and the amount and kind of compression that is applied to it.

When choosing dimensions for an image, if you keep in mind that most people view the Web in a browser window that's around 1000 pixels wide, you can consider dimensions of 800 x 600 pixels to be a realistic upper limit. Remember also that Web browsers always display images at 100% magnification. In the Save for Web & Devices dialog, you will be able to specify pixel dimensions for the optimized file and preview the results.

The GIF and JPEG formats cause a small reduction in image quality as they apply compression, but the resulting smaller file sizes download more quickly on the Web, so it's a worthwhile trade-off. Bear in mind that some types of images are more compressible than others. For example, a document with a solid background color and a few solid-color shapes will compress much more than a large document that contains many color areas, textures, or patterns. The JPEG format has more compression power than GIF.

## File formats

GIF and JPEG, the two file formats most commonly used for Web graphics, are best suited for different types of Photoshop documents:

### GIF

➤ GIF preserves flat colors and sharp edges (such as type) better than JPEG, but it's an 8-bit format, meaning it can save only up to 256 colors. This color restriction makes GIF more suitable for flat graphics than for continuous-tone (photographic) images, which contain more colors.

➤ For optimizing images that contain transparency, GIF is your only choice, because unlike JPEG, it supports transparency.

➤ You don't have to use the full complement of 256 colors when saving a file in the GIF format. If you lower the color depth of a GIF file, you reduce its size and the number of colors it contains, which in turn enables it to download more quickly. (The set of colors in a GIF is called the "color table.") The color reduction may produce dithered or grainy-looking edges and duller colors, but the necessary reduction in file size will be achieved.

### JPEG

➤ Because it retains a document's full 24-bit color depth, the JPEG format does a better job of preserving the color fidelity of continuous-tone images (photographs and the like) than GIF.

➤ Another advantage of JPEG is its compression power: It can shrink an image significantly without lowering its quality. When saving an image in JPEG format, you choose a quality setting; higher-quality settings produce larger files, lower settings produce smaller ones.

➤ Unfortunately, unlike the GIF format, JPEG doesn't preserve transparency.

➤ Each time an image is optimized in the JPEG format, some image data is lost; the greater the compression, the greater the loss.

Note: When optimizing a 16-bits-per-channel file via the Save for Web & Devices dialog, regardless of the format, the file is automatically converted to 8 bits per channel.

Don't panic! We'll break down the optimization steps for both formats.

# Previewing an optimized file

In the Save for Web & Devices dialog, you'll find everything you need to optimize your graphics for the Web, including multiple previews that let you test the effects of different optimization settings.

## To use the previews in the Save for Web & Devices dialog:

1. Choose File > **Save for Web & Devices** (Ctrl-Alt-Shift-S/Cmd-Opt-Shift-S). The dialog opens.**A**

2. Click the **4-Up** tab to display the original image and three previews. Photoshop will use the current optimization settings to generate the first preview (to the right of the original), then automatically generate two other previews as variations on those settings. You can click any preview and change the settings for just that preview, or choose a different download speed

for a preview from its individual **Download Speed** menu.▼≡

3. From the **Preview** menu on the right side of the dialog, choose a gamma value for Photoshop to simulate onscreen (see the sidebar on page 426). ★

4. After choosing settings for a GIF (see the next two pages) or a JPEG (see pages 425–426), to test the settings for the currently selected tab in your browser, click the **Preview** button or the browser icon at the bottom of the dialog. Your optimized image will open in the default Web browser application that's installed on your computer. Or to choose a different browser that's installed in your system, from the menu next to the browser icon, choose a browser name or choose Other and locate the desired browser.

*Preview tabs*

*Optimization options*

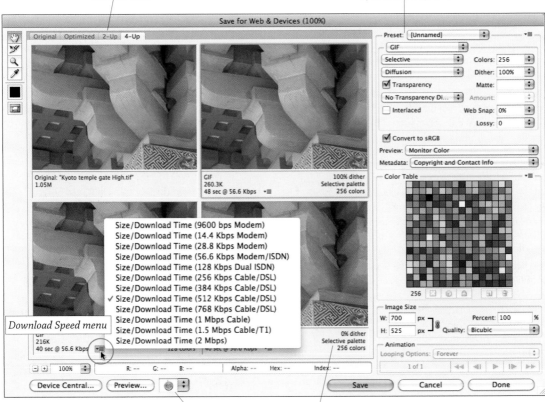

*Download Speed menu*

**A** *Using the Save for Web & Devices dialog, you can choose and preview the effect of different optimization settings.*

*Preview the optimized image in a browser (button and menu)*

*Optimization settings*

# Optimizing a file in the GIF format

The GIF format preserves flat colors and sharp edges (such as type), but it saves only up to 256 colors. You must use this format if you need to preserve transparency.

## To optimize a file in the GIF format:

1. Choose File > **Save for Web & Devices** (Ctrl-Alt-Shift-S/Cmd-Opt-Shift-S).

2. Click the **2-Up** tab at the top of the Save for Web & Devices dialog so you can compare original and optimized previews of the image. You can change the zoom level for the previews by pressing Ctrl/Cmd + or -.

3. Do either of the following:

   To optimize the file using a preset, from the **Preset** menu, choose one of the **GIF** options. Leave the preset settings as they are, then click Save. In the Save Optimized As dialog, keep the .gif extension, choose a location, then click Save.

   To choose custom optimization settings instead, follow the remaining steps.

4. From the **Optimized File Format** (second) menu, choose **GIF.**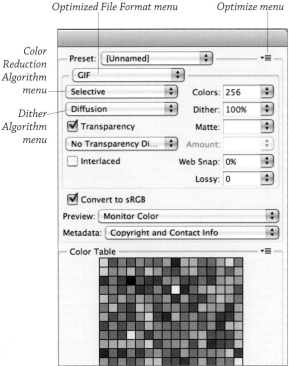

5. From the **Color Reduction Algorithm** menu, choose a method for reducing the number of colors in the image (see the sidebar at right) (**A**, next page).

6. Choose a maximum number of **Colors** for the color table by choosing a preset value from the menu or by entering an exact number in the field. The fewer the colors, the smaller the file size.

7. Choose a method from the **Dither Algorithm** menu. Dithering is a process by which Photoshop mixes dots of different colors to simulate more colors. Although the Diffusion option produces a larger file, it yields the best compromise between quality and file size. With the No Dither option chosen, gradients may have visible bands.

   Also choose a **Dither** percentage. The higher the dither value (color simulation), the larger the file size (**B**, next page).

8. Check **Transparency** to preserve any fully transparent pixels in the image. This option allows for the creation of nonrectangular image borders. With Transparency unchecked, transparent pixels will be filled with the color that's currently

*Continued on the following page*

*Optimized File Format menu*  *Optimize menu*

*Color Reduction Algorithm menu*

*Dither Algorithm menu*

**A** *To create a GIF file, choose optimization options in the Save for Web & Devices dialog.*

---

### THE COLOR REDUCTION ALGORITHMS

▶ Perceptual generates a color table based on the colors currently in the document, with a bias toward how colors are actually perceived.

▶ Selective, the default option, generates a color table based on the colors currently in the document, for the purpose of preserving flat colors, Web-safe colors, and overall color integrity.

▶ Adaptive generates a color table based on the part of the color spectrum that represents the predominant colors in the document. This choice produces a slightly larger optimized file.

▶ Restrictive (Web) generates a color table by shifting image colors to colors in the standard Web-safe palette, which contains only the 216 colors that the Windows and Macintosh browser palettes have in common. This choice produces the least number of colors and the smallest file size but not necessarily the best-looking image. With today's improved display technology, you don't need to choose this option.

listed on the Matte menu. Regardless of the Transparency setting, the GIF format doesn't preserve semitransparent pixels.

Leave the Interlaced option unchecked.

9. To control how semitransparent pixels along the edge of an image will blend with the background of a Web page, choose a **Matte** option. For the Matte color, choose the background color of the Web page, if you know what that color is. Any soft-edged effects (such as a Drop Shadow) on top of transparent areas will fill with the chosen Matte color. If the background color is unknown, set Matte to None; this will produce a hard, jagged edge.

Another option is to choose **Matte: None**, then check Transparency and choose one of three options from the **Transparency Dither Algorithm** menu. These effects will look the same on any background. **Diffusion** applies a random pattern to semitransparent pixels and diffuses it across adjacent pixels. This method usually produces the most subtle results and allows you to set the dithering amount. **Pattern** applies a halftone pattern to the semitranspar-ent pixels. **Noise** applies a pattern similar to Diffusion without affecting neighboring pixels.

10. *Optional:* You can adjust the **Lossy** value to fur-ther reduce the file size. As the name "Lossy" implies, this option discards some image data, but the savings in file size may justify the slightly reduced image quality.

11. Check **Convert to sRGB** to convert the color to sRGB, the standard profile for Web browsers.

12. From the **Preview** menu, choose a display gamma value to be simulated when the optimized image is previewed (see the sidebar on page 426).

13. From the **Metadata** menu, choose which metadata is to be saved with the file, such as Copyright and Contact Info. This data was assigned to the file by your camera, or by you in Bridge via the Metadata panel or the File Info dialog.

14. In the Image Size area, enter the desired **W** and **H** size values in pixels for the GIF file, or enter a scale percentage in the **Percent** field.

15. Follow steps 2–4 on page 422 to preview your settings. Make any needed adjustments, then click Save. The Save Optimized As dialog opens. Change the name (if desired), keep the .gif extension, choose a location, then click Save.

**A** *This image was optimized as a GIF with 32 colors using the Selective algorithm with no Dither.*

**B** *This the same image optimized with 100% Dither.*

**C** *This image was optimized as a GIF with Transparency checked and Matte set to black. A thin black line appears along the edge of each shape.*

**D** *This image was optimized as a GIF with Transparency checked and Matte set to None. The shapes have hard edges.*

# Optimizing a file in the JPEG format

JPEG is the best format for optimizing continuous-tone imagery (photographs, paintings, gradients, and the like) because by saving 24-bit color, you enable those colors to be seen and enjoyed by any viewer whose display is set to thousands or millions of colors. Two notable drawbacks to JPEG, however, are that its compression methods discard image data and that it doesn't preserve transparency.

## To optimize an image in the JPEG format:

1. Choose File > **Save for Web & Devices** (Ctrl-Alt-Shift-S/Cmd-Opt-Shift-S).

2. Click the **2-Up** tab at the top of the Save for Web & Devices dialog so you can compare the original and optimized previews of the image. You can change the zoom level for the previews by pressing Ctrl/Cmd + or -.

3. Do either of the following:

   To optimize the file using a preset, from the **Preset** menu,**A** choose one of the **JPEG** options. Leave the preset settings as they are, then click Save. In the Save Optimized As dialog, keep the .jpg extension, choose a location, then click Save.

   To choose custom optimization settings instead, follow the remaining steps.

4. From the **Optimized File Format** (second) menu, choose **JPEG**.

5. Do either of the following:

   From the **Compression Quality** menu, choose a quality level for the optimized image **B–C** (and **A**, next page).

   Choose a **Quality** value for the exact amount of compression needed.

   ▶ The higher the compression quality, the better the image quality — and the larger the file size.

6. Increase the **Blur** value to lessen the visibility of artifacts that the JPEG compression method produces, and to reduce the file size. Be careful not to overblur the image, though, or the details will become too soft.

7. Choose a **Matte** color to be substituted for areas of transparency in the original image. If you choose None, transparent areas will be changed to white in the optimized image.

*Continued on the following page*

*Optimized File Format menu*

*Compression Quality menu*

*Optimize menu*

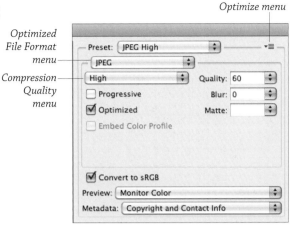

**A** *To create a JPEG file, choose optimization options in the Save for Web & Devices dialog.*

**B** *This image was optimized as a JPEG at High Quality.*

**C** *This is the image optimized as a JPEG at Medium Quality.*

*Note:* The JPEG format doesn't support transparency. To have the Matte color simulate transparency, make it the same solid background color as that of the Web page (of course you need to know what that color is). Click the Matte color swatch, and enter values in the Color Picker dialog.

**8.** Leave **Progressive** unchecked.

**9.** *Optional:* Check Optimized to produce a smaller file size. Note that some older browsers don't support this option.

**10.** Check **Embed Color Profile**. The newest generation of browsers can use a file's embedded color profile to display a color-managed image.

**11.** Check **Convert to sRGB** to convert the optimized color to sRGB, the standard profile for Web browsers. Note: Even with this option checked, the conversion of image colors will be more accurate if the embedded color profile is included, as we instructed you to do in the preceding step.

**12.** From the **Preview** menu, choose a display gamma value to be simulated when the optimized image is previewed (see the sidebar at right).

**13.** From the **Metadata** menu, choose which metadata is to be saved with the optimized file, such as Copyright and Contact Info. This data was assigned to the file by your camera, or by you in Bridge via the Metadata panel or the File Info dialog.

**14.** In the Image Size area, enter the desired **W** and **H** size values in pixels for the JPEG file, or enter a scale percentage in the **Percent** field.

**15.** Follow steps 2–4 on page 422 to preview your settings. Make any needed adjustments, then click Save. The Save Optimized As dialog opens. Change the name (if desired), keep the .jpg extension, choose a location, then click Save.

**A** *This is the image optimized as a JPEG at Low Quality.*

**CHOOSING A PREVIEW OPTION ★**

| Monitor Color | No gamma change |
|---|---|
| Legacy Macintosh (No Color Management) | Mac 1.8 gamma |
| Internet Standard RGB (No Color Management) | Windows 2.2 gamma, the most common gamma |
| Use Document Profile | Adjusts the gamma to match the document profile, if the file contains one |

**CREATING AN OPTIMIZATION PRESET**

To save the current optimization settings in the Save for Web & Devices dialog, choose Save Settings from the Optimize menu.▼☰ In the Save Optimization Settings dialog, enter a name (include the .irs extension), keep the location as the Optimized Settings folder, then click Save. Your saved set is now available on the Preset menu in the Save for Web & Devices dialog for any file.

Unless noted otherwise, the listings in this index pertain to Photoshop.

## Photography credits

### Shutterstock.com
Photographs on the following pages © ShutterStock.com: 1, 38, 39, 63, 65, 69, 72, 78, 79, 82, 89, 90, 121, 123, 125, 126, 127, 133, 147, 148, 149, 150, 151, 152, 154, 155, 156, 157, 159, 162, 164, 166, 167, 170, 185, 191, 192, 198, 202, 205, 206, 208, 209, 212, 214, 216, 217, 220, 222, 228, 234, 236, 237, 239, 244, 246, 248, 265, 266, 268, 270, 275, 276, 278, 280, 283, 285, 287, 289, 290, 293, 294, 295, 296, 302, 305, 306, 314, 315, 316, 321, 325, 355, 356, 358, 367, 374, 375, 383, 406, 413

### Photos.com
Photographs on the following pages © 2007 JupiterImages.com: 182, 267, 273, 299, 312, 317, 323, 346

### Gettyimages.com (PhotoDisc)
Photograph on page 17 © PhotoDisc

### Other photographs
Pages 410, 415, 422, 424, 425 © Victor Gavenda

All other photographs © Elaine Weinmann and Peter Lourekas